COOKS' INGREDIENTS

COOKS' INGREDIENTS

Introduction by Nika Hazelton

Photographed by Philip Dowell

Written by Adrian Bailey

Elisabeth Lambert Ortiz
Helena Radecka

WILLIAM MORROW AND COMPANY, INC.
New York

BANTAM BOOKS
New York Toronto London
1980

Cooks' Ingredients was conceived, edited and
designed by Dorling Kindersley Limited,
9 Henrietta Street, London WC2

Design and Art Direction
Stuart Jackman
Managing Editor
Amy Carroll
Project Editor
Miren Lopategui
Editors
Christine Davis
Scott Ewing
Maria Mosby
Picture Research
Lesley Prescott
Illustrations
Sheilagh Noble

ISBN 0–688–03681–3 (William Morrow and Company, Inc.)
ISBN 0–533–01282–7 (Bantam Books Edition)
Library of Congress Catalog Card Number 80–81457

1 2 3 4 5 6 7 8 9 10

Typesetting by Contact Graphics Limited, London
Reproduction by F E Burman Limited, London
Printed in United States of America

Contents

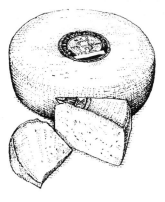

Bold numbers denote color plates; others denote text pages.

Introduction

Of all our passions, food is the only one that comforts us throughout our entire lifetime. It is a joyous passion and we never need to be furtive or apologetic about our interest in it or quiet about our preferences. I find it comforting to know that even in today's agitated world, food is a subject on which I can express my opinions forcibly without getting into trouble.

And our passion for food is not limited to eating. We are also curious about what we eat. Though cookbooks now proliferate like rabbits, I have seldom found one that satisfies my curiosity about the ingredients of the dishes the book tells me how to cook. I am told the ingredients I shall need, but I am not informed about the nature of these ingredients, much less what other uses they might be put to. Yet there is enormous interest in information about the foods from all over the world that are available to today's cooks. I know this from talking to people, from their letters, from questions asked in cooking schools and in magazines and newspapers.

People want concrete facts about what they can cook and eat. They want information about the animal, vegetable, or mineral nature of foods, their nutritive values, what they look like. They want to know their history and folklore and how familiar foods are used in cuisines other than our own. To get information of this kind can mean spending hours, if not days, in libraries and in tracking down the experts, finding obscure foreign groceries, studying mail-order catalogs – fascinating but time-consuming, often frustrating tasks. Anybody with an amateur, let alone professional interest in food has had this experience.

But now here we have *Cooks' Ingredients*, a veritable book of knowledge about food. In one glorious volume, it offers visual and written information on some two thousand foods that we cook and eat. Two hundred pages of unprecedented color photography allow us instant, easy identification of a host of familiar and unfamiliar ingredients. The arrangement of the photographs is calculated to provide comparison as well as identification: each food is shown with others related to it, all captioned by name or names, origin, seasonal availability, properties, variant forms. Each food is so exquisitely photographed as to deserve framing; once seen, it is never to be forgotten.

Besides feasting our eyes, *Cooks' Ingredients* also feeds our minds with informative background lore and specifics on shopping, cooking, and storage.

Anybody who shops for food knows that we need specific information; being specific saves time, money, and disappointments. For instance, consider meat, our most expensive necessity (sadly, I don't consider caviar a necessity): it is good to know that an accurate way to judge the age and tenderness of lamb is by its weight and that the highest quality in a leg of lamb is at the 5-pound weight. Another instance: if you grow fresh herbs, you may have wanted to dry them but did not know how – with the *Cooks' Ingredients'* comprehensive herb chapter, you will discover that, along with a great deal more. I find it worthwhile to know that strawberries should not be sugared in advance (the sugar draws their juice and makes the berries mushy), why lobsters turn red when they are cooked, how the fine grind of coffee produces the strength of espresso and Turkish coffees.

I am a person who really does think that variety is a spice of life, especially in one's daily food, so I was very pleased to read in *Cooks' Ingredients* how familiar foods are used in different ethnic cuisines. This book is a reference rather than a cookbook, so it does not include actual recipes, but it immediately gave me new ideas. I stuffed a pork roast with prunes in the Danish manner and investigated Japanese transparent noodles, which, to my surprise, I found to my liking. Various entries also reminded me of old favorites that had slipped my mind lately – such as split-pea soup and corned beef. Inspiration of this kind is valuable indeed to all of us who cook daily and mutter more and more often, "What on earth can I make today that is different, delicious, easy, and inexpensive?" Interestingly, leafing through the brilliant color pages of *Cooks' Ingredients* prompted me to make better use of my cookbooks, for Philip Dowell, Adrian Bailey, and their team of helpers have in fact created a book that is a natural and ideal companion to every cookbook. My thanks to them all for the most elegant *catalogue raisonné* of foods ever written and photographed.

NIKA HAZELTON

THE COLOR PLATES

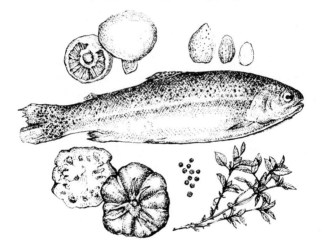

All ingredients photographed are actual size
unless otherwise specified.

TANSY (*Chrysanthemum vulgare*)
Native to Europe, it is now also common in America, where it is grown commercially. The leaves are chopped and used fresh.

TARRAGON (*Artemesia dracunculus*)
Native to southern Europe, it is now particularly common in France. The leaves of the plant are used.

Dried Tarragon

MARIGOLD (*Calendula officinalis*)
An annual plant native to southern Europe and Asia, the petals of the flowers are used, either fresh or dried, as a herb and a food dye.

Dried Borage

CORIANDER (*Coriandrum sativum*); **Chinese Parsley**
This plant is native to southern Europe and the Middle East, but is now available worldwide. The fresh leaves and the seeds (p. 19) are used. The herb has a fresh taste, similar to orange, and is an important ingredient in curry.

HOP (*Humulus lupulus*)
Native to northern temperate regions and southern Europe, the flowers and shoots of this annual climbing plant are used, either fresh or dried.

BORAGE (*Borago officinalis*)
An annual plant native to the Middle East, it is now common in southern Europe and southern England. The flowers and the leaves are used, fresh or dried, in vinegar, sauces and salads.

Herbs

See also p. 210

Dried Lemon Balm

Dried Basil

BASIL (*Ocimum basilicum*) **Sweet Basil**
An annual plant native to India, its use in the
West is relatively recent. The leaves are used,
fresh or dried: the fresh leaves have a taste
similar to cloves, but when dried they taste more
like curry. It has many uses, notably in the Italian
Pesto sauce.

LEMON BALM (*Melissa officinalis*) **Balm**
A perennial plant native to the Mediterranean area,
the leaves are used, fresh (in salads, or with other
vegetables) or dried (mainly in tea). As its name ·
implies, it has a lemon-scented taste.

Bowles Mint
(*Mentha villosa alopecuroides*)

Spearmint
(*Mentha viridis*)

Applemint
(*Mentha rotundifolia*)

Dried Spearmint

MINT
There are many varieties of this herb, native to the Mediterranean area
and western Asia, and now available worldwide. The leaves are used fresh
or dried. Its main use is in sauces and as a condiment to lamb.

Eau de Cologne Mint
(*Mentha citrata*)
Orange Mint

Dried Sweet Woodruff

Golden Sage
(*Salvia officinalis aureum*)

WOODRUFF
(*Asperula odorata*) **Sweet Woodruff**
A perennial herb native to Europe, it is
now also grown in England. It has a
distinctive scented taste, and the leaves
can be used fresh or dried. Its main use
when dried is in "May Cup" – a
traditional English drink – and in
tisanes. Otherwise, it is infused in
champagne, Bénédictine and punch.

BURNET
(*Poterium sanquisorba*)
Salad Burnet
Native to Europe,
today it is used
mainly in France
and Italy. The
leaves are used,
fresh or dried, in
salads, soups,
cordials, casseroles
and cocktails.

SAGE (*Salvia officinalis*)
There are many varieties of
this herb, which is native to
the north Mediterranean
coasts. The leaves are used,
fresh or dried, mainly
in stuffings.

Dried Sage

WINTER SAVORY
(*Satureja montana*)
Perennial and native to the
Mediterranean, its leaves
are used, fresh or dried.
Its peppery flavor makes it
a good seasoning.

BAY
(*Laurus nobilis*) **Laurel**
A tree native to Asia Minor,
and now grown in most
parts of Europe and America,
the leaves are used (usually
dried) in stocks and
bouquets garnis.

Dried Bay

Herbs

See also p. 210

Dried Thyme

PARSLEY
(*Petroselinum crispum*)
There are many
varieties of this herb,
which is native to the
Mediterranean area.
The leaves are used,
fresh or dried, in
sauces and herb
mixtures.

Dried Parsley

Common Thyme
(*Thymus vulgaris*)

Lemon Thyme
(*Thymus citriodorus*)

Lemon Creeping Thyme
(*Thymus azoricus*)

Dried Chives

THYME
There are many varieties of
this perennial herb, which
is native to southern
Europe and along the
Mediterranean. The
leaves (fresh or dried) have
many uses and form the
basic part of bouquets
garnis. Thyme has a strong,
sharp taste so lemon
thyme, which is less strong
and with a lemon tang, is
often used instead.

LEMON VERBENA
(*Lippia citriodora*)
Native to South America, it is
now also grown in Europe.
The leaves are used, fresh or
dried, as a herb or tea.

CHIVE
(*Allium schoenoprasum*)
Native to the cooler parts of
Europe, chives are now
available in many parts of the
world, including America
and Canada. The stems are
used: their bright green
color and oniony taste make
them an ideal garnish for
salads and soups.

Dried Marjoram

Dried Oregano

MARJORAM (*Origanum majorana*)
Sweet Marjoram
Native to the Mediterranean area, the leaves are used fresh or dried, mainly with meat and in stuffings.

OREGANO
(*Origanum vulgare*) **Wild Marjoram**
Native to Asia, Europe and North Africa, it is now available worldwide. The leaves are usually used dried, and are best known for their use in Italian dishes, especially pizzas.

Dried Lovage

LOVAGE (*Levisticum officinale*) **Love Parsley**
A perennial plant native to southern Europe, the whole plant (leaf, seed and root) is used. It is often used in salads and in soups.

ROSEMARY
(*Rosmarinus officinalis*)
An aromatic herb native to the Mediterranean and now available in most parts of the world. The leaves are used fresh or dried, most notably with lamb.

Herbs

See also p. 210

Dill Weed

BERGAMOT (*Monarda didyma*)
Oswego; Bee Balm
There are many varieties of this herb,
native to America and now also
available in Europe. The flowers and
leaves are used, fresh or dried, in
tisanes and teas.

Dried Dill

Comfrey Root

Dill Seeds

DILL (*Anethum graveolens*)
This plant of the parsley family is native to
southern Europe and western Asia, and is now
also grown in northern Europe. The leaves are used,
fresh or dried; also the seeds. The most important
use of the leaves is probably in dill pickles, though
they can also be used with salads or on cooked
vegetables and are essential to dill vinegar.

Dried
Fenugreek
Leaves

FENUGREEK (*Trigonella
foenum-graceum*) **Methi**
Native to western Asia, this plant
is now also available in
Mediterranean countries. The
leaves, which have a faintly bitter
taste, are used, fresh or dried;
also the rock-hard seeds. It is an
important ingredient in curries.

Dried Comfrey

Dried Curry
Leaves

NASTURTIUM
(*Tropaeolum majus*)
Native to Peru, this annual
plant is now available
worldwide. The leaves (usually
fresh), petals and seeds are all
used; their peppery, cress-like
taste makes them useful for
salads and sandwiches.

COMFREY (*Symphytum officinale*)
Native to Europe and Asia. The leaves of
this plant are used, either fresh (in salads)
or dried and powdered (in tea). The dried
root is also used, mainly as a flavoring for
country wine.

CURRY (*Chalcas koenigii*)
This plant is native to southwest Asia. The leaves, which
can be used fresh or dried, are
the basic curry ingredient.

Fresh
Camomile

Dried Camomile

CAMOMILE/CHAMOMILE
(*Matricaria recutita*)
There are many varieties of this
herb, native to Europe and now
grown in America, Britain and
Asia. The dried flower heads
are used.

Dried Chervil

CHERVIL
(*Anthriscus cerefolium*)
An annual plant from
southern Russia and the
Middle East, it is now grown
mainly in France. Fresh or
dried leaves are used.

ANGELICA (*Angelica*, spp.)
This plant is native to
northern Europe and Syria
and is now grown in Europe
and Asia. The whole plant
(leaves and stem) is used.

HYSSOP (*Hyssopus officinalis*)
A perennial plant native to southern Europe,
the Middle East and southern Russia. Both
the flowers and leaves are used, fresh or
dried. It has a minty taste, and is often used
in liqueurs, especially Chartreuse.

Dried Yarrow

Dried Fennel

**Fennel
Seeds**

YARROW (*Achillea millefolium*) **Milfoil**
A perennial plant native to southern
England and now grown in many
countries, including America. The leaves
(fresh or dried), seeds and root are used.

FENNEL (*Foeniculum vulgare*)
A perennial plant native to southern England and now grown in
many countries, including America. The anise-tasting leaves (fresh
or dried), seeds and dried root are traditionally used with fish.

CHINESE FIVE-SPICE POWDER
This is a Chinese spice mixture, consisting of equal parts of finely ground anise pepper, star anise, cassia or cinnamon, cloves and fennel seed. It has a subtle taste and, apart from its wide use in Oriental cookery, can be used in any pork or beef dish.

ANNATTO
(*Bixa orellana*) **Achiote; Bija; Bijol; Roucou**
The dried seeds of a small flowering tree native to tropical America, they are widely used in Latin American cookery. The outer orange pulp surrounding the seeds is also used as a food dye.

CURRY POWDER
A blend of any number of spices, bought ready-prepared. It can vary from mild to hot depending on the spices included, and its use in curries is confined mainly to the West.

PICKLING SPICE
A mixture of spices, consisting basically of black peppercorns, red chilis and varying proportions of mustard seed, allspice, cloves, ginger, mace and coriander seed. It is used in pickles, chutneys and vinegars.

MIXED HERBS
A ready-prepared mixture of dried herbs, usually consisting of thyme, marjoram, parsley, rosemary and basil. It can be used in most savory dishes, according to preference.

FRESH GRATED HORSERADISH
(*Armoracia rusticana*)
The grated outer part of the pungent root of the horseradish plant, native to eastern Europe. It is usually added to cream, vinegar or mayonnaise to make a relish.

BOUQUET GARNI
A combination of dried herbs such as thyme, parsley and bay used in soups, stews and sauces. The herbs are usually wrapped in a piece of muslin, which is removed before serving.

GARAM MASALA
The name means, literally, "hot mixture", and is applied to a combination of roasted spices (such as coriander seed, chili and black pepper) ground into a powder. Although freshly blended and ground in India and the East, in the West it is bought ready-prepared. It is used as a basic flavoring for many Indian dishes.

GALANGAL (*Alpinia officinarum*) **Lesser Galangal**
The ground, dried roots of a Chinese plant with a gingery-peppery taste used in curries and liqueurs.

DRIED GROUND HORSERADISH
The dried, ground root of the horseradish plant. It is less pungent than the type shown above, and has to be reconstituted with water before use. It can also be used to make a relish good with meat, fish or salad.

Cassia Bark

Ground Cassia

CASSIA (*Cinnamomum cassia*) **Chinese Cinnamon**
Similar to cinnamon and often confused with it,
cassia spice is the dried bark of an evergreen tree
native to Burma. Also used in powder form, it is
popular in Oriental cookery.

NIGELLA
(*Nigella sativa*) **Wild Onion Seed; Black Cumin**
The peppery seeds of a Middle Eastern plant;
they are often sprinkled on bread.

CELERY SEED (*Apium graveolens*)
The dried seeds of the celery plant, native
to Italy. They have a rather bitter taste and
are used in soups and stews.

SESAME SEED (*Sesamum indicum*)
The dried fruits of the sesame plant (an
annual native to India) the seeds are best
known as a source of oil. In the Middle
East they are ground to produce *tahina*
and *halva*. They are sometimes used to
decorate cakes and breads in the West.

FENNEL SEED (*Foeniculum vulgare*)
The aromatic dried seeds of the fennel plant,
native to the Mediterranean area. They have a
slight aniseed taste and can be used in a
wide range of dishes, including
apple pie, curries
and fish dishes.

SUNFLOWER SEED (*Helianthus annuus*)
The dried seeds of the sunflower plant native to
Peru, their main use is as a source of oil
(p. 33). They can also be eaten roasted in their
husks. There are many varieties.

TAMARIND SEED
(*Tamarindus indica*)
The dried fruit of the tamarind tree, native to East
Africa. Though referred to as a seed, the dried pulp is
used too. Its main use is in curries.

Black Sesame Seeds

White Sesame Seeds

PUMPKIN SEED (*Cucurbita maxima*)
The seeds of the native American plant
are used as a source of oil, but can also
be eaten roasted.

DILL SEED (*Anethum graveolens*)
The dried fruits of the dill plant, native
to southern Europe; the seeds taste like
caraway and are used with fish.

Spices and Seeds

See also p. 213

CAYENNE PEPPER (*Capsicum annuum*, var. *frutescens*)
The dried pods of a red chili pepper native to Central America are ground to produce this hot, pungent spice.

ANISE-PEPPER (*Xanthoxylum pipesitum*) **Szechuan pepper**
Made from the dried red berries of a Chinese tree, this is a hot, aromatic spice widely used in Oriental cooking.

Ground Nutmeg

Whole Nutmeg

NUTMEG (*Myristica fragrans*)
The dried kernel or "nut" of an evergreen of the myrtle family, native to Indonesia. It is encased in a fleshy apricot-like fruit which splits open when ripe, and is thought to be addictive. Small quantities are soporific and digestive. It can be used whole or ground.

WHITE PEPPERCORNS
The dried core of the ripened fruit of the pepper vine used whole (left) or ground. These are less strong than black peppercorns.

Ground White Pepper

CLOVES
(*Eugenia aromatica*)
The dried, aromatic flower buds of an evergreen of the myrtle family native to Southeast Asia, cloves are normally used whole (top), but the central "head" of the bud can also be ground into a powder (bottom). They are used in sweet and savory dishes, spiced wines and liqueurs.

BLACK PEPPERCORNS
These are sun-dried green peppercorns. They can be used whole (left) or ground.

Ground Black Pepper

Green Peppercorns in Brine

Garlic Flakes

Ground Garlic

PEPPER (*Piper nigrum*)
Both black and white pepper are derived from the green, unripened berries, or peppercorns, of the pepper vine, native to Asia. It should always be freshly ground.

GARLIC (*Allium sativum*)
The bulb of a perennial plant native to Asia, garlic can be dried and ground into flakes or a powder. It has a pungent taste and smell, and should be used sparingly.

Ground Mace

Blades of Mace

MACE (*Myristica fragrans*)
Mace, in blade form, is the outer net-like covering of nutmeg. The blades are pressed flat and dried before use, but they can also be ground.

Cinnamon Quills

Cinnamon Bark

Ground Cinnamon

CINNAMON (*Cinnamomum zeylanicum*)
The dried, aromatic bark of an evergreen of the laurel family, native to Ceylon. Cinnamon is used in the form of quills, bark and powder. It has keeping qualities.

PAPRIKA
(*Capsicum tetragonum*)
Made from a type of pepper native to South America, paprika varies in taste from mildly hot to mild and sweet and in appearance from rosy brown to scarlet.

White Poppy Seeds

Blue Poppy Seeds

POPPY (*Papaver somniferum*)
The seed of the poppy flower native to the Middle East, there are two types: white and blackish-blue. They are used in Indian and Jewish cooking.

CUMIN (*Cuminum cyminum*)
The dried fruit of an annual plant related to parsley and indigenous to the Upper Nile, cumin has a pungent, hot and somewhat bitter taste and is a very popular culinary spice in the East, Mexico and North Africa. It can be used whole (left) or ground (right).

Ground Coriander

Coriander Seeds

CORIANDER (*Coriandrum sativum*)
The seeds are the roasted and dried fruits of an annual plant related to parsley from southern Europe and the Middle East. They can be used ground or whole.

SAFFRON (*Crocus sativus*)
The dried stigmas of the crocus flower native to Greece, saffron is one of the world's most expensive spices.
Aromatic, pungent and slightly bitter, it is used both as a spice and as a food dye.

Spices and Seeds

Black Cardamom Pods

White Cardamom Pods

Green Cardamom Pods

Cardamom Seeds

CARDAMOM (*Elettaria cardamomum*)
The pods are the dried fruits of a perennial plant of the ginger family native to India. They can vary from green to black; the white pods are sun-bleached.

Ground Turmeric

Turmeric Root

TURMERIC
(*Curcuma longa*)
The rhizomes or root stems of this perennial plant of the ginger family are dried and then ground to produce the vivid yellow powder. It is a basic curry spice.

Black Mustard Seed
(*Brassica nigra juncea*)

CARAWAY
(*Carum carvi*)
The sickle-shaped seeds come from a plant native to Asia. Related to anise, it is used mainly in baking.

Star Anise Seeds

Ground Allspice

White Mustard Seed
(*Brassica alba*)

Mustard Powder

Allspice Berries

ALLSPICE (*Pimenta officinalis*) **Jamaica Pepper**
The berries (bottom) are the fruits of an evergreen tree native to the West Indies. They can easily be ground into a powder.

MUSTARD
The seeds come from three plants of the cabbage family. The black are hotter than the white; the powder is a mixture of both.

STAR ANISE (*Illicium verum*)
The dried, star-shaped fruit of an evergreen tree native to China. The seeds (top) are contained in the pods (bottom).

Ginger Root

Ground Ginger

Ground Anise

Dried Ginger (slices)

Anise Seed

GINGER (*Zingiber officinale*)
The rhizome or root stem of this plant native to Southeast Asia can be bought whole, sliced or ground. It is used in Chinese cooking and in baking.

ANISE (*Pimpinella anisum*) **Aniseed; Sweet Cumin**
The seeds are the dried aromatic fruits of an annual plant native to Greece and Egypt, and can be ground into a powder.

AJOWAN (*Carum ajowan*)
The seed of a plant native to India, it has a strong taste of thyme and is used extensively in Indian cookery.

JUNIPER (*Juniperus communis*)
The berries are the fruit of an evergreen shrub grown in the northern hemisphere. They are dried when fully ripened.

Ground Fenugreek

Chili Powder

Chili Flakes

FENUGREEK (*Trigonella foenum-graceum*)
The pods of a flowering plant native to western Asia contain seeds which are dried and then ground into powder.

CHILI (*Capsicum annuum var. frutescens*)
The fruit pod of the capsicum plant is dried (p. 22), and then converted into flakes or powder. Very hot and spicy, it is used for sambals, curries and Mexican dishes.

PASILLA PEPPER
(*Capsicum frutescens*)
A hot variety of dried pepper native to Central America and used as a flavoring in Latin American (and particularly Mexican) cooking.

MULATO PEPPER
(*Capsicum frutescens*)
A pungent dried pepper native to South America, it is widely used in Latin American cooking.

ANCHO PEPPER
(*Capsicum frutescens*)
This dried pepper, native to South America, is the most popular of all the dried peppers used in Mexican cooking. It is mild and has a full, rich flavor.

VANILLA
(*Vanilla planifolia*)
The cured pod of a climbing orchid native to Central America, vanilla is used as a flavoring in sweet sauces, cakes, chocolate and puddings.

DRIED CHILI PEPPER
(*Capsicum frutescens*)
This pungent pepper, native to South America, is sun-dried and used as a flavoring in many Latin American dishes. The seeds are sometimes crushed into a powder, and the outer skin shredded into flakes (p. 21).

DRIED MANGO
(*Mangifera indica*)
The mango fruit (p. 114),
native to India, is often dried
and sliced as shown and used
as a flavoring for curries.

GRENADINE
A type of French "syrup" made from
the sugar of pomegranate juice,
grenadine is used as a sweetener in
cocktails and desserts.

**Ground
Licorice**

Dried Licorice Slices

Licorice Root

LICORICE (*Glycyrrhiza glabra*)
One of the most ancient of flavorings,
licorice is the root of a small perennial
plant grown in southern Europe and the
Middle East. It has a bitter-sweet taste and
is used in candies and drinks. The root
can be sliced or ground.

ANGOSTURA BITTERS
These bitters, named after an old Venezuelan town,
are made in the West Indies. They consist of cloves,
cinnamon, mace, nutmeg, prunes, quinine, rum and
gentian. Their most popular use is in cocktails, but
they are also used in ice creams, fruit juices,
preserved fruits and puddings.

23

Rose Water

Butterscotch
Flavoring

Raspberry
Essence

Coffee Essence

FLAVORINGS AND ESSENCES

Some flavorings are sold in the form of "essences", which are highly concentrated extracts of fruits and plants. Others, marketed simply as "flavorings", cover a wide range, including butterscotch (a mixture of brown sugar and butter), and brandy and sherry, which simulate the smell and appearance of the drinks. All are used sparingly in recipes for mousses, creams, cakes, preserves and confectionery.

Peppermint Essence

Pineapple Essence

Brandy Flavoring

Rum Flavoring

Almond Essence

Pear Essence

Strawberry Essence

Lemon Essence

Vanilla Essence

Orange Blossom Essence

Orange Flower Water

Maraschino Essence

SEASONED SALT
This is refined salt containing several spices including oregano and black pepper. It can be used in all savory and meat dishes.

SETO FUUMI
A Japanese seasoning compound consisting of dried seaweed, tuna, sesame seed and monosodium glutamate, this is widely used in Oriental cooking.

STOCK POWDER
This is powdered dehydrated meat extract containing herbs. As its name implies, it is used for stocks, gravies and soups and occasionally in sauces.

GARLIC SALT
This is made up of refined salt crystals pounded and mixed with garlic, and can be used in any savory dishes where the taste of garlic is preferred.

BENTOO NO TOMO
A Japanese seasoning compound consisting of dried fish, salt, soy sauce, seaweed and monosodium glutamate, this is used in Oriental cooking.

GRAVY THICKENER
This is dehydrated meat extract with added thickening agents, such as corn starch or wheat flour. It can be used in stews and casseroles.

TABLE SALT
Rock salt obtained from underground deposits, it is usually refined and especially treated to prevent caking – magnesium carbonate is added to help make it run more easily.

MONOSODIUM GLUTAMATE; MSG; Ve-tsin
This white chemical consists of powdered crystals of glutamic acid. Though tasteless in itself, it is used to enhance other foods.

CELERY SALT
A special salt made by pounding celery seeds with refined salt. It can be used in any dish where the taste of celery is preferred.

CRYSTAL ROCK SALT
Obtained from underground deposits, this salt is less refined than table salt.

SEA SALT
The crystals are obtained by the evaporation of sea water. Sea salt is said by many to be the best salt.

KITCHEN SALT
Lump Salt; Block Salt; Common Salt
This is refined rock salt with no additives.

YEAST EXTRACT
The liquid from fresh yeast is separated, evaporated
and added to vegetable extract; it is used as a seasoning.

ASAFOE
This is a resin extracted from the stems of a plant
native to Asia. It is available as shown, and also
powdered, and is used in Indian cookery.

STOCK CUBES
Dehydrated meat, yeast
and vegetable
extracts used in
sauces and soups.

BEEF EXTRACT
A concentrated meat
soup reduced by
evaporation to a salty
paste and used for stews.

**FERMENTED SOYBEAN
PUREE; Miso**
Native to China and Japan, this
consists of soybeans, water and sea
salt. Extracts from the red, yellow and
black varieties of soybean are shown.

**GRAVY
BROWNING**
Consisting of caramel, water and other seasonings, this is
essentially used to enhance the visual appearance of
brown sauces and gravies by making them look darker.

MALT EXTRACT
The soluble part of the malted grain is extracted and evaporated; it is used mainly for
baking and in hot or cold milk drinks.

Pickles, Chutneys and Pastes

See also p. 218

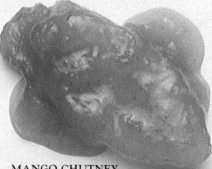

CUCUMBER CHUTNEY
A sweet-tasting mixture of cucumbers, mustard seed, sugar, vinegar, onions, peppers and spices, which goes well with cold meats, cheeses and grills.

TOMATO CHUTNEY
A rich and tangy blend of tomatoes, gherkins, chilies and spices, this can be eaten with cold meats and cheese.

MANGO CHUTNEY
This mild, sweet-tasting chutney, containing mangoes and spices, provides an excellent complement to spicy foods such as curries.

HORSERADISH RELISH
The grated root of the horseradish is mixed with cream, agar-agar, vinegar and salt in this commercial relish which is used with hot or cold meats and fresh or smoked fish.

SWEET PICKLE
Despite its name, this is more like a sweet chutney. It contains a wide range of fruits and vegetables and is best eaten with cheese and cold meats.

CAPER (*Capparis spinosa*, var. *rupestris*)
Members of the *Capparidaceae* family, capers are the unopened buds of a shrub native to the Mediterranean region. They are used only in their pickled form.

Olives with Almonds

Pitted Olives

Spanish Sevillano Olives

OLIVE (*Olea europea*)
A member of the *Oleaceae* family, this is the fruit of a tree native to Mediterranean coasts. There are several varieties, as shown here, and they are used only in their pickled form in recipes and as finger food.

Black Olives

Olives Stuffed with Red Peppers or Pimiento

Dried Olives

MANGO PICKLE
A spicy mixture of mangoes, chilies, spices and vinegar, this can be eaten with any bland foods.

PICCALILLI
A mustard pickle resembling a chutney and consisting of cauliflower, gherkins and onions blended in a mustard sauce. It is used mainly with cheese and cold meats.

PEANUT BUTTER
A paste made from crushed peanut seeds, this is used mainly as a spread in America. In Indonesia it is used to thicken sauces.

MIXED PICKLES
A mixture of cauliflower, onions and gherkins in a vinegar solution, these can be eaten as an accompaniment to cheese and cold meats.

INDONESIAN RELISH
Really a pickle containing a variety of vegetables such as cabbage, onions, leeks, carrots and cucumbers, it is mild-tasting – and is eaten with smoked fish.

JAPANESE PICKLED RADISH
The Japanese *daikon* radish is pickled in a solution of soy sauce and sugar, and is often eaten with fish.

PICKLED WALNUTS
These walnuts are packed in a solution of vinegar, caramel, black pepper and other spices, and are eaten with cold meats and cheese.

PICKLED RED CABBAGE
This cabbage is machine-shredded and soaked in a vinegar brine. It is then repacked in its pickling mixture.

TAHINA PASTE
A paste made from crushed sesame seeds, this is widely used as a flavoring in Middle Eastern and Latin American cookery.

PICKLED ONIONS
These onions, packed first in brine, then in vinegar, are best eaten with cheese.

PICKLED GHERKINS
These small cucumbers, grown exclusively for pickling, can be eaten with cold meats, sausages and in salads.

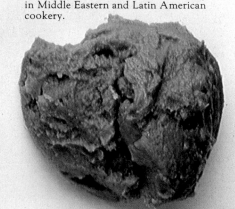

PATUM PEPERIUM ("Gentleman's Relish")
Based on anchovies and butter, this is used mainly as a spread.

Mustards

See also p. 219

GREEN HERB MUSTARD
A very mild mustard, delicately combined with a mixture of herbs, this should be eaten with cold meats and sausages.

MUSTARD WITH GREEN PEPPERCORNS
This mustard, containing crushed green peppercorns, is one of the Dijon varieties from Burgundy. It is fairly hot and therefore goes best with bland foods which need enhancing, such as broiled or grilled steaks and chops.

DIJON MUSTARD WITH WHITE WINE
This is a hot mustard, best used with bland foods. Its additional wine flavoring makes it suitable for many sauces and dressings.

FRENCH MUSTARD WITH TARRAGON
One of the darker Bordeaux mustards, this variety containing tarragon is mild and therefore best suited to cold meats and spicy food.

MOUTARDE DE MEAUX
This is Dijon mustard made with whole *Brassica nigra* seeds. It is fairly hot, and therefore goes best with bland foods.

COARSE-GRAIN MUSTARD
This is a coarse-grained variety of *moutarde de meaux* and contains white wine. It goes well with bland foods.

30

ENGLISH WHOLE-GRAIN MUSTARD
This is a hot, pungent mustard made from whole mustard seeds, white wine, allspice and black pepper. It goes with bland foods.

PLAIN DIJON MUSTARD
Made from the seeds of *Brassica nigra*, the hotter type of mustard, it is ideal with bland food.

AMERICAN MUSTARD
This mustard, made from *Sinapis alba* seeds, is mild and an excellent accompaniment to hot dogs and hamburgers.

ENGLISH MUSTARD
This hot mustard is made from *Brassica nigra* and *Sinapis alba* seeds, together with wheat flour and turmeric. It is also available as a powder, and can be used in toasted cheese sandwiches.

FRENCH MUSTARD
Not a Dijon mustard but a plain, mild Bordeaux type. It goes best with spicy foods.

DUSSELDORF MUSTARD
The most popular type of German mustard, it is similar to Bordeaux mustards. It is mild, and is eaten with spicy food.

GERMAN MUSTARD
This sweet-sour mustard contains herbs, spices and caramel. It is lighter than the usual Dusseldorf mustard (see left), is mild-tasting and is best eaten with cold meats and, of course, German sausage.

FLORIDA MUSTARD
This mild mustard is made with wine from the Champagne region. Like Bordeaux mustards, it is best with spicy food.

Reduction approx. 20%

WALNUT OIL
The kernels of the walnut, native to southeastern Europe and Asia, contain an edible oil, which is used mainly in salads.

OLIVE OIL WITH FENNEL
This oil has been extracted from black olives; the fennel it contains makes it suitable for use with fish.

AVOCADO OIL
This is taken from the pulp of damaged avocado fruit, and makes a good cooking oil.

SESAME SEED OIL
The oil is extracted from the seed capsules of the sesame plant, which is native to Africa. It can be used in salads or as a cooking oil.

SUNFLOWER OIL
The seed of the sunflower, which is native to North America, contains oil which, when refined, is used in salads and for cooking; also for making margarine.

OLIVE OIL
Good olive oil is greenish-yellow; it makes a good oil for salads and cooking.

GRAPE SEED OIL
Grape seeds contain between 6 per cent and 20 per cent oil, which is used in the manufacture of margarine, and also in salads.

CORN OIL
This oil, from the sweetcorn plant, is used in salads and margarine; also for cooking.

PEANUT OIL;
Groundnut Oil
This oil from groundnuts, native to South America, is used in salads and for cooking. It is also used in margarine and canned fish.

Reduction approx. 20%

GARLIC VINEGAR

DISTILLED MALT VINEGAR

CHILI VINEGAR

DILL VINEGAR

WHITE WINE VINEGAR
WITH ROSEMARY

WHITE WINE VINEGAR WITH
GREEN PEPPERCORNS

RED WINE VINEGAR

SPIRIT VINEGAR WITH LEMON

CIDER VINEGAR

WHITE WINE VINEGAR
WITH TARRAGON

MALT VINEGAR

WHITE WINE VINEGAR

CHILI SAUCE
A mild but spicy sauce, it includes red peppers, tomatoes and spices, and is principally used with cooked meat and for marinades and barbecue sauces.

TABASCO SAUCE
A fiery sauce with vinegar and red peppers named after the Mexican region where the peppers originated. It is used sparingly but effectively in many dishes, particularly in Creole cooking.

WORCESTERSHIRE SAUCE
A hot sauce that is used sparingly to give zest to a range of dishes. Made from an old Indian recipe it contains soy sauce, vinegar, molasses, chilis and tropical fruits and spices.

MAYONNAISE
An emulsion of oil, eggs and lemon juice, it is used on many salads and cold dishes. Other ingredients are often added – with anchovy essence it becomes Rémoulade.

SOY SAUCE
Made from soy beans, it is used extensively in Chinese and Japanese cooking. Adopted by other countries it now enhances many dishes – usually other sauces, stews and soups.

SAMBAL
Comparable to chutneys in Indian cooking, sambals are spicy accompaniments widely used in Oriental rice and noodle dishes. The one shown includes onions, red peppers and a selection of spices.

SWEET-AND-SOUR SAUCE
A Chinese style mixture, which combines sugar and vinegar with soy sauce.

OYSTER SAUCE
A thick sauce made from puréed oysters and sold bottled. It is widely used in Chinese cooking, and will keep indefinitely when refrigerated.

PESTO SAUCE; Basil Sauce
Of Mediterranean origins, this sauce is particularly associated with Genoa. It is served with pasta and comprises finely chopped basil, crushed garlic, pine nuts and Sardo or Parmesan cheese.

MINT SAUCE
A blend of sweetened fresh mint, seasoning and vinegar which is traditionally served with lamb.

MINT JELLY
An English recipe that is traditionally made with apple jelly and mint leaves.

ANCHOVY SAUCE
This has many versions, but consists, basically, of anchovies in a white sauce.

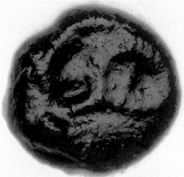

FRUIT SAUCE
Tomatoes, vinegar, raisins and fruits are combined in this sauce. Darker than tomato sauce it is similar in texture and used on the same types of cooked fish and meat dishes.

MELBA SAUCE
A raspberry-based sauce, it is known mainly from its connection with peach melba, a combination of ice cream, peaches and melba sauce, named after Dame Nellie Melba.

MUSTARD SAUCE
This is a type of Hollandaise sauce – made with egg yolks, butter, peppercorns and lemon juice. For this variation Dijon or English mustard is added to give a fairly hot result.

CATSUP; Ketchup; Tomato Sauce
Much used in the American and British kitchen, there are now many variations of this sauce, but usually the ingredients include tomatoes, vinegar and seasonings. It is used extensively on cooked dishes.

APPLE SAUCE
A purée of stewed apples and a little sugar for sweetening, occasionally enlivened by the addition of a spice such as nutmeg, cinnamon, mace or ginger. It is used traditionally with pork dishes but also served as a dessert.

THOUSAND ISLAND DRESSING
Mayonnaise forms the base of this dressing. Other ingredients – which vary – include chili sauce and green peppers.

CRANBERRY SAUCE
The traditional accompaniment to roast turkey, port or white wine and oranges are sometimes added to the cranberries.

BARBECUE SAUCE
There are many variations of this sauce, generally thick in texture, pungent in taste and highly seasoned.

HORSERADISH SAUCE; Sauce au Raifort
Usually a mixture of grated horseradish and fresh or sour cream. It is served with cold meats – generally beef.

TARTARE SAUCE
Mayonnaise made with hard-boiled egg yolks and chives. It is served with fish and cold meats.

BEARNAISE SAUCE
A mixture of fresh tarragon, shallots and white wine thickened with egg yolks.

COCKTAIL SEAFOOD SAUCE
A tangy mayonnaise-type sauce often containing tomatoes.

Sugars and Syrups

See also p. 224

SOFT BROWN SUGAR (light)
Several manufacturers produce a variety of brown sugars which differ in shade (see soft brown sugar, dark) and texture. These are refined sugars with cane molasses added. The refining process leaves a coating around the crystals (which is soluble in water) whereas with raw brown sugars the molasses is in the crystals.

CANDY CRYSTALS
These fairly large brownish crystals are particularly popular with coffee drinkers because they dissolve slowly. The coffee retains some of its bitter taste and is sweetened gradually as it is drunk.

RAINBOW SUGAR CRYSTALS
Vegetable dyes are added to white sugar to produce pastel-shaded crystals. They are sometimes served with coffee for an attractive table presentation and are often used for decoration of cakes, other baked goods and confections.

DEMERARA; Turbinado
One of several raw brown sugars – Barbados is another well-known type – which go through a preliminary cleaning process in their country of origin and are exported already packaged. They vary in taste and appearance and are used particularly in dark, rich fruit cakes.

SUPERFINE; Castor SUGAR
Much finer than granulated sugar, caster is used generally for baking – in cakes and pastries. Because of its texture it dissolves quickly and so is popular for use with fruits and cereals, too.

SOFT BROWN SUGAR (dark)
Another fine-grained sugar (see soft brown sugar, light). Both types are used with cereals and coffee and also in fruit- and spice cakes. There are other brown sugars on the market which do not contain cane molasses. These consist of white sugar with a vegetable dye added, and this will be stated on the packet.

GLUCOSE
Natural glucose occurs in large quantities in grapes and honey. Commercial glucose is available as a powder, a syrup and in chips. Used in jam and confectionery it is also useful to athletes as a quick source of energy because it is easily absorbed.

GRANULATED SUGAR
Several textures of white refined sugar are available. The most common is granulated, used both for the table and in cooking.

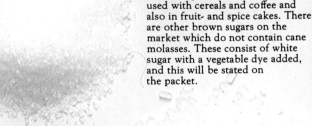

CONFECTIONERS' SUGAR (America); ICING SUGAR (Britain)
This is an even finer version of granulated sugar which is, in fact, powdered. It is used for covering cakes and making meringues.

PRESERVING SUGAR
A coarser variety of granulated sugar, used for pickling and making preserves.

MOLASSES SUGAR
The darker the sugar the more molasses it contains. This lightly processed brown sugar is moist and soft in texture. It is generally used in rich, dark fruit cakes.

LUMP SUGAR; Yellow Lump Sugar
These large golden crystals are very popular with Chinese cooks and are used in desserts and drinks.

GOLDEN SYRUP
Molasses residue that has been clarified.

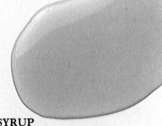

MAPLE SYRUP
The processed sap of the maple tree, this syrup has a distinctive taste.

MUSCOVADO SUGAR
A lighter brown than molasses sugar, muscovado is also soft and moist. It is used in fruit cakes and a variety of it is an important ingredient in many Indian dishes.

LUMP SUGAR
Blocks of dark brown concentrated sugar used in many Chinese and Indian dishes.

CANE SYRUP
The concentrated sap of sugar cane, it is sometimes substituted for molasses.

BLACK TREACLE
A darker and heavier version of golden syrup, it is used in rich fruit cakes and spicy sauces.

ROSE HIP SYRUP
Syrup from the pulp of softened rose hips.

MOLASSES
A by-product of sugar-making, it improves the keeping qualities of breads and cakes and is rich in iron.

CUBE SUGAR
Refined and crystallized sugar is moistened and compressed into cubes which are used for sweetening hot drinks.

CASSIS SYRUP; Blackcurrant Syrup
A rich fruity syrup made with sugar and the juice of blackcurrants.

Honeys

See also p. 226

HONEY, CONTAINING COMB; Chunk Comb Honey
This luxury item contains a section of the comb in a jar topped up with clear honey.

COMB
The natural form in which all honey is found, comb honey is eaten, wax and all. Normally the wax combs are cut by hand to remove the honey; when commercially processed they are uncapped by machine.

ENGLISH
This is a blend of honeys gathered from a variety of English blossoms. Also available creamed, it is often thought essential for a "proper" afternoon tea.

MANUKA
A dark creamed honey from New Zealand, it has a rich taste good in cooking.

PURE ORANGE BLOSSOM
Produced mostly in Spain, but also California, Mexico, South Africa and Israel, this light, delicate citrus-tasting honey is especially good in custards.

JAMAICAN
Clear and dark with an exotic tropical flower taste, this thick honey is good to use in cooking.

HUNGARIAN ACACIA
Romania, France and Italy also produce this mild variety which tends to always remain liquid.

EUCALYPTUS
A creamy Australian honey which can
be light or dark and medium to very
sweet depending on the variety of
eucalyptus nectar from which it is made.

HEATHER
Heather-covered heaths produce
a creamy honey which liquefies
when stirred.

HYMETUS
From thyme, marjoram and other herbal
blossoms growing on Mt Hymetus in Greece,
this dark, clear and slightly thick honey is
world famous. It is a perfect complement to
tart natural yogurt and is excellent used in
the confection *baklava*.

CLOVER
The most common honey in America, it is
also available clear. Its mild taste is best
for general cooking.

SUNFLOWER
Produced mainly in Greece, Turkey and Southern
Russia, sunflower honey loses its excellent
fragrance in cooking.

**TASMANIAN
LEATHERWOOD**
From Australia, this
rich, creamy honey has
a distinctive taste and is
high in glucose. If
necessary, it can be put
in warm water for 30
minutes to make it
clear, and used for
general cooking.

ROSEMARY
From small blue flowers once associated with the
Virgin Mary, this strong, aromatic herb honey is
produced mainly in Mediterranean countries.

Jams, Marmalades and Jellies

See also p. 227

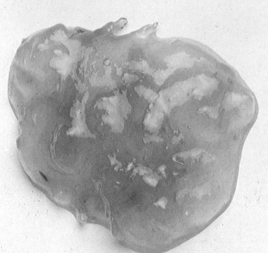

Mirabelle Plum Jam

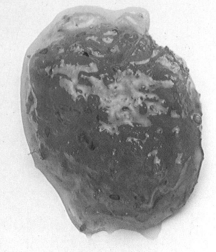

Gooseberry Jam

Black Cherry Jam

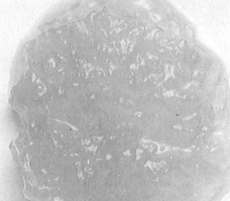

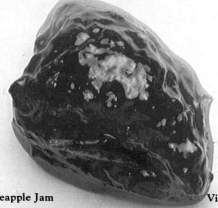

Pineapple Jam

Victoria Plum Jam

Greengage Stoneless Jam

JAMS

Most fruits can be made into jams, jellies and marmalades and this was originally a way of using up surplus produce for use later in the year. Nowadays much is made commercially, and all are basically a mixture of fruit, sugar and water – in jam-making the whole fruit is used. Jams are popular accompaniments to toasts, biscuits and muffins as well as being used in a variety of ways such as in sweetening desserts and sandwiching sponge cakes.

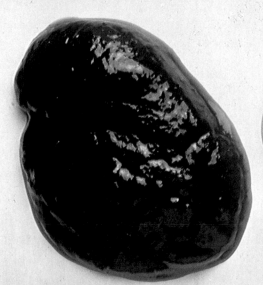

Damson Stoneless Jam

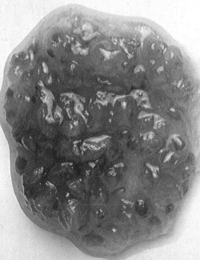

Cloudberry Jam

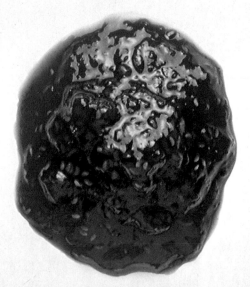

Raspberry Jam

Green Fig Jam

Orange Thick-cut Marmalade

Golden Apple Jelly

Orange Medium-cut Marmalade

Blackberry Jelly

Strawberry Jam

MARMALADES
Made with strained fruit pulp, they are used like jams and are particularly popular on breakfast toast. Marmalade is often brushed over a fruit cake to provide the sticky base for an almond paste covering.

JELLIES
In jelly-making the juice of the fruits is used. Jellies are used in the same way as jams. Their smooth texture makes them easily digestible and because of this they are particularly useful in invalid cookery.

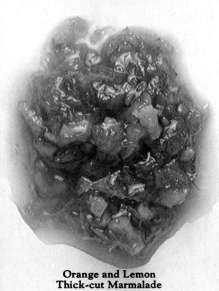

Crab Apple Jelly

Orange and Lemon Thick-cut Marmalade

Orange Thin-cut Marmalade

Unsalted Butter

Salted Butter

BUTTER
A natural dairy product made from cream, butter can be either unsalted or salted. The salted type has better keeping qualities.

DRIPPING
An animal cooking fat, this is separated fat produced from cooking meat.

LARD
This is melted and clarified pork fat. Softer than butter and margarine, it can be used for baking and frying.

MARGARINE
A butter substitute made from animal or vegetable fats, margarine can be bought in blocks or tubs.

SUET
Often used in puddings, suet is the fat surrounding the kidneys of certain animals. It is shown grated and ready for use.

SOFT MARGARINE
This variety is made from sunflower oil and contains polyunsaturates and emulsifiers. It is easier to spread than the margarine sold in blocks.

GHEE
A type of clarified butter made by heating ordinary butter to rid it of impurities (ghee is the yellow liquid left when the sediment has been removed). It has a higher burning point than most other oils, which makes it perfect for frying and sautéing.

MILK
The basis of all dairy products, milk is available in many forms: homogenized, skimmed, evaporated, condensed and powdered.

POWDERED MILK
A useful fresh milk substitute, powdered milk consists of pasteurized, air-dried milk particles, which should be reconstituted with water before use. The type shown is a skim milk substitute.

YOGURT
A product made from curdled milk with the addition of a lactic starter, *yogurt* is its Turkish name. Commercial varieties use evaporated milk and often contain fruit.

CLOTTED CREAM
Made from cream skimmed from scalded milk, warmed over a low heat, and then cooled, clotted cream is a speciality of western England.

BUTTERMILK
Originally the sour milk left over from butter-making, today buttermilk is usually made from pasteurized skim milk with an added culture to thicken its consistency. It is used as a drink, in baking and confectionery, and is a good sour milk substitute.

CREAM
Cream is the fatty part of fresh milk which rises to the surface when milk is left to stand. There are several varieties: the one shown, light (single) cream, has half the butterfat content of heavy (double) cream. As well as providing a basis for making butter, cream is used in its own right in a number of dishes, and as the basis for many sauces.

WHIPPING CREAM
This type of cream is halfway between light (single) and heavy (double) cream as regards butterfat content. As its name implies, it is used exclusively for whipping (when whipped it expands and solidifies).

RICOTTA
An Italian fresh, unripened cheese made from the whey of cow's milk. It is smooth and mild-tasting and is used in a variety of sweet and savory dishes, including pizzas. It is packaged in various shapes and sizes.

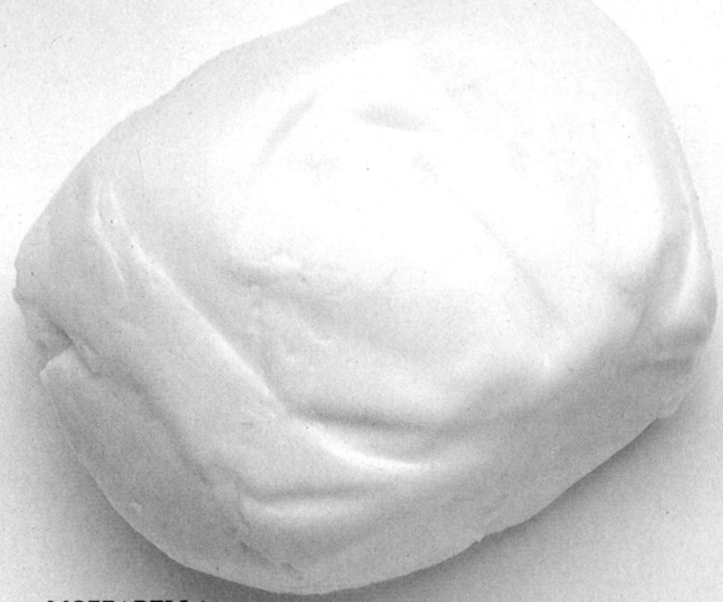

MOZZARELLA
An Italian unripened curd cheese originally made from buffalo's milk, but now obtained exclusively from cow's milk. Made in various shapes, such as rounds and slabs, it is also packed shredded. It is a soft cheese with a rather moist texture. It has a mild, creamy taste and is widely used as a cooking cheese – in pizzas, lasagne and toasted sandwiches.

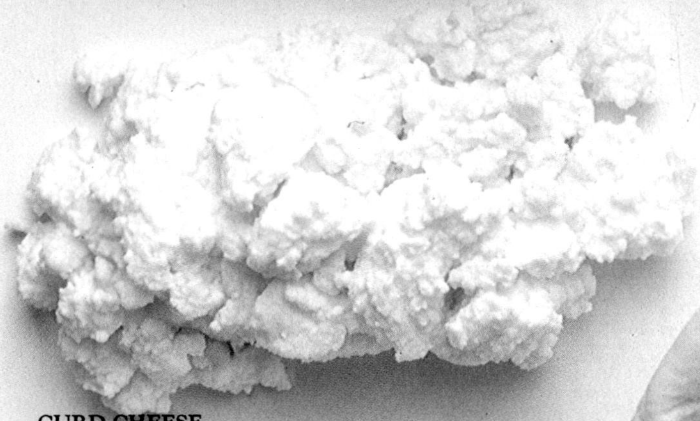

CURD CHEESE
"Curd" is the general name given to all unripened cheeses made from the separated curds of cow's or goat's milk. Curd cheese has a slightly acid taste, and is used in cheesecakes and sweet and savory fillings. It is also a popular base for dips and spreads. It is sold in most countries.

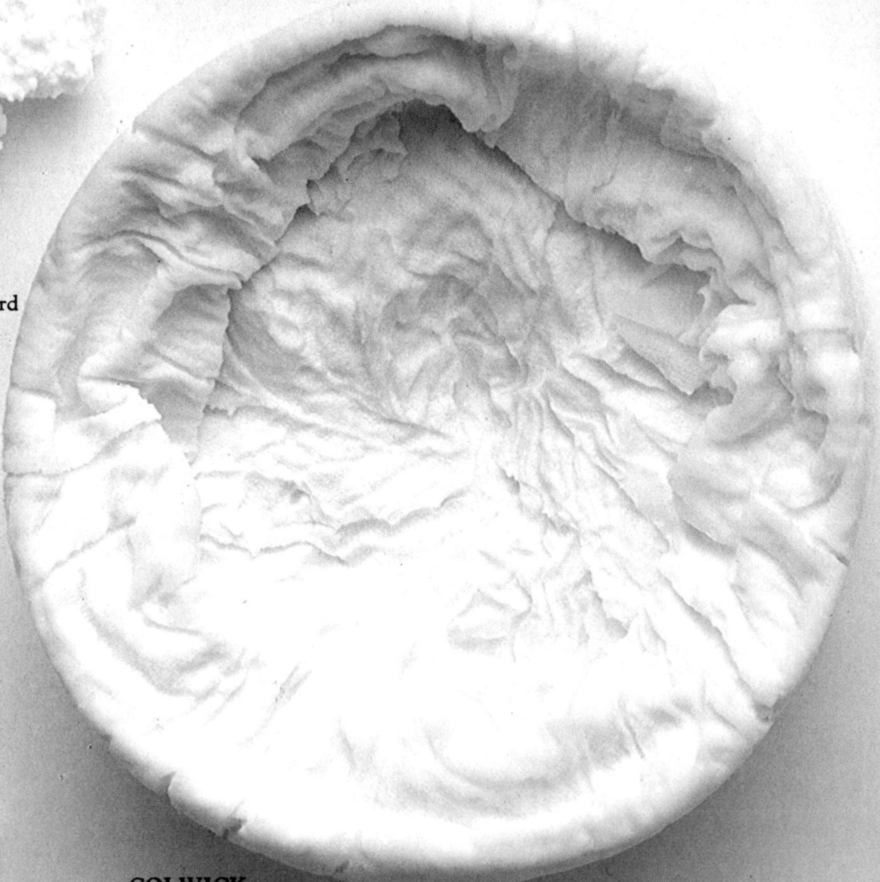

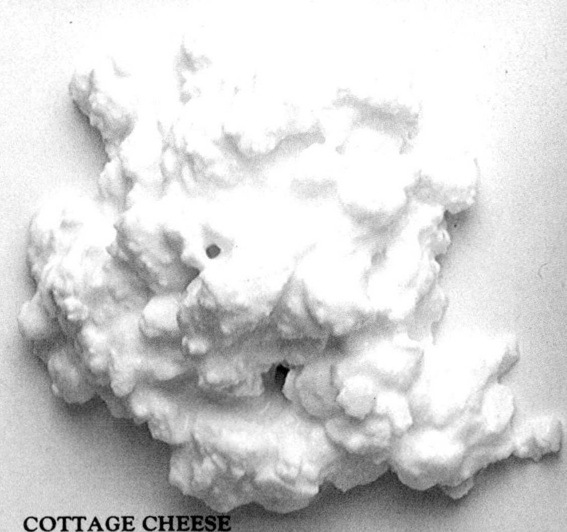

COTTAGE CHEESE
A lumpy, mild-tasting curd cheese, often containing cream. It has a moist texture, and is usually sold in tubs. Available in most countries it is used in cheesecakes and salads.

COLWICK
A traditional cow's milk cheese from England. Usually made in cylinder shapes, the variety shown here has a dished center, which can be filled with cream and fruit. This cheese is usually sold unsalted to be served as a dessert, but can be salted and used as a savory cheese.

COULOMMIERS
A French cheese made from cow's milk, this, like Brie and Camembert, has a white rind and a soft interior. It is rich and creamy tasting and is usually made in small wheel shapes. It is a popular cheese for desserts and snacks.

CAMEMBERT
This world-famous French cheese is made from cow's milk and there are several varieties. It has a distinctive taste which varies from mild to pungent as it ages. An excellent dessert- and snack cheese, it is made in small cylinder shapes, which means that it can be bought as an individual cheese.

BRIE
A French, soft cheese made from cow's milk, it has a creamy fruity taste and is delicious in snacks and as a filling for brioche. It is made in large, flat wheel shapes and there are many varieties. The thin crust is edible.

TOMME AU RAISIN
A French cheese made from cow's milk and covered with grape pulp, skin and pips. The word *tomme* is simply a dialect word for cheese from the Savoie region of France and there are many varieties. They usually have a fairly pronounced flavor and make excellent dessert cheeses. They are produced in small drum shapes.

PETIT MUNSTER
A cow's milk cheese from Alsace, traditionally thought of as being French in origin, though there are several German varieties. Made in wheel shapes it is good for snacks.

CREAM CHEESE
A fresh, unripened cheese made from cow's milk and usually foil wrapped.

BOURSIN AUX FINES HERBES
A French soft triple cream cheese (with a 75 per cent fat content), the variety shown contains rosemary, fennel and chives. It is most often served with crackers.

NEUFCHATEL
A French, mild flavored cheese made from cow's milk. Although it is eaten when ripened in Europe, in America it is often eaten as a fresh, unripened cheese. It is made in a variety of shapes and sizes and is good for desserts and snacks.

CABOC
A Scottish double cream cheese (with a 60 per cent fat content), made from cow's milk and rolled in oatmeal. It has a fairly sweet flavor and goes well with fresh fruit. It is made in small log or cylinder shapes.

BOURSIN AU POIVRE (with pepper)
A variety of Boursin coated with crushed black peppercorns which give the cheese a spicy taste, complementing its creamy interior. Like the herb variety it is packaged in small drum shapes and can be bought as an individual cheese.

FETA
A soft Greek cheese usually made from ewe's milk (sometimes from goat's milk). It has a sharp and salty taste and is used in savory stuffings and salads. It is made in various shapes and sizes.

Semi-Hard Cheeses

See also p. 230

MANCHEGO
Spain's most famous cheese, this is made from ewe's milk and has a creamy, firmish-textured interior, which sometimes has holes. It is strong-tasting and ideal for snacks, and is made in cylinder shapes.

DUNLOP
A Scottish cheese made from cow's milk, this is a Cheddar-type cheese with a rather bland, buttery taste. In Scotland it is often eaten with buttered oatcakes; otherwise it makes a good snack cheese and is ideal for toasting. It is made in cylinder shapes.

PORT SALUT
A French, rinded cheese made from cow's milk, it is good for desserts and snacks.

CABRALES
Traditionally a goat's milk cheese (though there are now ewe's milk varieties) it is from the mountain regions of northern Spain. Made in cylinder shapes, it has a strong, pronounced taste and makes a good snack cheese.

COLBY
A popular American Cheddar-type cheese from Colby, Wisconsin. It is a washed-curd cheese (if the curds are washed thoroughly in cold water, the moisture content of the cheese is increased, making it mature more quickly). Made in various shapes, it is a mild cheese with a slightly granular texture, and is popular in snacks and salads.

MONTEREY JACK
A Cheddar-type cheese originating in Monterey, California, but now also made in other parts of America, it is made from cow's milk, and has a rather bland taste with a smooth, open texture. It is made in block shapes or large wheels and is used in snacks, sandwiches and in recipes.

SAINT PAULIN
A rinded French cheese made from cow's milk, it can be bland or tangy, depending on its degree of ripeness, and is similar in taste to Port Salut. It is a good snack- and dessert cheese and is made in small wheel shapes.

Semi-Hard Cheeses

See also p. 230

TILSIT
A firm-textured cow's milk cheese, originally from East Prussia, but now produced all over Europe. It has a tangy taste, and is a good cheese for desserts and sandwiches. It can be made either in wheel- or block shapes.

DOUBLE GLOUCESTER
This cow's milk cheese has a full flavor and is considered one of the great English cheeses. It is good for desserts and snacks and is made in cylinder shapes.

CHEDDAR
England's most famous cheese, this is made from cow's milk and varies from mild to very sharp. It is packaged in many shapes.

GJETOST
A Norwegian whey cheese which can be made from either cow's milk or goat's milk. Rather fudge-like in taste and appearance, it is made in cubes or rectangular blocks and is usually foil-wrapped. It is used in sauces, desserts and snacks.

GRUYÈRE
This famous cow's milk cheese from Switzerland is similar to Emmenthal; in appearance and nut-like taste. Apart from being a good table cheese it is much used in fondues, sauces and quiches. It is made in large wheel shapes.

CANTAL
A cow's milk cheese from France, it is often referred to as *French cheddar*. Made in cylinder shapes, it is used in several regional dishes and is also a good all-purpose table cheese.

RED CHESHIRE
A cow's milk cheese from England, it has a crumbly texture and is colored with annatto dye. Its slightly salty taste makes it a good snack cheese. It is made in cylinder shapes.

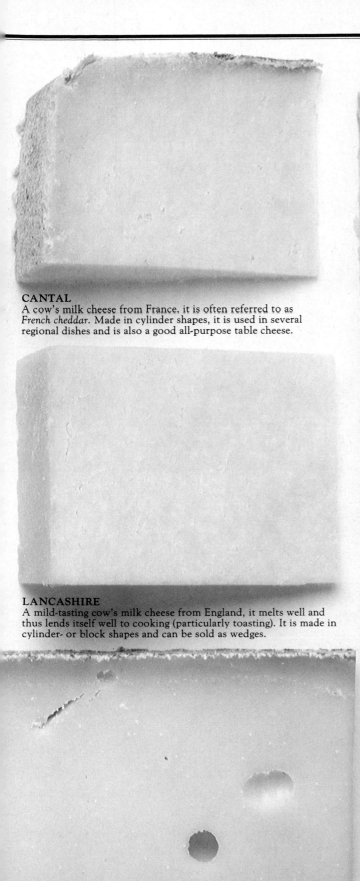

LANCASHIRE
A mild-tasting cow's milk cheese from England, it melts well and thus lends itself well to cooking (particularly toasting). It is made in cylinder- or block shapes and can be sold as wedges.

FONTINA
A cow's milk cheese from the Piedmont region of Italy, it has a delicate nutty, slightly smoky taste and is much used for *fonduta* (an Italian version of the Swiss "fondue"). It is made in flat wheel shapes.

LEYDEN/LEIDEN
A Dutch, semi-hard cheese covered with a dark yellow rind and then with red wax. It is made from whole or skimmed cow's milk and contains caraway and cumin seeds. Made in cylinder shapes, it goes well with gin and cocktails and makes a good snack cheese.

GOUDA
A world-famous Dutch cheese made from cow's milk which can be eaten "fresh" or matured; it is made in wheel shapes.

JARLSBERG
A Norwegian cheese, ranging from white to light yellow with large holes scattered throughout. It is made from cow's milk and has a firm, buttery interior and a mild, nutty taste. It is covered with a thick rind and then with a yellow wax. A good all-purpose cheese, it is used in *landgang*, the Norwegian version of a hero sandwich. Jarlsberg is made in wheel shapes.

EDAM
A famous Dutch cheese made from cow's milk and sold in ball shapes coated with red wax.

RACLETTE
A cow's milk cheese from Switzerland with a mild, nutty taste. Made in wheel shapes, it gives its name to a traditional toasted cheese dish.

CAERPHILLY
A cow's milk cheese from Wales with a mild, slightly sour taste. Usually made in cylinder shapes it is a good snack- and dessert cheese.

LEICESTER
An English cheese made from cow's milk and colored with annatto dye. Made in cylinder shapes it is a good snack cheese.

WENSLEYDALE
An English cheese . . . made as a blue-veined type. White . . . traditionally eaten with apple pie and is made in cylinder and block shapes.

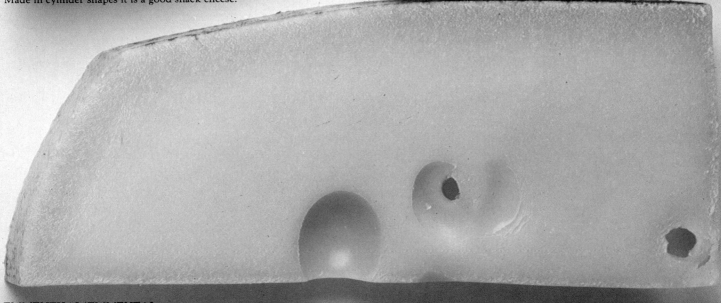

EMMENTHAL/EMMENTAL
This world-famous Swiss cheese made from cow's milk has a fairly sweet, nutty taste and can be used as a basis for fondues and toasted snacks. It is made in wheel shapes and is often sold in segments, pieces and slices.

PARMESAN; Parmigiano
One of Italy's best-known cheeses, Parmesan is one of the *grana*, or granular types. It is a cow's milk cheese made in large wheel shapes and when fully matured it is used for grating and cooking.

PROVOLONE
An Italian curd cheese made from cow's milk, Provolone is sold in many shapes, including "pears" and cylinders. A popular cooking cheese, it is often used in cannelloni and ravioli.

SAPSAGO
Green Cheese; Schabziger
A Swiss cheese made from soured skimmed milk and whole milk, Sapsago is pale green, due to the presence of clover which is added to the curd. It is a hard cheese which is normally grated before use, and makes a good all-purpose cooking cheese.

PECORINO
A hard, Italian *grana* cheese made from sheep's milk, Pecorino, when fully matured, is used for grating in many pasta-style dishes.

CACIOCAVALLO
An Italian cheese made from cow's milk, Caciocavallo is, like Provolone, one of the *pasta filata*, or "drawn curd" cheeses (in which the curds are softened by hot water, which means that they can be easily shaped by hand). Made in gourd-like shapes, the young cheeses are used for snacks or desserts; older cheeses become hard and granular and are then used for grating and cooking.

SBRINZ
A Swiss grating cheese made from cow's milk, this is a good all-purpose cooking cheese made in large wheel shapes.

GORGONZOLA
Italy's most famous blue-veined cheese, Gorgonzola is considered one of the best blue cheeses in the world. Made in cylinder shapes, the veining is greenish rather than blue, and the cheese has a strong and rich taste. It is good for desserts, snacks and salad dressings and, when grated and grilled, can be used as a topping for several foods.

SMOKED EMMENTHAL
Traditionally made in long sausage shapes, it is used mainly as a snack cheese. Other cheeses may be smoked and found in this form although the most commonly used cheeses are Emmenthal and Cheddar.

ROQUEFORT
Considered by many to be the king of cheeses, Roquefort is a sheep's milk cheese from the Causes area in France. It is made in cylinder shapes and has a rich, strong taste. It is used as a table cheese, and also in salad dressings.

MYCELLA
A Danish cheese made from cow's milk, Mycella has blue-green veins. It is usually made in tall, cylinder shapes, though smaller pieces are often sold foil-wrapped. It is used mainly as a table cheese, but can also be used in salads and salad dressings.

Blue Cheeses

See also p. 230

BLEU DE BRESSE; Bresse Bleu
A French, creamy blue-veined cheese made from cow's milk, it is soft-textured and has a rich taste. Made in small, cylinder shapes and often foil-wrapped, it is a good dessert cheese and is also used in *fromage cardinal* – a blend of cheese and paprika.

DOLCELATTE
A Gorgonzola-type cow's milk cheese from Italy, made in cylinder shapes.

BLUE CASTELLO
A Danish double cream soft-textured cheese made from cow's milk.

PIPO CREM'
A popular French blue-veined cow's milk cheese made in long cylinder shapes.

FOURME D'AMBERT
A French blue-veined cow's milk cheese made in tall cylinder shapes.

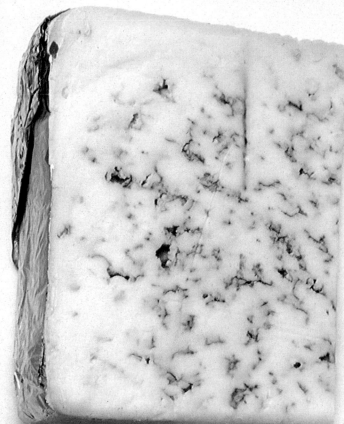

BLUE CHESHIRE
A worthy rival to Stilton, Blue Cheshire is an English semi-hard cheese made from cow's milk. It has a rich taste and is best served as a dessert cheese. It is made in cylinder shapes.

DANISH BLUE; Danablu
A Danish cheese made from homogenized cow's milk, it is soft-textured and creamy with a fairly strong taste, and makes a good dessert cheese. It is made in wheel shapes.

BAVARIAN BLUE
A double cream, soft-textured blue-veined cheese from West Germany. Made from cow's milk, it has a creamy texture and spreads well, making it good for sandwiches. It is made in small wheel shapes.

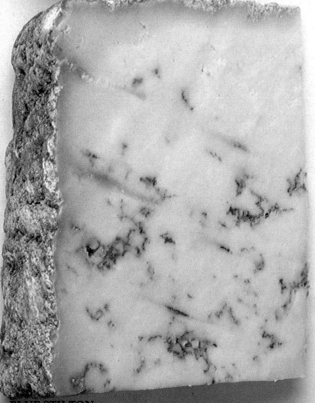

BLUE STILTON
A semi-hard English blue-veined cheese made from cow's milk, it comes in tall cylinder shapes.

BLUE SHROPSHIRE
A new arrival amongst blue cheeses and made, not in Shropshire, England, but in Scotland, it comes in cylinder shapes.

CHICKEN; Hen
Both brown and white eggs have the same nutritional value and it is a matter of personal taste which you choose to buy. These are the only eggs to be produced on a large commercial scale and are the familiar standard by which other eggs are compared, the average weight being about 2oz (50g).

1,000-YEAR-OLD; 100-Year-Old
Raw duck eggs preserved in lime, pine ash and salt for 50–100 days, these emerge translucent blue and green, looking much older than they are. Firm in texture, they are rich with a slightly fishy taste.

PHEASANT AND PARTRIDGE
These eggs are usually solid white, buff or olive, although some species nest in open areas and their eggs are blotched with brown or black for protection against predators. They are most often served hard-boiled; shelled and used in salads; pickled or set in aspic.

GOOSE
The goose egg has a slightly oily taste and should always be served very fresh in briefly cooked dishes.

QUAIL
Considered a delicacy, these small eggs are usually eaten hard-boiled or poached and in aspic.

DUCK
These eggs are oilier-tasting than chickens' eggs and can acquire a harmful bacteria as they are usually laid in a dirty spot. However, they are still suitable for eating if they are boiled for 15 minutes or used in baking. The white turns bluish and the yolk a reddish-orange after boiling.

GUINEA FOWL
Small and slightly pointed with a muddy complexion, this egg has a more delicate taste than the chicken's egg. It is usually eaten hard-boiled.

BANTAM
These are similar in taste to chickens' eggs and, although only about half the size, may be used in the same way. The difference in tints has no effect on the taste.

GULL
These eggs vary in size, depending on the species of gull, but are almost always camouflaged with dark blotches. They lack the strong, fishy taste which is common to the eggs of most sea birds.

PULLET
Another type of chicken's egg, laid by an immature breed.

OSTRICH
This egg is rarely available, but it is edible provided it hasn't been left to bake in the sun or been partially hatched. An ostrich egg is twenty times the size of a chicken's egg.

Leaf Vegetables

See also p. 237

Reduction approx. 25%

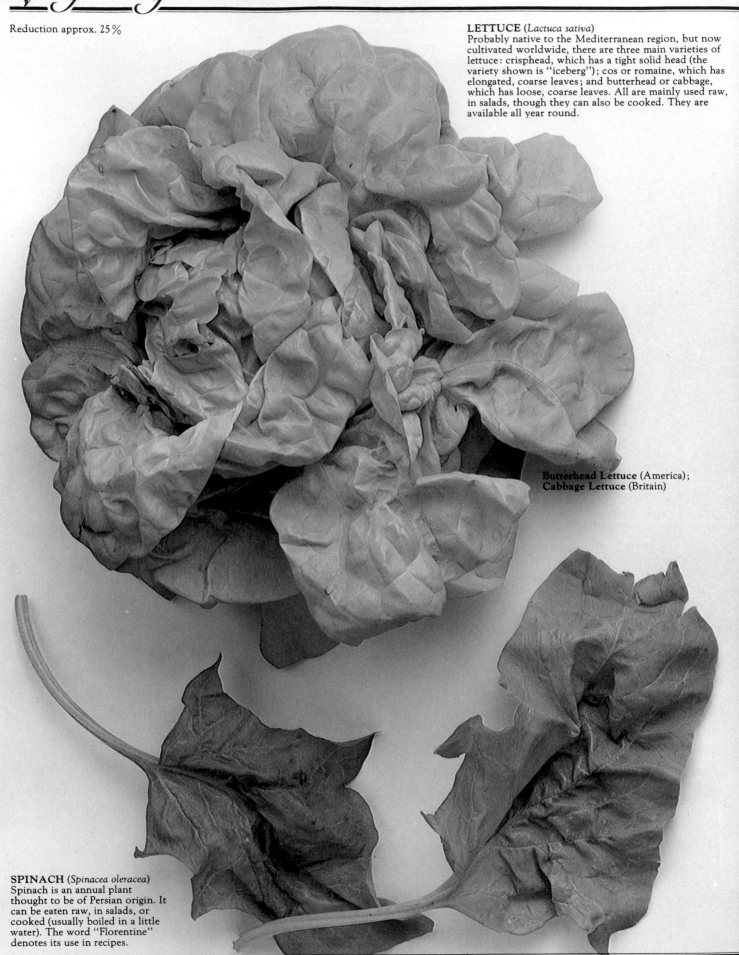

LETTUCE (*Lactuca sativa*)
Probably native to the Mediterranean region, but now cultivated worldwide, there are three main varieties of lettuce: crisphead, which has a tight solid head (the variety shown is "iceberg"); cos or romaine, which has elongated, coarse leaves; and butterhead or cabbage, which has loose, coarse leaves. All are mainly used raw, in salads, though they can also be cooked. They are available all year round.

Butterhead Lettuce (America);
Cabbage Lettuce (Britain)

SPINACH (*Spinacea oleracea*)
Spinach is an annual plant thought to be of Persian origin. It can be eaten raw, in salads, or cooked (usually boiled in a little water). The word "Florentine" denotes its use in recipes.

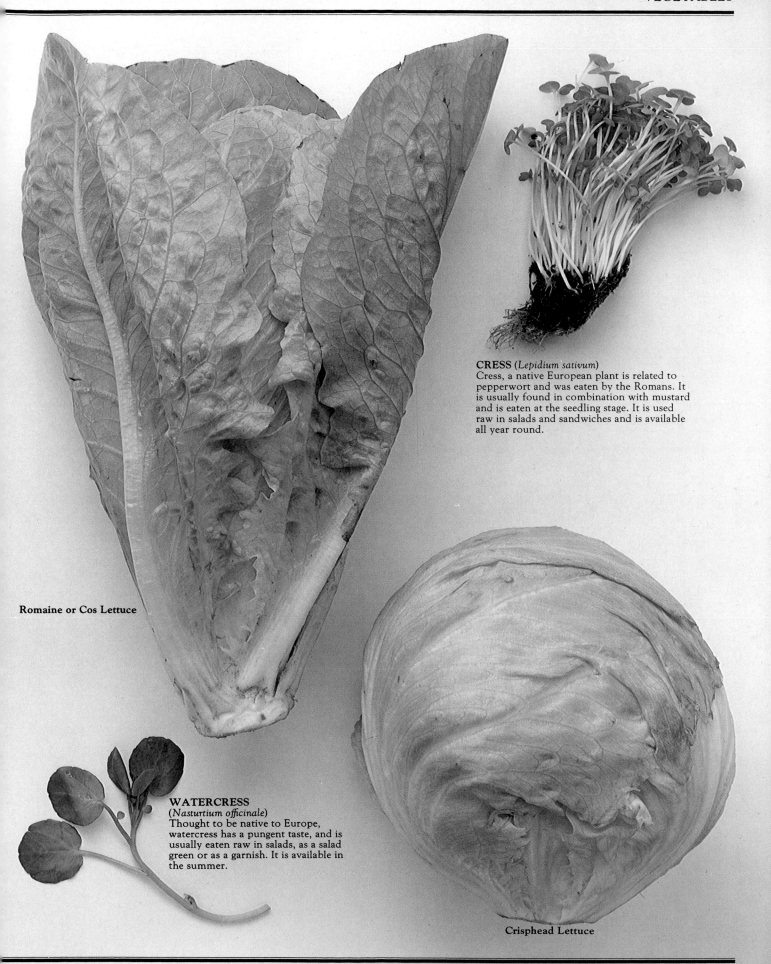

CRESS (*Lepidium sativum*)
Cress, a native European plant is related to pepperwort and was eaten by the Romans. It is usually found in combination with mustard and is eaten at the seedling stage. It is used raw in salads and sandwiches and is available all year round.

Romaine or Cos Lettuce

WATERCRESS
(*Nasturtium officinale*)
Thought to be native to Europe, watercress has a pungent taste, and is usually eaten raw in salads, as a salad green or as a garnish. It is available in the summer.

Crisphead Lettuce

Leaf Vegetables

Reduction approx. 50%

NETTLE
(*Urtica dioica*)
Available worldwide,
nettle is a perennial
plant which, like
sorrel and spinach,
can be cooked as a
purée. It is the basic
ingredient of nettle
soup, and is also used
to make beer and tea.

SWISS CHARD (*Beta vulgaris*) **Seakale beet**
Both the leaves and
shoots of this green
vegetable, native to the
Mediterranean region,
are used. It is available
from spring to
midwinter.

SORREL (*Rumex acetosa*)
A perennial plant native to Europe and Asia, and now
also found in America, sorrel has a refreshing, slightly
sour taste. It can be used as a vegetable (raw, in salads,
or cooked as a type of purée, like spinach) and as a
herb (in soups and sauces and, with other herbs, as a
stuffing for fish). It is mostly available in summer.

GOOD KING HENRY
(*Chenopodium bonus-henricus*)
Goosefoot
This perennial plant, native to
Europe, West Asia and North
America, is used as a green
vegetable, and is cooked in the
same way as spinach, for which it
is often substituted.

VINE LEAF (*Vitis vinifera*)
The vine, originally from the
Mediterranean region, is now found
worldwide. It is much used in Turkish,
Greek and Middle Eastern cooking, and
is best known in the form of *dolmades*
(vine leaves stuffed with rice and
minced meat).

CHICORY (America); **ENDIVE** (Britain) (*Cichorium endivia*)
This annual plant, native to southern Asia and northern China, is used mainly in
salads. It has a slightly sharp taste and is available from midsummer to midwinter.

Brassicas

See also p. 237

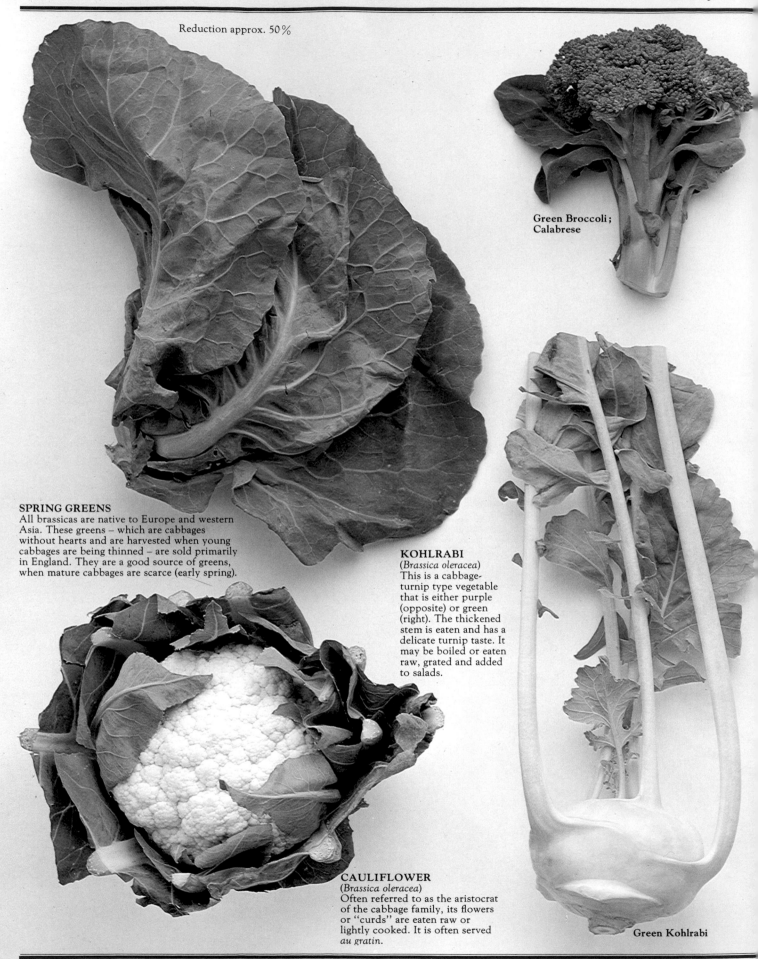

Reduction approx. 50%

**Green Broccoli;
Calabrese**

SPRING GREENS
All brassicas are native to Europe and western
Asia. These greens – which are cabbages
without hearts and are harvested when young
cabbages are being thinned – are sold primarily
in England. They are a good source of greens,
when mature cabbages are scarce (early spring).

KOHLRABI
(*Brassica oleracea*)
This is a cabbage-
turnip type vegetable
that is either purple
(opposite) or green
(right). The thickened
stem is eaten and has a
delicate turnip taste. It
may be boiled or eaten
raw, grated and added
to salads.

CAULIFLOWER
(*Brassica oleracea*)
Often referred to as the aristocrat
of the cabbage family, its flowers
or "curds" are eaten raw or
lightly cooked. It is often served
au gratin.

Green Kohlrabi

Purple Hearting Broccoli; Purple Cauliflower

BROCCOLI (*Brassica oleracea*)
A variety of cauliflower, there are two types, the green or "heading" broccoli (opposite) and the purple "hearting". They are not eaten raw but are best steamed. Although basically interchangeable, the purple type is a little more refined.

KALE; Curly Kale; Borecole
(*Brassica oleracea*, spp.)
There are many varieties both crinkly and smooth-leaved. A winter vegetable, it is rather coarse in texture but offers a good source of greens in the winter months. Kale is not eaten raw but is best poached, drained and served with butter.

Purple Kohlrabi

BRUSSELS SPROUTS
(*Brassica oleracea*)
These miniature cabbages get their name from their discovery in archaeological sites of prehistoric times in Brussels. Brussels sprouts are eaten raw or lightly cooked.

SAVOY CABBAGE (*Brassica oleracea*)
Probably of Italian origin its leaves are those usually chosen in recipes for stuffed cabbage leaves. Cabbages are grown in many shapes and shades. These wrinkly leaves make a decorative alternative to the roundhead cabbage (see overleaf).

Reduction approx. 50%

ROUNDHEAD CABBAGE (*Brassica oleracea*, spp.) **Common Cabbage**
Like the conical-shaped cabbage, this is available in summer and winter. Eaten raw or lightly cooked.

RED CABBAGE (*Brassica oleracea*, spp.)
Best known for its association with vinegar, either raw or cooked, it is often served in this way with game.

PAK-CHOI
(*Brassica chinensis*)
At its best late in the year, the plant does not form a heart and is reminiscent of a spinach leaf. It is usually eaten raw in salads, but can also be stir-fried with rice. It is used in Chinese cooking.

WHITE CABBAGE (*Brassica oleracea*, spp.) **Dutch Cabbage**
Because it keeps well, this is a variety that is good for storing. Its crisp, tight head is particularly good for grating and is used for coleslaws and sauerkraut.

PE-TSAI (*Brassica pekinensis*)
Can be lightly cooked – stir-fried – or eaten raw. Long in shape it is similar to the cos lettuce. It is used a great deal in Chinese cooking and is interchangeable with ordinary cabbage.

White Asparagus

Green Asparagus

GLOBE ARTICHOKE
(*Cynara scolymus*)
Really a type of thistle, the globe
artichoke is the flower head of a
perennial plant native to North
Africa, but now cultivated in
Europe as a winter vegetable and in
America as an all-year-round
vegetable. It can be pickled whole
when small, and its tender base or
"heart" is also sold canned and
frozen. It can be baked, fried,
boiled, or stuffed and served with
various sauces and dressings. The
stalk of the head is often used
blanched in soups and stews.

PALM HEARTS (Family: *Palmaceae*)
A tropical delicacy, these are the tender
terminal shoots of some varieties of
palm trees. They are usually sold
precooked and canned.

ASPARAGUS (*Asparagus officinalis*)
The young shoot of a plant native to Europe, there
are two basic types (green and white) each
comprising many varieties – the white varieties are
particularly popular in France, Belgium and
Germany. Available fresh from spring to early summer.

BAMBOO SHOOT (Family: *Gramineae*)
The white inner part of the young bamboo
plant, native to Asia, bamboo shoots are
usually sold cooked and canned. Their
crispness and slight acidity provide a good
complement to meat, especially pork.

FENNEL (*Foeniculum vulgare*)
Florence Fennel
A bulbous leafstalk native to Europe, fennel tastes very much like anise. It can be sliced and eaten raw in salads, or boiled whole or sliced and served with cheese sauce.

BELGIAN ENDIVE (America);
CHICORY (Britain) (*Cichorium intybus*)
Native to Europe and western Asia, but also grown in America, this is available from autumn to spring. Slightly bitter, it is used raw in salads; braised, or fried.

FIDDLEHEAD FERN
(Family: *Pteridium*)
Bracken; Brake
There are many varieties of this tender fern found in America and Europe which is available fresh, canned or frozen and is used mainly (raw) in salads.

CELERY (*Apium graveolens*)
Native to Europe but also grown in America, it is sold all year round, fresh (in heads or loose sticks), or canned. The leaves are a mildly pungent herb.

Fruit Vegetables

See also p. 237

"Slim Jim" Eggplant

White Eggplant

Cherry Tomato

Purple Truck Eggplant

Naples Early Purple Eggplant

Beefsteak Tomato

EGGPLANT (America); **AUBERGINE** (Britain) (*Solanum*, spp.)
This large, satin-skinned vegetable is probably a native tf India. It is available in different shapes and can range from deep purple to white, although the purple variety is the most common. Eggplants can only be bought as fresh vegetables, but are available all year round. The mealy, yellow-green flesh is always eaten cooked. Some of the more common recipes for eggplants are ratatouille, *moussaka* and *imam bayeldi*.

TOMATOES (*Lycopersicum*, spp.)
Originally from South America, tomatoes are available in varying shapes and sizes. Red or green tomatoes can easily be bought fresh or canned and can be eaten raw or cooked. Red tomatoes are also available as juice, purée or catsup (ketchup), while green tomatoes are often used in pickles and chutneys. Both varieties are available throughout the year.

PEPPERS (*Capsicum*, spp.)
Native to tropical America and the West Indies, peppers are usually classed as being either sweet or hot and come in many colors and sizes as shown. Both varieties are available fresh or canned, all year round. The sweet pepper is mild in taste and can be eaten raw or cooked. Chili or hot peppers are used almost exclusively as a seasoning.

Avocado

AVOCADO
(*Persea*, spp.)
Alligator Pear
This pear-shaped fruit originated in Central America. The dark green to purple skin covers an oily, soft, pale-green flesh – there is also a dark-skinned variety. Avocadoes can only be bought fresh and are always eaten raw as an appetizer or in salads.

Salad Tomato

Chili Peppers

Squashes

See also p. 237

CUCUMBER (*Cucumis sativus*)
An ancient cultivated fruit thought to be
indigenous to India, there are two basic types:
the long, thin, smooth variety grown under
glass and known as the *hot-house* cucumber
(right), and the thick, rough-skinned variety
known as the *ridge* cucumber (far right) – so
called because it is grown on raised ridges of
soil. Available all year round, cucumbers can
be bought fresh or pickled, and are usually
eaten raw in salads.

ACORN SQUASH (*Cucurbita pepo*)
Harvested in autumn, this thick-skinned American
variety keeps well for several days in a cool, airy
place before using. Sold fresh, canned and frozen,
it has yellowish, sweet-tasting flesh. It is usually
cooked unpeeled, because of its tough skin, but
can be cut into rings without peeling and steamed.
It is also suitable for stuffing and baking.

Ridge Cucumber

Hot-house Cucumber

SPAGHETTI SQUASH (*Cucurbita pepo*)
Vegetable Spaghetti
Shaped like a short vegetable marrow, this squash, available in winter, is usually boiled in its skin. The white flesh, which resembles spaghetti, is then taken out, seasoned, and eaten hot with butter, tomato sauce, or other seasonings, or chilled and served with meats or salads. It can also be deep-fried in batter.

GOLDEN NUGGET SQUASH
Orange with greenish flesh, this sq...
usually eaten when immature and tender and can be
steamed, boiled, or stuffed and baked like vegetable
marrow. A native American fruit, it can also be left
on the vine to ripen and develop a thicker skin that
must be peeled before cooking but which allows it to
be stored several days before cooking. When mature,
it can be boiled and mashed with butter and
seasoning or baked.

CUSTARD SQUASH (*Cucurbita pepo*)
Pattypan Squash; Custard Marrow
A summer squash with a somewhat floury taste
which is at its best when very ripe; its skin, flesh
and seeds can be eaten. It can be steamed, boiled,
or stuffed and baked.

SNAKE SQUASH
(*Trichosanthes cucumeriana*)
A curled, eye-catching variety, this type of squash is native to Southeast Asia and Australia but it can be grown in Europe and America. Eaten in the summer when immature and thin-skinned, it is usually sliced in rounds and steamed, or boiled and served with butter, salt, pepper, and herbs such as tarragon, dill or marjoram.

BUTTERNUT SQUASH (*Caryoka nuciferum*)
The fruit of a plant native to tropical America but now cultivated in North America and Europe, it is picked either in the summer, when tender, and enjoyed sliced and stewed or boiled, served in a light sauce or baked in a pie; or later in the autumn, when the squash is split, parboiled and baked with a stuffing. When mature, it is also used to make jams, preserves and pickles.

Striped Marrow

VEGETABLE MARROW
(*Cucurbita pepo*)
An edible gourd indigenous to
the Americas, this summer fruit
should be firm and heavy, and
about 12in. (30cm) long. It can
be steamed, boiled, or stuffed
and baked. It should be stored
in a cool dry place and used
within 3 days of purchase.

Plain Marrow

ZUCCHINI (America);
COURGETTE (Britain)
(*Cucurbita pepo*); **Italian Squash**
Generally available during summer, this
miniature marrow variety does not need
peeling. It can be simply topped, tailed,
sliced and eaten raw with dips; steamed,
or battered and fried. It is best used on
the day of purchase.

WEST INDIAN PUMPKIN (*Cucurbita*, spp.); **Calabaza**; **Winter Squash**

A close relative of the common pumpkin, this is actually a giant squash which lacks the dense texture and sweet taste necessary for pies, but can be stuffed and otherwise used as any smaller squash.

Pumpkins are similar in shape but usually have a bright orange skin and are particularly noted for their use in pies. They are often served with fresh cream – but they may also be used as a vegetable either lightly boiled or sliced and fried. They can also be puréed and used for soups; in France pumpkin jams are made and in Italy mashed pumpkin is used as a filling for sweet ravioli. Pumpkin seeds are rich in fats and proteins and an edible oil is produced from them.

LEEK (*Allium porrum*)
Not as pungent as onions or
shallots, the leek is a winter
plant native to Europe. It is
best used fresh in soups.

**YELLOW ONION (America);
SPANISH ONION (Britain)** (*Allium cepa*)
Like all varieties of the onion bulb, this originated in Central
Asia and today is found throughout the world. Unlike most
white varieties, yellow (Spanish) onions are mild and keep well,
so they are available all year round fresh, dehydrated, or as
reconstituted juice. Onions can be eaten raw, boiled, steamed,
braised, fried, and in many prepared dishes.

ITALIAN RED ONION (*Allium cepa*) **Red Onion**
Oblong, mild and sometimes sweet, this variety is grown in many places. It is attractive
when sliced thinly in rings and used raw as a garnish, as cooking blanches red onions.
Like all onions, leeks, and shallots, this variety acquires a bitter taste when its cut flesh
is exposed to the air too long before cooking or using in prepared dishes.

PICKLING ONIONS
(*Allium cepa*)
Picked when the plant has just
formed bulbs, their size is usually
preferred for pickling. Also good
boiled, served in sauce.

SPANISH ONION (America);
LARGE RED ONION (Britain) (*Allium cepa*)
Mild and often sweet, this, as all onion varieties, can be chopped a day ahead of time for a cooked dish when sautéed in butter, cooled, covered and placed in the refrigerator.

SCALLION
(America);
SPRING ONION
(Britain) (*Allium cepa*)
Green Onion
Pickled when young and tender before the bulb forms, the scallion is available from midwinter to midsummer and is used fresh in garnishes, relishes, and salads.

SHALLOT (*Allium ascalonicum*)
Unknown in ancient times and of uncertain origin, it is less pungent than the onion. Mainly used in sauces, elongated varieties tend to be stronger-tasting.

GARLIC (*Allium sativum*)
Probably of Central Asian origin, garlic is sold all year round in heads (right) but is usually used in small amounts, 1–2 cloves (left) at a time. To peel easily, first press the cloves under the flat side of a knife. Garlic cloves can be planted and their pungent leaves used in salads, garnishes, and hors d'oeuvres.

WHITE RADISH (*Raphanus sativus*)
While the wild radish probably originated in
southern Asia, white cultivated varieties are
found in many countries. It is usually at its
best in the spring.

NAVETTE (*Brassica rapa*, spp.)
A type of French turnip available in winter and early
spring; it can be boiled, or used in soups, stews
and casseroles.

PARSNIP
(*Pastinaca sativa*)
A sweet root vegetable
native to Europe but now
also grown in America, it
is sold fresh all year round
but is at its best in winter.

TURNIP (*Brassica rapa*)
The swollen root of a
plant thought to be native
to Europe, this vegetable is
available all year round.
Its main use is in stews
and soups.

SCORZONERA
(*Scorzonera hispanica*)
Black Salsify
The black-skinned fleshy root
of a plant of European origins,
scorzonera is now also grown
in some parts of America. At
its best in late autumn, it is
usually boiled and sautéed.

DAIKON RADISH (*Raphanus sativus*, spp.)
Japanese Radish
This traditional Japanese variety of radish is often sold in Oriental
food stores. Milder than other types, it is grated and used as a
garnish, and is also used for pickling (p. 29).

Root Vegetables and Tubers

See also p. 237

BEET (*Beta vulgaris*)
Native to the Mediterranean area but widely cultivated in America and Europe, this root vegetable is sold throughout the year. Available fresh or canned, it can be boiled or baked and served hot, or cooled and pickled. It can also be used in salads or soups.

RUTABAGA (America); **Swede** (Britain) (*Brassica napobrassica*)
This large versatile root vegetable originated in Europe but is now also common in America. It is at its best in winter and resembles the turnip but has yellowish flesh. It can be baked; roasted with meat; sliced and fried; cubed, blanched and added to stews; or boiled and mashed.

CELERIAC (*Apium graveolens*, spp.) **Celery Root; Celery Rave**
This special variety of celery is cultivated for its thick, tuberous root. A winter vegetable, it should be firm and must be peeled before cooking. To peel easily, cut it into slices first. It can be boiled until tender and served with white or cheese sauce, or blanched and dressed with vinaigrette sauce and used as an appetizer.

RED RADISH (*Raphanus sativus*)
Native to southern Asia, cultivated varieties of red radish are sold all year round in Europe and America, but taste less peppery in spring. Usually eaten raw in salads or with butter and bread as an hors d'oeuvre, its leaves add pungency to salads.

CARROT (*Daucus carota*)
Cultivated worldwide but native to Europe, carrots are available all year round but are most tender in early summer, when they are also smaller and sweeter (right). Sold fresh, canned and frozen, they are good steamed or boiled, then served or sautéed in butter and herbs; roasted with meat; or used in stews and soups. Their fresh juice is nutritious and delicious.

NEW POTATOES (*Solanum tuberosum*)
One of the many modern varieties of a tuber which originated in western South America but is now cultivated worldwide. New potatoes grow quickly, have white flesh and are usually dug in the early summer when they are sold in most markets. They are best scraped and simply boiled in their peels and served with butter, salt and pepper.

Tubers

See also p. 237

CYPRUS NEW POTATO (*Solanum tuberosum*)
Planted for all potato varieties, new or young
potatoes are mostly from late winter to early spring.
When tiny, they should be bought in small
quantities as they quickly lose their earthy taste.
They do not need peeling, but should merely be
scrubbed before use. They are not good for mashing
and are also available canned.

PENTLAND CROWN POTATO
(*Solanum tuberosum*)
A thin-skinned, creamy-white variety that is
best just before Christmas when the tuber is
mature. It has a floury texture like Idaho
potatoes and is excellent for baking, though,
like all floury varieties, it becomes less mealy
as it cools.

KING EDWARD POTATO
(*Solanum tuberosum*)
Often larger, its high-quality
creamy-white, sometimes yellowish
flesh is good for all cooking.

CRAIG ROYAL RED POTATO
(*Solanum tuberosum*)
A maincrop potato variety ready in July, it is non-
floury and white, fleshed with red or pinkish-white
skin, and has a uniform size and shape. Its waxy
texture is best for frying, boiling and using in salads.

PENTLAND HAWK POTATO
(*Solanum tuberosum*)
Firm with pale yellow, creamy-
textured flesh, this is a medium grade,
all-purpose potato. It can be steamed or
boiled, sliced with or without skin, and
served with butter, herbs, salt and
pepper or mayonnaise. It is also good
for mashing and baking.

YAM (America);
RED SWEET POTATO (Britain) (*Ipomeo batatas*)
Perhaps native to Asia but first found in
Central America, this sweet, orange-fleshed
tuberous root was introduced to Europe in the
16th century before the common potato.
Available canned, when fresh it can be cooked
like other potatoes. It is good with roasts, or
mashed and used in cakes,
soufflés and stuffings.

PENTLAND SQUIRE POTATO
(*Solanum tuberosum*)
Firm and white-fleshed, a medium grade all-
purpose potato. Like many it is commercially
frozen for frying, or sold dehydrated or canned.

DESIREE POTATO (*Solanum tuberosum*)
High-quality like the American Burbank
variety, it is floury and excellent for baking
and frying; also for boiling and mashing.

MARIS PEER POTATO (*Solanum tuberosum*)
This variety's medium-firm, creamy-white flesh
is prized for boiling as it rarely blackens. It can
be used in salads, sautéed or fried.

WHITE SWEET POTATO
(*Ipomeo batatas*)
A smaller variety of sweet potato with yellow flesh, it is also drier, less rich and has a fluffier texture when cooked, but the two varieties may be interchanged. It can be fried, boiled or used in casseroles with butter, ginger, nutmeg or allspice.

YAM (Britain) (*Dioscorea batatas*)
A mild, tuberous root native to the Orient, it is also grown in tropical America. Sold at speciality markets, it is cooked in the same way as potatoes (with the outer bark removed) and is a popular feature of West Indian cooking.

JERUSALEM ARTICHOKE
(*Helianthus tuberosus*)
This tuber has several varieties, ranging from beige to brownish-red. It is native to North America but is also grown in Europe from autumn to spring. It has a nut-like taste, and is cooked in the same way as potatoes.

Pods and Seeds

See also p. 237

PEA (*Pisum sativum*)
Native to the Middle East, peas are sold fresh, frozen, canned and also dried (p. 92). Different varieties include the snow pea (*mangetout*), and the *petit pois* which are so popular in France. Though the pods are usually discarded they are sometimes used to make pea soup.

SNOW PEA; Mangetout; Sugar Pea
Early varieties of pea (usually available in spring) which have very tender pods. They need only be topped and tailed before cooking and are eaten pod and all.

Garden Pea

PETIT POIS
Small-seeded peas which are picked very young while they are sweet and tiny. Particularly popular in France, they are often considered to be the finest of all varieties.

OKRA (*Hibiscus esculenta*)
Lady's Finger; Gumbo
The pod is the fruit of an annual plant of the cotton family, native to tropical Africa. Eaten fresh, cooked, canned or dried, it is used to thicken soups and stews, and is also eaten as a vegetable.

CORN (*Zea mays*) **Sweetcorn; Maize; Indian Corn**
This variety of corn, indigenous to America, is eaten as a vegetable in its immature state, fresh, frozen or canned, and is also used in several American recipes; in corn bread, corn pone and hominy.

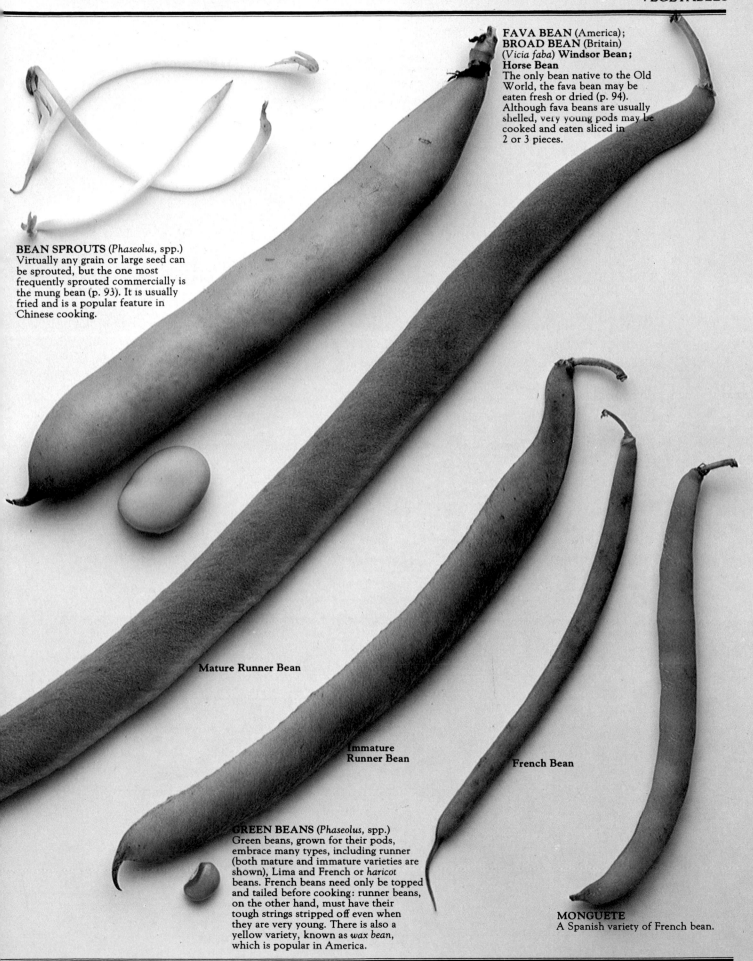

BEAN SPROUTS (*Phaseolus*, spp.)
Virtually any grain or large seed can be sprouted, but the one most frequently sprouted commercially is the mung bean (p. 93). It is usually fried and is a popular feature in Chinese cooking.

FAVA BEAN (America);
BROAD BEAN (Britain)
(*Vicia faba*) **Windsor Bean;**
Horse Bean
The only bean native to the Old World, the fava bean may be eaten fresh or dried (p. 94). Although fava beans are usually shelled, very young pods may be cooked and eaten sliced in 2 or 3 pieces.

Mature Runner Bean

Immature
Runner Bean

French Bean

GREEN BEANS (*Phaseolus*, spp.)
Green beans, grown for their pods, embrace many types, including runner (both mature and immature varieties are shown), Lima and French or *haricot* beans. French beans need only be topped and tailed before cooking: runner beans, on the other hand, must have their tough strings stripped off even when they are very young. There is also a yellow variety, known as *wax bean*, which is popular in America.

MONGUETE
A Spanish variety of French bean.

BLUE PEA (*Pisum sativum*)
One of the most tasty of several varieties of dried peas. Its texture is floury but it retains its shape when cooked.

Mediterranean Chick-pea

CHICK-PEA (*Cicer arietinum*) **Garbanzo**
There are several varieties of this large pea, native to western Asia. Available whole and split, they can be served in casseroles, soups and stews and are the main ingredient of the Arab dip *hummus*.

ORANGE LENTIL (*Lens esculenta*)
It is the only pulse which may not need soaking before cooking. There are many types which vary in size and shade, and which may be sold split or whole. This familiar orange lentil cooks to a purée.

SPLIT GREEN PEA (*Pisum sativum*)
This variety is sweeter than the blue pea. It cooks to a purée to make the traditional English pease pudding.

Middle Eastern Chick-pea

Large Green Lentil

GREEN LENTIL (*Lens esculenta*)
Continental Lentil
Lentils are particularly rich in protein. This variety is popular in European cooking. It retains its shape after cooking and may be served as a vegetable. There are large and small varieties.

SPLIT YELLOW PEA (*Pisum sativum*)
Like the split green pea these make excellent purées for soup and for vegetable dishes served with ham.

Split Skinless Chick-peas

Small Green Lentil

**Whole
Mung Beans**

**Split
Urd Beans**

PUY LENTIL (*Lens esculenta*)
These dark French lentils, which vary in size, are highly regarded and considered the best of their type. Like the green or continental lentil it retains its shape when cooked.

MUNG BEAN (*Phaseolus aureus*) **Moong Dal; Green Gram**
Widely cultivated in India and China, mung beans are available whole, split and skinless, and are probably best known in the form of bean sprouts (p. 89).

URD BEAN (*Phaseolus mungo*) **Urd Dal; Black Gram**
A bean that is sold in several forms. It is thought to be native to India and it is widely grown both in India and the Far East.

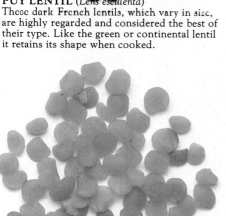

YELLOW LENTIL (*Lens esculenta*)
Yellow Dal
Because of their Asian origin many lentils are often referred to by their Indian names as various types of dal. They are often served as a main or side dish with curry.

Skinless Mung Beans

Skinless Urd Beans

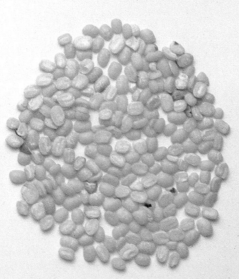

INDIAN BROWN LENTIL (*Lens esculenta*)
Masoor Dal
These are red lentils from which the seedcoat has not been removed. They become purées when cooked.

Split Mung Beans

Whole Urd Beans

Dried Beans

See also p. 244

FLAGEOLET
(Phaseolus vulgaris)
A small, green variety of common bean (haricot), native to the Americas. It can be eaten fresh or dried and is also available precooked and canned. In France it is traditionally eaten with roast lamb.

FAVA BEAN (America); **BROAD BEAN**
(Britain) *(Vicia faba)* **Field Bean; Windsor Bean**
Native to North Africa, this was cultivated by the ancient Egyptians and Greeks. It is available fresh, dried or canned and can be eaten on its own or in stews and salads.

RED KIDNEY BEAN *(Phaseolus vulgaris)*
This sweet-tasting bean comes in many varieties ranging from dark pink to maroon. It is most readily identified with Mexican cooking, particularly for its use in chili con carne.

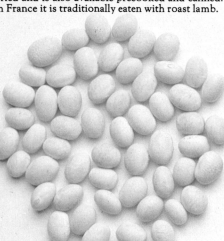

BOSTON BEAN *(Phaseolus vulgaris)*
Pearl Haricot; Navy Bean; Pea Bean
A small, white variety of common bean used to make the French dish cassoulet and the traditional Boston baked beans – the forerunners of canned baked beans.

BLACK BEAN
(Phaseolus vulgaris) **Frijol negro**
A shiny, black variety of common bean which is tender and sweet-tasting. Virtually a staple food of Central and South America, it is usually served with rice.

CANNELLINO BEAN *(Phaseolus vulgaris)*
A creamy-white kidney bean, slightly larger than the navy bean and with a fluffier texture. Used mostly in Italian cooking, cannellini beans are often used with tuna fish to make *tonno e fagioli.*

LARGE WHITE BEAN
(Phaseolus vulgaris) **White Haricot**
A large, creamy-white flat variety of the common (haricot) bean, used in stews and casseroles, and generally interchangeable with other types.

BORLOTTO BEAN *(Phaseolus vulgaris)*
Borlotti beans cook to a creamy consistency and are used in dips and in salads.

LIMA BEAN
(Phaseolus, spp.)
Butter Bean;
Madagascar Bean
Native to South America, but also found a great deal in Madagascar (hence their alternative name), Lima beans are available fresh, dried and frozen.

FUL MEDAMES (*Lathyrus sativus*)
Widely eaten in the Middle East, where they originated, their white counterpart is called ful nabed. Ful medames have given their name to one of the national dishes of Egypt in which they are baked with eggs, cumin and garlic.

BLACK-EYED BEAN (*Vigna*, spp.)
Although native to China, this bean has come to be identified with the "soul food" of the American Deep South, where it is traditionally served with salt pork.

Black Soybean

Yellow Soybean

ADUKI BEAN
(*Phaseolus angularis*) **Adzuki Bean**
The seeds of a bushy annual native to China, aduki beans can be served as a savory side dish. They are also used by both the Chinese and Japanese for confectionery.

RICE BEAN (*Phaseolus calcaratus*)
Native to Southeast Asia, rice beans are grown in limited amounts in China, India and the Philippines. They are named because of their rice-like taste.

SOYBEAN (*Glycine max*)
One of the "five sacred grains" of ancient China, the soybean has many cultivars, including the black and the yellow, and countless uses: it can be cooked fresh or dried in stews, sprouted, turned into soy paste, bean milk, curd and textured meat substitute.

BLACK FERMENTED CHINESE BEANS
Usually soybeans preserved in salt, these are used in meat and vegetable dishes.

LABLAB
(*Dolichos lablab*) **Hyacinth Bean**
Native to India but now also eaten throughout Asia and the Middle East, these hard-skinned beans must be shelled before cooking.

PIGEON PEA
(*Cajanus Cajan*) **Gunga Pea; Toor Dal**
These beans take their name "pea" from their shape and size. Native to Africa, they are also eaten in India and the Caribbean.

Mushrooms and Truffles

See also p. 246

Périgord Black Truffle

Piedmontese White Truffle

TRUFFLES (*Tuber magnatum, melanosporum*)
Both the classic Périgord black (*melanosporum*) and the Piedmontese white are renowned for their scent and taste.

WOOD EARS (*Auricularia polytricha*) **Chinese Black Fungus** A gelatinous species collected and cultivated in China.

BOLETUS (*Boletus granulatus*) **Yellow Mushroom** A fruity-smelling mushroom found in conifer woods in the summer and autumn.

SHIITAKE (*Lentinus edodes*) **Chinese Mushroom** Eastern tree fungus from oak logs and *shii* trees.

MOREL (*Morchella esculenta*) **Sponge Mushroom** A dried version.

DRIED MUSHROOMS Need soaking in tepid water for reconstituting.

CUP MUSHROOM The medium-sized version of the cultivated mushroom.

BUTTON MUSHROOM The smallest, most immature form of the cultivated mushroom.

Field Mushroom (*Agaricus campestris*)

CULTIVATED MUSHROOM (*Agaricus bisporus*) The cultivated mushroom is traditionally grown from spawn on stable manure. It comes in three sizes, the smallest or button, the medium sized or cup and the largest or open (flat) mushroom. A "wild" version is the Field Mushroom (*Agaricus campestris*) shown above. Another variety is shown on opposite page.

FLAT MUSHROOM; Open Mushroom This is the largest, most strongly tasting form of the cultivated mushroom.

BEEFSTEAK FUNGUS (*Fistulina hepatica*) Named after the beef-like appearance of its flesh, it is found occasionally on living trees, especially oaks.

Dried Chanterelles

CHANTERELLE (*Cantharellus cibarius*) **Girolle; Egg Mushroom**
Commonly found in woods, especially beech, from summer to midwinter, it is extremely popular throughout Europe. It smells faintly of apricots and, when cooked, tastes slightly peppery with a delicate perfume. Its firm flesh requires longer cooking than other fungi.

RUBBER BRUSH (*Hydnum repandum*) **Wood Hedgehog**
Commonly found in all types of woodland in the autumn and early winter, it is unique in having spines instead of gills, hence its names. It is a good cooking mushroom especially for fricassees.

BLEWIT (*Lepista*, spp.)
Named for their bluish-violet cast, blewits are found under deciduous trees or conifers as well as on grassy pastures and in woods. They appear from October to December, and are best fried or baked.

PARASOL MUSHROOM (*Macrolepiota procera*) **Umbrella Mushroom**
A summer and autumn fungus found standing tall on grassy hillsides, often near trees. Its size makes it easy to find. It gets its name from the way in which its cap opens out from its stem on maturing. It should be picked young when it is quite tasty.

CEP (*Boletus edulis*) **Cèpe**
A common summer and autumn fungus found most often in beech woods.

FIELD MUSHROOM (*Agaricus vaporarius*)
One of the many varieties of wild mushroom found in meadows and pastures in summer and autumn.

DATE (*Phoenix*, spp.)
The fruit of the date palm, native to the northern shores of the Persian gulf, it is exceedingly rich and nourishing. Dates can be bought fresh or dried, and are available all year round.

PEACH (*Prunus*, spp.)
Probably of Chinese origin, this fruit has over 2,000 varieties. The velvety soft skin encloses a firm, juicy flesh with one large stone. Peaches are normally classified as being either freestone or clingstone, and can be eaten fresh, canned or dried, or used to make preserves and liqueurs.

NECTARINE (*Prunus*, spp.)
A smooth-skinned member of the peach family, nectarines have sweet, juicy flesh and are usually served as a dessert fruit. They are normally sold ripe and therefore should be eaten on the day of purchase. Nectarines can also be made into preserves.

APRICOT
(*Prunus armeniaca*)
Native to China, apricots are in season through late spring and summer. The sweet flesh encloses a single stone and is covered by a tender skin. Available fresh, dried or canned, apricots can be eaten raw or used to make wines, brandies, preserves and confectionery.

CHERRY (*Prunus*, spp.)
Sweet or sour cherries are available for a short time in the summer. They are normally eaten fresh but are also available canned and are used in many liqueurs and brandies.

Red Ace Plum

Switzen Plum

Californian Nectarine

Greengage

Burbank Plum

Nectarine

PLUM (*Prunus*, spp.)
A late summer to early autumn fruit,
plums are normally classified as
being used for desserts or for
cooking. Both types can be eaten raw,
although cooking plums are more
acidic and rather dry in comparison
to the juicy, richer-tasting dessert
plum. There are many varieties of
this fruit available fresh, dried (as
prunes) and canned. Plums are
usually eaten raw, but can be cooked
or used in jams.

Damson; Prune Plum

Californian Santa Rosa Plum

BLACKCURRANT
(*Ribes nigrum*)
Usually sold stripped from
their stalks, these summer
fruits are always served
cooked, as a filling for pies
and puddings. They also
make excellent preserves, and
form the basis of the famous
French liqueur *cassis*.

CRANBERRY
(*Vaccinium
macrocarpon*)
Grown almost exclusively in
America, but also harvested in
Finland, cranberries are too acid
to be eaten raw, but are usually
used as cranberry sauce, the
traditional accompaniment to
turkey. They are also used in
pies, ices, liqueurs and jellies.
Available fresh in winter they can
also be bought frozen.

RED CURRANT
(*Ribes sativum*)
Rather tart for eating raw, these summer fruits have many
other uses: they make a sparkling jelly, excellent with roast
lamb, poultry and game; a delicious summer salad tossed
with grated raw vegetables; and, dipped by the bunch in
lightly beaten egg white, then "frosted" with fine sugar,
they make a simple but dramatic table decoration. They
are also used in jams.

BLUEBERRY (*Vaccinium*, spp.)
Originally wild, this somewhat tart fruit is now grown commercially.
Blueberries are eaten raw with sugar and cream, stewed, made into
soups, preserves and jams or used in pies.

WILD STRAWBERRY (*Fragaria*, spp.);
Frais du bois; Alpine Strawberry
A variety of strawberry, smaller and more aromatic than the
ordinary cultivated variety, it is usually eaten fresh and does not
need to be hulled before eating.

GOOSEBERRY
(*Ribes grossularia*)
Known and enjoyed in
Europe since the Middle Ages,
gooseberries are summer
fruits with a very short season
lasting only a few weeks.
Sweet varieties are delicious
eaten raw; tart ones make an
excellent preserve, and can be
used in many desserts.

RASPBERRY
(*Rubus idaeus*)
Raspberries often appear in two
crops, one summer, one autumn –
the latter are often smaller but
juicier. Raspberries can be eaten on
their own with just cream and
sugar or made into soups, fine
preserves, sorbets and other
desserts.

BLACKBERRY (*Rubus ulmifolius*) **Bramble**
A shiny black fruit that decorates country hedgerows in
early autumn, this has also been cultivated commercially for
over a hundred years in America. Eaten fresh, blackberries
make a tart, refreshing dessert, but the majority are
preserved as jam or jelly.

STRAWBERRY (*Fragaria*, spp.)
This fruit, native to America, can vary widely in size. Available all
year round, it can be eaten with cream and sugar and used in
preserves, cakes and tarts.

LOGANBERRY (*Rubus loganobaccus*)
A cross between the raspberry and the blackberry, the
loganberry, invented in California by a Scotsman, embodies
the best of each.

Citrus Fruits

See also p. 248

GRAPEFRUIT (*Citrus paradisi*)
A popular species of the citrus family which originated in the West Indies; 90 per cent are now grown in America. Available all year round, there are two basic varieties: white (below), which is particularly good for juicing, and pink (far right), which is much sweeter. Grapefruit can be served as a breakfast appetizer, used to make juice and marmalades or served broiled or grilled as an accompaniment or dessert.

Florida Duncan (white) Grapefruit

SWEET ORANGE
(*Citrus sinensis*)
The most popular of citrus fruits, the sweet orange was first cultivated by the Chinese. It is available all year round and is used in a multitude of ways: the fruit is served plain, cut up in salads or sliced for drinks or as a garnish; its juice is drunk plain or used in sauces and batters; its rind is grated for baking and used whole as a shell for salads and ices or sliced and candied. It is available in a variety of sizes, as shown.

Jaffa Orange

Spanish Orange

Texan Pink (pink) Grapefruit

KUMQUAT (*Fortunella japonica*)
Of Chinese origin and no bigger than
a large olive, the kumquat can be eaten
raw, rind and all; included in mixed
fruit salads, or used to make marmalade.

CITRON
(*Citrus medica*)
Native to China, the citron,
unlike other members of the
Citrus family, is not cultivated
for its flesh or juice but for its
thick, fragrant rind, which is
candied and used in cakes and
confections. It is an important
part of the Jewish festival of
Succoth.

LEMON (*Citrus limon*)
Of Indian origin, the lemon is easily the most versatile of all
the citrus fruits: a few drops of lemon juice will enhance
delicate fish or poultry dishes, creams and pies. Its acid also
prevents cut fruit from turning brown when exposed to
the air.

LIME (*Citrus aurantifolia*)
This small, thin-skinned fruit of Indian origin is closely
related to the lemon, and is, in fact, often used as a lemon
substitute. It is used in juices, cocktails, pickles and curries.

Citrus Fruits

See also p. 248

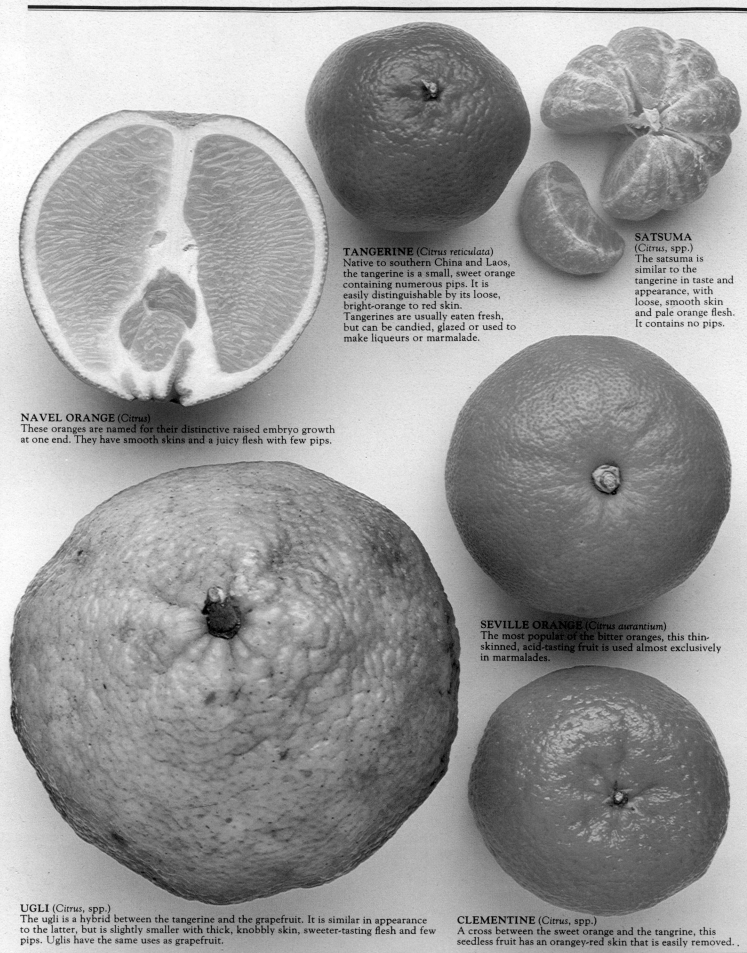

TANGERINE (*Citrus reticulata*)
Native to southern China and Laos, the tangerine is a small, sweet orange containing numerous pips. It is easily distinguishable by its loose, bright-orange to red skin.
Tangerines are usually eaten fresh, but can be candied, glazed or used to make liqueurs or marmalade.

SATSUMA
(*Citrus*, spp.)
The satsuma is similar to the tangerine in taste and appearance, with loose, smooth skin and pale orange flesh. It contains no pips.

NAVEL ORANGE (*Citrus*)
These oranges are named for their distinctive raised embryo growth at one end. They have smooth skins and a juicy flesh with few pips.

SEVILLE ORANGE (*Citrus aurantium*)
The most popular of the bitter oranges, this thin-skinned, acid-tasting fruit is used almost exclusively in marmalades.

UGLI (*Citrus*, spp.)
The ugli is a hybrid between the tangerine and the grapefruit. It is similar in appearance to the latter, but is slightly smaller with thick, knobbly skin, sweeter-tasting flesh and few pips. Uglis have the same uses as grapefruit.

CLEMENTINE (*Citrus*, spp.)
A cross between the sweet orange and the tangrine, this seedless fruit has an orangey-red skin that is easily removed. .

PEARS (*Pyrus*, spp.)
Today there are over 5,000 varieties of pear in existence throughout the world. Dessert pears (illustrated) have a juicy, white flesh that is slightly acid-tasting but also sweet. They have a strong, but pleasant scent. Stewing pears are rather hard and tasteless, with little juice. Pears ripen and are harvested during an extremely short period and, once ripe, go bad very quickly. The stewing varieties keep for a slightly longer period than the dessert pears. Both types can be eaten raw or cooked, in preserves, desserts, candies or as dried (p. 118) or canned fruit.

Sliced Comice

Packham

Comice

Conference

Williams

GOLDEN DELICIOUS; Yellow Delicious
One of the major varieties of dessert apples in America, South Africa and England, it is firm and crisp when the skin is greenish or less crisp but sweeter when completely golden. It provides a good contrast to blue cheese.

BRAMLEY
This is the foremost British cooking apple. Large and green, sometimes flushed with red, its flesh is sharp and juicy and is not usually eaten raw. It can be used for making apple chutney, or cored, peeled and sautéed in butter to serve with bacon and sausage at breakfast or supper.

GRANNY SMITH
Originally grown from a pip in nineteenth-century Australia, this apple's crunchy hard flesh, sharp, distinctive taste, and bright green skin have made it popular and easily recognizable. A worldwide choice both for cooking and eating.

CRAB APPLE
Available briefly in autumn, this small, acidic, apple-like fruit can be red or yellow. High in pectin, it is widely used for jellies, preserves and other food accompaniments.

COX'S ORANGE PIPPIN
Crisp, firm and juicy, this is Britain's most popular eating apple. Also good to cook.

STARKING
From France, a crisp dessert apple with red streaked skin and very white, sweet flesh. Also called *Starking Delicious*, it is best served early in the season on its own at the end of a meal, with cheese, or cored, sliced in rounds and fried in a sweet batter as fritters.

SPARTAN
The Danes developed this firm apple with a custard-like taste that is popular for eating and cooking. It goes well in a cold salad with onions and cured meats.

RED DELICIOUS
An American variety, this is one of the world's best eating apples. Firm, sweet and long-lasting, its red skin makes it look attractive in a fruit bowl as well as served baked with roasts.

McINTOSH
Slightly tart, best freshly picked, this all-purpose American apple is good on its own, in salads, or with meat and takes less cooking time than other varieties.

Table Grapes

See also p. 248

Muscatel

Hothouse

Napoleon Red

GRAPES (*Vitis vinifera*)
Most likely originating in western Asia, grapes
are one of the oldest cultivated plants. They are a
vinous fruit, growing in clusters, and have
digestive and therapeutic properties which are rare
in other types of fruit. Grapes are normally
classified as being either table grapes, which
would include all the varieties shown here, or
wine-making grapes, both of which are good for
eating raw. They are available all year long. They
can be eaten on their own or in fruit salads, and
are often used as a garnish in desserts. When dried
they become raisins (p. 119).

Californian Seedless

South African
Walthamcross

WATERMELON (*Cucumis citrullus*)
Indigenous to Africa, the rich red, occasionally yellow flesh of the watermelon is especially refreshing as it is 91 per cent water. It is grown in tropical countries and in warmer parts of America and Europe it is available from summer to early autumn. Round or oblong, when ripe the skin should be a rich deep green or green variegated with dark gray, sometimes with a yellow underside, and its thin surface should come away easily when scraped with a fingernail. For vine-ripened sweetness, the stem end should be slightly sunken and calloused. Mostly eaten as a thirst-quencher in very hot weather, it can also be eaten in fruit salads, or, sliced, with vinaigrette dressing.

OGEN (*Cucumis melo*)
A small, round hybrid variety named after the kibbutz in Israel where it was first cultivated, it is widely sought after for the sweet succulence of its flesh. Available from spring to midwinter, 1 melon should be allowed per person.

CHARENTAIS (*Cucumis*, spp.)
The charentais's orange, sugary and fragrant flesh make this fruit popular both as a dessert or first course. Available all year round in many places, it keeps well when stored in a cool, dry place and ripens after several days in a warm room. When ripe, it is fragrant even before being cut. Although at its best when freshly cut, it can be stored in the refrigerator for up to 2 days if covered in plastic wrap.

HONEYDEW (*Cucumis melo*)
An oval melon available all year round in most places, its delicate taste and pale green flesh contrasts well with a thin slice of raw, cured ham or sweet wine such as muscatel or port.

GALLIA (*Cucumis melo*)
A small, round melon developed in Israel, its skin has a bark-like or netted appearance which turns from green to golden yellow when ripe and sweet. To serve chilled, refrigerate briefly to preserve its taste.

CANTALOUPE (*Cucumis melo*)
Thought to have originated in Asia, it is widely available during summer. When ripe, the melon is extremely fragrant and its flesh sweet. It can be served with ice cream.

Tropical Fruits

See also p. 248

GUAVA (*Psidium guajava*)
This fruit of the Guayaba tree is probably native to Haiti, but is now found in most tropical and subtropical countries. Available in the spring and summer, it has a sharp taste, and is therefore usually used for stewing and making tarts and preserves. It can be bought fresh (as shown) or canned (in slices).

PASSION FRUIT
(*Passiflora edulis*) **Purple Granadilla**
The fruit of a perennial climbing plant native to Brazil, passion fruit can be eaten fresh when the skins are deeply wrinkled and the fruit is juicy, or used to make preserves and ice cream. It is most readily available in the summer.

PAPAYA (*Carica papaya*) **Pawpaw; Papaw**
Native to Central America, this fruit has a fairly sweet taste when ripe (similar to apricots and ginger), and makes a good dessert or breakfast fruit. It can also be cooked as a vegetable before it is ripe, and is often used to make preserves and pickles. It is most readily available in the spring and summer months.

MANGO (*Mangifera indica*)
This pitted fruit, native to India, can be green or yellow/red (as shown), and contains a sweet and sticky pulp, tasting like nectar and peaches, which can be eaten on its own or used in preserves and chutneys. Available from midwinter to autumn, it can be bought fresh or canned.

KIWIFRUIT (*Actinidia sinensis*)
Chinese Gooseberry
A native of China, the kiwifruit is now grown in many countries. It has a slightly sour taste and a hairy skin, which should be removed before eating. It is available from midsummer to winter.

FEIJOA (*Feijoa sellowiana*)
Now grown mainly in New Zealand, the feijoa is native to Brazil and Uruguay. It tastes like a combination of pineapple and strawberry and is delicious in fruit salads. It is available in late spring and summer.

PINEAPPLE (*Ananas comosus*)
Rather than a single fruit, the pineapple is really a cluster of fruits of the Ananas tree, which all combine to form one "multiple fruit". Native to South America, it is one of the most popular of all tropical fruits. It is available all year round and makes an excellent dessert fruit. It can be bought fresh (as shown) or canned (in chunks, slices and rings).

Other Fruits

See also p. 248

Japonica

Quince

QUINCE
(*Cydonia vulgaris/oblonga*)
There are many varieties of
this hard and acid Asiatic
fruit which is used mainly in
preserves. Japonicas are
closely related and have the
same uses.

PRICKLY PEAR (*Opuntia ficus indica*) **Indian Fig**
Native to America, and now found in all temperate regions, the
prickly pear is available from midsummer to midwinter. A member of
the cactus family, it has a thorny skin which must be removed before
eating. It can be eaten raw or stewed and is often used in preserves.

PERSIMMON (*Diospyros kaki*)
Kaki Fruit; "Apple of the Orient"
There are several varieties of this fruit,
which is native to China and Japan. It
can be eaten fresh or cooked and is
often candied. It is available from
midsummer to midwinter.

FIG (*Ficus carica*)
This fruit, indigenous to Syria, is available
in summer and autumn. It can be bought
fresh, dried (see p. 118), or canned, and is
often used in preserves.

BANANA (*Musa nana*)
Native to the Tropics, bananas are sweet-tasting and are usually eaten raw, on
their own or in fruit salads. They can also be flambéed with brown sugar, brandy
or rum. They are available all year round.

RHUBARB
(*Rheum rhaponticum*)
The stem of a large perennial plant thought to be native to Tibet, rhubarb is, technically, a vegetable, though it is used as a fruit. Available from midwinter to midsummer, it can be bought fresh or canned, and is stewed and used in sauces, pies, preserves and wines.

POMEGRANATE
(*Punica granatum*)
The pomegranate, indigenous to Persia, is among the most ancient of fruits. It is available in the autumn months. It is usually eaten as a raw fruit, though its juice is often extracted and used in drinks. Pomegranate seeds are used to make grenadine syrup (p. 23).

PLANTAIN (*Musa paradisiaca*)
Native to the Tropics, the plantain is a type of cooking banana, larger than dessert bananas and with a lower sugar content. Unsuitable for eating raw, it is cooked in a wide range of savory dishes and is popular in West Indian and African cooking. It is available all year round.

FIGS
California and the Mediterranean countries (particularly Turkey) are the world's main producers of figs, which are usually sun-dried. They can be eaten as they are, reconstituted with water in compotes, or chopped and used for baking and confections.

PEACHES
Although peaches are usually preserved by canning, a small part of the crop is halved and dried for use in compotes, baking, jams and preserves.

DATES
Varying in quality and form from the large, plump table dates, pitted or unpitted, to pressed slab dates, which are considerably cheaper, dried dates can be eaten as they are or used in baking and confections.

CURRANTS
The dried fruit of the small, seedless grape of Corinth, Greece, from which they take their name, currants are used mainly for baking.

PRUNES
Like dates, prunes (dried plums) vary widely in quality. Long enjoyed as a breakfast compote with great digestive qualities, prunes also make a fine fruit brandy.

PEARS
Dried pears are now available in many health food and wholefood stores. They are used for making compotes and the famous Swiss *birnenbrot* (pear bread).

BANANAS
Drying concentrates the elusive taste of the banana to produce a deliciously chewy and highly nutritious sweetmeat. The fruits are usually split lengthwise and dried in the sun.

RAISINS
A type of dried grape and one of the most popular of all dried fruits, raisins are produced mainly in California and the Middle East. They make a good snack, especially if mixed with nuts, and also have a wide application in all kinds of baking.

APRICOTS
Dried apricots are almost preferable to the fresh fruit, unless the latter is very ripe and sweet. They vary in form, from the withered yellow "rags" which must be soaked and cooked with sugar to make them palatable, to plump, sun-dried sweet fruit which can be eaten as it is.

GOLDEN RAISINS;
Sultanas; White Raisins
Another type of dried grape, these are larger and sweeter than raisins, and are used when the acidity of raisins and tartness of currants is not required.

APPLES
Dried apples have been a winter standby of country housewives since ancient times when cold storage and other modern methods of preservation were unknown.

Nuts

See also p. 254

Shelled Walnut

Whole Walnut

Ground Walnut

Chopped Walnut

WALNUT (*Juglans regia*)
There are many varieties of this nut, which is indigenous to Persia. Sold in the shell, shelled, ground and chopped, it can be eaten on its own – fresh, dried or pickled (p. 29) – or used in stuffings, cakes and confections.

Whole Brazil Nut

Shelled Brazil Nut

BRAZIL NUT (*Bertholletia excelsa*)
The seeds of a tall, forest tree of South America, Brazil nuts are sold whole and shelled. They can be eaten on their own, and are also used in confectionery and cakes.

Whole Pecan Nut

Shelled Pecan Nut

Chopped Pecan Nut

PECAN NUT (*Carya illinoensis*)
The pecan nut, indigenous to North America, is related to the walnut. Its best known use is in the popular American dessert, pecan pie.

Shelled Bitter Almond

Shelled Almond

Whole Almond

Blanched Almond

Flaked Almond

Chopped Almond

Ground Almond

ALMOND (*Prunus dulcis*)
The seeds of a Mediterranean tree of the peach family, almonds, when growing, are covered with a green outer skin which is later removed. There are bitter and sweet varieties.

Whole Filbert

Shelled Filbert

Chopped Filbert

Ground Filbert

FILBERT (*Corylus maxima*)
Native to the Mediterranean region, but now grown all over Europe, filberts can be eaten on their own, or used in desserts and confectionery.

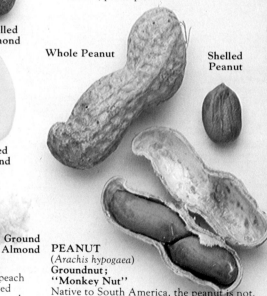

Whole Peanut

Shelled Peanut

PEANUT
(*Arachis hypogaea*)
Groundnut;
"Monkey Nut"
Native to South America, the peanut is not, strictly speaking, a nut but a legume. Its outer "shell" is the dried fibrous pod of the plant, and contains the seeds or "nuts". One of its best known uses is as the basis for peanut butter.

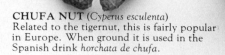

TIGERNUT (*Cyperus esculenta*) **Earth Almond**
Always referred to, and thought of, as nuts these are really the rhizomes of a plant native to Africa. Usually sold dried, tigernuts have an almondy taste and can be eaten on their own, like peanuts.

CHUFA NUT (*Cyperus esculenta*)
Related to the tigernut, this is fairly popular in Europe. When ground it is used in the Spanish drink *horchata de chufa*.

Shelled Chestnut

Whole Chestnut

SWEET CHESTNUT (*Castanea sativa*)
The fruit of a tree native to southern Europe, the chestnut can be eaten on its own, boiled, roasted, or preserved in sugar and syrup, as in the famous French delicacy marron glacé (p. 128).

Whole Pistachio Nut

Shelled Pistachio Nut

PISTACHIO NUT
(*Pistacia vera*)
The fruit of a small tree native to the Middle East and Central Asia, the pistachio nut can be eaten salted, like peanuts, or used in ice cream, cakes and general confectionery.

COCONUT (*Cocos nucifera*)
The fruit of the coconut palm, native to the Tropics, the form in which it is usually sold is as the fibrous husk of the nut once the outer skin has been removed. It is also available dried and flaked (p. 128).

MACADAMIA NUT
(*Macadamia ternifolia*) **Queensland Nut**
Native to Australia, and now also grown in Hawaii, macadamia nuts are usually sold shelled and roasted in countries where they are not grown.

PINE KERNEL (*Pinus pinea*)
The seeds of the stone pine, native to the Mediterranean. Like peanuts they are eaten raw or roasted and salted. They are often used in soups, sauces, stews and confectionery.

CASHEW NUT (*Anacardium occidentale*)
The fruit of a tropical tree native to America, the cashew nut is used as a dessert nut, and is often served with cocktails. Cashew nuts are usually sold shelled and salted.

RYE (*Secale cereale*)
Probably of southwest Asian origin, rye is similar in composition to wheat. In Europe it is used mainly for making rye bread and crispbread (particularly in Scandinavia). It is also used in the manufacture of drinks: whisky in America, gin in Holland and beer in Russia.

BUCKWHEAT (*Fagopyrum esculentum*)
An annual grain plant thought to be native to China, its seeds are roasted and made into a flour used for pancakes, crisp thin cakes, and noodles called *soba* in the Far East.

MILLET (*Panicum miliaceum*)
The seed of an annual, gluten-free grass which is widely eaten as a cereal in Africa and Asia. It is also used as a source of starch in Russia.

CORN (*Zea mays*) **Maize; Indian Corn**
Indigenous to Mexico, corn is one of the most important cereals in the form of grain, meal and flour. It is used to make many American items such as corn bread and hominy, and is also an important source of starch and of cooking oil.

WHEAT (*Triticum aestivum/durum*)
Thought to have first been cultivated in the Nile region, it is the source of the highest quality bread and baking flours. There are many different varieties: the durum wheat type is best known for making pasta.

OATS (*Avena sativa*)
Native to Central Europe, oats are used to make oatmeal and flour, and are often added to cakes and cookies.

BARLEY (*Hordeum vulgare*)
Indigenous to the East, barley is used for making malt liquor, as a side dish similar to rice, and also in soups.

BASMATI RICE (*Oryza sativa*, spp.)
Grown in the foothills of the Himalayas, this narrow long-grain rice is one of the finest. It should be soaked before cooking, and is the best rice to eat with Indian food.

White
Glutinous
Rice

Black
Glutinous Rice

Brown Italian Rice

GLUTINOUS RICE (*Oryza sativa*, spp.)
Despite its name, this rice, widely used in Chinese cooking, is completely gluten-free. When boiled it becomes sweet and sticky and is thus used mainly in baking and confectionery; also for making beer. Two varieties are shown: black (left) and white (right). The white variety is dehulled in processing.

White Italian Rice

CONVERTED RICE (*Oryza sativa*, spp.)
This rice is parboiled to remove its surface starch, thus leaving most of the nutrients and vitamins in the grains, unlike other white rice varieties. It provides the best of all possible options, since it has the nutritional value of brown rice, without its chewy texture and longer cooking methods.

ITALIAN RICE (*Oryza sativa*, spp.)
A large, round-grained type of rice, its texture makes it ideal for the classic Italian rice dish, *risotto*. Brown and white varieties are shown.

BROWN RICE (*Oryza sativa*, spp.)
The whole natural grain of the rice before it has been processed. It needs more water and longer cooking than white rice.

PUDDING RICE (*Oryza sativa*, spp.)
A short-grain strain of polished rice which becomes soft and mushy when cooked. It is usually reserved for cream puddings.

CAROLINA RICE (*Oryza sativa*, spp.)
Long-grain Rice; Patna Rice
Grown all over the world, it is the most versatile and popular of all. The grains, which are hulled and polished, remain firm, fluffy and separate when cooked.

Cereal Products

See also p. 256

COUSCOUS
A cereal processed from semolina into tiny pellets, it is best known for its use in the traditional North African dish of the same name.

MATZOH MEAL
Ground *matzohs* (unleavened crispbreads) made of wheat flour and water, used in place of leavened breadcrumbs during the Jewish Passover.

TAPIOCA
Pellets made of manoic flour, a starch extracted from the root of the manoic or cassava plant (*Manihot esculenta*).

SAGO
A processed starch extracted from the pithy stem of *Metroxylou sagu*, a palm native to Asia.

SEMOLINA
The hard part of the wheat sifted out of flour and used for pasta, which would be difficult to make with "soft" or cake flour.

CRACKED WHEAT; Burghul; Bulgur
Processed wheat popular throughout the eastern Mediterranean and the Middle East, it is baked, cooked as a pilaf or soaked and served as a raw salad (Lebanese *tabbouleh*).

WHEATGERM
The germ or "embryo" of the wheat grain, from which new wheat plants can be grown, wheatgerm is usually extracted from the grain during flour-making. Although it only forms a small part of the grain it is considered to be high in nutritional value, and can be eaten on its own or used to make the basis of a flour.

CORNMEAL;
Polenta; Manaliga; Maize Meal
A type of meal ground from Indian corn, it can be eaten on its own as a type of porridge or used to garnish meat and fish dishes.

PEARL BARLEY
Dehulled and polished barley grains which may be added to soups, used to make invalid beverages or served as a pilaf in place of potatoes.

Coarse Oatmeal

OATMEAL
Dehulled oats ground to varying degrees of fineness (as shown) or softened and rolled to make rolled oats.

Medium Oatmeal

BARLEY FLOUR
Once the main ingredient of bread, it is now usually combined with wheat flour to increase its gluten content (bread made exclusively from barley flour tends to go dry quickly).

RYE FLOUR
Frequently used in combination with wheat flour because of its unsuitable gluten content, rye flour makes the characteristic "black" breads of northern and eastern Europe.

SOY FLOUR
Not a flour in the conventional sense but a highly nutritious food supplement which can be added to soups and cakes.

CORN MEAL (America); MAIZE FLOUR (Britain)
A gluten-free flour that must be reinforced with wheat flour for bread-making. It is also used to make cakes.

LOTUS ROOT FLOUR
A gluten-free flour milled from dried and powdered lotus root, it is used in Chinese and Japanese cooking as a thickener for sauces.

BRAN
The brown outer layer of any cereal, usually separated from the grain during flour-making, it is a valuable source of fiber in the diet, and can be used to make a flour in its own right.

WHEAT FLOUR
There are many varieties, ranging from the all-purpose (plain, as shown) to cake flour (fine plain).

POTATO FLOUR
Made from cooked potatoes that have been dried and ground, this flour is often used as a subtle thickening agent.

BUCKWHEAT FLOUR
A type of pancake flour particularly popular in America, France and Eastern Europe.

RICE FLOUR
A gluten-free flour milled from both ordinary polished white and brown rice grains, it is widely used as a thickening agent, both alone or in conjunction with other flours for cakes and cookies or biscuits, and in the Chinese kitchen for making a variety of noodles called *fun*.

GRAHAM FLOUR; Whole-wheat Flour
Flour milled from the whole grain of the wheat, it includes the bran and wheatgerm, normally removed in ordinary flours.

Raising, Thickening and Coloring Agents

BREWERS' YEAST
In spite of its name, this is not a raising agent, but is used mainly for brewing wines and beers, as its name implies. Available dried, powdered or in tablets.

RED YEAST
A type of wild yeast, sold dried and used mainly for fermenting purposes, particularly in the manufacture of Oriental vinegars.

FRESH YEAST
One of the main raising agents used in bread, fresh yeast should be bought in small quantities, as it loses its potency quickly once broken. It is also available frozen.

PECTIN
A carbohydrate which occurs naturally in certain fruits, pectin is used mainly in jams and jellies to help them set. Pectin extracts can be bought commercially or can be made at home.

YEAST CAKES
This is another form of fresh yeast, compressed into a rounded shape rather than being sold in a block. It can be bought in most specialist Oriental food shops.

BICARBONATE OF SODA; Sodium Bicarbonate; Baking Soda; Saleratus
Bicarbonate of soda has no leavening properties, but can be used as a raising agent when combined with an acid such as sour milk.

CREAM OF TARTAR
This substance is found in the juice of grapes, after they have been fermented in wine-making and is then refined and used as one of the main ingredients in baking powder.

DRIED BAKERS' YEAST
Today, bakers' yeast is manufactured only in factories and is almost always based on a solution of molasses and water. Although it is used for the same purposes as fresh yeast, its main advantage lies in the fact that it will keep for a much longer period.

BAKING POWDER
This leavening agent can be bought commercially or made at home from cream of tartar, bicarbonate of soda and salt.

CORNSTARCH; Cornflour
A fine, white flour obtained from corn, used for thickening puddings and sauces and for baking cakes.

KUZU; Kudzu
The edible, tuberous roots of the Kuzu vine are rather bitter-tasting but when boiled and mashed are often used as a thickener in Chinese and Japanese cooking.

AGAR-AGAR; Bengal Isinglass; Japanese Moss; Ceylon Moss
A neutral-tasting product obtained from various Far Eastern seaweeds, agar-agar is used mainly in the making of jellies and gelatin-like desserts.

Powdered Gelatin

Sheet Gelatin

Powdered Food Dyes

ARROWROOT
This delicate, nutritive starch takes its name from the American Indian word for flour-root, *araruta*. It is a combination of starchy extracts obtained from the roots of various tropical plants and is most often used as a thickening agent.

FOOD DYES
These are sold in a powdered form or, more commonly, as a liquid. They may be of artificial or natural origin and should be used sparingly as too much can give food a vivid tint.

GELATIN
Extracted from boiled beef bones and tendons, gelatin is available as powder, or in transparent sheets and is most often used in the making of desserts and prepared meats.

Confections

See also p. 258

COCONUT
Dried coconut in flaked or finely shredded form is often used plain or toasted as a garnish, or it can be included in baking recipes such as macaroons.

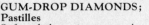

MARRON GLACE
Often boxed as a gift confection these chestnuts are first preserved – a lengthy process – and then glazed with syrup.

MARZIPAN FRUITS
Almond paste is shaped and then tinted with food dyes to resemble fruits. These are used as cake decorations or are often boxed as gift confectionery.

GUM-DROP DIAMONDS; Pastilles
Soft and chewy in texture, these sugar decorations are useful for making patterns on cakes and desserts, particularly for children's parties.

GLACE CHERRY
Cherries, coated in a sugar and glucose syrup mixture, are used as ingredients in fruit cakes and chocolates and as decorations.

MARSHMALLOW
A soft, white confection that is eaten plain or toasted. It is made of sugar, egg white and gelatin and coated in powdered sugar.

CANDY VIOLETS AND ROSE PETALS
These hard sugar-coated flowers are popular cake decorations and are available in different sizes and shades.

MIXED PEEL
A mixture of citrus fruit peel, sugar and glucose syrup, it is included in rich fruit cakes and Christmas puddings.

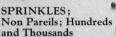

SPRINKLES; Non Pareils; Hundreds and Thousands
Available in tiny tube- and ball shapes these hard sugar sprinkles are quick and easy to apply as dessert- and cake decorations.

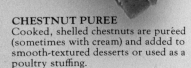

CHESTNUT PUREE
Cooked, shelled chestnuts are puréed (sometimes with cream) and added to smooth-textured desserts or used as a poultry stuffing.

DRAGEES
Shiny and smooth-coated hard sugar balls are often used on special occasion cakes.

CRYSTALLIZED VIOLETS, ROSE PETALS AND MINT LEAVES
Dipped in egg white and granulated sugar these flowers and leaves make pretty decorations on small cakes and ice creams.

CRYSTALLIZED PINEAPPLE
Pineapple with a sugary coating can be eaten as a confection or used chopped as a decoration.

SUGAR DROPS
Sugary sprinkles, available in different shades, are useful for small and large cakes.

CANDY ORANGES AND LEMONS
Simulated fruit slices made of sugar and gelatin make decorative finishes for desserts and cakes.

SUGAR-COATED CUMIN SEEDS AND MIMOSA BALLS
Seeds with a coating of tinted sugar. Quite hard and crunchy, they provide a contrasting texture to a creamy dessert.

STRAWBERRY AND CHOCOLATE CRUNCH
Sugar toppings for cakes and ice creams.

CHOCOLATE CHIPS
Tiny chocolate chips are used in cookie and cake recipes as well as for decoration.

CRYSTALLIZED GINGER
Stem ginger with a sugary coating that can be eaten as a confection or used chopped as a decoration.

ALMOND PASTE
Crushed, blanched almonds mixed with vanilla and sugar. The mixture is rolled out and used to cover fruit cakes before they are frosted (iced).

BAKING CHOCOLATE
This slab chocolate is produced when crushed cacao bean liquid is cooled and shaped into blocks. It is also known as *cooking* or *unsweetened* chocolate. Sweet and semi-sweet chocolates, which contain more sweetening and cocoa butter, are also available and are used in baking and sauce-making.

CHOCOLATE FLAKE
Served whole or crumbled, it is used as an accompaniment to vanilla ice cream.

ANGELICA
Stalk of the herb that is coated in sugar and used chopped or cut into slivers as a cake decoration.

RICE PAPER
This white wafer is unleavened bread. Flour is mixed with salt and water to a paste, cooked between hot irons and dried. It is used as a base in many recipes, notably nougat and macaroons.

Pasta

See also p. 259

Extra-long Spaghetti (*pasta asciutta*; *secca*)

SPAGHETTI

Known as *vermicelli* in southern Italy, the word *spaghetti* means "little strings". It remains the most popular type of pasta and is available fresh or dried.

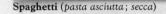

Spaghetti (*pasta asciutta*; *secca*)

Whole-wheat Spaghetti (*pasta asciutta*; *secca*)

Buckwheat Spaghetti (*pasta asciutta*; *secca*)

CAPELLINI; Vermicelli; Capolnevere
(*pasta asciutta*; *secca*)
The finest ribbon pasta, it can be homemade or bought readymade in a shop. Capelli d'angelo, meaning "angel's hair" is the thinnest variety.

LASAGNETTE (*pasta asciutta*; *secca*)
Lasagnette, a smaller version of lasagne, is a flat, ribbon pasta about ¾in. (18mm) wide, with a ruffled edge.

TAGLIATELLI; Fettucini (*pasta asciutta*; *all'uovo*)
Tagliatelli is the pasta specialty of Bologna. These flat, ¼in. (6mm)-wide ribbon noodles are, like all pasta, made from durum wheat and can easily be made at home or bought dried. They are served with a variety of sauces, ranging from a simple milk and butter mixture to one with a rich meat, fish or poultry base. Tagliatelli verdi (left) has puréed spinach added to the basic dough.

secca = dried   asciutta = cooked in water
all'uovo = fresh   in brodo = cooked in stock

FEDELI; Fedelini (*pasta asciutta; secca*)
This is a very fine, cylindrical pasta, similar
to vermicelli. It is available fresh or dried.

TAGLIARINI (*pasta asciutta; all'uovo*)
A flat, ribbon-like pasta, similar to tagliatelli, but slightly smaller in width. It can
be homemade, obtained fresh in a specialty shop or bought readymade and is also
available as tagliarini verdi (left). Usually served with a sauce as for tagliatelli.

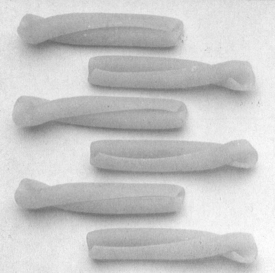

CASARECCIA (*pasta asciutta; secca*)
Pasta lengths that are curled into shape, with a twist at one end.

BOZZOLI (*pasta asciutta; secca*)
This is named for its cocoon-like shape.

CRESTI DI GALLO (*pasta asciutta; secca*)
This is named for its ridged mane that looks like a cock's comb.

LUNGO-VERMICELLI COUPE
(*pasta asciutta; secca*)
This name describes the pasta accurately as long vermicelli, cut into pieces.

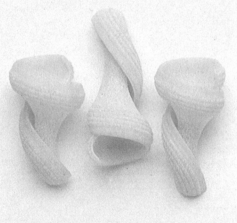

RICCINI (*pasta asciutta; secca*)
This ridged, shell-like pasta takes its name from the Italian word *riccio*, meaning "curl".

GRAMIGNA (*pasta asciutta; secca*)
Small, grass-like shapes. The name actually means "grass", or weed.

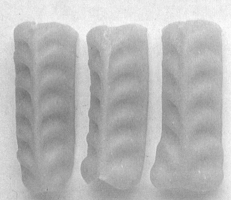

FESTONATI (*pasta asciutta; secca*)
The word means "festoon", or garland.

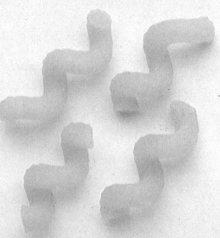

CAVATAPPI (*pasta asciutta; secca*)
Ridged pasta in a twisted shape.

FUSILLI BUCATI (*pasta asciutta; secca*)
Pasta made in the shape of tiny springs.

GNOCCHI (*pasta asciutta; secca*)
These small dumplings, shown here made from durum wheat, are also available made from potatoes or semolina flour.

ORECCHIETTE (*pasta asciutta; secca*)
Pasta shaped like an ear. The name derives from the Italian word *orecchio*, meaning "ear".

GNOCCHETTI SARDI
(*pasta in brodo; secca*)
A smaller version of gnocchi, named for its sardine-like shape.

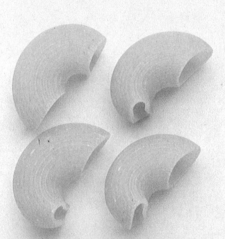

PIPE RIGATE (*pasta asciutta; secca*)
A ridged pasta in the shape of a pipe.

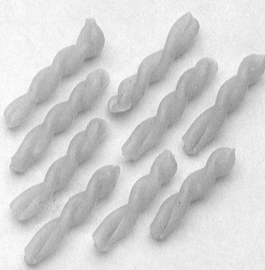

SPIRALE (*pasta asciutta; secca*)
Pasta lengths twisted together to form a spiral.

ANELLI (*pasta asciutta; secca*)
Anelli, meaning "ring", is an appropriate title for these pasta shapes, shown here made from whole-wheat flour.

LUMACHE MEDIE (*pasta in brodo; secca*)
These shapes resemble snails' shells, thus the name *lumache* which means "snail"

VEGETABLE-DYED MACARONI
(*pasta in brodo; secca*)
Made from durum wheat, dyed green with spinach or red with tomatoes.

ANELLI (*pasta asciutta; secca*)
These small ring shapes are shown here made from durum wheat.

Pasta

See also p. 259

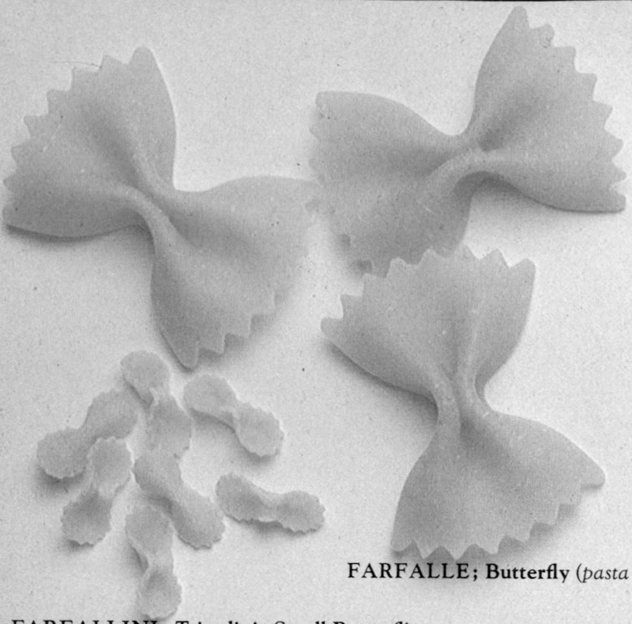

FARFALLE; **Butterfly** (*pasta asciutta; secca*)

FARFALLINI; **Tripolini; Small Butterflies**
(*pasta in brodo; secca*)

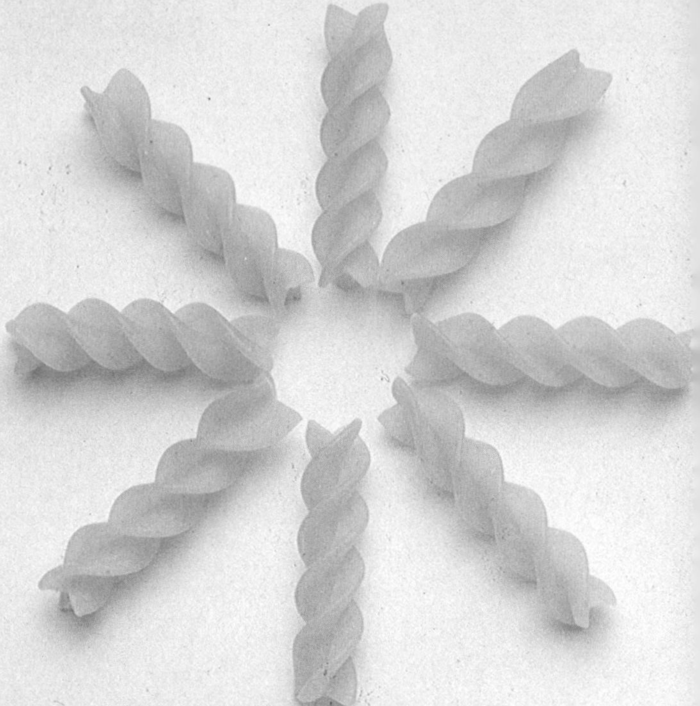

FUSILLI; **Archimede** (*pasta asciutta; secca*)
Pasta made in the spiral shape of a corkscrew.

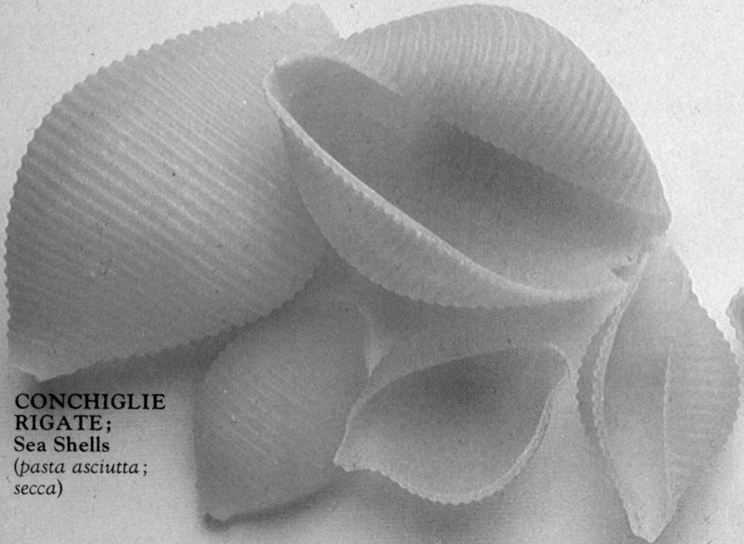

CONCHIGLIE RIGATE; Sea Shells
(*pasta asciutta; secca*)

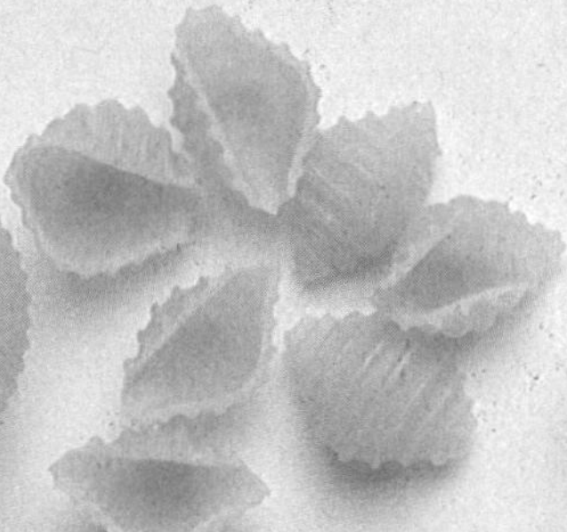

CONCHIGLIE PICCOLE RIGATE; Small Sea Shells
(*pasta asciutta; secca*)

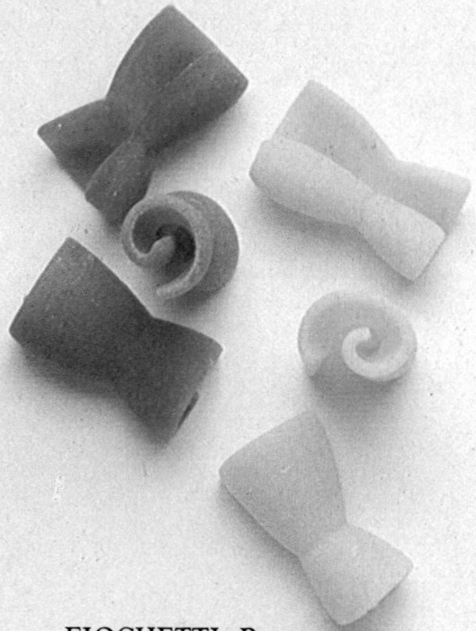

FIOCHETTI; Bows
(*pasta asciutta; secca*)
Also available as *fiochetti verdi* (left).

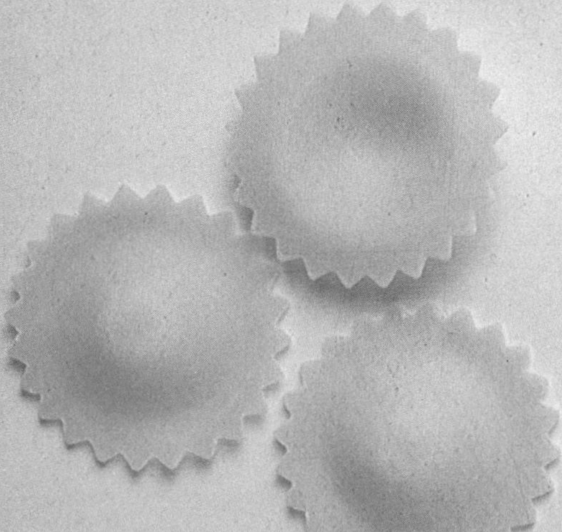

CAPPELLETTI
(*pasta asciutta; secca*)
Little pastry hats made, like most pasta, from durum wheat.

DIAMANTI (*pasta asciutta; secca*)
Pasta made in an elongated diamond shape.

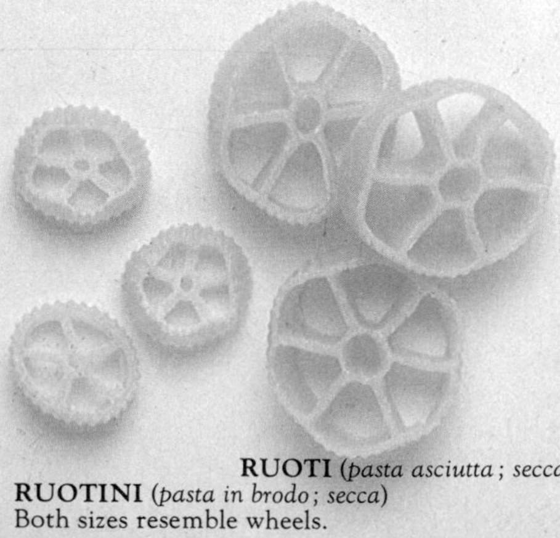

RUOTI (*pasta asciutta; secca*)
RUOTINI (*pasta in brodo; secca*)
Both sizes resemble wheels.

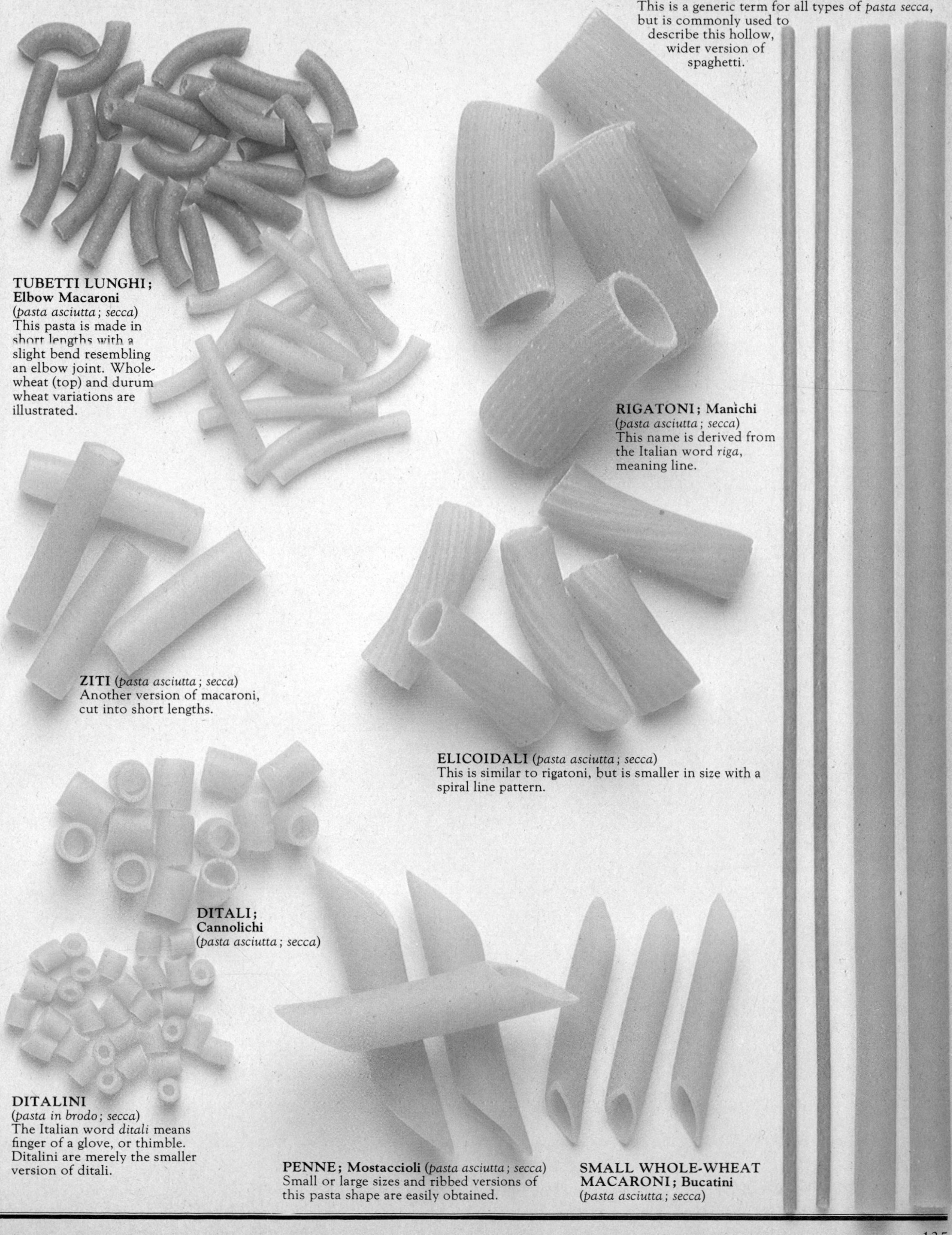

MACARONI (*pasta asciutta*; *secca*)
This is a generic term for all types of *pasta secca*, but is commonly used to describe this hollow, wider version of spaghetti.

TUBETTI LUNGHI;
Elbow Macaroni
(*pasta asciutta*; *secca*)
This pasta is made in short lengths with a slight bend resembling an elbow joint. Whole-wheat (top) and durum wheat variations are illustrated.

RIGATONI; Manichi
(*pasta asciutta*; *secca*)
This name is derived from the Italian word *riga*, meaning line.

ZITI (*pasta asciutta*; *secca*)
Another version of macaroni, cut into short lengths.

ELICOIDALI (*pasta asciutta*; *secca*)
This is similar to rigatoni, but is smaller in size with a spiral line pattern.

DITALI;
Cannolichi
(*pasta asciutta*; *secca*)

DITALINI
(*pasta in brodo*; *secca*)
The Italian word *ditali* means finger of a glove, or thimble. Ditalini are merely the smaller version of ditali.

PENNE; Mostaccioli (*pasta asciutta*; *secca*)
Small or large sizes and ribbed versions of this pasta shape are easily obtained.

SMALL WHOLE-WHEAT
MACARONI; Bucatini
(*pasta asciutta*; *secca*)

pasta
all'uovo

pasta secca

pasta
secca

pasta secca

LASAGNE; LASAGNA (*pasta asciutta*)
Often homemade, but widely available dried, this is the broadest of the ribbon pasta.
Lasagne can be bought smooth, ridged or with a ruffled edge and can be made with
whole-wheat dough or with the addition of puréed spinach.

TORTELLINI (*pasta asciutta; all'uovo*)
A small, stuffed pasta dumpling which, according to legend, was modeled on Venus's navel. It is usually stuffed with a variety of the following: chopped chicken breast, pork, mortadella or bologna sausage, cheese and nutmeg. Tortellini is almost always homemade, but is available readymade in some shops.

RAVIOLI (*pasta asciutta; all'uovo*)
This is the most well-known pasta dumpling. Square in shape, it is traditionally stuffed with spinach and ricotta cheese or herbs, but can be filled with a savory meat mixture. Cooked in boiling water, it is often served with a gravy or sauce, although small ravioli may be cooked *in brodo*. Ravioli is usually served fresh, but can also be bought readycooked in a can.

Whole-wheat Lasagna
(*pasta secca*)

PASTINA (*pasta in brodo; secca*)
Pastina is the general term for the wide variety of tiny pasta shapes that are usually cooked *in brodo*.

CANNELLONI (*pasta asciutta; secca*)
The word *cannelloni*, meaning "big pipes", describes this hollow, cylindrical pasta shape, which is stuffed and baked *al forno*.

Fresh Egg Noodles

EGG NOODLES
All of these noodles are made with eggs, the darker yellow ones containing more egg than the others. These noodles are normally sold in compressed bundles of varying size and have usually been pre-cooked by steaming so they require only a minimal amount of preparation at home. The main difference between noodles and Italian pasta lies in the way they are prepared rather than their substance or shape. All of the noodles shown are dried unless otherwise specified.

Rice, Bean and Wheat Noodles

RICE NOODLES
Noodles are a symbol of longevity in China and are often served at birthday parties as a wish for long life. These rice noodles are made in long strands before being folded over and packaged.

RICE NOODLES
These flat, ribbon-like rice noodles are made in long strands and are often called *rice sticks*.

TRANSPARENT NOODLES; Cellophane Noodles
The transparent noodles shown here are made from mung-bean starch paste, but they are also available made from pea starch or wheat. They are used in soups, or with meat and vegetables.

Rice Noodles

RICE NOODLES
Noodles made from rice are more commonly eaten in southern China, where more rice is grown. The curled pad of noodles illustrated here is commonly known as *rice vermicelli*.

WHEAT NOODLES
These flat, stick-like wheat noodles are available in different widths, and are interchangeable with rice noodles according to taste.

Freshwater Fish

See also p. 261

Reduction approx. 50%

TROUT
Native to Europe and now found worldwide, trout comes in many varieties: brook, lake, steelhead, brown and salmon (pp. 144–145). The type shown is a rainbow trout. It is usually cooked whole and can be bought fresh, frozen, canned or smoked. Available all year round it can be baked, poached, sautéed, broiled or grilled.

PIKE
Readily available in the northern hemisphere, pike can be bought fresh or frozen; whole (if small) in fillets (if large). It can be baked, braised, poached, sautéed, broiled or grilled and is available all year round. It is particularly popular in Central European cooking.

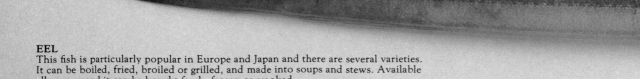

EEL
This fish is particularly popular in Europe and Japan and there are several varieties. It can be boiled, fried, broiled or grilled, and made into soups and stews. Available all year round it can be bought fresh, frozen or smoked.

CARP

There are several varieties of this fish, native to eastern Asia but now found in ponds, lakes and rivers in most parts of the world. It is particularly popular in America, France and England, and, although available all year round, is at its best in winter. It tends to have a muddy taste and should be scaled, cleaned and soaked in mildly salted water for 3 to 4 hours before cooking. It can be bought fresh, frozen or smoked; whole or in steaks and fillets. It can be baked, poached, fried, steamed or braised.

Reduction approx. 50%

SALMON

Found in cooler waters throughout the northern hemisphere, salmon is one of the world's finest food fish. Delicate and tasty, its firm, oily flesh can be pink to dark red, Pacific varieties tending to be darker. Most salmon mature at sea but return to coastal streams to spawn, depending on the variety, during several weeks from December to August when the fish is generally available fresh. Canned salmon, frozen salmon steaks, and smoked salmon are available all year round. Pickled salmon is excellent as an hors d'oeuvre, while the delicious red roe is known as *salmon caviar*. Marinated salmon is a mainstay of Scandinavian cuisine.

SALMON TROUT; Sea-Trout

Larger than trout but smaller than salmon, this North Atlantic, Baltic, and North Sea fish is often confused with salmon as it returns from the sea to spawn in European coastal rivers. At its best during the summer months, its pale pink and delicate-tasting flesh is particularly good poached and served cold or used to prepare dishes such as salmon trout in aspic. Too delicate for smoking, all other methods of preparing trout or salmon are applicable to salmon trout. Because it is less expensive than salmon it is quite often served as a salmon substitute.

RED MULLET
Available frozen in America, this 1–2lb (450–900g) fish is native to the Atlantic, and now found in the coastal waters of the Mediterranean. Available all year round, but at its best during the summer months, it has tasty firm, white flesh and is suitable for frying, baking, broiling or grilling. It is usually cooked whole: connoisseurs leave the liver inside when cooking the fish.

RED SNAPPER
This Gulf of Mexico fish can weigh up to 30lb (13.5kg) and has choice, white, creamy flesh. Those under 5lb (2.3kg) are usually baked whole and stuffed. Larger fish are cut into fillets or steaks and can be prepared in a variety of ways: broiled or grilled (with lemon butter), deep-fried (served with Rémoulade sauce), sautéed, poached, or used in soups. Available all year round, it is usually sold fresh, although it can be bought frozen in America. Species such as gray snapper are also available, but they are smaller and inferior in taste.

SEA BASS; Loup de mer
One of a large group of seawater fish which includes groupers, the sea bass is found in Europe off the southern Atlantic and Mediterranean coasts and in America off the East coast. It is a firm, white fish which can weigh up to 10lb (4.5kg) (the Pacific coast bass can weigh twice this), although the ones sold for cooking purposes are much smaller. Usually bought fresh, it is available whole or in steaks and fillets, and is suitable for poaching, baking, broiling or grilling.

RED BREAM; Porgy; Dorade
Found in the Atlantic, Pacific and Mediterranean, the bream group of fish has red, gray and bluish varieties weighing up to 3½lb (1.6kg). All have firm, white flesh though the red bream has the best taste. Available all year round it is usually bought fresh and whole. The larger fish can be casseroled, baked and stuffed; the smaller ones can be broiled or grilled whole.

GRAY MULLET
No relation to the smaller, firmer-fleshed red mullet, the gray mullet has a similar taste to sea bass. Available all year round, it can be bought whole or in fillets. The smaller fish are suitable for broiling or grilling; larger ones can be baked, and the fillets can be poached.

Reduction approx. 50%

HAKE

Varieties of hake are found almost all over the world. Hake is a large
seawater fish of the cod family with slightly firmer white flesh and is
available all year round. Small pieces of hake weighing 2–3lb (900g–
1.4kg) can be poached whole; larger hake are cut into fillets, steaks or
cutlets and sold fresh or frozen, canned or smoked. These can be
sautéed, fried, broiled or grilled, but they are usually poached in
seasoned fish stock or *court bouillon* and served with lemon or herb
butter. They are also poached, chilled and served with mayonnaise.
Hake is an excellent fish to use in stews, casseroles and soups, and it
can be used in cod or haddock recipes. Salted hake is prepared and
used in the same manner as salt cod.

COD
One of the world's most important food fishes, cod is found in the cold northern waters of the Atlantic, mainly off the coasts of New England, Newfoundland, Iceland and Norway. It has soft white flesh and can grow to a weight of 80lb (36kg). Young cod weighing under 2½lb (1.1kg) are sometimes called "scrod". Available all year round, cod is sold whole when fresh and small (when it is particularly suited to poaching and baking), and in fresh or frozen fillets and steaks (which can be fried, broiled or grilled). It is also available salted, smoked and dried (pp. 168–169), in which form it is an important ingredient in Mediterranean and Caribbean cooking. Cod's roe is also sold fresh, canned and smoked (p. 173).

WHITING
Whiting is a European seawater fish found off coasts from the Baltic to the Mediterranean. In America, however, the slightly larger (12–14in. [30–35cm]) silver hake is also sometimes known by this name. Available fresh, frozen, smoked and salted, it can be fried, poached, broiled or grilled. It is available all year round.

SARDINE
The many species of this strong-tasting oily fish, found in the Atlantic and the Mediterranean, can vary a great deal in size. The name "sardine" is reserved for the younger fish; older ones are called "pilchards" (3 or 4 larger fish will make a good portion). Available all year round, sardines are sold fresh or canned and can be baked, fried, broiled or grilled.

WHITEBAIT
The name given to young herrings or sprats, these tiny silvery fish are found in the Mediterranean and the Atlantic. Available all year round they are at their best in spring and summer. They are sold fresh or frozen and are so small that they do not need gutting or topping and tailing, but are eaten whole. They are usually deep-fried with flour until golden brown and crisp.

SPRAT
A rich, oily fish related to the herring, it is available fresh or smoked (p. 172) and can be barbecued, baked, broiled or grilled. Smoked sprats packed in oil are a popular delicacy in northern and eastern Europe. Sprats are at their best in winter.

MACKEREL
A fatty, dark-fleshed fish found in the Mediterranean, Atlantic and Pacific, it lends itself particularly well to barbecueing, baking, smoking, broiling or grilling. It can be eaten raw with plenty of lemon juice or a similarly acid garnish to counteract its richness. It is available all year round.

SMELT
Often confused with the sprat, the smelt is, in fact, a member of the salmon family and as such is far more delicate and less oily by nature. Its bones are so soft that it is often eaten whole. Smelt is available in winter, and is usually eaten deep-fried.

HERRING
An oily fish found in the Atlantic and Pacific, the herring was once so cheap that it was dismissed as fit only for the poor. Now, however, it has become a great delicacy. Sold whole or filleted, it can be baked, fried, broiled or grilled. Its extreme oiliness makes it ideal for curing, as in rollmops, soured and marinated herrings, buckling, matjes, bloaters, red herrings and kippers (pp. 170–171). Herrings are at their best during summer.

Seawater Fish

Reduction approx. 75%

POLLACK

Pollack is caught all year round off North Atlantic coasts from Newfoundland to northern Europe and is available fresh in many local markets. It has fairly firm white flesh and can be prepared like fresh hake or cod, though its taste is considered slightly inferior. It is good used in mixed fish soups such as the French *bourride* or *chaudré*, or poached and served with a sauce like Creole sauce.

COLEY; Coalfish; Saithe

A soft-fleshed white fish related to cod and pollack, coley is fished extensively all year round in the North Sea and North Atlantic. Usually sold as fresh or frozen fillets, the flesh looks pinkish-gray but becomes white when cooked. Though it is not suited to broiling or grilling, it can otherwise be cooked like cod. It is generally used in soups, fish pies and casseroles.

MONKFISH; Anglerfish
A deep-sea fish found off the Mediterranean and Atlantic coasts of
Europe, Africa and America, the monkfish has such an ugly, heavy head
that usually only the tail is sold. Its flesh, which averages 2–4lb (900g–
1.8kg), is firm, white and succulent and is said to resemble lobster in taste.
It can be poached, baked, broiled or grilled and is excellent served hot
with a butter sauce such as Choron or Hollandaise; cold with rich
mayonnaise; or cubed, battered and deep-fried with tartare sauce.

HADDOCK
Usually smoked and known worldwide as *Finnan haddock* or
Arbroath smokies, this North Atlantic fish is also available
fresh or frozen all year round as fillets and cutlets. Its firm
flesh is good sautéed with almonds.

LING; Sea Turbot
The largest member of the cod family, ling was once so popular it was
called "beefe of the sea". Today, however, its soft white flesh is
usually only available salted or smoked, rarely fresh.

Flat Seawater Fish

See also p. 261

Reduction approx. 80 %

DOVER SOLE
Caught in European waters it is exported all over the world. Available fresh or frozen it can be fried whole or divided into fillets. One of the finest of the smaller flatfish, it is available all year round.

PLAICE
From the North Sea and Icelandic waters, it is sold fresh and frozen, whole or in fillets. It can be fried, broiled or grilled and is available all year.

LEMON SOLE
A fish that is at its best from December to March. Although less tasty than the Dover sole, it can be cooked in the same way and is available fresh or frozen.

SKATE
Many varieties are available in the Mediterranean and in North American waters. Sold fresh, only the "wings" are eaten. Principal season is from October to April. Skate can be poached and served with a black butter sauce, fried, broiled or grilled.

FLOUNDER
In America the word applies to several types of flatfish: blackback, fluke, gray and American lemon sole from Atlantic and South Pacific waters. Available all year, they are sold fresh, frozen, and smoked. In Europe it belongs to one fish (*Platichthys*, spp.) common in the Baltic. Fry whole or in fillets.

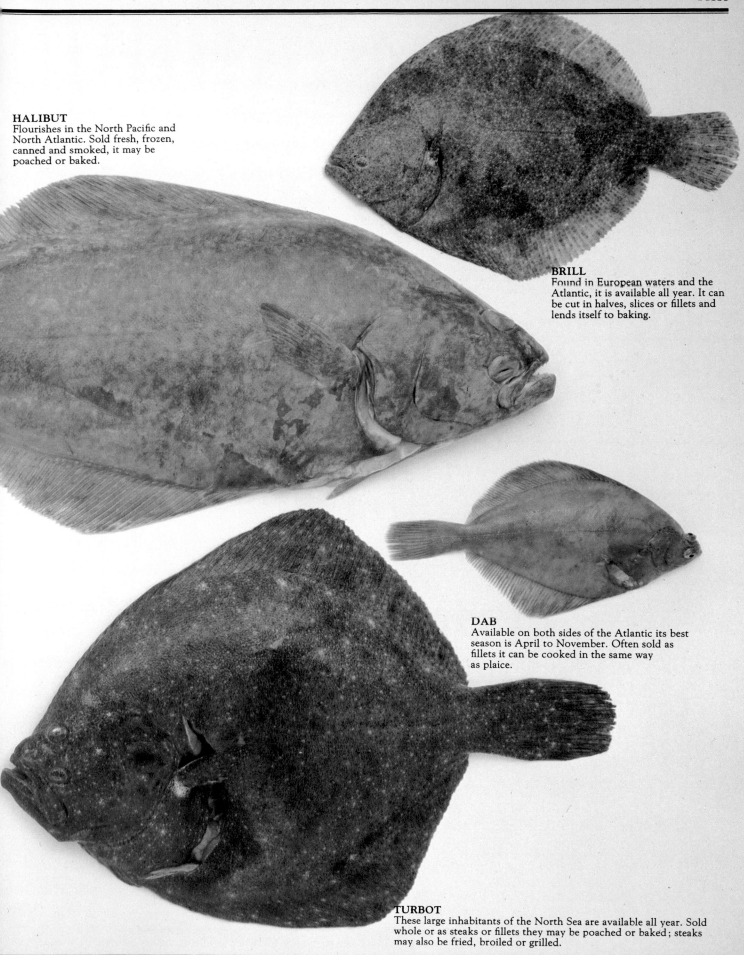

HALIBUT
Flourishes in the North Pacific and
North Atlantic. Sold fresh, frozen,
canned and smoked, it may be
poached or baked.

BRILL
Found in European waters and the
Atlantic, it is available all year. It can
be cut in halves, slices or fillets and
lends itself to baking.

DAB
Available on both sides of the Atlantic its best
season is April to November. Often sold as
fillets it can be cooked in the same way
as plaice.

TURBOT
These large inhabitants of the North Sea are available all year. Sold
whole or as steaks or fillets they may be poached or baked; steaks
may also be fried, broiled or grilled.

LOBSTER
A crustacean found in the Atlantic and the Mediterranean, there are
several varieties. It is available all year round and can be bought fresh
or frozen, alive or cooked in its shell. When alive it is dark blue;
when cooked (as shown) it turns bright red. Lobster can be baked,
steamed, boiled, broiled or grilled. The female or "hen" lobster can
contain eggs in the form of red roe or coral.

SALTWATER CRAYFISH (America);
DUBLIN BAY PRAWN (Britain);
Norway Lobster; Langoustine; Scampi
Found in the East Atlantic and the
Mediterranean, this crustacean is sold
fresh or frozen, alive or cooked (as
shown), with or without its shell.
When alive it is very pale pink. It is
available all year round.

**FRESHWATER
CRAYFISH; CRAWFISH** (America); **CRAYFISH** (Britain); **Ecrevisse**
Found mainly in France, this is a freshwater crustacean. Fairly rare, but
theoretically available all year round, it can be bought alive or cooked (as shown).
When alive it is pale pink. It is especially popular in Scandinavia. It can be
fried or boiled and is the main ingredient of Nantua sauce.

Crustaceans

SHRIMP
There are several varieties of this tiny crustacean, which reaches a maximum of 4in.
(10cm) in length. Pale pink when raw (the ones shown are cooked), shrimps are
available fresh, frozen or canned.

JUMBO SHRIMP (America); **PRAWN** (Britain)
There are several varieties of this crustacean, which is indigenous to the Mediterranean but is now also found in the Atlantic. It can be steamed, stewed, broiled or grilled, and is often used in salads. Available fresh or frozen it is usually bought cooked, though it can also be bought uncooked, shelled or unshelled.

Cooked Jumbo Shrimp (Prawn)

Uncooked Jumbo Shrimp (Prawn)

SPINY LOBSTER; ROCK LOBSTER (America)
CRAWFISH (Britain); **Langouste**
Found worldwide in most temperate coastal waters, these crustaceans have no claws and weigh 3–8lb (1.3–8kg). Most of their flesh is contained in the tails and they can be used in any recipes calling for lobster. Available fresh or frozen, they can be steamed or boiled. Unlike other crustaceans, such as lobsters, they do not turn bright red when cooked (as shown).

Crustaceans

See also p. 264

EDIBLE CRAB
Found in the Mediterranean and the Atlantic, this
large crustacean has powerful claws – larger in the
male than the female – which, as in other crabs,
contain white meat (the shell contains dark meat). It
can be bought alive, uncooked in the shell (as shown),
cooked (with or without the shell), fresh and canned,
and is also sometimes bought "dressed" (prepared
ready for eating). Available all year round, it can be
baked, steamed or boiled. When cooked it turns
bright red.

BLUE CRAB
Native to the east coast of America, where it is still
popular, the blue crab is also found in the North and
South Atlantic and the eastern Mediterranean. Available
all year round, it can be bought as a soft-shelled crab in
the summer; otherwise it is sold alive, uncooked in the
shell (as shown), cooked (with or without the shell),
fresh, frozen and canned. Blue crabs can be baked,
steamed or boiled; when cooked they turn red.

SPIDER CRAB
Found in the South Atlantic and the Mediterranean,
the spider crab is particularly popular in Italy.
Available all year round, it can be bought alive,
uncooked in the shell (as shown), cooked (with or
without the shell). It can be baked, steamed or boiled,
and turns bright red when cooked.

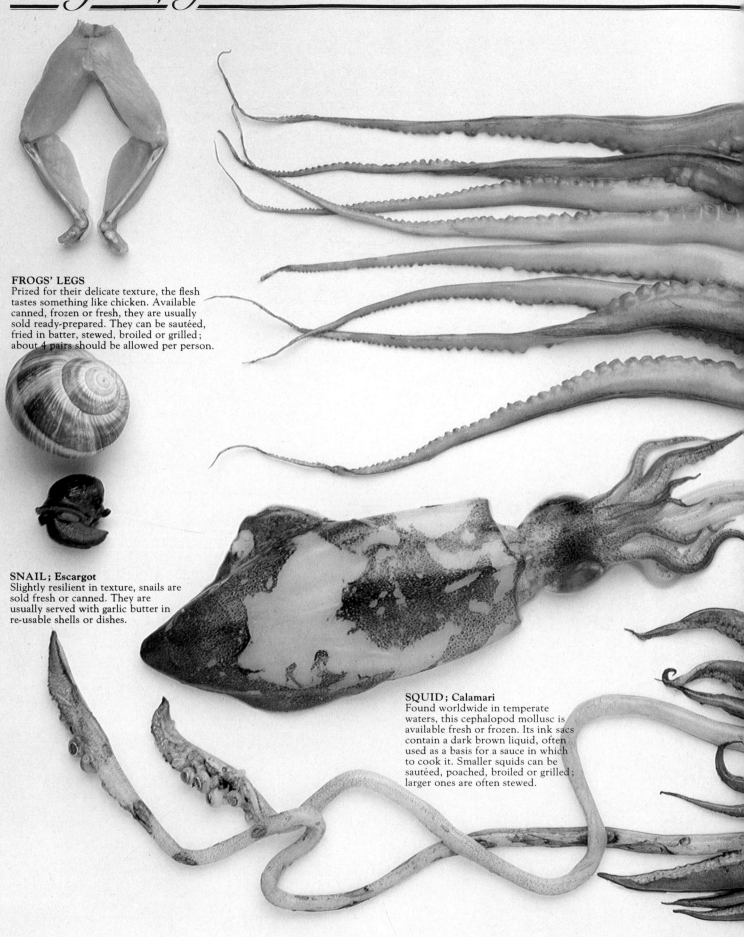

FROGS' LEGS
Prized for their delicate texture, the flesh tastes something like chicken. Available canned, frozen or fresh, they are usually sold ready-prepared. They can be sautéed, fried in batter, stewed, broiled or grilled; about 4 pairs should be allowed per person.

SNAIL; Escargot
Slightly resilient in texture, snails are sold fresh or canned. They are usually served with garlic butter in re-usable shells or dishes.

SQUID; Calamari
Found worldwide in temperate waters, this cephalopod mollusc is available fresh or frozen. Its ink sacs contain a dark brown liquid, often used as a basis for a sauce in which to cook it. Smaller squids can be sautéed, poached, broiled or grilled; larger ones are often stewed.

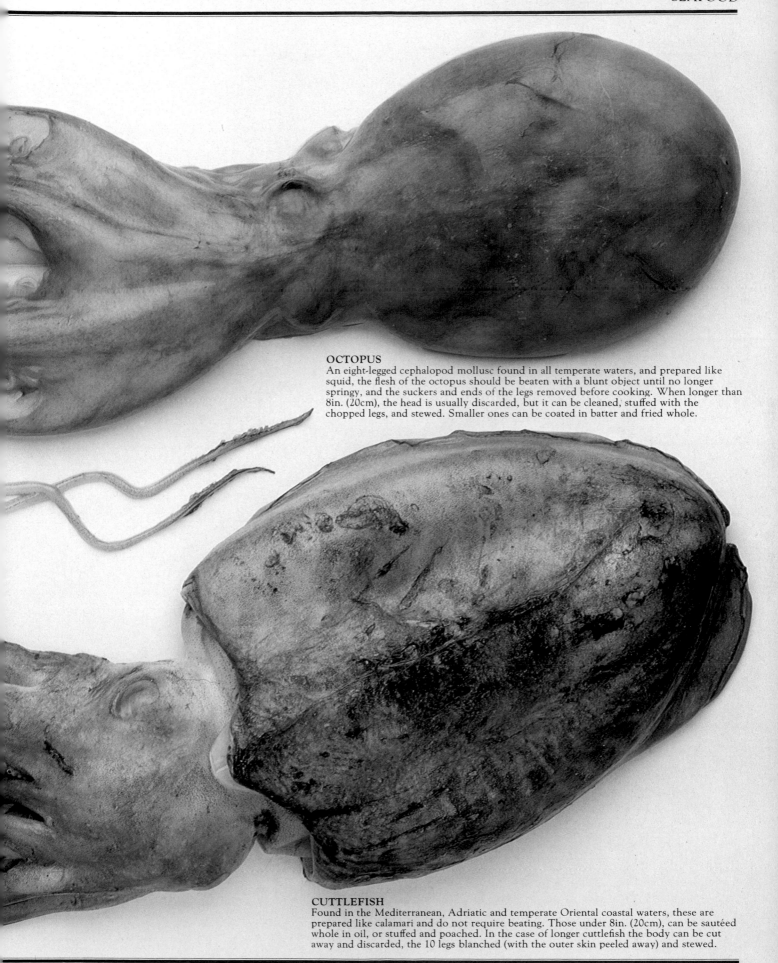

OCTOPUS
An eight-legged cephalopod mollusc found in all temperate waters, and prepared like squid, the flesh of the octopus should be beaten with a blunt object until no longer springy, and the suckers and ends of the legs removed before cooking. When longer than 8in. (20cm), the head is usually discarded, but it can be cleaned, stuffed with the chopped legs, and stewed. Smaller ones can be coated in batter and fried whole.

CUTTLEFISH
Found in the Mediterranean, Adriatic and temperate Oriental coastal waters, these are prepared like calamari and do not require beating. Those under 8in. (20cm), can be sautéed whole in oil, or stuffed and poached. In the case of longer cuttlefish the body can be cut away and discarded, the 10 legs blanched (with the outer skin peeled away) and stewed.

Molluscs

See also p. 264

Chowder Clam

Cherrystone Clam

CLAM

There are both soft-shelled and hard-shelled varieties of this mollusc – some types of hard-shell are shown. These clams with brownish shells are found prolifically on America's Atlantic coast but they are specially cultured in some European waters, too; for example, the Bay of Bourgneuf. Larger, stronger-tasting hard-shells are usually reserved for chowders while some of the smaller cherrystone varieties are eaten raw; the larger littleneck clams may be steamed open and served with melted butter.

Littleneck Clam

WINKLE

A darkish brown shell is most common. Although available on both sides of the Atlantic it is much more popular in Britain than America. Winkles are usually cooked in boiling salted water and they are sometimes served with a sauce.

WHELK

Generally with a brownish or a grayish shell, it is found on both sides of the Atlantic Ocean although the North American variety is inclined to be much larger. Whelks are usually cooked in a covered pot in a little water but some are sold canned and precooked or pickled.

MUSSEL

Its dark blue shell is familiar in America and Europe. Mussels may be steamed open and served in the half-shell. Their best-known use is in *moules marinière*.

European Oyster

Portuguese Oyster

OYSTER
There are many varieties of this mollusc, which is found in Mediterranean, Atlantic and Pacific waters – all of them varying in size and shade of brown. The recommended way of eating oysters is straight from the half-shell complete with juices. If served hot, they should be only lightly cooked. The giant American Pacific oyster can be more than double the size of the European varieties.

SCALLOP
A shell with a pink tinge and distinctively shaped edge, it is found on both sides of the Atlantic. In America only the white muscle is eaten; in Europe the pink roe is eaten too.

COCKLE
Cockles with their pale shells are widely available in the Mediterranean, Baltic and American Atlantic. They can be eaten raw or cooked.

Seaweeds

See also p. 267

KOMBU
A type of dried kelp which is particularly popular in Japan, where it is used to make the soup stock *dashi* and infused to make a tea-like drink. It should be washed before use.

NORI
An edible laver-type seaweed which is sold pressed into sheets and dried. In Japan it is used for making *sushi*, a dish of rice and fish; also as a garnish for other dishes.

JELLYFISH SEAWEED
Although sold as a seaweed and usually thought of as such, this is, in fact, strips of jellyfish which have been dried and salted. It is used in China, Japan and Southeast Asia.

MEKABU
A Japanese lobe-leaf seaweed similar to *wakame* (the traditional Japanese seaweed), available in the form of curled, dried strands. Used mainly in soups and salads and as a garnish, it should be soaked before use.

CARRAGEEN MOSS; Irish Moss
A seaweed that is hand-raked on the coasts of northern Europe and New England. A gum similar to agar-agar is extracted from it, and it is also cooked and eaten as a vegetable which is very like spinach.

DULSE
A coarse Northern seaweed which, when fresh, is red. It is harvested along the coasts of the British Isles, Iceland and parts of Canada. Usually sold dried, it can be cooked, like spinach, or chewed like candy or gum.

CANNED ANCHOVIES
Anchovies are usually filleted, brined and then preserved in oil, though they are also available salted in jars. Very strong-tasting, they are used in canapés, pastes, pizza toppings and anchovy butter.

CANNED TUNA; Tunny; Bonito
Tuna is one of the fishes that lend themselves well to canning; it is usually preserved in oil. Its firm flesh makes it useful in sandwiches, cold dishes and casseroles.

CANNED SARDINES
These small fish of the herring family (p. 130) are usually canned whole, in oil (as shown) or tomato sauce. The preserving process softens the bones, which means that they can be eaten as they are. Their main use is in appetizers and sandwiches.

ROLLMOP HERRING
The raw herring is beheaded, gutted, deboned and left in the form of double fillets. It is then spread out flat and rolled up around pieces of pickled cucumber or onion and marinated in a spiced vinegar. After several days it is ready for eating with dark bread and butter.

MATJES HERRING
A pickled herring of German origins, it is usually bought whole, salted from the barrel, though salted fillets (below) are also available. It should be soaked in water before use.

Dried Fish

Reduction approx. 50%

BOMBAY DUCK; Bombil
Despite its name, this is really an unsalted, sun-dried fish. In its fresh state it is from a long, silvery species called "bummalao", which is native to India, where it is often eaten fresh. It is, however, more well known in its dried form, when it is used as a flavoring in curries.

BACALAO
This is salted and dried cod. The fresh fish is caught in the north Atlantic, and then imported by European countries (often already dried). It can be bought either whole, as shown, or cut up in pieces, and is much used in Iberian cookery for stews and casseroles, one of the most famous of which is *bacalao a la vizcaina*. It needs overnight soaking before use.

SHARK'S FIN
The dried cartilage of a shark's fin, this is much used in Oriental cookery, where it is considered a delicacy. It requires overnight soaking before use and is best known as the basic ingredient for shark's fin soup.

Smoked Fish

See also p. 267

Reduction approx. 50%

SMOKED TROUT
Both the rainbow and the brown trout can be smoked, but it is, in fact, the rainbow trout which is normally used. It is gutted with the head left on, brined and then hot-smoked (at a temperature of over 80°F [26°C]). Smoked trout requires no cooking and is usually served as an appetizer with thinly sliced brown bread and butter and lemon wedges.

BUCKLING
Of the many versions of smoked herring, this is undoubtedly the best. Originally from Germany, it is also prepared in Britain, the Netherlands and Norway. It is hot-smoked and requires no cooking, and is usually eaten cold in the same way as smoked trout.

KIPPER
The most common smoked herring, it should be plump, juicy and properly smoked, not dyed to disguise inadequate treatment, as is often the case. Kippers are sold whole – usually in pairs – or as fillets, which are often available frozen. They can be used to make pâté, and otherwise can be broiled or grilled. They are part of the traditional English breakfast.

SMOKED EEL
A good smoked eel is a succulent delicacy, so smooth and buttery in texture that it becomes virtually spreadable. Dutch smoked eels are acknowledged to be among the best.

SMOKED MACKEREL
Smoking intensifies the already rich, strong taste of the mackerel. It is ready for eating and is usually used for hors d'oeuvres, served with lemon wedges.

SMOKED SALMON
The unrivaled king of all smoked fish, this is usually served as an appetizer, in paper-thin slices accompanied by a half-lemon. It is sold in fillets, which are dry-salted before being cold-smoked.

SMOKED HADDOCK;
Finnan Haddie; Findon Haddie
Originally from the village of Finnan in Aberdeenshire, Scotland, from which it takes its name, this haddock is traditionally cured over peat smoke. It can be eaten as it is, served with a rich egg sauce, or flaked and used as an omelet filling. It is also an ingredient of kedgeree, the classic English breakfast dish of fish and rice.

ARBROATH SMOKIE
Another version of smoked haddock from the east coast of Scotland, this is usually headed and gutted but otherwise left whole. Often sold in pairs, Arbroath smokies are usually served as an appetizer.

Smoked Fish and Roes

See also p. 267

SMOKED STURGEON
This is a delicacy regarded as a sort of *objet d'art* of the gourmet world – very expensive and yet worth every effort to track down! It should be thinly sliced and served as an appetizer.

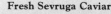

SMOKED SPRAT
A German variety of sprat is smoked whole and eaten in the traditional German way with a dark rye bread and butter.

Fresh Sevruga Caviar

SEVRUGA CAVIAR
Caviar is called after the species of sturgeon providing it. This one is the smallest grained. Sold fresh (above) and pressed (below). Pressed caviar is made from damaged eggs, salted and crushed together.

SMOKED HALIBUT
Usually it is the Greenland halibut which is smoked – it is quite a fatty fish and smoking seems to suit it. Serving suggestions include slices of the fish on open sandwiches with lemon pieces.

Pressed Sevruga Caviar

SOFT HERRING ROE
Sperm of the male fish, it has a creamy smooth texture. It is often fried in butter and served with lemon slices. A hard variety is also available, though it is quite scarce.

COD'S ROE
Also available uncooked and boiled, it is here shown smoked and in this form can be used to make a variety of *taramasalata*, the Greek dip. Boiled roe can be fried, broiled or grilled.

Fresh Beluga Caviar

Orange Lumpfish Roe

BELUGA CAVIAR
The largest grained caviar – and the most expensive. Above is the fresh; right, pasteurized and below, pressed.

Pasteurized Beluga Caviar

Black Lumpfish Roe

Pressed Beluga Caviar

LUMPFISH ROE
Lumpfish is usually from Iceland and there are both orange and black varieties. Experts do not put it in the same class as caviar but it can be a good introduction to it.

SALMON ROE
Eaten in the same way as caviar, it is sometimes referred to as caviar though the word should really apply only to sturgeon roe.

Reduction
approx. 50%

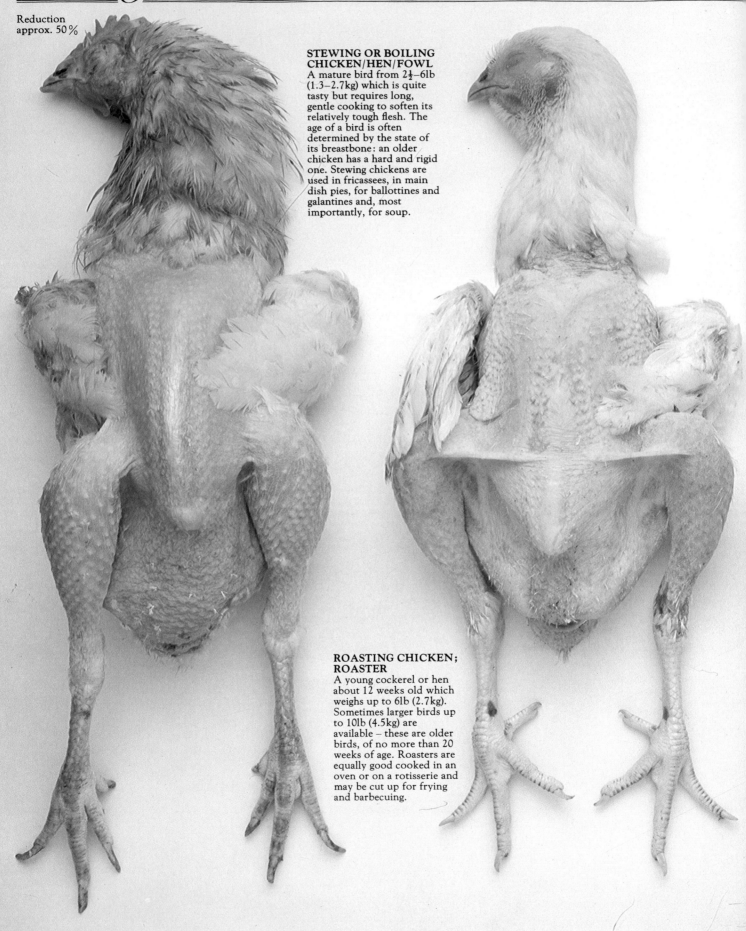

**STEWING OR BOILING
CHICKEN/HEN/FOWL**
A mature bird from 2½–6lb
(1.3–2.7kg) which is quite
tasty but requires long,
gentle cooking to soften its
relatively tough flesh. The
age of a bird is often
determined by the state of
its breastbone: an older
chicken has a hard and rigid
one. Stewing chickens are
used in fricassees, in main
dish pies, for ballottines and
galantines and, most
importantly, for soup.

**ROASTING CHICKEN;
ROASTER**
A young cockerel or hen
about 12 weeks old which
weighs up to 6lb (2.7kg).
Sometimes larger birds up
to 10lb (4.5kg) are
available – these are older
birds, of no more than 20
weeks of age. Roasters are
equally good cooked in an
oven or on a rotisserie and
may be cut up for frying
and barbecuing.

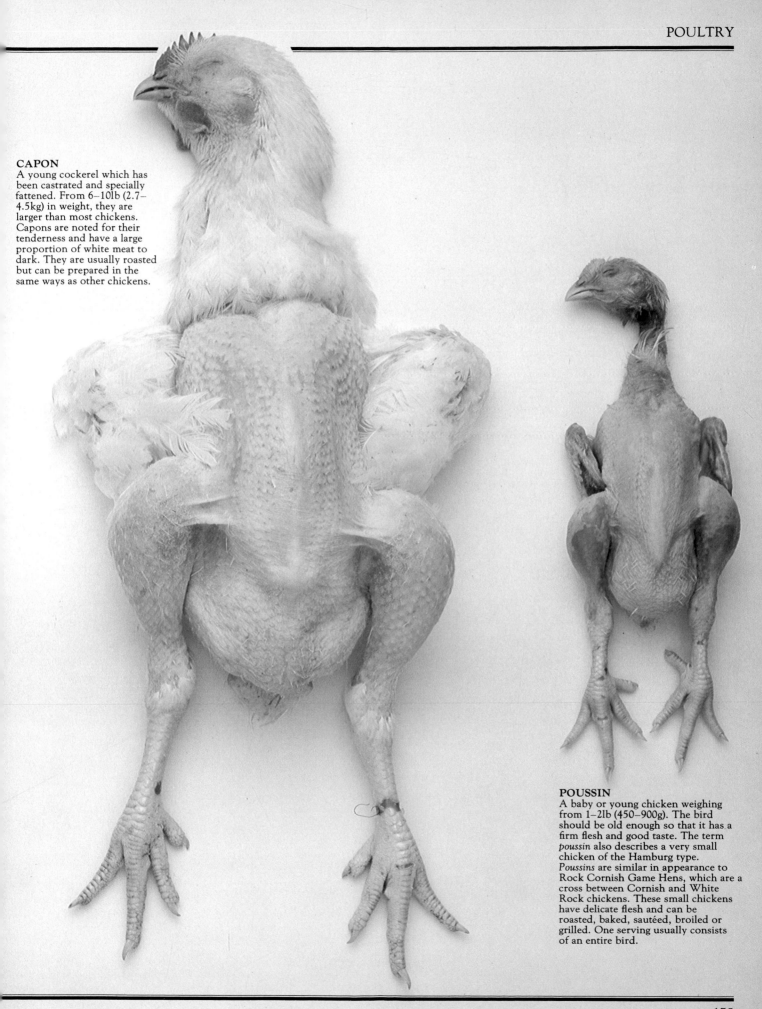

CAPON
A young cockerel which has been castrated and specially fattened. From 6–10lb (2.7–4.5kg) in weight, they are larger than most chickens. Capons are noted for their tenderness and have a large proportion of white meat to dark. They are usually roasted but can be prepared in the same ways as other chickens.

POUSSIN
A baby or young chicken weighing from 1–2lb (450–900g). The bird should be old enough so that it has a firm flesh and good taste. The term *poussin* also describes a very small chicken of the Hamburg type. *Poussins* are similar in appearance to Rock Cornish Game Hens, which are a cross between Cornish and White Rock chickens. These small chickens have delicate flesh and can be roasted, baked, sautéed, broiled or grilled. One serving usually consists of an entire bird.

Reduction approx. 30%

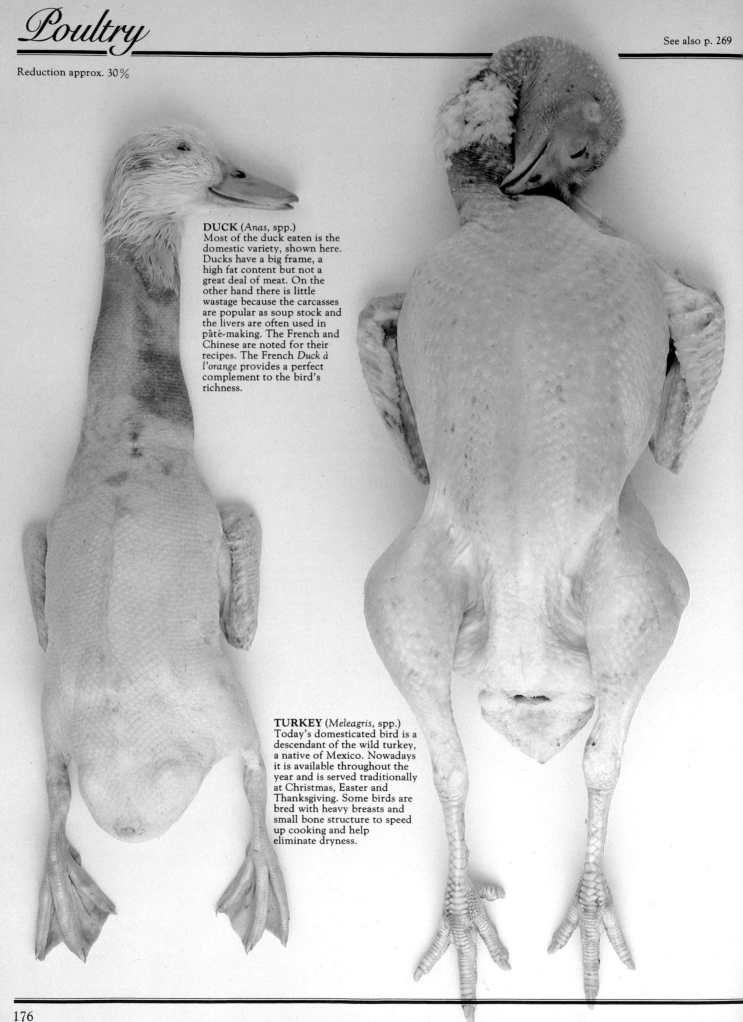

DUCK (*Anas*, spp.)
Most of the duck eaten is the
domestic variety, shown here.
Ducks have a big frame, a
high fat content but not a
great deal of meat. On the
other hand there is little
wastage because the carcasses
are popular as soup stock and
the livers are often used in
pâté-making. The French and
Chinese are noted for their
recipes. The French *Duck à
l'orange* provides a perfect
complement to the bird's
richness.

TURKEY (*Meleagris*, spp.)
Today's domesticated bird is a
descendant of the wild turkey,
a native of Mexico. Nowadays
it is available throughout the
year and is served traditionally
at Christmas, Easter and
Thanksgiving. Some birds are
bred with heavy breasts and
small bone structure to speed
up cooking and help
eliminate dryness.

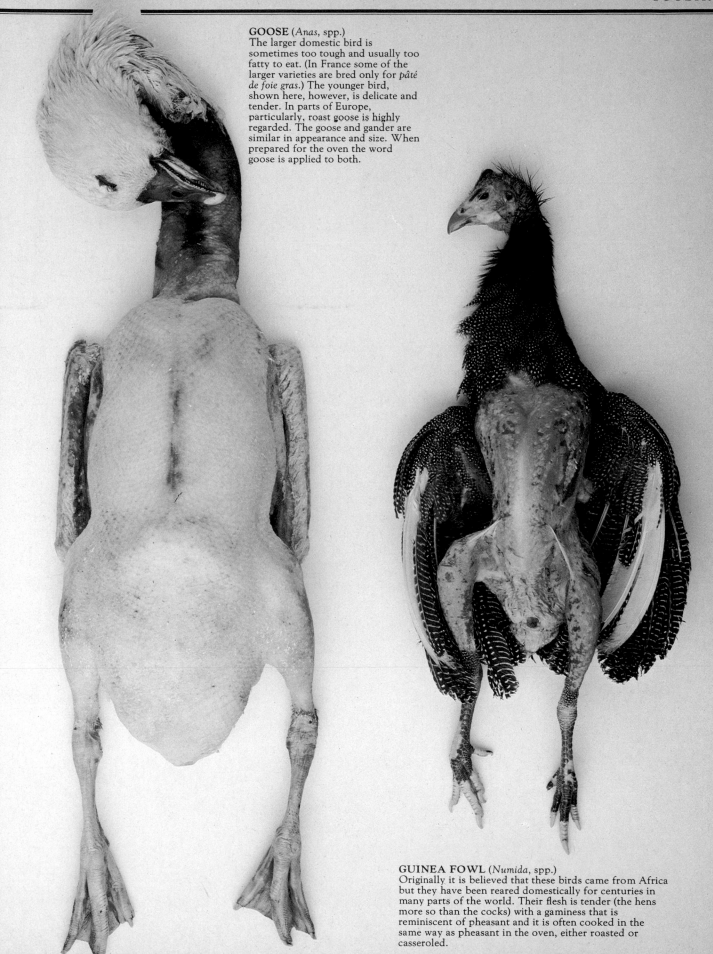

GOOSE (*Anas*, spp.)
The larger domestic bird is
sometimes too tough and usually too
fatty to eat. (In France some of the
larger varieties are bred only for *pâté
de foie gras*.) The younger bird,
shown here, however, is delicate and
tender. In parts of Europe,
particularly, roast goose is highly
regarded. The goose and gander are
similar in appearance and size. When
prepared for the oven the word
goose is applied to both.

GUINEA FOWL (*Numida*, spp.)
Originally it is believed that these birds came from Africa
but they have been reared domestically for centuries in
many parts of the world. Their flesh is tender (the hens
more so than the cocks) with a gaminess that is
reminiscent of pheasant and it is often cooked in the
same way as pheasant in the oven, either roasted or
casseroled.

Feathered Game

See also p. 271

Reduction approx. 30%

WOODCOCK
Native to Europe and America, but
now found worldwide, the availability
of this game bird is often limited by
hunting seasons. Woodcock should be
well hung but the skin should remain
intact on plucking. One woodcock
should be served for each person. It is
suitable for roasting, braising, broiling
or grilling; if roasted, it is not drawn
or decapitated although the gizzard
is removed.

GROUSE
Native to Scotland, there are several varieties of
this bird; the type shown is the British grouse.
Like other game birds its availability is limited
by hunting seasons. Young birds are suitable
for roasting, broiling or grilling; older birds
can be casseroled or braised. One bird is
normally served per person.

SNIPE
This bird, native to Europe, is subject to the same availability restrictions as most other game birds. It is best roasted, although it is so small it can also be cooked under the broiler or grill. One bird should be allowed per person.

PARTRIDGE
The type shown is native to Europe, but there are many other varieties. Its availability is restricted by hunting seasons and it can be roasted, stewed or casseroled. Young birds especially should be roasted and served with their own gravy as a sauce. When roasting, 1 bird should be allowed per person.

QUAIL
Native to the Middle East, there are many varieties of this small game bird, which features in many *haute cuisine* dishes. Available all year round, it can be roasted, sautéed, broiled or grilled; allow at least 1 bird for each person.

Reduction approx. 65%

Hen Pheasant

Cock Pheasant

MALLARD DUCK
Originally from the northern hemisphere,
the mallard is the largest of wild ducks
(the male is shown). It can be bought
fresh (though its availability is
restricted by hunting seasons), or frozen.
It is excellent for roasting and 1 bird
will serve 2 or 3 persons.

PHEASANT
Native to China, but now found all
over the northern hemisphere, the
cock and hen pheasant are often sold
together as a brace. Though the hen
pheasant is considered to be more
tender, it will only serve about 3
persons, whereas the cock will serve
4. Bought fresh (though its
availability is restricted by hunting
seasons) or frozen, it is excellent for
roasting, stewing, braising and
serving en *papillote*.

HARE
Originally from Europe, now found worldwide, the availability of hares is restricted by hunting seasons. They can be roasted or used in casseroles, stews and terrines. Older hares are usually jugged. Many classic French dishes call for the back or saddle (*râble*) or the saddle and hind legs (*train*) only.

WILD RABBIT
Originally from Africa, but now found worldwide, the availability of wild rabbits, unlike that of domestic rabbits, is restricted by hunting seasons. Usually bought whole (domestic rabbits can also be bought cut up and frozen), they are used in casseroles, stews and roasts.

Reduction approx. 20%

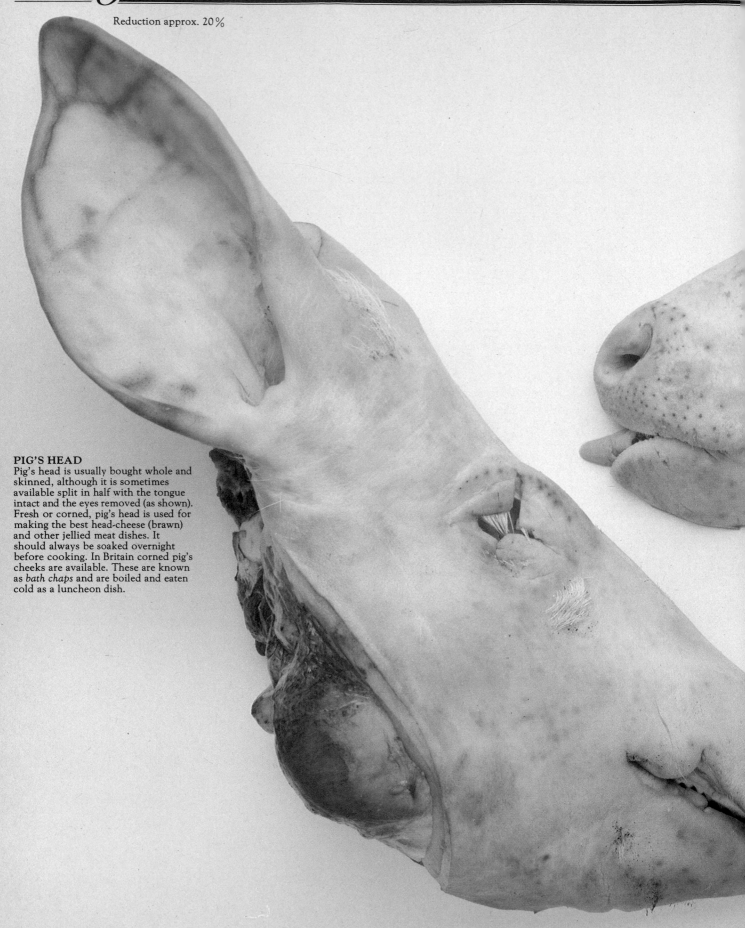

PIG'S HEAD

Pig's head is usually bought whole and skinned, although it is sometimes available split in half with the tongue intact and the eyes removed (as shown). Fresh or corned, pig's head is used for making the best head-cheese (brawn) and other jellied meat dishes. It should always be soaked overnight before cooking. In Britain corned pig's cheeks are available. These are known as *bath chaps* and are boiled and eaten cold as a luncheon dish.

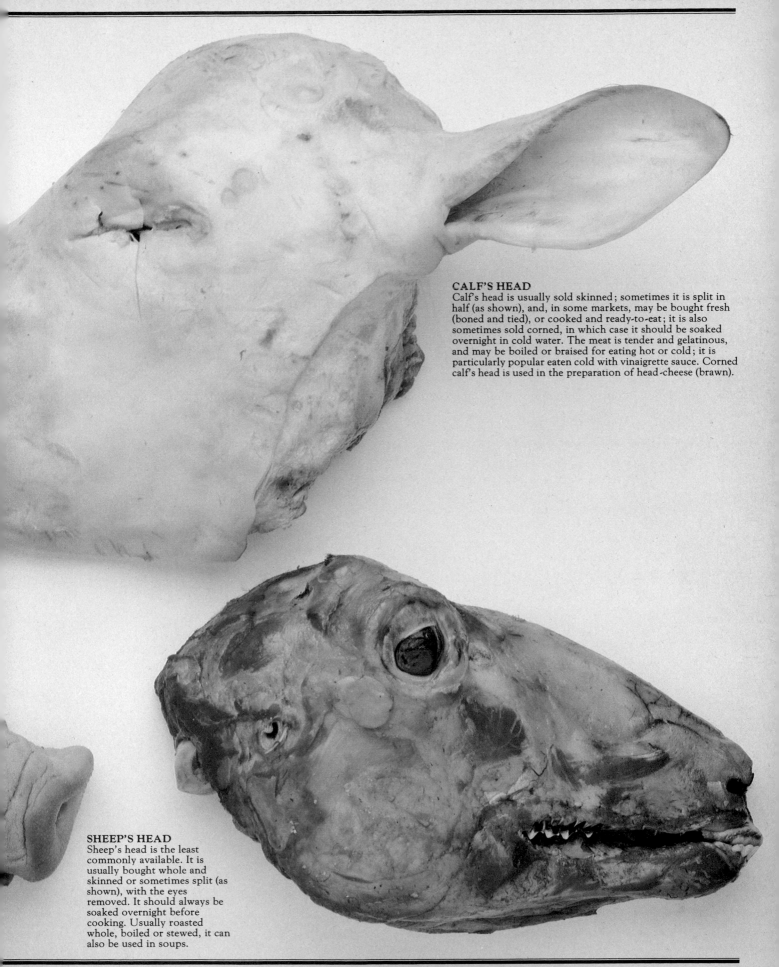

CALF'S HEAD
Calf's head is usually sold skinned; sometimes it is split in half (as shown), and, in some markets, may be bought fresh (boned and tied), or cooked and ready-to-eat; it is also sometimes sold corned, in which case it should be soaked overnight in cold water. The meat is tender and gelatinous, and may be boiled or braised for eating hot or cold; it is particularly popular eaten cold with vinaigrette sauce. Corned calf's head is used in the preparation of head-cheese (brawn).

SHEEP'S HEAD
Sheep's head is the least commonly available. It is usually bought whole and skinned or sometimes split (as shown), with the eyes removed. It should always be soaked overnight before cooking. Usually roasted whole, boiled or stewed, it can also be used in soups.

Variety Meats

See also p. 281

Reduction approx. 60%

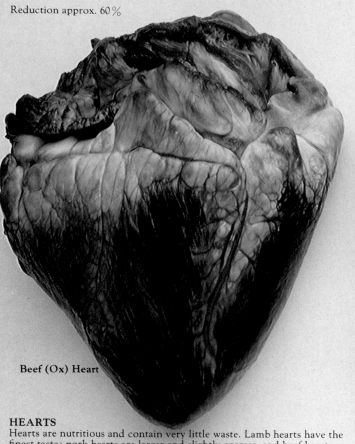

Beef (Ox) Heart

HEARTS

Hearts are nutritious and contain very little waste. Lamb hearts have the finest taste; pork hearts are larger and slightly coarser, and beef hearts are the least tender of all. All require long, slow cooking.

Pork (Pig) Heart   **Lamb Heart**

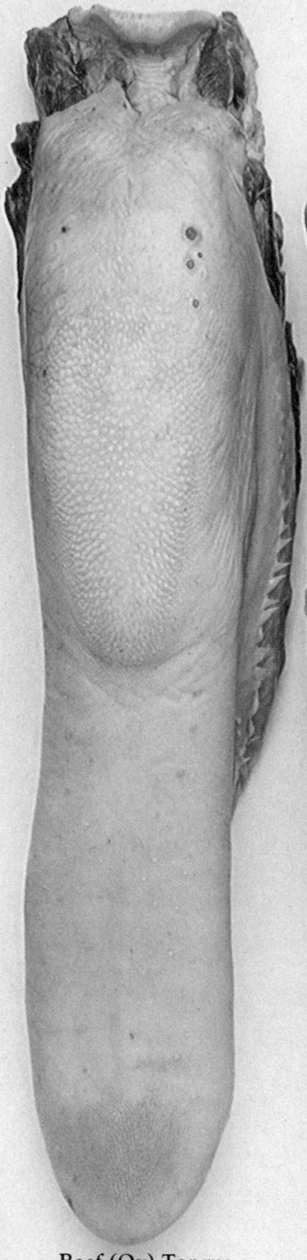

Beef (Ox) Tongue

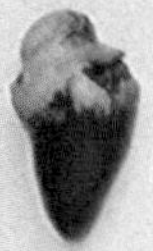

Chicken Heart

EYEBALLS

Eyeballs (particularly sheeps' eyeballs, as shown) are considered a great delicacy in the Middle East. They are usually removed from the head after it has been roasted or boiled and are eaten straight away, with or without extra sauce or seasonings.

Veal (Calf) Tongue

Lamb Tongue

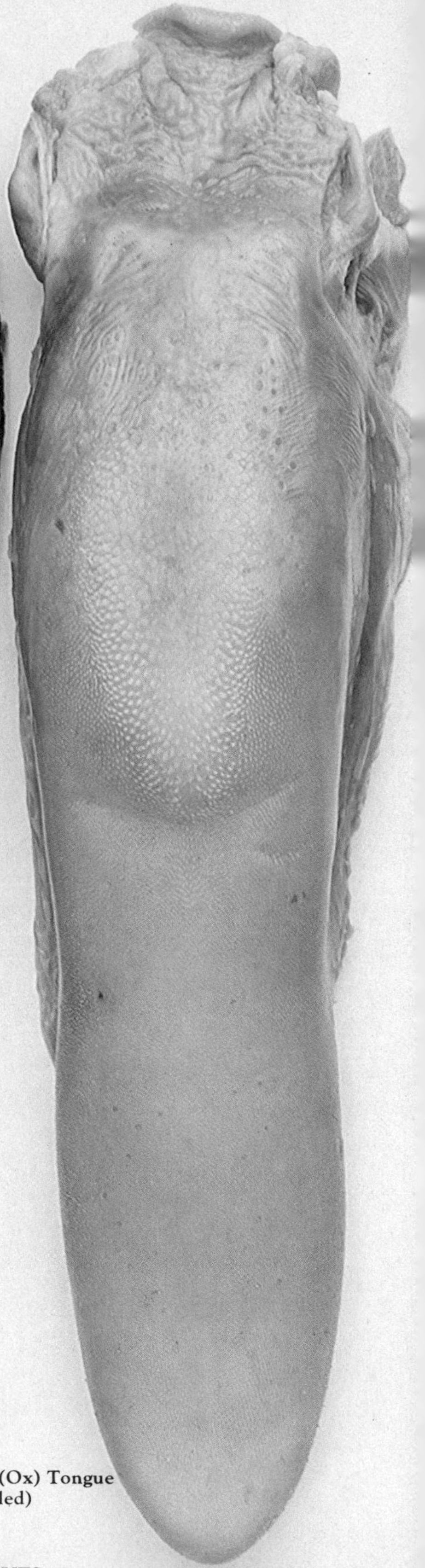

Beef (Ox) Tongue (pickled)

TONGUES

In some markets, tongue is sold ready to serve, but it is more usual to buy it fresh, smoked or corned for cooking and eating hot or cold, with or without sauce. Beef and veal tongues are the commonest, lamb tongues the most tender.

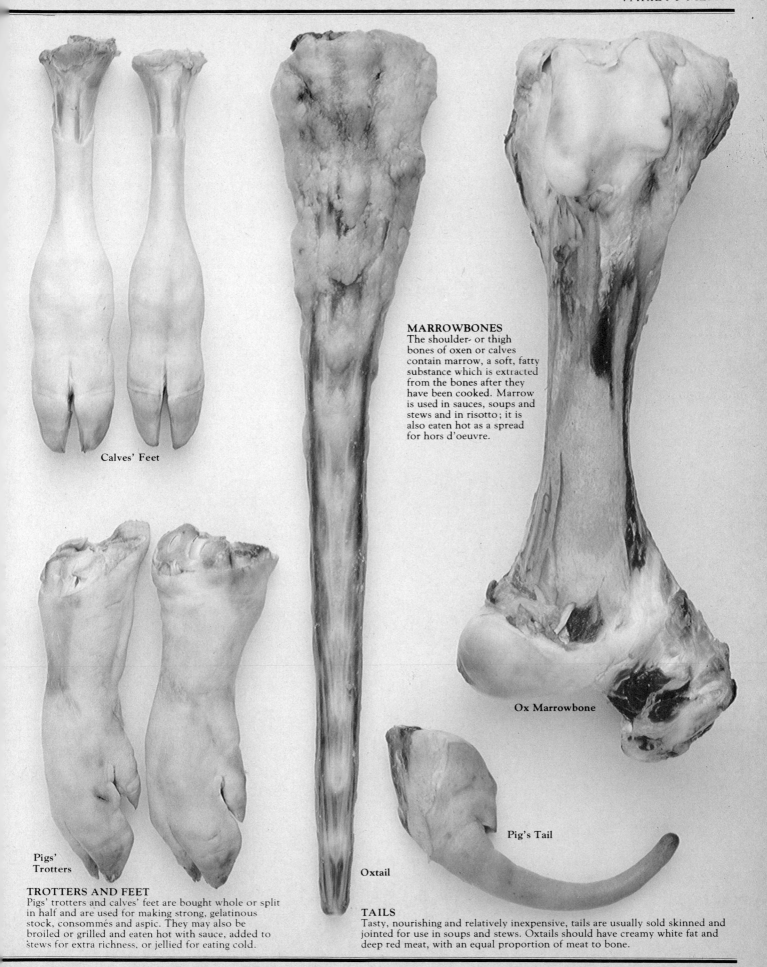

Calves' Feet

MARROWBONES
The shoulder- or thigh bones of oxen or calves contain marrow, a soft, fatty substance which is extracted from the bones after they have been cooked. Marrow is used in sauces, soups and stews and in risotto; it is also eaten hot as a spread for hors d'oeuvre.

Ox Marrowbone

Pig's Tail

Pigs' Trotters

Oxtail

TROTTERS AND FEET
Pigs' trotters and calves' feet are bought whole or split in half and are used for making strong, gelatinous stock, consommés and aspic. They may also be broiled or grilled and eaten hot with sauce, added to stews for extra richness, or jellied for eating cold.

TAILS
Tasty, nourishing and relatively inexpensive, tails are usually sold skinned and jointed for use in soups and stews. Oxtails should have creamy white fat and deep red meat, with an equal proportion of meat to bone.

Reduction approx. 60%

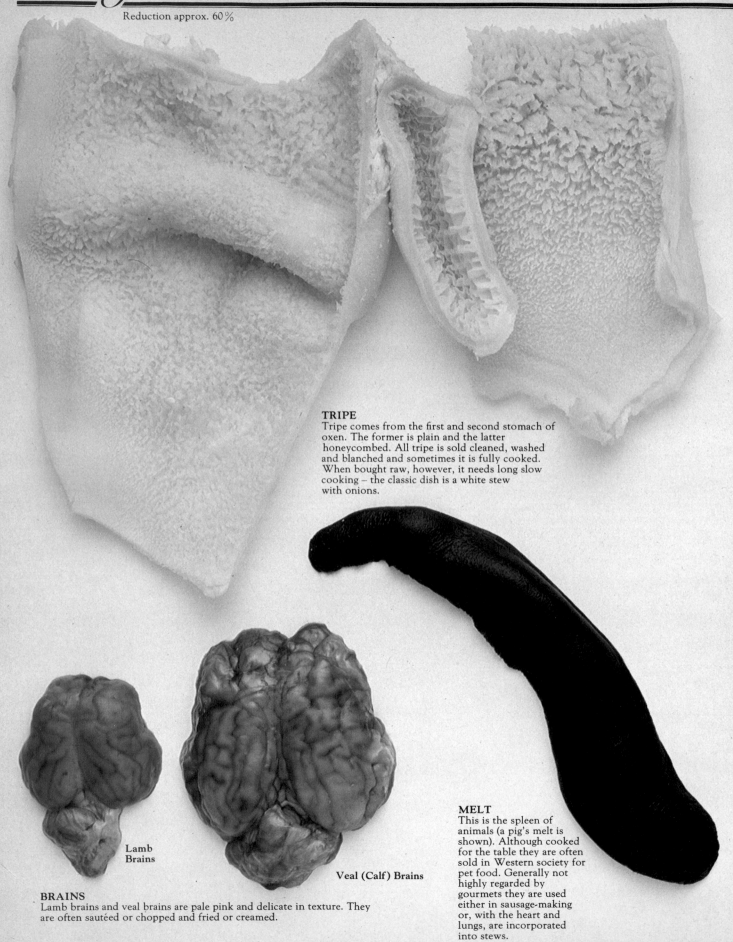

TRIPE
Tripe comes from the first and second stomach of oxen. The former is plain and the latter honeycombed. All tripe is sold cleaned, washed and blanched and sometimes it is fully cooked. When bought raw, however, it needs long slow cooking – the classic dish is a white stew with onions.

Lamb Brains

Veal (Calf) Brains

MELT
This is the spleen of animals (a pig's melt is shown). Although cooked for the table they are often sold in Western society for pet food. Generally not highly regarded by gourmets they are used either in sausage-making or, with the heart and lungs, are incorporated into stews.

BRAINS
Lamb brains and veal brains are pale pink and delicate in texture. They are often sautéed or chopped and fried or creamed.

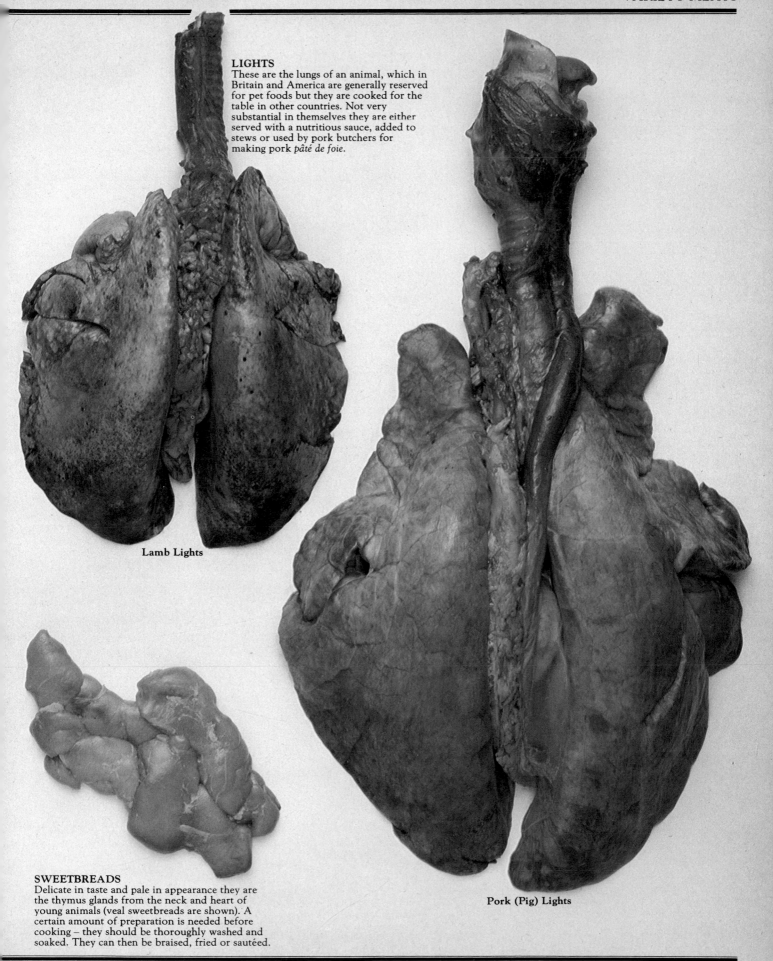

LIGHTS
These are the lungs of an animal, which in Britain and America are generally reserved for pet foods but they are cooked for the table in other countries. Not very substantial in themselves they are either served with a nutritious sauce, added to stews or used by pork butchers for making pork *pâté de foie*.

Lamb Lights

Pork (Pig) Lights

SWEETBREADS
Delicate in taste and pale in appearance they are the thymus glands from the neck and heart of young animals (veal sweetbreads are shown). A certain amount of preparation is needed before cooking – they should be thoroughly washed and soaked. They can then be braised, fried or sautéed.

See also p. 281

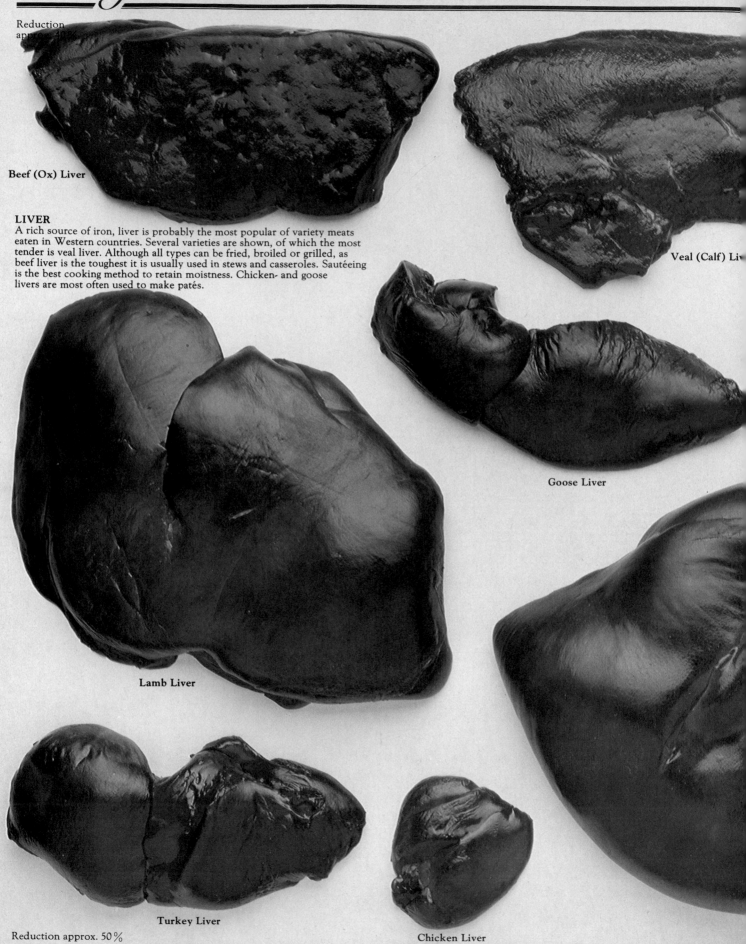

Reduction
approx. 40%

Beef (Ox) Liver

Veal (Calf) Liver

LIVER

A rich source of iron, liver is probably the most popular of variety meats eaten in Western countries. Several varieties are shown, of which the most tender is veal liver. Although all types can be fried, broiled or grilled, as beef liver is the toughest it is usually used in stews and casseroles. Sautéeing is the best cooking method to retain moistness. Chicken- and goose livers are most often used to make patés.

Goose Liver

Lamb Liver

Turkey Liver

Chicken Liver

Reduction approx. 50%

Veal (Calf) Kidney

Duck Liver

Beef (Ox) Kidney

Lamb Kidney

Pork (Pig) Kidney

Pork (Pig) Liver

KIDNEY

Kidneys have a strong, distinctive taste and are considered by many to be a great delicacy. Pork kidneys are usually used in terrines; veal and lamb kidneys are often sautéed, and ox kidney is used in pies and dishes that require longer cooking.

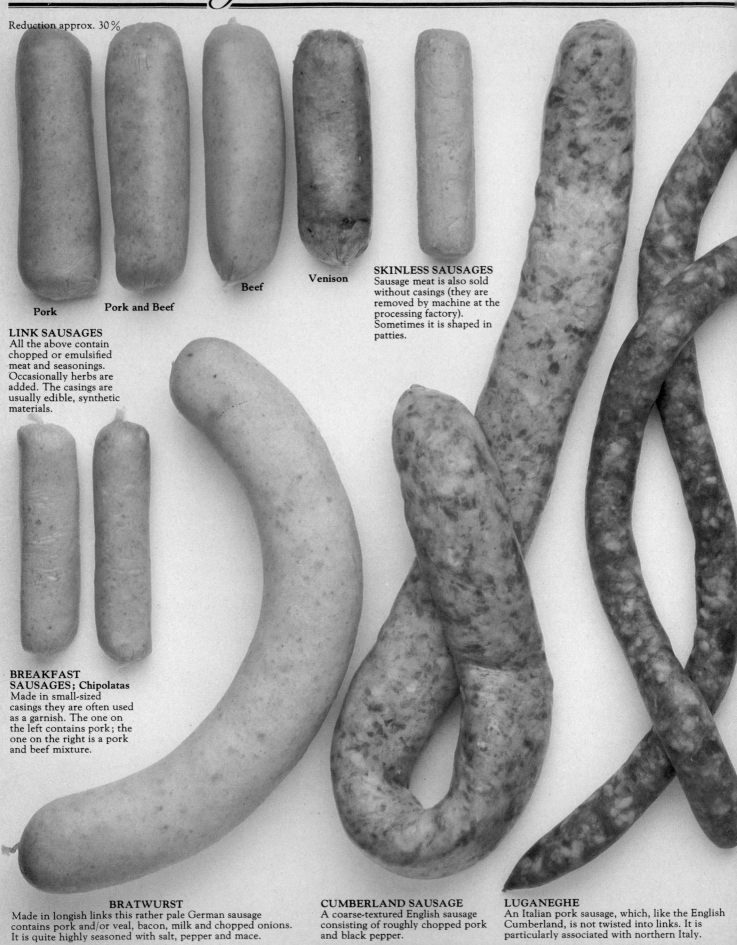

Fresh Sausages

See also p. 282

Reduction approx. 30%

Pork

Pork and Beef

Beef

Venison

LINK SAUSAGES
All the above contain chopped or emulsified meat and seasonings. Occasionally herbs are added. The casings are usually edible, synthetic materials.

SKINLESS SAUSAGES
Sausage meat is also sold without casings (they are removed by machine at the processing factory). Sometimes it is shaped in patties.

BREAKFAST SAUSAGES; Chipolatas
Made in small-sized casings they are often used as a garnish. The one on the left contains pork; the one on the right is a pork and beef mixture.

BRATWURST
Made in longish links this rather pale German sausage contains pork and/or veal, bacon, milk and chopped onions. It is quite highly seasoned with salt, pepper and mace.

CUMBERLAND SAUSAGE
A coarse-textured English sausage consisting of roughly chopped pork and black pepper.

LUGANEGHE
An Italian pork sausage, which, like the English Cumberland, is not twisted into links. It is particularly associated with northern Italy.

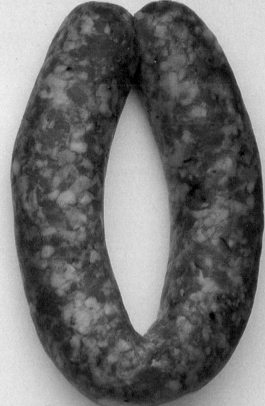

MERGUEZ
An Algerian sausage that is known for its high spiciness. It is usually broiled or grilled.

TOULOUSE SAUSAGE
The texture of this sausage should be very coarse. In France it is cooked with haricot beans in a cassoulet.

LAP CHEONG
A Chinese sausage with pork, soy sauce and paprika. (*Lap* means "wax" and *cheong* means "intestine".)

SALAMELLE
This is the name given by the Italians to a variety of spiced sausage.

SPICED ENGLISH SAUSAGE
A pale pink sausage that incorporates pork and spices. Its texture is quite smooth.

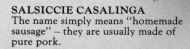

SPICED FRENCH SAUSAGE
A fairly coarse-textured sausage, highly spiced and well seasoned with garlic.

SALSICCIE CASALINGA
The name simply means "homemade sausage" – they are usually made of pure pork.

PAPRIKA SAUSAGE
A dark, fairly coarse-textured sausage, made of lamb and beef and containing paprika, coriander, fennel and a variety of seasonings.

BLACK PUDDING
Traditionally this black sausage is associated with the north of England although it appears under different names in many areas. Main ingredients are pig's blood, groats, fat, oatmeal and seasonings.

MORCILLA
The Spanish version of black pudding, Morcilla is used as an ingredient of a national dish, *fabada*, which includes chorizos and bacon.

BUTIFARA
There are many variations of this Spanish firm-textured sausage. Generally they include pork, white wine, seasonings and spices.

BOUDIN
A French version of black/white pudding. The black contains pig's blood; the white may have pork, chicken or veal.

GREEK SAUSAGE
A dark, stubby sausage from Greece. It is usually quite heavily spiced.

ANDOUILLETTE
This type of French sausage is made from offal such as tripe or mesentery.

CREPINETTE
The term *crépinette* covers many varieties of small minced meat sausages, consisting of either lamb or pork, all wrapped in caul.

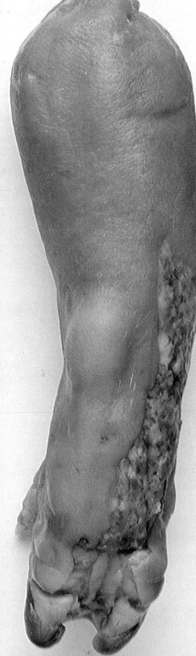

COTECHINO
Lean and fat pork with white wine and spices. It is often served with beans.

FRANKFURTER
The genuine frankfurter is lean pork and salted bacon fat blended into a paste and smoked but there are now many variations in ingredients as well as in size and shape, as shown here. Often the ingredients include beef and pork trimmings, tripe and pig hearts.

ZAMPONE
A pork sausage that is stuffed into a hollowed-out pig's trotter instead of a casing.

TEEWURST
A quality sausage made of the best meat. A mixture of finely minced pork and beef, it is sometimes highly spiced.

CERVELAT
There are many different varieties in many parts of Europe but generally it is a finely minced mixture of beef and pork smoked until golden.

SAVELOY
An English version of cervelat, saveloy contains pork and lights. The addition of saltpeter gives it a red tinge.

Cooked and Lightly Smoked Sausages

See also p. 282

Reduction approx. 30%

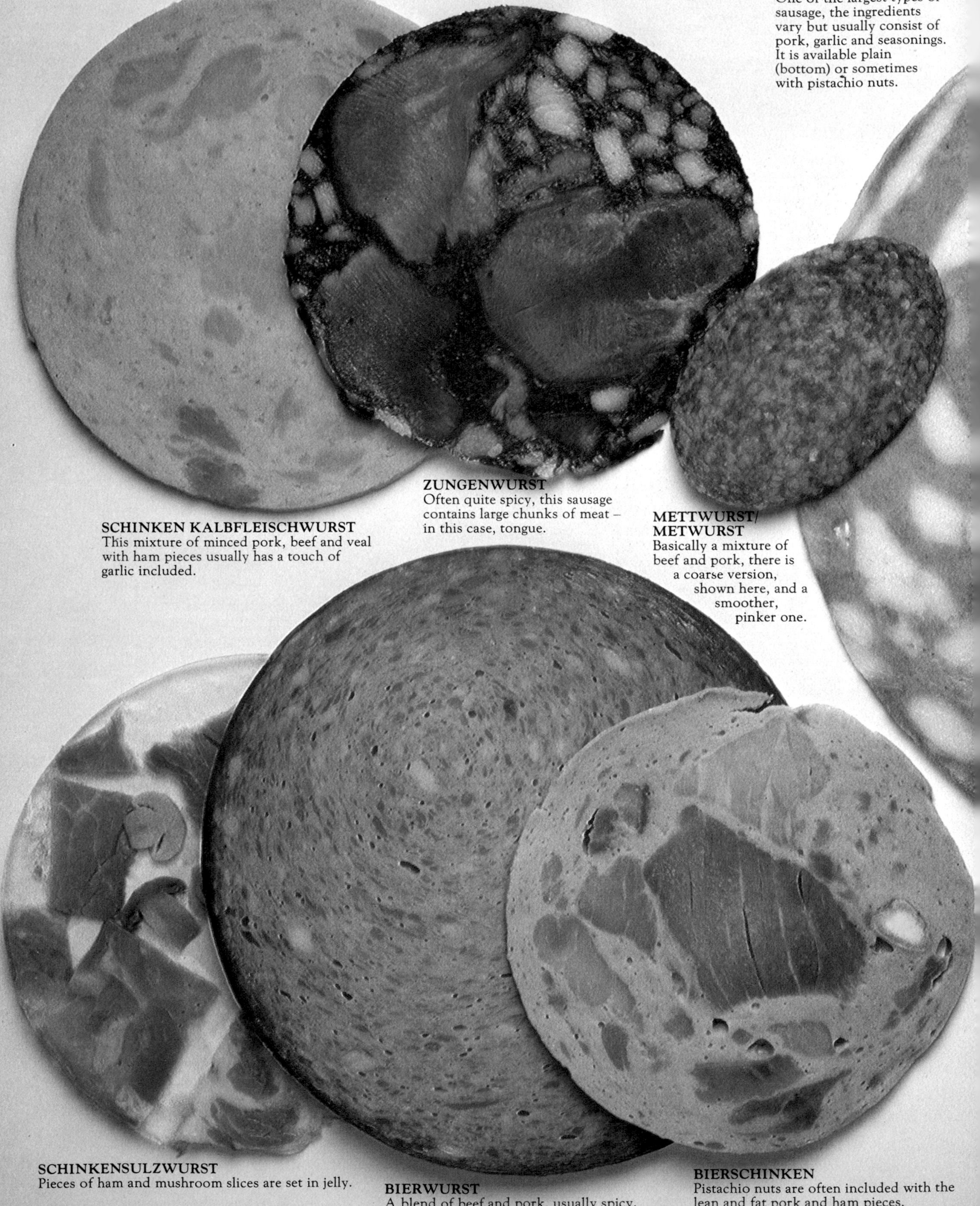

MORTADELLA
One of the largest types of sausage, the ingredients vary but usually consist of pork, garlic and seasonings. It is available plain (bottom) or sometimes with pistachio nuts.

ZUNGENWURST
Often quite spicy, this sausage contains large chunks of meat – in this case, tongue.

SCHINKEN KALBFLEISCHWURST
This mixture of minced pork, beef and veal with ham pieces usually has a touch of garlic included.

METTWURST/ METWURST
Basically a mixture of beef and pork, there is a coarse version, shown here, and a smoother, pinker one.

SCHINKENSULZWURST
Pieces of ham and mushroom slices are set in jelly.

BIERWURST
A blend of beef and pork, usually spicy.

BIERSCHINKEN
Pistachio nuts are often included with the lean and fat pork and ham pieces.

Mortadella with
Pistachio Nuts

EXTRAWURST
A pale pink mixture of beef and
pork or bacon fat. It is smooth in
texture and slices easily.

KNOBLAUCHWURST
The strong, distinctive taste of garlic is associated
with this sausage, which contains fat and lean
pork, salt, pepper and spice.

Plain Mortadella

**SCHINKEN
JAGDWURST**
Finely minced pork with diced pork fat and pieces of ham.

KATENRAUCHWURST
This dark-skinned sausage is firm in texture and contains coarsely cut smoked pork. Originally it was produced in *Katen* – peasant huts – hence its name. It was left in the chimneys of the huts for long periods to be smoked.

PEPPERONI/PEPERONI
A dry Italian sausage that consists of a mixture of coarsely chopped beef and pork and is highly seasoned with ground red pepper and other spices. It is commonly served on pizzas.

BIRNENFORMIGE SALAMI
The name means "pear-shaped" – a perfect description of this German salami before slicing.

NETZ SALAMI
À German salami that takes its name from the fact that it is bound with string ready for hanging.

CERVELAT
German minced beef and pork sausage that is smoked to a golden brown. Its meat is more finely ground than Italian salami and usually less highly seasoned. See p. 193 for another variety.

LAND SALAMI
A country-style salami usually with spices or herbs mixed into the pork.

EDEL SALAMI
The name means "noble" – a rich salami of mixed pork and beef.

SAUCISSON FUME AUX HERBES
Garlic is blended into a basic sausage mixture which is dried and smoked. It is finished with a generous coating of herbs.

PFEFFER PLOCKWURST
One of the few square sausages. It is coated with a covering of coarsely ground black pepper.

KIELBASA
A Polish sausage of ground pork and beef that is garlicky and well seasoned.

Reduction approx. 60%

SALT BEEF
A cut of beef – usually brisket – soaked in brine.

GALANTINE
Made from boned meat or poultry prepared in a gelatin stock and set.

DUCK TERRINE
Duck, lean ham and bacon fat with seasonings, spices and sometimes brandy.

CHORIZO
A Spanish sausage with many variations but always including pork and pimiento.

KABANOS
A Polish sausage made of minced pork.

TONGUE
Usually beef tongue, it is salted, poached and served in cold slices with salads.

RILLETTES
From France potted belly of pork, sometimes with goose or rabbit added.

SMOKED TURKEY
First the meat is soaked in pickling brine and then smoked. Served sliced with cold dishes.

BRESAOLA
This dried salt beef is a specialty from Lombard, Italy. Cut thinly it is served as an hors d'oeuvre.

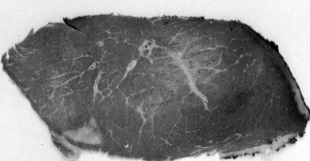

PASTRAMI
This is the cured, smoked plate (underside) of beef. It is usually thinly sliced and used for sandwiches.

BOLOGNA
One of the most famous sausages of which there are now a number of versions but basically a mixture of cooked smoked pork and beef.

LIVERWURST; Liver Sausage
There are many varieties from different countries. Generally if is a smooth mixture of ground pork, liver, onions and seasonings.

NETZ SALAMI
À German salami that takes its name from the fact that it is bound with string ready for hanging.

CERVELAT
German minced beef and pork sausage that is smoked to a golden brown. Its meat is more finely ground than Italian salami and usually less highly seasoned. See p. 193 for another variety.

LAND SALAMI
A country-style salami usually with spices or herbs mixed into the pork.

EDEL SALAMI
The name means "noble" – a rich salami of mixed pork and beef.

SAUCISSON FUME AUX HERBES
Garlic is blended into a basic sausage mixture which is dried and smoked. It is finished with a generous coating of herbs.

PFEFFER PLOCKWURST
One of the few square sausages. It is coated with a covering of coarsely ground black pepper.

KIELBASA
A Polish sausage of ground pork and beef that is garlicky and well seasoned.

197

Smoked Sausages

See also p. 282

DANISH SALAMI
An even-shaped salami which is useful in sandwich-making. A mixture of pork, veal, spices and sometimes garlic.

MILANO SALAMI
An Italian salami made with lean pork, beef and pork fat. It is seasoned with garlic, pepper and white wine (see Milano style).

FRENCH PEPPER SALAMI
Pork and beef are mixed with coarse fat and seasoned with whole black peppercorns. Often used in hors d'oeuvres.

FRENCH HERB SALAMI
A small beef and pork salami coated with herbs. Useful for picnics it is also used for hors d'oeuvres.

TOSCANA
Fiorentino is the best known of the Tuscan salamis. Larger than average they often consist of pure pork mingled with pieces of lean meat and fat.

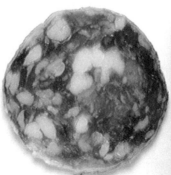

FELINETTI
From Parma, this is a delicate salami containing white wine, peppercorns and a little garlic.

MILANO STYLE SALAMI
Another variety of Milano salami. Both are often used for antipasto.

GENOA SALAMI
Popular as an antipasto served with broad beans, it is seasoned with garlic, peppercorns and red wine and contains a mixture of pork and *vitellone*.

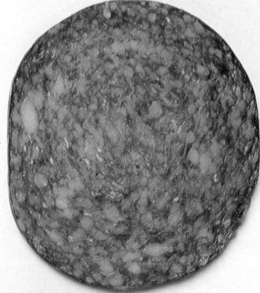

GERMAN SALAMI
Generally the German varieties are a finely ground beef and pork mixture and tend to be more heavily smoked than any of the Italian salamis.

NAPOLI SALAMI
A long, thin salami made with pork and beef and seasoned well with both black and red pepper to make it quite hot.

FARMER-STYLE SALAMI
A type of salami that is usually a coarse-cut beef and pork mixture with whole peppercorns and garlic.

COUNTRY STYLE SALAMI
A basic sausage mixture, it is bound with twine and left to dry and mature instead of being eaten immediately. It contains pork, pork fat, garlic, herbs and peppercorns.

HUNGARIAN SALAMI
Very fat pork mixed with a blend of several spices. The casings are lightly smoked and the taste of this salami improves with age.

Reduction approx. 60%

SALT BEEF
A cut of beef – usually brisket – soaked in brine.

GALANTINE
Made from boned meat or poultry prepared in a gelatin stock and set.

DUCK TERRINE
Duck, lean ham and bacon fat with seasonings, spices and sometimes brandy.

CHORIZO
A Spanish sausage with many variations but always including pork and pimiento.

KABANOS
A Polish sausage made of minced pork.

TONGUE
Usually beef tongue, it is salted, poached and served in cold slices with salads.

RILLETTES
From France potted belly of pork, sometimes with goose or rabbit added.

SMOKED TURKEY
First the meat is soaked in pickling brine and then smoked. Served sliced with cold dishes.

BRESAOLA
This dried salt beef is a specialty from Lombard, Italy. Cut thinly it is served as an hors d'oeuvre.

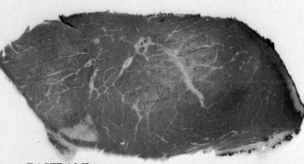

PASTRAMI
This is the cured, smoked plate (underside) of beef. It is usually thinly sliced and used for sandwiches.

BOLOGNA
One of the most famous sausages of which there are now a number of versions but basically a mixture of cooked smoked pork and beef.

LIVERWURST; Liver Sausage
There are many varieties from different countries. Generally it is a smooth mixture of ground pork, liver, onions and seasonings.

Unsmoked Sliced Bacon (Streaky)

Smoked Sliced Bacon (Streaky)

SLICED BACON (America); SLICED STREAKY BACON (Britain)
Individual slices, left unsmoked and right, smoked. Because of the evenness of the slices it is usually more popular than the slab bacon.

Smoked Sliced Canadian (Back) Bacon   **Unsmoked Sliced Canadian (Back) Bacon**

PATE DE FOIE
Made from the liver of specially reared geese, mixed with seasonings and spices to a smooth texture.

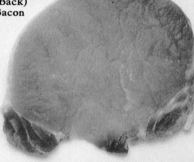

CANADIAN BACON (America); BACK BACON (Britain)
On the left is smoked, on the right is unsmoked. Canadian bacon is cut from the loin of the animal and is much meatier than other bacon cuts.

TERRINE DE PYRENEES
A semi-smooth-textured terrine which includes mushrooms.

PATE DE FORESTIER
A much coarser texture than the terrine above, it is also a true pâté as it is surrounded by a pastry crust.

Canadian (Back) Slab Bacon

Smoked Slab Bacon (Streaky) with Rind

Unsmoked Slab Bacon (Streaky) without Rind

SLAB BACON
Left, smoked bacon with rind; right, unsmoked bacon without rind and top, Canadian (back) bacon. The first two are cut from the belly and are quite fatty.

Hams

See also p. 282

Reduction
approx.
50%

BAYONNE
Almost every region of France has its own salted and smoked ham.
This one from the Basque country is one of the best known.

PARMA; Prosciutto
A delicate-tasting ham – one of the best known from Italy.

WESTPHALIAN
One of the most famous of the German hams. After curing and
smoking this rich, dark ham undergoes a lengthy aging process.

ARDENNES
A Belgian ham of great quality which is considered to rank in taste
with Parma, York and Bayonne hams.

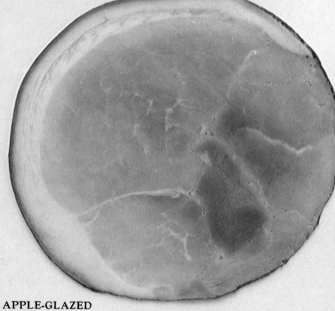

APPLE-GLAZED
Fully cooked boneless ham with an apple glaze
usually made of apple jelly, lemon juice and cloves.

SUGAR-GLAZED
A rolled boneless cooked ham with a sugar glaze;
it is sold whole, in halves
or sliced.

SUFFOLK
This expensive English ham is soaked in molasses
rather than salt – a process which turns its skin a
distinctive black.

YORK
This English ham enjoys a worldwide reputation. Firm and tender, it is
noted for its delicate taste. It is cured with dry salt instead of brine and
then lightly smoked. The one shown has been coated with breadcrumbs.

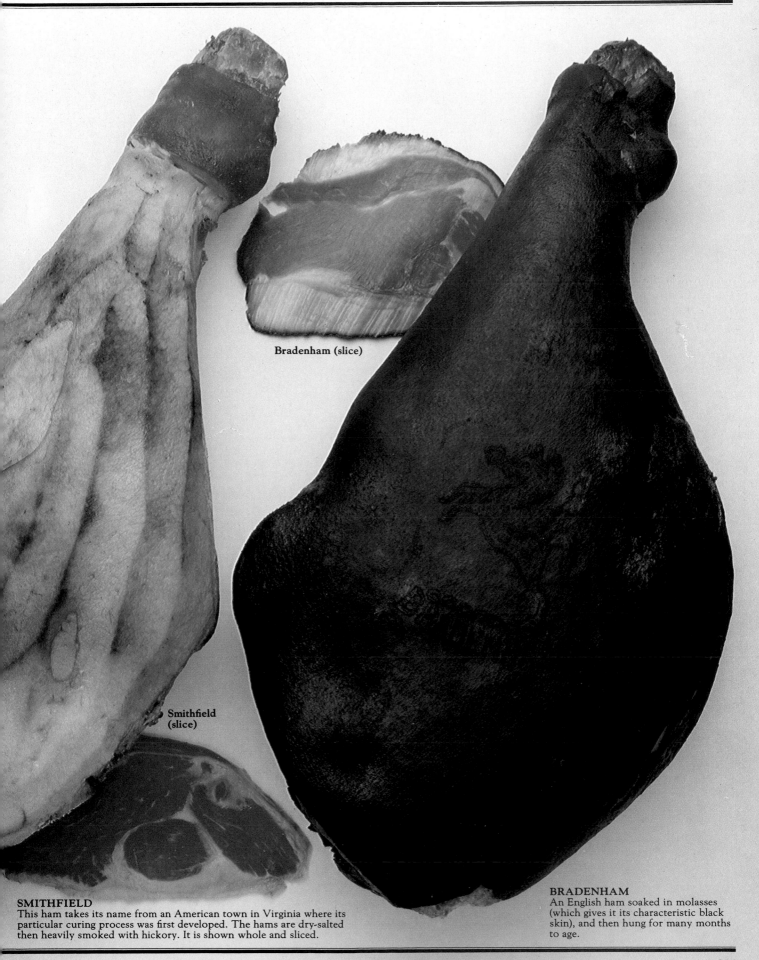

Bradenham (slice)

Smithfield
(slice)

SMITHFIELD
This ham takes its name from an American town in Virginia where its particular curing process was first developed. The hams are dry-salted then heavily smoked with hickory. It is shown whole and sliced.

BRADENHAM
An English ham soaked in molasses (which gives it its characteristic black skin), and then hung for many months to age.

Coffee

See also p. 286

HIGH ROAST BEANS
Shown here an Algerian *arabica* bean. Like all high or dark roasts it has a rather bitter taste as the oil, which sustains a coffee's sweetness, has come out.

High Roast Coarse Grind

COARSE GRINDS
Coarse grinds are better for percolating. Use high roasts which are stronger, at dinner; light ones at breakfast.

High Roast Medium Grind

MEDIUM GRINDS
The best texture to preserve the delicate taste and aroma. Suitable for percolator, Cona and jug methods.

High Roast Fine Grind

FINE GRINDS
Ideal for Melior infusion method, most espresso machines and filter methods which use papers to strain.

LIGHT ROAST BEANS
Shown here a Kenyan *arabica* bean. The light roasts have a delicate taste and can be drunk with milk. On the right, three textures of grinding.

Light Roast Coarse Grind

Light Roast Medium Grind

Light Roast Fine Grind

FULL ROAST BEANS
Shown here the mocha bean. Highly regarded, it has a strong distinctive taste on its own but blends well with milder beans.

MEDIUM-LIGHT ROAST BEANS
Shown here a bean from Turkey, where the unique style of brewing strong coffee from powdered beans originated.

COSTA RICAN UNROASTED BEANS
Beans can be stored 2–3 years before roasting which gives them aroma and caramelizes them. All coffee is best when freshly roasted.

COSTA RICAN ROASTED BEAN
A fine, mild and rich-bodied *robusta* bean, it has a sharply acid taste. Always medium or lightly roasted, it is usually enjoyed unblended.

DANDELION COFFEE
Extracted from the root, it can be brewed as a caffeine-less coffee substitute.

DECAFFEINATED
When ground, treated with solvent and dried, coffee loses most of its caffeine.

INSTANT FREEZE-DRIED
Made by freezing a brew of good coffee, grinding it to particles and removing the water.

INSTANT
Usually made with cheaper grades of coffee, it's harsher tasting but more convenient.

KEEMUN
A black tea from China that makes a light infusion with a smoky taste and a special bouquet. Good to serve with food, it is best without milk.

SCENTED ORANGE PEKOE
The finest grade of Indian tea, it is picked from the buds and top leaves of the plant. Not always scented, it is rarely used in blends.

LAPSANG SOUCHONG
A black China tea with large leaves and a rich, smoky, taste. It needs slow brewing, is best without milk or lemon, and is often used in blends.

NEW SEASON ASSAM
A high-quality, all-purpose black tea from Northeast India. Usually drunk unblended, it makes a reddish brew with a full, malty taste. It is good with milk or on its own.

GREEN ; Gunpowder
A greenish-gray China tea, its leaves are characteristically rolled in pellets. Unfermented, it makes a delicate brew which is best drunk on its own.

FAN YONG
This is an unscented tea from China whose black leaves make a mild, light infusion that is low in tannin. Like Keemun tea, it is best without milk and good to serve with food.

JASMINE
A green tea from China with a distinctive fragrance, it is delicately scented with dried jasmine blossoms. A tea to enjoy on its own, never with milk.

KANOY
This is a black, unscented tea with tiny black leaves from the island of Sri Lanka, once called Ceylon. It makes a bright golden infusion.

FORMOSA OOLONG
A black semi-fermented tea from Taiwan, it has the biggest leaf, but makes quite a light infusion tasting of ripe peaches.

DARJEELING
A black, slow-brewing Indian tea with a rich, rather fruity taste.

HIBISCUS
Made from hibiscus flowers, its brew is red, tart and fruity, and has no tannin.

ROSE HIP
Made from the fruit of the wild rose plant crushed with the seeds, it makes a tart brew.

BAMBOO
A strong-tasting, bitter black tea from China, so-called because it is encased in dried bamboo leaves. Two rounded sections should be cut off and used for an average serving, and the tea shaken out into the pot.

Green Chartreuse Yellow Chartreuse Crème de Menthe Anis; Anisette Sambuca Tia Maria

CHARTREUSE (green and yellow). A French brandy-based liqueur containing honey, herbs and spices, and originally made by Carthusian monks at the monastery of La Grande Chartreuse. It is used in cocktails, cakes and chocolates. The green (original) Chartreuse is more alcoholic than the yellow. **CREME DE MENTHE.** Usually made in France this popular liqueur contains peppermint, cinnamon, ginger, orris and sage. It is used in cocktails.

ANIS: ANISETTE. A popular South European drink made in Barcelona, Bordeaux and Amsterdam, it contains coriander and fennel seeds as well as aniseed. **SAMBUCA.** A clear Italian drink with an aniseed taste, it can be drunk as an aperitif as well as a liqueur. **TIA MARIA.** A Jamaican liqueur based on rum and coffee extract with the addition of spices.

Crème de Cacao Crème de Banane Crème de Cassis Grand Marnier Maraschino Bénédictine

CREME DE CACAO. A sweetened distillate of cocoa beans, containing vegetable extracts from the Antilles, French Guiana and Senegal. **CREME DE BANANE.** Crushed bananas and sugar are steeped in spirit to produce this sweet liqueur which, like *crème de cacao*, can be used in desserts as required. **CREME DE CASSIS.** A blackcurrant liqueur also used in many desserts and chocolates.

GRAND MARNIER. A French liqueur made from brandy and bitter orange peel, it is used in desserts and pancakes, and can be served with duck – *à l'orange*. **MARASCHINO.** Made from fermented maraschino cherries with added sweeteners, it is used in many cakes and puddings. **BENEDICTINE.** Originally brewed by Benedictine monks at the Abbey of Fécamp in Normandy its ingredients include brandy, honey and myrrh.

Galliano   Advocaat   Strega   Kummel   Drambuie   Southern Comfort

GALLIANO. An Italian herb-based liqueur, named after a famous Italian soldier, Giuseppe Galliano, its most famous use is in the cocktail, Harvey Wallbanger. **ADVOCAAT.** A popular Dutch liqueur made from brandy, egg yolks and sugar. **STREGA.** An orange-based Italian liqueur, it contains many herbs and is used in cakes and mixed drinks.

KUMMEL. A North European liqueur containing caraway seeds, cumin and fennel. **DRAMBUIE.** A Scottish liqueur made from Highland malt whisky, herbs, spices and honey, its name is an anglicization of a Gaelic phrase meaning "the drink that satisfies". **SOUTHERN COMFORT.** An American liqueur thought to be based on Bourbon whisky and also containing many fruits, including oranges and peaches.

Curaçao   Amaretto   Cointreau   Peach Brandy   Cherry Brandy   Apricot Brandy

CURAÇAO. Produced mainly in Holland, it was originally made from the dried peel of oranges from the island of Curaçao. **AMARETTO.** Made at Saronno in Italy, this pleasantly fruity drink containing almonds can be successfully used in many dessert recipes. **COINTREAU.** A French orange-based liqueur, drunk as both an aperitif and a liqueur; it can also be used with strawberries and in soufflés and pancakes.

PEACH BRANDY, CHERRY BRANDY, APRICOT BRANDY. Despite their names these liqueurs are not true fruit brandies, since they have not actually been distilled from the fruits themselves. An ordinary brandy base is used, and the various fruits are added as required, together with sweetening agents. These sweetened "fruit brandies" are produced in many countries.

207

Reduction approx. 50%

Red Wine

White Wine

Marsala

Madeira

Dry Sherry

Medium Sherry

Rosé Wine

Champagne

Sweet Sherry

Red Vermouth

White Vermouth

Dark Rum

White Rum

Ruby Port

White Port

Brandy

Slivovitz

Kirsch

Gin

Vodka

Grappa

Calvados

Whisky

Golden Tequila

Arrack

Ouzo

Clear Tequila

Cider

Lager

Schnapps

Pernod

Brown Ale

Pale Ale

Guinness

Reduction approx. 30%

THE INGREDIENTS
their origins, nature, properties and
culinary applications

Herbs

Herbs are non-woody plants – usually annual and mostly grown from seed – of which the flowers, leaves, seeds, stems and roots are used as flavorings in cooking, or for medicinal purposes. The name "herb" comes from the Latin word *herba*, meaning grass or herbage. They are plants of great antiquity going back to earliest civilizations, with records from ancient Persia, Egypt, Arabia, Greece, India and China giving details of their cultivation and use. The names of many are a reminder of the medieval period after the fall of Rome when the monasteries of Europe were centers of agriculture, each having its own herb or "physic" garden.

Herbs gathered for the medicine chest have an alchemistic ring to them, with names like skullcap, St Johnswort, wormwood, woodruff, balm and self-heal, which suggests a restorative purpose. All herbs do, in fact, have medicinal qualities and some – rue, for example – still provide a source for a substantial number of vital drugs used in pharmacy. Many have a dual purpose as they are used both in cooking and in medicine, and, although the original purpose is unknown, the general consensus is that their primary use was culinary. Centuries before the birth of Christ it was suggested that medicine was a by-product of cooking. One use must have followed the other rapidly since the Sumerians were using thyme and laurel medicinally by 5000 BC and in 2700 BC the Chinese had a herbal listing 365 plants.

Herbs are also credited with magical and religious significance. The Romans, for example, believed that a wreath of bay leaves would protect the wearer from lightning during a storm. Nicholas Culpepper's herbal of 1653 was extremely popular and influential, mixing herbs with magic, medicine and astrology.

Herbs in the kitchen

The use of herbs in the kitchen is ruled by culinary traditions which vary from country to country. Every cuisine has its favorite herbs: oregano, mint and dill in the Middle East and Greece are used a great deal in lamb dishes; in Thailand, coriander leaves garnish almost every dish on the table, and lemon grass flavors fish and chicken dishes. In Britain, sage is a favorite with pork and gives its green color to Sage Derby cheese, while roast lamb is often served with mint sauce.

Dill is an important flavoring: for fish in Scandinavia; soups in Russia and Denmark; and for pickling cucumbers in America. Italians acknowledge the happy union of basil with tomatoes, and rosemary with lamb; the Germans of savory with beans, and the French of tarragon with chicken, and fennel with fish. The herbs of Provence are justly famous for their pungency and aroma: thyme, marjoram, tarragon, juniper, lavender, bay, rosemary and fennel owe much to the soil of the region and to the long hours of sunshine. The amount used in cooking depends partly on individual taste, as does all seasoning, and partly on the type of herb. Strongly flavored herbs such as lovage, hyssop, bay, sage, thyme, oregano and rosemary should be used sparingly.

Fresh herbs are always preferred to dried ones, and many, such as parsley, basil, fennel, marjoram or thyme, can be grown in pots on a window sill. Dried herbs are much more concentrated than fresh because the water content has been removed. For every teaspoon of dried herbs, use 3 teaspoons or 1 tablespoon of fresh.

Bouquet garni, much used in French cooking, is a bouquet of herbs tied with a piece of string, or tied in a small square of cheesecloth and put into sauces, stews or *court bouillon*. Strictly the herbs are parsley sprigs, thyme sprig and bay leaf but other seasonings may be added such as celery, garlic, rosemary, marjoram, savory and so on. The bouquet is always removed at the end of the cooking time. Bay leaves put directly into a dish are also removed at the end of cooking, and so are dried sprigs of herbs like thyme or marjoram, as they would be unattractive in a finished dish.

Storing and drying herbs

To store fresh herbs, wrap them separately in paper towels then put them into plastic bags and keep in the vegetable compartment of the refrigerator.

To dry herbs, pick them just as they begin to flower when their flavor will be at its strongest. Gather them on a dry day, tie them in bunches and hang in a warm room away from strong light, or dry them in a very slow oven. Rub the dried leaves and flowers onto paper towels then sift them into airtight containers and store away from the light in a cool place. Remember, dried herbs will gradually lose their flavor.

Angelica

Angelica (*Angelica officinalis; archangelica*) □
A member of the parsley family, angelica is probably a native of northern Europe. The entire plant can be used, as even the root provides a drug, but its more familiar form is as a candied stem used in baking.

Basil (*Ocimum basilicum*) **Sweet basil** □
A strong and pungent herb, this is a native of India where it is regarded with some reverence. Much use of this herb is made in Italy, perhaps because of its affinity with tomatoes and it is also used in the Pesto sauce of Genoa. Basil can be purchased

dried, preserved in oil, or fresh in late spring and summer.

Bay (*Laurus nobilis*) **Sweet bay; Laurel** □
Not to be confused with varieties of laurel which are poisonous, this refers to a leaf of the sweet bay tree native to the Mediterranean, which is usually purchased dried, although powdered bay is available. Used to flavor meat dishes, milk puddings, soups, stews and sweet white sauces, bay is one of the ingredients in bouquet garni.

Bergamot (*Monarda didyma*) □
The strongly flavored leaves of this American plant are part of

the mint family. They can be used in salads, but their main purpose is in making Oswego tea, iced cups and cordials.

Borage (*Borago officinalis*)
A native of the Middle East, this is a small herb with bright blue flowers. Its fresh leaves and flowers decorate and perfume Pimms wine cups, and the taste is reminiscent of cucumber. Finely chopped leaves can be used to flavor cream cheese and yogurt.

Burnet (*Pimpinella saxifraga, P. sanguisorba*) **Salad burnet** □
A native of Europe, this is similar to borage in flavor and is

Bay

Comfrey

likewise used in wine cups, salads, and sauces. The leaves are used fresh, when young.

Camomile/Chamomile
(*Anthemis nobilis*) □
A daisy-like plant found growing wild throughout Europe and parts of America. The leaves and flowers are used to make a refreshing tisane, camomile tea. It is available dried.

Celery (*Apium graveolens*)
The fresh ribs and leaves, or the seeds of this plant are used in cooking, to flavor soups and stews and also to flavor salt.

Chervil (*Anthriscus cerefolium*) □
A native to southern Russia and the Middle East, this parsley-like plant with feathery leaves is considered one of the *fines herbes* in French cuisine. It is used to flavor soups, salads and stuffings and is also employed as a garnish. Available dried, but best when used fresh.

Chives (*Allium schoenoprasum*) □
A native of Europe, chives are a member of the onion family. The fine, hollow stems are used fresh and chopped finely, in cream soups, scrambled eggs, omelets, salads and hors d'oeuvres. Chinese chives (*Allium odoratum*) have larger leaves, flowers that smell of roses, and taste of garlic.

Comfrey (*Symphytum officinale*) □
This herb is a relative of borage, and is used in the same way.

Coriander
(*Coriandrum sativum*) □
A member of the carrot family, this ancient herb is indigenous to the Mediterranean and the Caucasus, and is often sold as *cilantro* or *Chinese parsley* in Latin America and Chinese markets. It is greatly used in India, Asia, Mexico and South America, and in the Middle East in its fresh, leafy form. The seeds are used as an ingredient in curry and to flavor alcoholic drinks such as gin. In Thailand, the roots are used in curries.

Costmary (*Chrysanthemum balsamita*; *Tanacetum balsamita*) Alecost
Costmary is similar to tansy, being spicy but less bitter. Native to the Far East, the

leaves were traditionally used in Britain and America as flavoring for beer – hence the name "alecost". It is used with game and veal and in soups. It is mostly available dried.

Curry leaf (*Chalcas koenigii*) □
A relative of the lemon tree, and a native of Southeast Asia, this leaf bestows a curry-like flavor to certain commercial curry powders. It is also used throughout southern India in vegetarian dishes. The curry leaf is available in fresh or dried form, although the fresh leaves are preferred.

Dill (*Anethum graveolens*) □
A native of Europe and western Asia, dill is now grown throughout the world. Dill weed (as it is sometimes called) is best known for its affinity with fish and its use in flavoring dill pickles. Also used in soups, egg dishes and sauces it is available as seeds (p. 14), or as dried leaves. The seeds have a more pungent, arresting flavor.

Epazote (*Chenopodium ambrosiodes*) Mexican tea; Wormseed; Goosefoot; Jerusalem oak
Epazote can be found growing wild all over the Americas and in many parts of Europe. It is widely used as a green herb in Mexican cooking and as a tisane in Europe.

Fennel (*Foeniculum vulgare*) □
A tall plant with feathery leaves and yellow seeds, fennel is a native of southern Europe. Like dill, it has long been used as a fish herb, and now grows wild throughout the world, although it is produced commercially. The leaves can be used in salads and stuffings, and the stems are cooked as a vegetable (p. 240). In Provence, gray mullet and bream are often flambéed on a bed of dried fennel stalks. The seeds have a slight licorice taste.

Fenugreek
(*Trigonella foenum-graecum*) □
Fenugreek has its origins in southern Europe, around the Mediterranean. Its name means "Greek hay" and the leaves are used in curries, or as a vegetable; the very young leaves may be put into salads. The seeds are ground and used as a spice.

Hop (*Humulus lupulus*) □
Well-known as a flavoring for beer, hops are the flowers of a vine-like plant native to Europe. The young shoots are used as a vegetable, and can also be made into a salad. Pillows stuffed with hops are said to aid insomnia, as is hop tea.

Hyssop (*Hysoppus officinalis*) □
The leaves have a pungent and slightly bitter taste and are used for flavoring liqueurs such as Bénédictine, and may also be used sparingly in salads and stews. Available dried.

Lemon balm
(*Melissa officinalis*) Balm □
So-called because of its lemony scent, the leaves of this plant native to Europe are used in vegetable and fruit salads, drinks – especially punch and cordials – soups and sauces, as a tisane, or wherever a faint lemon flavor is required. Fresh or dried leaves are available.

Lemon grass (*Cymbopogon citratus*; *C. flexuesus*, and *C. nardus*)
This includes several species of grass, all possessing the flavor of lemon due to the presence of citric oils. This aromatic grass is native to Southeast Asia, where in some places the lemon tree is absent. It is useful in flavoring salads, fish dishes and soups. The grass is available powdered as "Sereh Powder". In Thailand, and other parts of Southeast Asia, the leaves of the Kaffir lime (*Citrus hystrix*) are also used for fish dishes.

Lovage (*Levisticum officinale*) □
A large, celery-like plant native to the Mediterranean that yields an essential oil giving lovage its strong, aromatic flavor. The entire plant is used: stems and root can be cooked in the manner of celery, or candied as for angelica; leaves, roots and seeds are used in salads, soups and sauces, and seeds can be used in baking. Available dried, as whole seeds, or in root form.

Marigold (*Calendula officinalis*) □
A native of southern Europe, the petals of this golden flower were used in medieval cookery, both as a flavoring and a dye to color cheese, in custards and cakes. Today they are used to

color and flavor rice, meat and fish dishes, or in soups and salads. The petals are sold dried.

Marjoram (*Origanum majorana*) Sweet marjoram

Although the name "marjoram" covers numerous plants, including **wild** marjoram (see Oregano) and **pot** marjoram (*Origanum onites*) normally sweet, or cultivated, marjoram is meant. It can be used fresh or dried in omelets, stuffings, sausages, bouquet garni, meat sauces, potato dishes, soups and stews.

Mint (*Mentha*, spp.)

There are many varieties, but from the cook's point of view, **spearmint** □ (*Mentha spicata; viridis*) and **applemint** □ (*M. rotundifolia*) are the two most important. Spearmint is native to southern Europe and is the common or garden mint, used for mint sauce, mint jelly, stuffings, salads and to flavor drinks such as Moroccan mint tea. Applemint, or *round-leaved* mint, has a fine flavor. The leaves are covered with a fine down, and such varieties as **Bowles mint** □ (*M. villosa alopecuroides*) are recommended for all culinary uses. **Eau de cologne mint** □ (*M. citrata*) or *orange* mint, has a pleasant perfume, and can be used chopped in salads, or to flavor iced, summer drinks. Other mints include **peppermint** (*M. piperita*), used for flavoring candies, and in crème de menthe, and **horsemint** (*M. longifolia*), used in curries and chutneys.

Nasturtium (*Tropaeolum majus*)

Cultivated for its decorative qualities, this plant is a native of Peru. The brilliant orange and red flowers and the peppery-tasting leaves can be used in salads. The seed pods can be pickled and used like capers.

Oregano (*Origanum vulgare*) Wild marjoram

This aromatic herb has been used for centuries in Asia and Europe and is now specially popular in Italy, where it is used in pizzas. It is also used with tomatoes, cheese, beans and eggplants. There are also many Greek varieties, collectively called *rigani*, the flowers of which are used to garnish meat dishes.

Parsley (*Petroselinum crispum*) □

Native to the Mediterranean area, there are several varieties, including **broad-leaved** parsley, **curly-leaved** parsley, **Hamburg** parsley, and **Neapolitan** or *Italian* parsley, grown for its celery-like stems. Parsley has many uses, not the least of which is as a garnish. It is used in bouquet garni, and in *fines herbes* and is chopped and added to sauces and stuffings. Parsley may also be fried as an accompaniment to fish. It is available fresh and dried.

Rosella (*Hibiscus sabdariffa*)

A native of tropical Asia, rosella is grown for its fleshy red sepals which are used to make drinks and preserves. Also known as *sorrel*, and *flor de Jamaica*, it is most popular in Mexico, Guatemala, the West Indies and Southeast Asia.

Rosemary (*Rosmarinus officinalis*) □

A plant of Mediterranean origin, rosemary is found growing wild over most of Europe, and in America. Its hard, spiky leaves contain oil of camphor, and are widely used for flavoring meat dishes, and chicken and fish. Rosemary is seldom used in salads or soups except in powder form, when some of its qualities become muted. It is available fresh, as dried leaves or in powder form.

Sage (*Salvia officinalis*) □

Native to the northern Mediterranean, sage is a well-known plant with downy leaves and a strongly aromatic flavor. There is much variation in the color of the leaves and the flavor. **Garden sage** is used for stuffings, particularly with pork or duck, and may be used with discretion in meat stews and casseroles, though it tends to overpower subtle flavors.

Savory (*Satureja montana* [**winter** □ savory] and *S. hortensis* [**summer** □ savory])

Both plants are very similar and seasonal according to their names, although winter savory is considered by some cooks to possess a coarser flavor than its warm weather relative. They are fairly strong, aromatic herbs, which can have the same applications as thyme.

Tansy (*Chrysanthemum vulgare*) □

A European herb, once widely used to flavor egg and fish dishes. Tansy now features as an ingredient in drisheen sausage.

Tarragon (*Artemesia dracunculus*) □

Tarragon is a very aromatic, distinctive herb, related to wormwood. There are two main species, **French** tarragon and **Russian** tarragon, the latter being inferior in flavor, with a coarser leaf. French tarragon, native to Europe, is used for Béarnaise and Hollandaise sauce, *poulet à l'estragon*, savory butters, soups, fish dishes and salads. Available fresh, as dried leaves, or in powdered form.

Thyme (*Thymus vulgaris*) □

One of the most popular and best known herbs. There are several varieties of this Mediterranean plant: **garden** □ thyme (*Thymus vulgaris*); **wild** □ thyme (*T. serpyllum*) (English and Continental); **lemon** □ thyme (*T. citriodorus*), with a faint lemony scent, as its name suggests; and many others. Thyme can be used to flavor soups, stews, roast meat dishes, and stuffings for poultry.

Verbena (*Aloysia citriodora*) Lemon-scented verbena

This herb is a native of South America, and was introduced to Europe by the Spanish. It can be used to impart a lemon flavor to drinks and salads. Available fresh or dried.

Vervain (*Verbena officinalis*)

Often confused with verbena this ancient European herb is mainly used to make herb tea. Available as dried leaves.

Woodruff (*Asperula odorata*) Sweet woodruff

Indigenous to Europe, Asia and North Africa, woodruff leaves are used in German and Austrian cooking – in braised beef dishes, and in wine cups, in particular, German May wine. Available as dried leaves.

Yarrow (*Achillea millefolium*) Milfoil

A plant that grows wild in Europe. Yarrow is similar to chervil in flavor, though slightly bitter. It may be used in salads.

Drying and preparing herbs

Spices and Seeds

Spices – most of which come from the Tropics – are dried parts of aromatic plants and include flowers, seeds, leaves, bark and roots. Their use is of great antiquity and they have played a large and important role in human history. Once valued as highly as gold, governments in countries with a big spice trade became rich on the taxes they levied. The Queen of Sheba brought spices, among other gifts, to Solomon, and the Wise Men brought frankincense and myrrh as gifts to the infant Jesus.

Although there are no exact dates it is believed that the trade in spices that came along the hazardous caravan routes from China, Indonesia, India and Ceylon to the eastern Mediterranean lasted about 5000 years. A favorite route went through Peshawar, over the Khyber Pass, through Afghanistan and Persia eventually to reach Europe. The Phoenicians were great spice traders, so were the Arabs and the Romans and later the Venetians and Genoese. After the fall of the Roman Empire there was a long, stagnant period, until the Portuguese eventually found a sea route to the East via the Cape of Good Hope, which led to competition and conflict between the Portuguese, Dutch, French and English.

During the centuries of struggle among peoples to control the trade, wars raged and empires rose and fell but the spices that cooks have needed and used since early in time – nutmeg, cloves, cinnamon, pepper, ginger, saffron and, from the New World, allspice, annatto, vanilla and chocolate – continued to arrive. Though once as costly as gold they are today reasonably priced, neatly packaged items on the spice shelves of every supermarket. No longer do they come from a few precious sources; indeed, there is now hardly a country that does not produce at least one spice of its own.

The use of spices grew out of the natural cooking techniques of India, China and Southeast Asia, where herbs and spices are still widely employed. The spices indigenous to these areas, such as ginger and nutmeg, provide a lively and enjoyable accent to the blandness of rice and bring out latent flavors in vegetable, fish, poultry and meat dishes; in Southeast Asia, spices complement the fiery sambals and fermented fish sauces, and are essential in the wide variety of curries prepared throughout the subcontinent.

Spices in the kitchen

Today, spices still have a wide range of uses. Some, like pepper, are used exclusively in savory dishes. Others, such as ginger, can also be used for baking or pickling.

Ginger should be bought fresh, as ginger root; alternatively, the dried root can be bought, which will need to be soaked before grinding.

Grinding your own spices is particularly important when making curries, since you will need to vary the ingredients according to the recipe. The basic mix, called a *garam masala* when made with dry spices, may include up to twenty spices in a variable ratio of quantities. A wet *masala*, or curry paste, usually has fresh spices such as chili peppers, garlic, onion, ginger, mashed together with dried coriander seed, cumin, cardamom, or whatever the recipe specifies, but in most curry powders or pastes, coriander predominates.

Roasting or dry-frying dried seeds, bark or roots helps to release their aromatic, essential oils, and thus increases the flavor. Heat must be gently applied, then the spices can be pulverized – it's rather like first roasting then grinding coffee beans for maximum flavor. Spices can be used in whole pieces – in *birianis* and *pilaus* you can add pieces of cinnamon, or whole cloves or cardamoms to perfume the rice. They can also be used singly – as in China – where star anise is used to flavor pork and beef, ginger to add piquancy to fish and chicken – or in combination, as when using five-spice powder, in such dishes as Szechwan duck. In Japan a favorite on-the-table condiment is *shichimitogarashi*, seven-flavor spice, a seasoning powder which is made from ground hot red peppers, ground Japanese pepper leaf (*sansho*, the leaf of the prickly ash), sesame, mustard, rape and poppy seeds, and dried tangerine peel.

The French *quatre épices* is another popular combination of spices consisting of ground peppercorns, nutmeg, cloves and cinnamon. Ginger is sometimes substituted for the cinnamon. Many modern cooks combine allspice berries and black and white peppercorns in pepper mills for on-the-table use. The art of blending spices is as subtle as that of blending teas, perfumes, or liqueurs; cooks vary ingredients according to individual preference.

Pepper or spice mill
A predecessor of the larger, modern varieties, the small drawer collects the freshly ground pepper

Ajowan (*Carum ajowan*) □
Strongly flavored by oil of thyme, it is used in Indian and Middle Eastern cookery. It is available in seed form.

Allspice (*Pimenta officinalis*)
Pimento; Toute-épice;
Jamaica pepper □
The dried fruit of the pimento tree, native to the West Indies. So-called for its versatile nature, it tastes like nutmeg, cinnamon and cloves. It is used in baking, pickling, and savory dishes, and is available whole or powdered.

Anise (*Pimpinella anisum*) □
Grown for the seed which yields a sweet-scented anise flavor, it is used mainly in confectionery and baking; it also features in Pastis, Ricard and other anise-flavored alcoholic drinks. Both the seeds and fresh leaves are used.

Anise-pepper
(*Xanthoyxlum piperitum*)
Szechwan pepper □
The dried berries of a tree native to China, it has a peppery flavor and is used in Chinese five-spice powder.

Annatto (*Bixa orellana*)
Achiote □
The fruit and seeds of a tree native to tropical America. The dye from the fruit is orange and used for coloring foods. Seeds are ground and used as a spice in Latin America, and in Southeast Asia, where they feature in *ukoy*, shrimp and potato cakes.

Caraway (*Carum carvi*) □
Well-known in Europe, where the seeds are used in baking, in cheese-making, and many savory dishes, caraway is native to Europe and Asia. It has a pungent, characteristic taste and is also used to flavor liqueurs.

Cardamom
(*Elleteria cardamomum*) □
There are several varieties of this aromatic pod – green, white and black – containing a number of small seeds. Cardamom is the world's most expensive spice, after saffron. It

Nutmeg and mace
The fleshy fruit of the nutmeg tree splits open when ripe, revealing the brown, wrinkled seed or nutmeg. The seed has a red, web-like covering which, when dried, is broken into blades and used as mace

is used to perfume rice dishes and is available in pods or seeds.

Cayenne pepper
(*Capsicum frutescens*) □
Made from a type of red chili pepper said to be native to Cayenne in French Guiana, other seeds, salt and spices are often added to the powder in its commercial form. It is very pungent and thus should be used sparingly. It is used in curries, white sauces, soups and stews; also with smoked fish, oysters, shrimps and whitebait and cooked cheese.

Chili powder
(*Capsicum frutescens*) □
A type of red pepper made from dried ground chili peppers. Not to be confused with paprika, it can vary from mild to very hot. **Nepal pepper** is a mild, yellow variety of ground chili pepper used a great deal in India.

Chinese five-spice powder
A blend of spices consisting of anise-pepper, star anise, cassia, cloves and fennel seed. A licorice flavor predominates. Used in Chinese cuisine for a variety of savory dishes, it is available in powder form.

Cinnamon
(*Cinnamomum zeylanicum*) □
A member of the laurel family and native to India, used for its aromatic bark as is the **cassia** plant (*Cinnamomum cassia*), closely related to cinnamon but coarser. Available in sticks or as a powder, cinnamon is used for baking, and desserts; also to flavor rice dishes and fish, chicken or ham. Cassia is best suited to spiced meats, pilaus and curries.

Cloves (*Eugenia caryophyllata*) □
Hard, dried flower buds (their name comes from the Latin *clavus*, meaning "nail") they are powerfully scented. They contain an essential oil, famous for alleviating toothache, but are also very useful as a spice for baking, pickling and in drinks. Available whole or in powder.

Cloves
The aromatic pink buds of the clove tree are picked before they open, and, after sun-drying, turn reddish-brown, the form in which they are normally sold

Coriander
(*Coriander sativum*) □
The leaves are used as a herb, the seeds as a spice – they are quite different in flavor. Coriander is a leading item in

curry pastes and powder. It is used with lamb and pork, in pickles, marinades and *à la grecque* recipes.

Cumin (*Cuminum cyminum*) □
Resembling the caraway seed but with a more pungent, savory taste, it is used in curries and meat dishes; also as a pickling spice.

Fenugreek
(*Trigonella foenum-graecum*) □
Native to the Middle East. The name means "Greek hay", which presupposes its widespread use in Greek cooking. Actually it features more in Indian cooking, both as a spice (the seeds), and a herb (the leaves).

Galangal, Greater and Lesser
(*Kaempferia pandurata*, or *K. galanga*) □
Both varieties are root spices related to ginger but with a faint flavor of camphor. They are used in the Far East in curries and in Malay dishes; also in liqueurs and bitters. They are available in root or powder form.

Ginger (*Zingiber officinale*) □
Native to Southeast Asia, the spice is derived from the rhizome of the plant. Its uses include baking, confectionery, and liqueurs; also Oriental dishes and pickles. Sold in root, powder or pickled forms.

Grains of paradise
(*Amomum melegueta*)
Guinea pepper; Malegueta pepper □
Piquant, strongly flavored brown seeds of a plant related to allspice, used as a substitute for pepper. It is indigenous to West Africa.

Horseradish
(*Armoracia rusticana*) □
The pungent root of the plant is grated, and sometimes sold dried. Its most important use is as the basis for a sauce traditionally eaten with roast beef.

Juniper (*Juniperus communis*)
Native to the northern hemisphere, juniper is used to flavor gin, game and pork. In Germany it is used in sauerkraut and in preserves. The berries are usually sold dried.

Nigella (*Nigella sativa*)
Wild onion seed □
These black seeds have a peppery taste and are sprinkled on bread and cakes. Nigella is often confused with the black variety of cumin.

Nutmeg and mace
(*Myristica fragrans*) □
The nutmeg is the dried seed of the fruit of an evergreen tree native to Southeast Asia. The seed has a lacy husk that we call "mace". The two are similar in flavor and aroma, but nutmeg, grated, is used for sweet dishes, while mace is used for pickles and savory recipes. It is a fine distinction; but one of ancient usage. Nutmeg is available whole or powdered; mace comes in flakes ("blades"), or powdered.

Paprika (*Capsicum tetragonum*) □
A bright red powder made from certain varieties of pepper. The national spice of Hungary – there is also a Spanish version called *pimentón*. It is used in goulashes, white sauces, meat and chicken dishes, cream soups and cream cheese.

Pepper (*Piper nigrum*) □
A type of vine pepper not to be confused with the capsicum varieties. Native to Asia, but used in most cuisines. **Black peppercorns** □ are the sun-dried berries of the pepper vine, picked while still green. **White peppercorns** □ are from the same plant, but the berries are picked when ripened. When these turn red, the skin is removed, and the "corns" are dried. Both are used as a seasoning though white pepper is much less aromatic and is mainly used in white sauces, where the visual appearance of black pepper would be unsightly. **Mignonette** pepper is a coarse-grained pepper made by grinding and sieving black or white peppercorns. It is used a great deal in French cookery.

Poppy (*Papaver somniferum*) □
Seeds from the opium poppy are gray (in some varieties yellow) but contain no habit-forming alkaloid. Instead they are used in baking to decorate bread and confectionery, especially as a filling for cakes and buns, such as the Jewish *hamentaschen*.

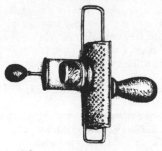

A 19th-century American nutmeg grater

Saffron (*Crocus sativus*) □
The stigmas of a crocus, they yield a brilliant yellow dye with a distinctive flavor. The world's most expensive spice, because some 75,000 stigmas are needed (hand-harvested) to produce 1lb of saffron. It is used for coloring and flavoring rice dishes, cakes and breads, in soups, particularly in *bouillabaisse* and paella. It is available as stigmas or powder.

Sesame (*Sesamum indicum*) **Benne seed** □
Native to India, it is one of the world's oldest spices, and oil-seed crops – used as a principal vegetable oil in Mexico (*ajonjoli*),

and as a flavoring oil in Chinese cooking. The small pearly-white seeds are used in Mexican and Japanese cooking. It is made into a paste called *tahina*, used in the Middle East in *meze* (hors d'oeuvres), and is much used in cakes and cookies in America. There are several varieties.

Star anise (*Illicium verum*) □
Small, star-shaped seed of a tree native to China, and related to the magnolia, it contains the same essential oils as anise. It is used in Oriental cooking, especially with braised beef, chicken and lamb and is used in Chinese five-spice powder.

Tamarind (*Tamarindus indica*) □
The fruit pods of an African tree, now grown throughout India. The pods contain a very sour juice used as a flavoring for some Indian curries. Sold as sticky, broken pods minus the seeds, and dried.

Turmeric (*Curcuma longa*) □
A bright yellow spice obtained from the rhizomes of a plant of the lily family, native to Southeast Asia. It is an inexpensive spice, used in curries, curry powder, and in pickles. It is available as a powder and a dried root.

Flavorings

People have never been content merely to accept nourishment for its own sake: the pursuit of taste to enliven a staple diet has always been an important part of eating habits and as new and interesting flavors were discovered so were they adapted and incorporated.

In Central America the staples of maize and potatoes were heightened by the use of chilis – the Mexicans had some sixty varieties to choose from. Chilis were eventually to make an enduring impact on the curries of India and the sambals of Southeast Asia. In the same way two plants originally enjoyed only by the Aztecs – chocolate and vanilla – were destined to contribute enormously to international cooking.

Although we do not fully understand the physiological mechanism of taste, we have made considerable advances in understanding the chemistry of flavor and many synthetic flavorings have been developed which are by and large preferred by some sections of the industry because they are concentrated, more stable under high temperatures, and have a reduced moisture content.

There is, however, still a demand for the real thing. Extracts, mainly essential oils, are produced from the plant usually by steam distillation, or by macerating the plant in water and alcohol, processes which soften and break down the oil-bearing cells. Essences are extracted from various parts of the plant according to its nature: from crushed seeds or pits; from flowers, or leaves, or the dried bark and roots.

Flavorings in the kitchen

Flavoring extracts will keep indefinitely stored in tightly sealed bottles, and in a cool, dark place. If a recipe demands "a few drops" of some essence, the mixture should be tried and tasted before cooking – add the essence drop by drop until the desired strength is reached.

Ice cream needs stronger flavoring than temperate foods, because mixtures lose their flavor as they get progressively colder – also, cold numbs the taste buds.

Vanilla pods are preferable to vanilla essence. Whole pods can be cooked in sweet sauces to flavor them, after which the pods can be washed, dried, and used again. Vanilla sugar is a useful form of flavoring, and a pod of vanilla can be kept in a jar of fine sugar for adding to cakes and confectionery, bearing in mind that it can be overpowering.

Cocoa
The yellow or red pods of the cacao tree which is native to the American tropics, contain beans which are processed into cocoa powder and chocolate

Angostura □
A flavoring agent made in Trinidad from the bark of a tree (*Galipea officinalis*) which yields an extract containing the intensely bitter angosturin. This is blended with other aromatic ingredients, such as cinnamon, cloves, mace and nutmeg, to make angostura bitters, which is used to flavor cocktails, fruit salads and ice cream.

Bitter almond
This commercial almond essence, much stronger than oil of sweet almond, is derived from the bitter *Prunus amygdalus*, and from the kernels of peaches and apricots. It is used in baking, confectionery and desserts.

Carob
A flavoring from the pulp of the carob or locust bean (*Ceratonia siliqua*) originating in the Middle East, it is used in soft drinks manufacture, and in the baking and confectionery industry.

Chocolate
Chocolate and cocoa come from the fruit of the Mexican *Theobroma cacao*, in beans containing 20–30 white seeds which, when fermented, dried, then roasted are a source of **cocoa butter, cocoa powder, drinking chocolate** and **baking chocolate** □. Milk chocolate contains full cream, dried milk powder. Apart from the familiar use of chocolate in baking and confectionery, it is also used, unsweetened, to flavor some Mexican meat dishes.

Cola
Extract from the nuts of *Cola nitida*, native to West Africa, and a main ingredient of cola drinks. The nuts are macerated to obtain an extract, then mixed with syrup.

Dried chili peppers
(*Capsicum frutescens*) □
Many varieties of pungent chili peppers are dried and used to flavor savory dishes, particularly in Latin American cooking. They include **ancho** □, **jalapeño, mulato** □, **pasilla** □, and the traditional **red chili** □.

Vanilla orchid
The long, yellow pods of the vanilla orchid are picked when unripe and are subjected to a curing process. The cured pods are dark brown and have a fragrant, sweet aroma

Dried mango
(*Mangifera indica*) □
The mango fruit is often dried and used in curries.

Grenadine □
A popular term for the extract of pulp from the pomegranate (*Punica granatum*) native to Kurdistan. It is used in soft drinks, cocktails, ice cream and confectionery.

Licorice (*Glycyrrhiza glabra*) □
A plant native to Europe, the root can be sliced or ground and used in soft drinks, ice cream, candy, desserts, cakes and chewing gum.

Neroli bigarade
The fruit and flowers of the bitter orange tree (*Citrus aurantium* var. *bergamia*, the Bergamot orange), yield a powerful, aromatic oil, called *neroli* oil, which is used in soft drinks, ice cream, candy and baked goods.

Orris
The peeled rhizomes, "orris root", of *Iris germanica*, native to the Far East, yield orris extract which is used in ice cream, candy and baked goods.

Peppermint
Steam distillation of the flowering plant *Mentha piperata* gives peppermint oil, which is used in soft drinks, beverages, confectionery, ice cream and icings.

Sandalwood
The dried bark of a tree native to southern India is distilled to yield an essential oil, containing aromatic sanatol. It is used in ice cream, candy, baked goods.

Sarsaparilla
The roots from the Mexican tree *Smilax aristolochiaefolia*, yield an extract with a bitterish, licorice taste. It is used in soft drinks, ice cream, candy and baked goods.

Sassafras (*Sassafras albidum*)
The roots, bark and leaves of this tree native to North America are used, and steam-distilled to produce a lemon-scented oil with a spicy flavor. It is used in soft drinks, candy, ice cream.

Vanilla (*Vanilla planifolia*) □
The cured pod of the fruit of the vanilla orchid plant, native to tropical America, it is widely used in confectionery, in baked goods and ice creams.

Ylang-ylang
The flowers of a large tree (*Cananga odorata*) native to the Philippines. They are steam-distilled to obtain their oil, which has a strong, flowering odor, and a bitter aromatic taste. Used in soft drinks, ice cream, candy, baked goods.

Seasonings, Preservatives and Extracts

The purpose of seasonings is to enhance and accentuate flavors, especially flavors dormant in food, or to create a dominant taste in bland foods. In the West salt is the principal seasoning, and in the East soy, either in the form of soy sauce (p. 27) or as a paste (see below). Pepper, also widely thought of as a seasoning, is more in the nature of a spice (p. 214).

Salt

Salt is the mineral sodium chloride; when obtained from the evaporation of sea water it is *sea* or *bay* salt; when mined from deposits left by primeval seas, it is *rock* salt.

Although salt contains no calories, proteins or carbohydrates, traces of other minerals are present in unrefined salt, including calcium, magnesium, sulfur and phosphorus; magnesium in salt gives it a bitter aftertaste. Salts of potassium – potassium nitrate or saltpeter, and sal prunella – are *preserving* salt (the pink color of pickled beef is due to the action of saltpeter, used in small quantities as a preservative). Both salt and sugar have the ability to preserve foods – the curing of fish and meats by pickling in brine, or by rubbing with coarse or lump salt, is an ancient technique. Salt preserves by the action of osmosis, drawing water from the cell membranes of meat into the salt – remember that salt (and sugar) attract and retain water. This inhibits the potential activity of harmful bacteria that thrive in moisture.

The mineral elements in unrefined sodium chloride can affect foods cooked with salt. For example, rock salt contains calcium, which will toughen the skin of beans and pulses – for this reason we are advised not to boil sweetcorn in salted water. Calcium also increases the moisture retention of salt, so that anti-caking agents are needed; the hygroscopic properties of salt cause it to solidify or to become heavy with moisture in damp conditions. This characteristic led to the creation of one of the most famous advertising slogans – Morton's Salt Co. added a magnesium carbonate conditioner to their table salt so that "When it rains, it pours." Manufacturers have now improved this technique by treating salt with YPS (sodium ferrocyanide), a harmless chemical that causes small tentacles to form on each grain of salt, preventing them from sticking together.

Salt in the kitchen

A measure or a "pinch" of salt is an essential ingredient in a limitless variety of recipes, savory and sweet. Salt enhances the taste of foods, and actually reduces the sourness of acid, and increases the sweetness of sugar – or appears to increase it – when added to sweet dishes. Salt and sugar react together as balancing agents: sugar will reduce saltiness, while oversweet foods can be moderated by adding a touch of salt.

You will need salt in the majority of bread recipes, for it strengthens the gluten – the building fiber of wheat – and helps to form a crisp crust on bread. Yet too much salt will inhibit the action of yeast, so bakers must measure carefully, according to the recipe. The best salt to use in the kitchen is the fine, free-flowing table salt, or the larger crystals of pure sea salt such as Maldon salt, crushed in the fingers or in a mill.

Food extracts

Meat and vegetable extracts further fulfil the purpose of seasoning, since they are concentrates – and they have excellent keeping properties. Although commercial extracts are a fairly recent invention – the German chemist Justus von Liebig developed a concentrated beef paste at Fray Bentos, Uruguay, 1847 – the usefulness of food concentrates must have been evident to the first cooks who used meat gravy, and the Chinese who, many thousands of years ago, made a paste from fermented soybeans, an early type of yeast extract. In the late nineteenth century, German chemists experimented with yeast cultures, and found that autolysis of brewer's yeast with salt created a vegetarian equivalent of beef extract.

Food extracts have a long shelf life, though stock cubes may absorb moisture if stored in a damp place. Soy pastes have a shelf life of over six months, and once opened tend to slowly dry out; they can be moistened with a little oil.

Wooden salt box

Asafoetida □
A resin from the plant *Ferula asafoetida* it is sold as a powder, or in pieces, and only minute quantities are needed. It is particularly useful in fish recipes and is often used in Indian cooking as a salt substitute.

Bovril □
Bovril was first made in Quebec in 1874. Then known as "Johnston's Fluid Beef", the name was changed to "Bovril" when Johnston combined the Latin word "Bo" (meaning ox) with "Vrilya", the name given to the life force in Bulwyer Lytton's novel *The Coming Race*. Bovril is a concentrated meat soup, reduced by evaporation to a thick, dark brown, salty paste.

Gravy browning □
This is basically a coloring agent which enhances the appearance of brown sauces and gravies. It should be used with caution – added drop by drop until the desired color is obtained. The usual composition of gravy browning is simply caramel, salt and water. Sometimes flavors are added, such as hydrolized vegetable protein, and MSG. The mixture is boiled, filtered and bottled.

Gravy powder □
These are concentrated extracts, dehydrated into powder. The powder is blended with a thickening agent and can then be reconstituted to make gravy.

Malt extracts □
Malt extract is made by soaking powdered malt in water, heating, and then reducing the mixture to a syrup or paste. It is used in brewing and distilling, in the manufacture of breakfast cereals, as a coffee substitute, and in baking. Malt is hygroscopic, it retains moisture and thus bestows a moist texture to brown bread. It also liberates carbon dioxide during the proving and baking, which helps the dough to rise, while imparting a sweet flavor.

Malted milk
Malted beverages arose from the pioneer work done during the mid-19th century on invalid diets and infant foods. In 1869, an English immigrant to America, William Horlick, developed a maltose-dextrin-milk powder that found favor with the medical profession, and was marketed as Horlicks in 1887. Malted milk, a foundation member of America's drugstores and soda fountains, is itself an ingredient, used in the manufacture of crackers, cookies, cake mixes, frostings, and ice cream.

Marmite □
This is a yeast paste produced by the autolysis of yeast cells – the cells are broken down and the resulting liquid drawn off for evaporation.

The paste has similar characteristics to meat extracts.

Monosodium glutamate; MSG; Ve-tsin □
The salt of glutamic acid, one of the amino acid food proteins, it is flavorless in itself but adds flavor to other foods. It is used as a salt substitute.

Salt □
Bay salt is obtained by the evaporation of sea water in pits by the natural heat from the sun. **Block** salt is a refined rock salt without additives most commonly used for pickling or curing meat. **Flavored salts**, including **garlic** □ salt and **celery** □ salt, and the spiced **sel épice**, are a mixture of salt and other ingredients and are useful seasonings. **Freezing** salt is a rough, coarse version of salt in crystals, also known as *gros sel*. It is usually not considered fit for human consumption. **Pretzel** salt is currently mined on the Gulf of Mexico, where there is a rare deposit of salt that forms large, regular, flat flakes that are perfectly suited to coating pretzels. **Rock** □ salt is purified by a similar process as sea salt – boiling down and crystallizing the saline to varying degrees of fineness, to produce cooking or kitchen salt, and table salt. **Sea** □ salt is produced from tidal pools of concentrated saline, filtered and heated in shallow pans, and left to crystallize. It is artificially evaporated.

Seaweed compounds
Two Oriental seasoning compounds based on fish-seaweed combinations are **Seto Fuumi** □ and **Bentoo no tome** □.

Soy pastes □ and tempeh
There are two types of paste made from soy, the fermented and the unfermented. The Japanese **miso** is a fermented type, made by cooking the beans, mixing them with *koji* (steamed rice, treated with a growth of the fungus *Aspergillus oryzae*), salt and water, then inoculating the mass with yeast. The *miso* is then left to ferment for several months.

Natto is a similar preparation, where cooked beans are inoculated with *Bacillus natto*, producing a dark, sticky paste.

In Indonesia, **tempeh** is a fermented bean cake made by inoculating the beans with a previous batch of *tempeh*. The mold used is *Rhizopus oligosporus*. Unfermented bean pastes are prepared as **tofu**, or Chinese bean curd, and the sweet red bean paste used in confectionery.

Stock cubes □
There are many brand name types, but in principle, stock cubes usually contain MSG, herbs and spices, yeast extract, starch, caramel, lactic acid, sugar, salt, fat, onion, celery and pepper.

Pickles, Chutneys and Pastes

Pickles, chutneys and pastes are flavorings designed to enliven or to provide a contrast to their accompanying foods. Most are products of preserving techniques using oil or vinegar, sugar and salt.

Broadly speaking, *pickles* are vegetables or fruits (either whole or coarsely chopped) which are preserved in brine or vinegar. The word "pickle" also describes a brine or spiced vinegar solution used for preserving meat, fish, fruit or vegetables. Olives and lemons, for example, are pickled in brine; walnuts, capers, onions, gherkins and red cabbage are preserved in a vinegar pickle, as are many Japanese vegetables, such as the Japanese radish (eaten in Japan with raw fish) small, Japanese plums (*ume oshi*), fiddleheads (*warabi*), ginger root (*beni-shiga*) and Chinese cabbage (*hakusai*). Other vegetables are pickled in *miso* (p. 217).

Chutneys are mixtures of fruits or vegetables, either fresh or cooked in a thick sauce. They are sweet-tasting, thick and spicy, and are, in fact, similar to sweet mixed pickles, though these are generally darker in color and sharper in flavor. Fresh chutneys, as made in the East, need no preservative, but the chutneys made in the West (tomato chutney, for example) are cooked preparations, and so include vinegar.

Pastes are finely ground products based on a main ingredient such as nuts, meat or salted fish. Their keeping qualities are due to the presence of oil (as in peanut butter and tahina paste) or salt (as in *patum peperium*).

The word "relish" is often used to describe any chutney or sweet pickle preserved in a sweet-sour foundation. Certain foods are traditionally connected with certain types of relishes. Indian curries, for example, are linked with many such accompaniments, including mango chutney, tamarind and coriander chutneys, pickled sour limes and cauliflower – a variety of tastes ranging from the subtle to the strong. Indonesian pickles, or *sambals*, are equally variable in taste.

Capers
The unopened flower buds of a Mediterranean shrub, capers are usually pickled and it is the preserving process which enhances their flavor. They are used as a flavoring and as a garnish

PICKLES
Capers □
French capers are reputed to be the best and include **Capucines** and **Nonpareilles**.

Capers are used in *salade Niçoise* and black butter sauce.

Dill
There are 4 main types: **fermented** (usually in brine); **unfermented** (packed in brine with vinegar); **sour** (prepared in fermented salt stock, then packed in a vinegar solution); and **sweet** (brined and packed in a sugar syrup with vinegar). Dill pickles are often eaten with cold meats and hamburgers.

Gherkins □
Gherkins are small cucumbers grown exclusively for pickling. They usually accompany meat pâtés and cold meats.

Olives □
The difference between green and black olives is simply that the black ones are fully ripened. Varieties, include **Sevillana** and **Manzanilla** from Spain, **Ascolane** and **Corate** from Italy and **red** olives. Some olives are pitted by machine, then stuffed and used for canapés and hors d'oeuvres.

Onions □
Onion pickling is one of the most ancient forms of pickling – evidence of it was found in the ruins of Pompeii. They are used with cheese and cold meats.

Piccalilli □
There are two main types: **American** and **English**. The American is made with green tomatoes, onion and sweet pickles in spices and sweet vinegar. The English is a mustard pickle, with mixed vegetables. Piccalilli is used mainly with cheese.

Red cabbage
The cabbage is machine-shredded, brined, then drained and repacked in spiced vinegar. Pickled cabbage is used in salads.

Sauerkraut (pickled cabbage); Choucroute
Finely shredded green or white cabbage, fermented in brine and flavored with juniper berries. It is sold canned or in plastic packs in supermarkets and loose (from the barrel) in specialty food stores. It is often eaten with meats.

Walnuts □
The nuts are picked while still green, retained in their shells, steamed and packed in a malt vinegar solution. They are used mainly with cold meats.

CHUTNEYS
Apple
Made with cooking apples, this relish can be sweet or savory. Similar chutneys can be made with green tomatoes or pears. They are all eaten with cold meats.

Coriander
Fresh coriander leaves pounded with green chilis, yogurt, and spices make this slightly sour chutney which is eaten with cooked fish, meat or vegetables.

Mango □
Perhaps the best known Indian chutney, it can be hot or mild; usually eaten with curries.

Tomato □
Sweet tomato chutney is cooked with ginger, sugar, and vinegar. **Spicy** tomato chutney – good with vegetable dishes – usually has no sugar or vinegar.

PASTES
Patum Peperium; "Gentleman's Relish" □
A preparation based on anchovies, butter, herbs and spices, invented in 1828 by an Englishman living in Paris. Advertisements in *The Times* attracted the nobility, hence the name "Gentleman's Relish". It is used for canapés.

Peanut butter □ and Sesame paste
Pastes made by crushing the seeds of peanuts and sesame seeds. Sesame paste (or *tahina*) is used in the Arab hors d'oeuvre *taratoor*; also in the dip *hummus bi tahina*. In America peanut butter is used as a spread.

RELISHES
Horseradish □
The grated root of the horseradish plant is mixed with peanut oil, powdered milk, agar-agar, vinegar and salt. It is used with meat and fish.

Mustards

Mustard is a condiment produced from three different plants of the *Cruciferae* family, the color of the seeds giving the name of the mustard type: *Sinapis alba* is white mustard (sometimes called "yellow mustard"), *Brassica nigra* is black mustard and *Brassica juncea* brown mustard (sometimes also called "black mustard"). In fact, when black mustard is used, it is normally the *juncea* variety rather than the *Brassica nigra*, which is now considered unsuitable for modern farming.

The word "mustard" (or *moutarde*) comes from the Latin *mustum ardens*, meaning "burning must". (This probably comes from the fact that it used to be mixed with grape must in France.) Although mustards are probably thought of as hot – as their name would imply – the majority are mild, and only freshly prepared English, Chinese and Japanese mustards are really fiery.

The use of mustard dates back thousands of years – it was certainly used by the ancient Greeks and Romans, who introduced it into Britain. An important center for mustard since the Middle Ages has always been France – in particular Dijon, which in 1634 was granted the exclusive right to make mustard; it still makes half the world's mustard today.

Medieval English mustard was a coarse paste made of pounded seeds, mixed with water or verjuice (the juice of unfermented green grapes). The modern, fine yellow powder was originally developed by a Mrs Clements of Durham in the eighteenth century: she apparently traveled from town to town, promoting her mustard powder, which eventually found favor with the royal court – English mustard had arrived. In the nineteenth century, Jeremiah Colman began experimenting with mustard seeds, using the plants grown around the city of Norwich, now center of the Colman mustard industry.

Mustard was originally pulverized and sprinkled onto the food, though later, particularly in France, it became the basis for more involved preparations.

Types of mustard

The pungency of mustard is due to an essential oil which is only formed by the action of water on pulverized seeds. The active principals of mustards are the glycosides sinigrin (from *Brassica nigra* and *Brassica juncea*) and sinalbin (from *Sinapis alba*), and the enzyme myrosin. Only *nigra* and *juncea* – the black and the brown – contribute the familiar "hot" or pungent flavor of mustard, the black being the stronger of the two. White mustard contributes its own, characteristic flavor, and commercial mustard powders – basically the dry residue after oil has been extracted from the seeds – are a combination of the two types.

Mustards are made in a wonderful variety of flavors, derived from the addition of herbs and liquids such as verjuice, wine, vinegar, lime or lemon juice. They may be prepared with whole mustard seeds, or with tarragon, allspice, peppercorns, mint, chilis and garlic. There are also green mustards, which are mild and flavored with herbs.

Mustard in the kitchen

Mustard can be used in the form of whole seeds (p. 20), but is more usually used in its prepared form, or as a powder. When using mustard powder, it should be prepared with cold water to make a smooth paste. Hot water or vinegar (which is sometimes used) will inhibit the action of the enzyme, and result in a mild mustard.

The chemical reaction that takes place when you add water is fully developed after about ten minutes. (The same is true of horseradish, since it contains the same essential oil of mustard.) After a while the pungency deteriorates, although the typical mustard flavor may be retained.

In the preparation of sauces, mustard should be made into a paste (or used straight from the jar) and added only after the sauce has completed cooking. Mustard powder alone makes a sauce lumpy, and excess heat destroys pungency. Prepared mustard may be used in mayonnaise, and the French Dijon mustard is an ingredient for many sauces (see below).

All types of mustard can be used in the kitchen. Although the black mustard is stronger, white mustard also has its advantages: its enzymes are strong and not so easily damaged as the enzymes of black mustard. White mustard is also strongly preservative – it discourages molds and bacteria, which is why it is often included in pickles (p. 218). It also helps prevent mayonnaise from breaking.

Yellow or white mustard plant
Found wild but also cultivated throughout the Mediterranean region, the leaves can be used as a flavoring in salads; the seeds are used as a spice and are milder than the black variety. They form the basis of commercial ready-made mustards

American □
This is usually based on *Sinapis alba* seeds. It is light-colored, mild, and makes an excellent accompaniment to hot dogs.

Chinese
Usually prepared from dry mustard and water or flat beer, it is an extremely hot preparation. It is traditionally served with egg rolls.

English □
English mustard is made of *Brassica nigra* seeds blended with *Sinapis alba* seeds, plus a quantity of wheat flour, and, sometimes, a very small amount of turmeric. It is used as an accompaniment to boiled and roast beef, boiled ham, hamburgers, grilled herrings, chops and steaks, sausages and meat pies. As an ingredient, it features in toasted cheese dishes (Welsh rarebit) and in mustard sauce. Bear in mind that English mustard, if freshly made, is quite hot. It *should* be hot, for that is its true character.

French □
There are 4 traditional types: **Dijon** □ (from Burgundy); **whole seed** □; **Bordeaux** □; **Florida** □. Dijon mustard, from Burgundy, is the most well known outside France. It is usually paler than its Bordeaux counterpart, because it is made from *Brassica nigra* without the seed husk (it is the seed that darkens a mustard). Dijon mustard is hotter than the Bordeaux, and there are several varieties. There is a plain variety, and others with green peppercorns and with white wine. It should be used with foods whose flavor need enhancing, such as steaks, hamburgers and beef, and is also used in sauces such as Ravigote, Rémoulade, Dijonnaise and Russian sauce. Whole seed mustards are Dijon mustards containing the seeds of brown mustard, so that biting into the seed releases a quantity of the pungent oil. Whole seed mustard is known as *moutarde de meaux*, and here, too, there are

Mustard pot
An early Victorian mustard pot. The glass jar inside the silver casing holds the mustard

many varieties. They may contain coarse mustard seeds and include white wine, spices, vinegar and salt. These mustards should, like the Dijon and English mustards, be used with any food which needs enhancing. Bordeaux mustards contain the seed husk and are, therefore, dark, though they can vary slightly in color. They may contain a variety of herbs, particularly tarragon, vinegar and sugar. They are mild – with a sweet-sour taste – and as such are best used with cold meats and spicy sausages (anything which needs to have its flavor masked, in fact). Bordeaux mustard can also be used in salad dressings and makes a delicious sauce when mixed with honey or brown sugar and lemon juice. Florida mustard is made with wine from the Champagne region. It is mild and thus has the same uses as Bordeaux mustards.

German mustard □
This is similar to Bordeaux mustard. It is usually dark in color (though there are light varieties), sweet-sour and flavored with herbs and spices. The main German mustard center is Dusseldorf. Since it is mild, it is best eaten with cold meats and spicy sausage (particularly, of course, German sausage).

Oils

The main types of oil used in the kitchen are *fatty* oils (cooking or salad oils). Oil is the vehicle that moves mayonnaise so smoothly over vegetables, salads and eggs. Italians pour it into soup, over pasta, over salads and practically everything else, *con amore*. Its lubricity makes salads palatable, when mixed with vinegar or lemon juice to make a vinaigrette dressing. Bakers use oil to encourage the expansion of bread dough, and to coat their baking tins. Cooks brush oil over meat prior to roasting or broiling, and, although some of the most reactionary chefs insist that only kidney fat can be used for frying *pommes frites*, most cooks fry potatoes in one of of the many oils on the market. Oil has been an essential ingredient throughout history: the ancient Egyptians expressed oil from the radish, while the Hittites are said to have preferred oil of almonds. Other historical sources of oil include sesame seeds in the Middle East, poppies in Europe, and olives in Crete and Palestine.

Modern agriculture has substantially added to the primitive and unrefined oils used by our ancestors. The sunflower, first cultivated by the American Indian, was introduced to Europe during the sixteenth century and first became established as an oil crop in Russia, where it was produced commercially in the 1830s. Also, corn, cottonseed, soybean, colza and peanut oil have all substantially overtaken poppy, olive and almond oil in productivity.

Types of oil
Each oil has its specific character, color and culinary purpose. Some are naturally darker than others, and darken with age, but because consumers prefer light-colored oils, color is removed by bleaching – except for olive oil, which is often green or deep yellow.

The majority of oils possess two main characteristics: they tend to collapse or *revert* during cooking, and they may solidify in cold weather or in the refrigerator.

You may have noticed how, in cold weather, oil has a tendency to go opaque in the bottle. The first manufacturers of commercial mayonnaise found that their products were inclined to "de-emulsify" in low temperatures as the oil gradually hardened. It was for this reason that *winterized* oils were developed. Winterizing means artificially freezing the oil until the solids are artificially separated off. The remaining oil can then be marketed as "salad oil" to distinguish it from "cooking oil".

Several types of oil are unstable and break down during increases in temperature, to give strong or unpleasant flavors. Safflower, sunflower and soybean oil can develop a fishy taste, and this is why most oils are now stabilized during processing, by a hardening technique known as *hydrogenation*.

There are basically three types of fat: saturated, unsaturated and polyunsaturated. Saturated fats are considered to increase levels of cholesterol in the blood, and oils containing polyunsaturated fatty acids, such as safflower, sunflower and corn oil, are thought by some to be beneficial to the diet-conscious. Oils used in the kitchen must possess a high standard of quality and stability. Compounds such as emulsifiers may be added – a chemical called *lethicin* is important to cooking oils, since it is a natural emulsifier, helps to prevent food from sticking to the pan, and water droplets from splattering.

When frying food in oil, you need to maintain a constant correct temperature to prevent the oil from entering the food and making it greasy. The temperatures should not be too high – from 325°F (162°C) to 385°F (195°C) depending on the type of food: French fries, for example, need 370°F (188°C), donuts 375°F (190°C) and chicken pieces 365°F (184°C). If the oil gets too hot it darkens and burns the outside of the food, leaving the inside undercooked.

Almond
The nuts of the sweet almond contain about 50–60 per cent oil, which is used in baking and confectionery. Italy is the main producing country.

Avocado □
The pulp of the avocado fruit contains about 15–20 per cent oil and a high percentage of lethicin. The oil is probably extracted only from damaged fruit because of the popularity of avocados as a fruit crop. It is used mainly as a cooking oil.

Coconut
The dried copra (or white meat of the coconut) is the source.

Some extraction is done in coconut-growing countries but the copra is often exported to other countries and the extraction done there. It is an excellent frying oil that contains natural lethicin.

Colza; Rape
This is produced from the seeds

Olive oil

Olives

of several varieties of the colza or rape plant (*Brassica napus*). It is used for culinary purposes in Europe and India and particularly for oiling loaves of bread before baking.

Corn; Maize ☐
This is one of the numerous polyunsaturated types that finds great favor with dieters. It is a good frying oil, but some people find it too heavy for salads.

Cottonseed
This winterized oil is equally good for salads, mayonnaise and for frying.

Grape seed ☐
Grape seeds contain between 6 and 20 per cent oil, which is used for salads and making margarine.

Olive ☐
This is certainly the most expensive, and one of the most popular of all the oils. Greece, France, Italy, and Spain are the main producers. Olives have a very high yield – between 75 and 82 per cent, and about 1½ million tons are produced yearly, insufficient to meet the world demand. Two types of oil are marketed: **virgin** oil, and that sold as "**pure** olive oil". The virgin oil is obtained only from the pulp of high-grade fruit, and is never deodorized or bleached. "Pure olive oil" means that the oil has been pressed from the pulp and kernels of lower-grade olives. Good olive oil (pressed cold from the fresh ripe fruit) should be a pale, clear yellow and completely odorless: the green oil (usually made from secondary pressings under heat) is not usually of such good quality, and tends to smell rancid if left for a while. Olive oil is often blended with soybean or cottonseed oil (about 10 per cent olive) and sold as salad oil. It can be used either in salads, or for cooking and frying.

Palm
The seed of the palm fruit is an important source of oil, which is used mainly in the manufacture of margarine, and in African and Brazilian cooking.

Peanut; Groundnut; Arachis ☐
Peanuts contain about 50 per cent oil and yield some 13 million tons per annum. The oil is excellent for salads and for frying; it doesn't revert too easily (when it does it has a pleasant, nutty taste), but cannot be winterized.

Poppyseed
The seeds contain about 40–55 per cent oil. It is used as a salad or cooking oil.

Rice bran
Used in Pakistan to make artificial ghee or *banaspati*.

Safflower
Safflower, or Mexican saffron (*Carthamus tinctoria*) has a higher concentration of polyunsaturated fatty acids than any other oil, and is used in special-diet mayonnaise and salad dressings.

Sesame seed ☐
Probably of African origin, the sesame plant (*Sesamum indicum*) yields 50 per cent oil, and between 20 and 25 per cent protein. The oil is used for cooking and salads; it is also popular in Chinese cooking.

Soybean
The seeds of the soybean contain 16–19 per cent oil, which has many uses. When refined it is used in salads, for cooking, and also for making margarine. It is a natural winter oil which does not keep well as it tends to revert.

Sunflower ☐
The seeds contain about 40 per cent oil. It is unsaturated, tasteless and pale yellow in color, and is excellent as both a cooking and a salad oil.

Walnut ☐
Walnuts contain 60 per cent oil. The oil has a pleasant nutty taste, is high in iodine content and is used mainly for salads. France and Italy are the main producers.

Vinegars

Vinegar is a by-product of fermentation and should, strictly speaking, be made from wine (the word "vinegar" comes from the French *vin aigre*, meaning "sour wine"). The discovery that such sour wine was a tasty condiment to use with food must have been an early one as both the Greeks and Romans had special vinegar vessels for the table in which bread was dipped. Thirteenth-century vendors in Paris sold vinegar from barrels rolled in the street. There were even flavored vinegars, such as mustard and garlic vinegar, available at that time. Today, the term "vinegar" is also used for other sour liquids produced in the same way – for example, cider vinegar and malt vinegar.

Vinegar develops through a completely natural process involving two fermentations, the alcoholic and the acetous. The first occurs when natural yeasts present in the air, or on fruit (grapes, for example) turn the sugar content into alcohol. Vinegar yeasts, also natural but usually added by the manufacturer, are then introduced. These *acetobacters* multiply to form the vinegar plant, a floating raft of yeast cells called the *vinegar mother*, which converts the alcohol into acetic acid (the main component of vinegar), thus completing the second stage of the process, acetous fermentation. (Anyone can, in fact, make their own vinegar by obtaining a vinegar mother.)

Genuine vinegars (substitutes are made from diluted acetic acid) contain aromatic esters, iodine and, it is claimed, minute and harmless traces of radioactive carbon.

Strengths and types
The strength of acetic acid varies considerably with each type of vinegar: wine vinegar is stronger than malt or cider vinegars, while distilled or fortified vinegars are the strongest of all. The minimum level of acetic acid required by law in Britain and America is 6 per cent and above for wine vinegars and 4 per cent and above for other types.

Regional and national varieties depend on the raw materials available: wine-producing countries, for example, produce both red and white vinegars from grape fermentation; where apples are a main crop, the delicately flavored cider vinegar will form the bulk of vinegar production, while beer-producing countries favor malt vinegar. In the Far East vinegar is made from rice wine; also from fruit, as in the case of the Japanese *ponza* or *pon* vinegar, a mild variety made from *dai dai*, a lime-like Japanese citrus fruit.

Vinegar in the kitchen

Vinegar was originally used as a preservative. Over the years, however, it has also become a valued aromatic condiment.

Wine vinegars particularly lend themselves to herb, spice and fruit flavorings; these include rosemary, tarragon, dill, garlic, chili peppers, peppercorns, lemons, raspberries, rose petals and violets. Cooks should keep a selection of these

vinegars, as different types suit different recipes. As a general rule the choice of vinegar depends upon the country of origin of the recipe: rice vinegar should be used in Chinese and Japanese recipes, wine vinegar in Mediterranean recipes, cider vinegar in traditional American recipes, and malt vinegar in English recipes.

Other points worth bearing in mind are that cider or wine vinegar can be used for general cooking purposes; wine, rice, sherry or any herb vinegar for salads, and distilled, spirit or malt vinegar for pickling.

Below are descriptions of the main types of vinegars and their uses.

Vinegar cruet

Cider □

The sugar in apple pulp is converted to alcohol and then to acetic acid in the usual way. Home-produced cider vinegar is cloudy, while commercial types are crystal clear, due to filtering. It is used a great deal for general cooking purposes, and also makes an excellent substitute to rice vinegar in Chinese and Japanese cooking. It also makes good salad dressings.

Distilled □

Although any vinegar can be distilled, malt vinegar is usually used. Distilled vinegars are colorless and very strong – simply because the distillation process has increased the percentage of acetic acid which they contain. It is because of their strength and their slowness to deteriorate that they are used for pickling (particularly onions). Manufacturers also use them in bottled sauces.

Flavored □

These usually consist of herbs steeped in wine vinegar, and may

include tarragon, basil, lemons, savory, thyme, shallots, sugar, salt, horseradish, bay leaves and rosemary. Tarragon vinegar, particularly suitable for Béarnaise sauce, is the most popular.

Malt □

Malted barley is mashed, heated with water and fermented into a crude type of beer which is then fed into steel or plastic vats filled with beech shavings. The acetobacters are introduced and left for several weeks until acetic acid is formed. The vinegar is then filtered, matured and colored with caramel.

Malt vinegar is used for pickling (particularly walnuts) and in the well-known Worcestershire sauce.

Rice □

Chinese vinegar can be red, white or black. There is also a Japanese variety called **su**. Although different ones are used in different recipes, as a general rule the white is most used, especially as a flavoring in soups

and in sweet-and-sour dishes. Cider- or wine vinegar are the best substitutes.

Spirit □

The liquid (often molasses or sugar beet alcohol) is distilled before all the alcohol has been converted to acetic acid.

It is colorless, and is used mainly for pickling.

Wine □

The finest wine vinegars are made in oak vats by a slow process which encourages a higher concentration of aromatic qualities. There are several kinds of wine vinegar: **red □**, **white □**, **rosé** and **sherry**. Wine vinegars are used for Béarnaise sauce. White wine vinegar is best for mayonnaise, Lyonnaise. Poivrade, Hollandaise and Ravigote sauce. Red wine vinegar should be used in a *sauce hachée*, and in *sauce à la diable* (in Britain, this deviled sauce is made with malt vinegar).

Sauces and Dressings

The commercial preparation of sauces and condiments on a large scale is a fairly recent enterprise. During the late eighteenth century and the first half of the nineteenth, the expansion in world trade brought about the exchange of new ideas and new ingredients: soy sauce was introduced to the West by the East India Company; Lea & Perrin's Worcestershire sauce, and Harvey's Sauce were manufactured in England; McIlhenny's Tabasco arose in America; Liebig's meat extracts were produced in Uruguay, and Osborne's *Patum Peperium* was manufactured in Paris (not a sauce, it is true, but nonetheless one of the fine "new" delicacies, p. 218). All drew immediate and permanent public acclaim. Both Worcestershire sauce and Tabasco appeared on the world's tables as well as in the kitchen – many of the great recipes of French cuisine depend on a dash or two of Worcestershire

sauce and with good reason, for although manufactured, it relied (and still relies) on the excellent quality and choice of ingredients.

The story of Worcestershire sauce reads like a legend: a retired governor general brought home to England a recipe from the mysterious Orient (Bengal in India) and had his local druggists Lea & Perrin make up the recipe. They obligingly did so, but the general was disappointed with the result, and the sauce lay gently maturing in Lea & Perrin's shop for several years. One day they rediscovered it and, with some misgivings, tried a spoonful, and found the sauce much to their liking. The original recipe, though a closely guarded secret, is considered to contain soy, fruits, vinegar and spices. Other sauces need maturation – Tabasco improves with age, and its origin is similar to Worcestershire sauce.

Tabasco sauce was first introduced by McIlhenny in 1868, after he had been given some small, fiery peppers by a friend returning from the Mexican-American campaigns. The taste and piquancy of Tabasco improves during the long manufacturing process, and when used sparingly in recipes imparts its own subtle influence.

Sauces and dressings are largely based on one ingredient, to which further ingredients are added – mayonnaise, itself a prominent sauce, is the basis for many salad dressings, including Thousand Island and Green Goddess and Tartare sauce. Worcestershire sauce inspired many derivations, such as beef steak sauce (vinegar, soy, tamarinds, sugar and a variety of spices); "London Club Sauce" (a similar type of recipe, with the addition of molasses). Tabasco, a relative of the chili sauces of China and the sambals of Indonesia,

inspired the recent barbecue sauce (see below), an important adjunct to charcoal-broiled spareribs and steaks. Some sauce and meat combinations are of ancient lineage – mint sauce or mint jelly with lamb; Cumberland sauce (a fruit sauce with port wine) with venison; cranberry with turkey; horseradish with beef.

Commercially made sauces and dressings have the advantage of convenience. They all have a fairly long to indefinite shelf life, and stored in the kitchen are immediately available to the cook for use in recipes. Although it is true that mayonnaise, mint sauce and horseradish sauce should ideally be prepared at home from fresh ingredients, Worcestershire, Tabasco and soy are best left to the traditional manufacturers. Below you will find some of the best loved and regularly used sauces and dressings, and how they are made.

Barbecue sauce □
A thick and rich, piquant sauce of which there are many variations, but basically consisting of vinegar, butter, mustard, locust bean gum, tomato paste, salt, sugar, paprika, pepper, garlic, chilis, Tabasco and Worcestershire sauce. Barbecue sauce can be used for basting during cooking or served with cooked meat.

Chili sauce □
Usually a fairly thick, hot sauce as distinct from the thin Tabasco relish. Chili sauce is prepared from pulped peppers (*Capsicum frutescens*), flavored with garlic and vinegar, and thickened with cornstarch. Preservatives may be added to extend the shelf life. Chili sauce is usually eaten as a condiment with Chinese dishes.

Horseradish sauce □
Grated horseradish, vinegar, salt and cream.

Mayonnaise □
Mayonnaise is a classic French sauce. It should ideally be made fresh, but there are several excellent unsweetened commercial preparations. The basic recipe is simple – egg yolk, oil and vinegar blended into a thick, creamy emulsion; a Provençal version called *aïoli* exists, with the consistency of butter and highly garlicked.

Commercial mayonnaise may contain eggs, white wine vinegar, salt, sugar, vegetable oil, mustard and food starch. Once opened, it should be refrigerated, but do not keep it at too low a temperature, as this may cause the product to separate.

Mint sauce and Mint jelly □
Mint sauce is a very simple

preparation of finely chopped mint leaves (Spearmint – *Mentha spicata* – or applemint – *M. rotundifolia*) with sugar and cider or malt vinegar. It is traditionally eaten with lamb.

Mint jelly is an English recipe traditionally made with apple jelly and mint leaves, but commercially made with gelatin and green vegetable coloring.

Pesto sauce; Basil sauce □
Recently introduced commercial version of the Ligurian sauce served with *trenette*; several preservatives added to extend its limited shelf life. Once opened, *salsa alla pesto* must be used at once, or refrigerated. Pesto is made from fresh, pounded basil leaves, crushed garlic, pine nuts, salt, grated Parmesan cheese, and olive oil.

Salad dressings □
Mayonnaise-based dressings include: **Thousand Island** □, made with hard-boiled eggs, chili sauce, parsley, sweet pickles and paprika; **Green Goddess**, made with tarragon vinegar, garlic, cayenne and anchovies; **Russian**, made with mustard, onion, Worcestershire sauce and tomato catsup.

A combination of olive oil and wine vinegar is the basis for other bottled dressings including **vinaigrette**, which also contains salt, pepper and lemon juice; **Italian**, flavored with paprika, tomato, salt, turmeric, sugar and garlic; **French**, made with honey, mustard and salt.

Soy sauce □
A dark, almost black, thin sauce, the main condiment in China and the Far East, and largely used in place of salt. Typically, soy is made from

fermented soybeans (*Glycine max*). For example, in the Japanese fermented *shoyu*, soybean flakes are mixed with roasted wheat and inoculated with a yeast mold called *Aspergillus oryzae*. Salt is added and fermentation continues for up to 1 year. The liquid soy is then filtered from solid residues, pasteurized and bottled. Soy has an unlimited shelf life, has a salty yet sweetish taste, and may be used in soups, stews and a wide variety of meat dishes. Soy is one of the main ingredients in **hoisin** □, a sweet Chinese sauce.

Sweet sauces □
Mainly used over ice creams, these are primarily sugar-based sauces with additional ingredients such as cocoa for **chocolate**; caramel flavoring for **caramel**; butter and corn syrup for **butterscotch**; currant jelly and raspberries for **Melba** □.

Sweet-and-sour sauce □
A Chinese sauce based on the combination of vinegar and sugar. In China, rice vinegar would be used, with soy sauce, cornstarch, garlic, plus a finely chopped carrot and onion, or the addition of pickle relish.

Tabasco sauce □
The peppers used in the manufacture of this famous, hot relish are the *Capsicum annuum* and *Capsicum frutescens* varieties, originally from the Tabasco region of Mexico. The peppers are harvested by hand, ground to a pulp and packed into oak barrels with salt. The pulp is left to mature for over 3 years, before being mixed with distilled vinegar. The seeds and skins are removed by machine, and the finished product – a

thin, fiery sauce – is bottled. It has a long shelf life and, like Worcestershire sauce, is used in a great number of recipes, especially American and Creole ones such as seafood gumbo, pumpkin soup, crab or lobster dishes, casseroles and the Bloody Mary cocktail.

Tartare sauce □
The classic French recipe for *Sauce tartare* is mayonnaise, chopped hard-boiled eggs, chopped onion and chives, while the commercial version may contain dill pickles, parsley and onions. Usually served with fried fish and shellfish, it also makes a good dressing for salads.

Tomato catsup; Ketchup; Tomato sauce □
It is a ubiquitous, versatile sauce, widely used as a table condiment and consists of tomato paste, sugar, vinegar, salt and spices. Catsup has a shelf life of at least 6 months.

Worcestershire sauce □
Worcestershire sauce is aromatic, pungent and sweet-sour, very dark brown, and with 25 per cent visible sediment. The precipitate is an essential feature, and you must shake the bottle before use. Although Lea & Perrin's recipe is secret, the principal ingredients for the standard recipe are walnut and mushroom catsup, vinegar,

sherry and brandy, soy sauce, pork liver, salt, sugar, tamarinds, cayenne and black pepper, coriander, mace, anchovies, shallots and garlic and caramel. The tamarinds, anchovies and pork liver are simmered in vinegar, the liquor of which is then strained and combined with other ingredients. The sauce must then mature for at least 6 months to bring out the full flavor, before being pasteurized, and bottled. Worcestershire sauce has a long, almost venerable shelf life, and it is used to effect in many recipes, especially in soups, sauces and gravies, in tomato juice cocktail, and in salad dressings.

Sugars and Syrups

Until the sixteenth century, when cane sugar from the West Indies became readily available and inexpensive, the world depended mainly on honey as its sweetener. Like honey, sugar cane is also of ancient origin. It was first cultivated in India 2500 years ago and called, in Sanskrit, *karkara*. Sugar derives from the Arabic form of the word *sakkara* (*sukkur*), and appeared in the thirteenth century in England. The recorded history of cane sugar begins when a member of Alexander's army mentions it in 325 BC. It reached China by 100 BC but the Japanese did not get it until 700 AD, though by 400 AD it was being widely cultivated in the Middle East. Pliny the Elder called it a kind of honey made from reeds. So did the Crusaders, who encountered it in the eleventh century and introduced it to Europe. It remained expensive until Columbus introduced the canes into Hispaniola, now Haiti-Dominican Republic, in the West Indies in 1493. Despite setbacks, its cultivation spread throughout the islands and cane sugar became, and still is, a main source of sweetness.

Types of sugar
There are several types of sugar. The white crystalline product used in the kitchen or found on the table as "sugar" is a purified chemical, a carbohydrate consisting of almost pure sucrose or cane sugar, which in its turn contains *glucose* (dextrose or grape sugar) and *fructose* (fruit sugar). Other sugars are *lactose* or milk sugar, obtained from whey and skim milk; and *maltose*, a cereal sugar derived from the malting process.

How we obtain sugar
Sugar is created in green plants by photosynthesis. The plants convert carbon dioxide and water into carbohydrates, using the energy provided by lightwaves. The carbohydrates are synthesized in the leaves and converted to sugar – sugar is the main source of the plant's energy and is important to its metabolism. Some plants have an additional reserve of sucrose, and these sugar-rich varieties are used by the sugar industry. They are the sugar cane, sugar beet, the maple, and several varieties of palm tree.

Sugar from canes
Sugar cane (*Saccharum officinarum*) is the world's principal source of sugar. The cane is harvested mechanically; only in a few places is it still gathered by the traditional method of hand-cutting. The cut cane is fed into a crushing machine to extract the juice, which is then treated with chemical flocculants to precipitate the impurities, and boiled to give a saturated solution. This syrup must then be processed to allow the "cropping out" of sugar crystals. The technique is progressive, so that the residue mother liquor, or *molasses*, may yield a further crop of crystals.

Brown sugar is produced when cane juice is boiled to provide the first crop of sugar crystals and molasses. The crystals are brown simply because they are coated with liquid molasses. Washed, the crystals would be almost white, with a faint golden tint. Commercial brown sugars are mostly manufactured in the refinery, to clear the products of impurities. Some sugar refiners color their own sugars with caramel.

During the cropping out process in the refinery, sugar crystals are produced that leave a residue of *syrup*. These syrups are variable in quality – a secondary syrup is bound to be more concentrated than a primary one. Such syrups also vary in color from very light to dark brown, almost black. The final, non-yielding syrup is *blackstrap molasses*, a concentrate of about 50 per cent sugars with minerals and organic materials. Molasses may be a blend of syrups from different varieties of cane, and marketed in grades according to quality, or a blend of refinery syrups obtained during the refining of white sugar.

Sugar from roots
The sucrose obtained from the sugar beet (*Beta vulgaris*) is identical to the sugar processed from the cane, both in strength and quality. It is extracted by pulping or slicing the washed roots, which are soaked in hot water to provide a sugar solution, processed in the same fashion as cane sugar. Sugar beets will not, however, produce brown sugars, though a bitter-tasting molasses is obtained from them.

Sugar from trees
American settlers learned from the Indians to exploit the maple tree as a source of sugar. The old-fashioned technique of collecting the maple sap was to drive a tap into the tree and hang a can on it. Today, plastic tubes and a vacuum pump extract the sap. It goes into evaporation pans and then the juice is heated and reduced to maple syrup. Straight from the tree, the sap is sweet but without color or flavor, and it must be boiled to produce the dark syrup with its characteristic maple taste that has defied analysis.

Palm sugar comes from the date, coconut, toddy and palmyra palms. The sap is collected by tapping the trunk, or top of the tree, and reducing it to syrup, a clear and transparent product which is then allowed to crystallize.

Sugar in the kitchen
Brown sugars are used for their characteristic taste and for the fact that they add moistness to the finished product; brown sugars are often specified in recipes for bread and cakes. *Confectioners' sugar*, or *icing sugar*, is used to make candies, and replaces superfine sugar in some cake recipes. Typically it is used for frostings. Treacle, molasses, corn syrup, and maple syrup all have important applications in the kitchen. They are used in baking and confectionery and as toppings.

Frostings and syrups may need boiling, as will many types of confectionery, jams and jellies, reaching temperatures that are critical to the success of the recipe. Temperatures can be checked with a sugar thermometer, and the density of the syrup with a saccherometer. Boiling sugar syrups are inclined to crystallize or grain if the crystals are not entirely dissolved before bringing to the boil. Any stray crystals clinging to the side of the pan may precipitate graining and should be brushed down into the syrup with a brush dipped in water. The addition of a little cream of tartar and glucose will help to prevent graining, and scum forming on the syrup.

Harvesting sugar cane
Grown mainly in the Tropics and the southern American states, cane is a tall grass, with jointed stems, large, firm, thin leaves and numerous flowers. It is usually harvested by hand prior to processing

Sugar beet
The main source of sugar in temperate countries, the juice is extracted from the root by shredding and heating. The impurities are removed and the liquid crystallized to produce the sugar

WHITE SUGARS
Confectioners'; Icing
Powdered sugar with the addition of tricalcium phosphate or cornstarch as a conditioner against damp, which may cause the sugar to go lumpy or to solidify. It is used to make meringues, cakes, cake frosting and confectionery.

Cube; Loaf
Refined and crystallized sugar that has been moistened and compressed into square or rectangular blocks. Brown varieties are also made in Europe. Used for the table to sweeten beverages.

Granulated
A refined white sugar with granules slightly larger than superfine. A general-purpose cooking and table sugar.

Preserving
A sugar boiled in the refinery to obtain a large grain or crystal, which helps to eliminate scum forming when making preserves and jellies.

Superfine; Castor
A very fine, crystallized white sugar, used in recipes for baking, confectionery and desserts, and for dredging on fruit.

COLORED SUGARS
Dark brown, moist; Barbados
Small crystals of refined white sugar treated with dark-grade molasses. **Soft, light brown** sugar is treated with light-colored molasses.

Demerara
A refined white sugar treated with light-colored molasses, and no added color.

Rainbow crystals; Rock candy; Sugar candy; Coffee sugar
A white, refined, large crystal type, sometimes colored with vegetable dye paste in a variety of colors. It is used for decorative purposes, and to sweeten coffee.

SYRUPS
Corn syrup
A by-product of sweetcorn (*Zea mays*) cultivation, corn syrup is converted from cornstarch. An acid-enzyme catalyst, or an acid catalyst such as hydrochloric acid converts the starch to glucose syrup. Other products of the starch include the syrups of dextrose and levelose, and high maltose. Corn syrup is used for a great variety of manufactured products, including cookies, beverages, canned fruits, ice cream, infant foods and preserves.

Fruit syrups
Not products of the refinery, but simple preparations of white sugar, fruit and water, they are especially popular in the Middle East. They are prepared from fruit pulp, such as rose hips, or blackcurrants, or from the petals of flowers, treated with a pectin enzyme that destroys natural yeasts, (or the syrup would ferment), boiled, bottled and sterilized. Fruit syrups are used as a base for drinks, and to top ice creams and desserts. They keep about 1 year.

Golden syrups
These are specially processed to obtain the golden color, hydrolized to reduce the water content, and stabilized microbiologically to prevent fermentation in the can.

Maple syrup
Its best known use is for over pancakes and waffles but it is also used in maple butter, maple sugar cake, cookies, frostings, in baked beans, ice cream, baked ham, candied sweet potatoes, baked apples. Enthusiasts claim there is no substitute.

Molasses
A sugar-cane sap derivative it is commonly found as two types – **Light** and **Dark** (blackstrap). Mild-flavored light molasses is used as a table syrup; stronger-flavored dark molasses is used in recipes.

Sugar syrup; Simple syrup
Granulated sugar which is dissolved in either hot or cold water. It is used in alcoholic drinks as sugar does not readily dissolve in alcohol.

Treacles
These are a blend of refinery syrups and extract molasses. They are used to make candies and desserts (although the English treacle tart is actually made with golden syrup) and in baking.

Honey

Honey is the oldest sweetening substance: it was used long before sugar (it is, in fact, only in the last few hundred years that it has been replaced by refined sugar). Ancient brewers used it to make the fermented drink mead (from the Sanskrit *madhu*, a honey drink), which sustained Beowulf and lesser mortals during the Age of Heroes.

Its traditional use, however, has been in baking. The ancient Greeks used honey in a bread called *melitutes*, which the Romans subsequently borrowed, and called *panis melitus*, and also baked a sacrificial honey cake known as *libum*.

The practice of sweetening bread with honey led in turn to a wealth of spice-honey cakes, such as the French *pain d'épices*, the German *lebkuchen* and the English gingerbread. Eastern confectioners discovered the happy marriage of almonds with honey, and the recipes spread far and wide to Italy, where the sweetmeat *torrone* was fashioned; to France, where nougat was produced at Montélimar after the introduction of the almond tree to the Midi in the 1500s; and to Spain (where it was used as a Moorish sweet) in the form of *turrón*. Finally, the ancient (and modern) Maya made a liqueur, *Ixtalseutun*, out of it, and the Aztecs sweetened their chocolate with it.

Methods of processing honey

Although honey can be made artificially from dextrose, flavorings and coloring substances, it is the natural product – as made by the bees – which is normally used. The honeycombs are uncapped by machine and the honey extracted from the cones by a centrifugal force which spins the honey from the combs (it is sometimes heated to facilitate extraction). The honey is then pumped into a strainer, filtered and packed.

Types of honey

Honey is produced by the bee from nectar taken from a variety of flowers and trees. It is the true essence of flowers, and each species of flower in different parts of the world will produce a honey of characteristic flavor. The famous Hymetus honey of Greece is produced as a result of bees visiting sage, marjoram, thyme and savory herbs and, as you might expect, combinations of orange blossom, lemon and lime, produce citric lemony-tasting honeys.

There are many types of honey – over 200 in America alone – and they can vary a great deal in flavor and appearance. Apart from the fact that they are available in wax combs or as liquid in jars, the liquids themselves can differ greatly, ranging from very thin to almost hard – and may be white to golden, amber to varnish brown, and even black.

The difference in the consistency of honeys is due to a variety of factors: plant sources, water content and temperature while processing. Flavors too, are easy to analyze, but it is not known why honeys each develop a particular color.

Honey in the kitchen

Honey can be eaten on its own or used as an ingredient. Its main use is in baking – it is the sweetener for many Oriental and Arab cakes – also for the Turkish *baklava*, the Greek *pasteli* and the popular *halva*, as well as for those sweetmeats already mentioned. It is also used for curing ham, making honey butter, coating breakfast cereals, and is delicious cooked with chicken and almonds.

When cooking with honey, bear in mind that its sugars tend to caramelize when heated, and that some of its delicate aroma may also be driven off. Also, all honeys tend to crystallize and harden with age. This varies from honey to honey, and usually depends on the glucose content.

Some of the finest honeys are described below: the choice of which to use is purely a matter of personal preference.

Beehive
An original beehive, or steep, was often made from twisted string or rope

Alcahual
This amber-colored honey with a fine flavor is exported from Mexico. Also from Mexico are **campanilla**, **morning glory** and **aguinaldo** – said to be the lightest in the world, almost pure white.

Barberry
This honey is derived from flowers of *Berberidacae* and is amber-colored.

Buckwheat
Wild buckwheat honey is mainly produced in California as "Californian sage honey". Cultivated buckwheat makes a very dark brown honey with a strong flavor. It is the main type used for making honey cakes and Jewish honey wine.

Chunk comb □
This is a liquid, golden honey. The jar contains a section of the honeycomb.

Clover □
This is perhaps the commonest and most popular honey in Europe and America. It comes from the red or white *Trifolium repens*, is thick, and pale amber.

Eucalyptus □
There are about 500 varieties of this honey, all native to Australia. Some honeys are light to medium amber, others quite dark. Flavors range from the delicate *Eucalyptus albaros*, to the extra light but sweet and cloying *E. melliodora*, and the dark, strong *E. tereticoruis*.

Heather □
Heather honey is extremely popular in Britain and Europe. It can come either from **ling** (*Calluna vulgaris*) or **bell** heather (*Erica cinera*).

Hungarian acacia □
This is a thin, very pale honey from *Robinia pseudocacia*.

Hymetus □
This aromatic Greek honey – famous in ancient Greece – combines thyme, savory and marjoram flavors. It is considered one of the best in the world.

Ilex
This honey comes from the holly tree and is mild and light-colored. It is popular in Europe.

Lavender
A popular European honey, especially in the south of France, it is amber-colored, often with a greenish caste and a butter-smooth texture.

Logwood
This honey, produced mainly in Jamaica, is made for export and is usually light-colored.

Mango
This honey is amber-colored and dense in body.

Honeycomb pot

Manuka □
The prolific *Leptospermum scorparium*, the "ti" or tea tree of New Zealand, produces this thick, dark honey.

Orange blossom □
Popular in eastern Europe, South Africa and America, this honey comes from the *Citrus aurantium*.

Pohutakawa
This rare honey from New Zealand has a unique and salty flavor and comes from the tree *Metrosideros excelsa*.

Rosemary □
Rosmarinus officinalis produces this thin, amber-colored honey, popular in Britain and other European countries.

Sunflower
Popular in Bulgaria, Russia and Argentina, this is a golden-colored, thin but good-quality honey from *Helianthus annuus*.

Sweet basil
A honey of very light color, with a characteristic herbal flavor, it is popular in Europe.

Tasmanian leatherwood □
Considered by many to be the world's finest, this honey is usually light-colored.

Tulip tree
This honey is dark brown with a heavy body and delicate, quince-like flavor.

Jams, Marmalades and Jellies

The making of jams and jellies did not become a popular household industry until refined sugar from the West Indies became widely available in Europe. Before that, the production of preserved fruits and jams relied upon crude, unrefined sugars, or upon honey being mixed with the cooked fruits, a method which is still in use today.

Marmalade did not achieve popularity in England until the late nineteenth century, but its roots go back even further. The Portuguese made a quince preserve called *marmelado*, derived from the word *marmelo*, meaning "quince". The term was adopted in Britain in the early 1700s to describe a preserve made with bitter oranges – later known as *marmalade*.

The composition of jams, marmalades and jellies
Jams are traditionally made from soft, whole fruit or its pulp, that has been cooked with sugar until it forms a firm set. Fruit butters and cheeses are also cooked until they are very thick, usually of a spreading consistency.

Jellies are cooked in a similar manner to jams, but the juice is strained and then cooked with sugar before being allowed to set. They have a much greater clarity than jams, as only the juice of the fruit is used.

Marmalades are made from citrus fruits and require longer cooking and less sugar than jams. They are quite thick and often include pieces of the fruit.

How fruits gel
One of the most important ingredients in any preserve is pectin. Strictly speaking, pectin (p. 258) is a carbohydrate present in certain fruits and vegetables, which, when combined with sugar helps a jam, jelly or marmalade to set or gel. Many fruits, such as apples, quinces, red currants, gooseberries, plums and cranberries, are rich in pectin and jams made with one of these fruits do not require an added agent but gel naturally. However, fruit that is low in pectin, such as strawberries, blueberries, peaches, apricots, cherries, figs, pears, raspberries, blackberries, grapes and pineapples, need to be combined with a pectin-rich fruit or a commercial pectin.

Pectin content is at its highest when the fruit is about to reach maturity, after which enzymes and molds quickly break down and the pectin deteriorates. Therefore, ripe or overripe fruit should be avoided as it will be difficult to obtain a set and there may be some loss of flavor.

While the use of a commercial pectin has its advantages in that it gives a greater yield and speeds up preparation, there is no comparison to the superior flavor derived from pectin obtained naturally from fruit.

No one is quite sure how the gel is achieved, but it is thought that the pectin molecules link with those of the sugar in the presence of an acid, or that the pectin is precipitated by the sugar. The degree of acidity is important as acids help to extract the natural pectin from the fruit. Fruits lacking acid will need the addition of lemon juice or tartaric acid crystals and should be added at the beginning of cooking time.

Fats and Milk Products

In addition to meat, animals have been the main source of fat and dairy products since they were first domesticated. While Westerners rely mainly on cattle and, to a small extent, on goats, vast areas of the world make use of the milk of camels, sheep, goats and even yaks to produce foodstuffs.

In Western society milk has been regarded as *the* calcium builder in childhood, while in the diet of Eastern peoples it has long been considered – in the form of yogurts and fermented milks – to have intestinal health-giving properties.

Ironically, nowadays it is in the aspect of health that milk and animal fats have suffered some adverse publicity because of the link suggested between the consumption of these products and a high level of cholesterol in the blood, leading to heart troubles. Thus, in recent years we have seen the emergence, as an alternative to butter, of the polyunsaturated margarines – the soft, tub margarines which are mostly of vegetable origin – and the increased use of skim milks. Fats and milk products can be looked at in four categories: milks;

creams; butters, margarines, cooking and baking fats; and sour creams and yogurts.

Milks

Milk is composed of water, calcium and albumen, milk protein (casein), milk sugar (lactose), milkfat and vitamins. The final product depends on how the milk is processed and how one or more of milk's main constituents is treated.

In many countries, the milk sold has, by law, to be pasteurized – that is, freed of any bacteria which could cause milk-borne disease. Usually the milk is heated to below boiling, held at this temperature for a few seconds, then cooled immediately. *Whole* milk usually contains about 3·25 per cent milkfat and a cream line is clearly visible. *Homogenized* milk, on the other hand, has no cream line because the fat has been broken up and dispersed evenly throughout. *Skim* milks have less than 1 per cent milkfat but all the protein and minerals of whole milk apart from the fat-soluble vitamins, whereas fortified skim milk has some of these vitamins added. *Condensed* milk has its water content reduced by about half and a sweetener is added; *evaporated* milk undergoes a similar process but without the addition of sugar. *Powdered* milk is made by reducing the water content to less than 3 per cent, while *longlife* milk is milk that has been subjected to ultra-high temperatures, rapidly cooled and vacuum-packed.

Creams

As milk cools the fat rises to the surface and this is "creamed" off to make butter or cream. The fat content of cream varies from country to country; common types are: half-and-half – up to 18 per cent milkfat; light cream – up to 30 per cent milkfat; whipping cream, which can be either light (30–36 per cent milkfat), or heavy (36–40 per cent milkfat). For clotted cream – a speciality of England's West Country – milk is scalded, skimmed and then cooled quickly.

Butter, margarine and fats

Alternatively, cream can be collected and churned into butter, which should have a fat content of 80 per cent. The cream made in butter-making can be either fresh or soured although most of the butter produced is from the former. The residue that is left after butter-making is buttermilk, although nowadays buttermilk is often made from pasteurized skim milk.

Margarine was originally "invented" as a low-cost alternative to butter by a French chemist. He made an emulsion of beef fat extract, water and skim milk. Today's margarine consists of refined and purified edible oils such as sunflower, palm, soy and coconut. These are then hydrogenated – a process which adds hydrogen and solidifies the oils. A similar but more expensive technological process blends together the oil and a high proportion of water (up to 60 per cent), enabling some commercial producers to market a low-calorie poly-unsaturated spread. The hard or block margarines contain saturated or animal fats.

All animal fats need some processing before use. Suet (the fat deposits from the loins round the kidneys of beef and sheep) must be skinned and cleaned. Dripping (the fat that has separated from meat during cooking) has to be strained or clarified, while lard (pork fat) is purified. It is heated, liquefied and then strained.

Sour creams and yogurts

Yogurt is made by inoculating fresh milk with a lactic acid culture of which there are several types, while fermented milks are made when both a lactic and alcoholic fermentation takes place. Similarly, sour cream is produced by introducing a lactic acid culture such as *Streptococcus lactis* into a low-fat homogenized cream.

Fats and milk products in the kitchen

Milk is a versatile ingredient that can be used in many beverages and foods, including puddings, baked goods, soups and ice cream. Pasteurized milk should keep four to five days in a refrigerator. It spoils but does not sour, so that in recipes calling for sour milk, buttermilk is usually used. Condensed milk is used in the making of confectionery; powdered milk is used in baking.

Cream can be kept two to three days in a refrigerator, but will harden if left uncovered. It enhances many dishes and can be added to soups and sauces as well as being used as a garnish. Overwhipped cream becomes buttery.

Margarine and butter should be kept in the refrigerator. They have good keeping qualities in temperate climates and can be deep-frozen for at least six months. Refined lard, grated suet and reduced suet can be kept for months in a refrigerator covered in a suitable container or vacuum-wrapped. Butter burns at a fairly low temperature and is unsuitable for frying unless mixed with a vegetable oil which has the effect of raising the optimum temperature. Clarifying butter by melting it so that the solids can be drawn off means that foods may be lightly fried without fear of burning. Apart from this, butter has a great number of uses in cooking, including the making of pastry, and compound butters which are mixed with fresh herbs, or other ingredients such as caviar, sardines, garlic and paprika. Some types of margarine are interchangeable with butter in baking; like butter it is not suitable for deep-frying. Margarines designed for spreading only will be so marked and should not be used for cooking.

In many countries yogurt is regarded as a guard against disease and varieties are used as a refreshing drink, also in cooking. In India, yogurt is mixed with fruits and vegetables and served as *raita*. Sour creams play an important role in cooking, too. They are added to sauces giving them a slightly acid taste. They should be added at the end of cooking time and either off the heat or on a low heat; otherwise they will curdle.

MILKS

Buttermilk □
The residue of butter-making but now usually made from pasteurized skim milk. Popular in biscuit-making, it can be used as a substitute for sour milk.

Condensed
Canned milk from which half of the water content has been removed and sugar added. It can be poured over fruit salads, and is useful for reconstituting and confectionery-making.

Dried; Powdered □
Milk from which most of the moisture has been removed – it is stored in powder form and can be included with the dry ingredients in baking, or reconstituted for drinking or adding to coffee and tea.

Evaporated
Canned milk with a large percentage of its water removed. It is similar to condensed milk but because it has no sugar does not keep as well. Once opened it should be stored and treated like fresh milk.

Wooden butter paddles

Fortified skim
Skim milk with vitamins added. It has less than 1 per cent milkfat yet contains the fat-soluble vitamins because these have been added after the milk is skimmed.

Homogenized
Contains the same percentage of ingredients as whole milk but it has been processed so that the cream does not separate. It can be used in beverages, puddings, soups and a variety of baked goods.

Longlife
Milk that is ultra-heat treated to render it sterile for long keeping.

Pasteurized □
Milk that has been subjected to heat treatment to destroy bacteria. It should keep 4–5 days in the refrigerator. It spoils but does not sour.

Skim
Milk with less than 1 per cent milkfat but all the protein and minerals of whole milk except for the fat-soluble vitamins.

Whole
Milk that has none of its fat removed – it usually contains about 3·25 per cent – and which has not been homogenized, so that it has a cream line. It can be kept 4–5 days in a refrigerator and is used in drinks, puddings and for baking.

CREAMS
Clotted □
The milk is scalded, skimmed, then cooled. It is a specialty of England's West Country, where it is usually served with scones and jam.

Half-and-half
A mixture of milk and cream, often homogenized. It contains up to 18 per cent milkfat and is served with cereals and fruit and in coffee.

Whipping □
Expands to twice its volume when whipped. There are two types: light (30–36 per cent milkfat) and heavy (36–40 per cent milkfat). It can be kept 2–3 days in a refrigerator. It enhances many dishes and can be added to soups and sauces.

Sugars and flavors are sometimes added, as in *crème chantilly*, used as a decoration or filling for cakes and desserts.

BUTTERS, MARGARINES AND FATS
Butter □
The cream skimmed from milk and then churned. It can be made from fresh or sour cream and sometimes has salt added to help it keep. It should have a fat content of 80 per cent. It can be used for light sautéing or softened and flavored with herbs and other additions such as mustard or anchovies. Salted and unsalted varieties are available.

Dripping □
Fat that has separated from meat during cooking. It has to be strained or clarified.

Ghee □
A type of clarified butter used in India. It is made by heating butter and evaporating the moisture. It can be used as a sauce for lobster, also to make *beurre noire*.

Lard □
Fat from pork, it has to be purified. It is heated, liquefied and then strained. Available in commercially produced blocks it can be kept for months in a refrigerator covered and in a suitable container. It is used for deep-frying, roasting meats, and in pastry-making.

Margarine □
Butter substitute made from vegetable or animal fats or a combination of both. Only the polyunsaturated type is less fattening than butter. Block □ margarine is an emulsion of vegetable oils and animal fats. It is used like butter for frying, baking and as a spread. Polyunsaturated □ margarine is made from refined and purified vegetable oils only and contains a high percentage of water. It spreads easily but is less successfully used in baking.

Suet □
The fat surrounding the kidneys of beef or sheep, it is skinned and cleaned and sold fresh for grating or already shredded and packed. It is used for steamed puddings.

SOUR CREAMS AND YOGURTS
Sour cream
Cream inoculated with a lactic acid culture. It is used as a dressing for salad ingredients and added to sauces to give a slightly acid flavor. It is also added to many cooked dishes such as beef stroganoff. It should be added at the end of cooking time and either off the heat or on a low heat or it will curdle.

Yogurt □
Milk inoculated with different types of lactic acid culture. Yogurt is eaten plain but often has fruit or honey added to it for extra flavor. It can be added to savory dishes such as lamb and chicken, as in the curries and pilaus of India and Pakistan and is also used as a dressing for salads, particularly cucumber – a favorite in the Scandinavian countries.

Yogurt- or fermented milk drinks □
There are a number of sour milk variations from different parts of Asia and the Middle East. **Dough**, which is popular in Iran, is yogurt beaten with salt and water. It is available there bottled as a soft drink. **Kaelder milk** is a Norwegian fermented milk drink; **kefir** is made from fermented camel's milk and is popular in eastern Europe. **Kumiss**, which is drunk in the U.S.S.R., is made from mare's milk, while **kyringa** is a gassy alcoholic sour milk from central Asia. **Laban** and **lassi** are yogurt drinks made in the Middle East and **mazoum** is a yogurt product popular in Armenia. **Skula**, from the Carpathian region of central Europe is a fermented milk drink and **skyr** is a yogurt-type drink made in Iceland which is sometimes served with fruit.

Cheese

It is impossible to say where and when cheese was first produced, but the farmers in Mesopotamia, who first domesticated sheep and goats about 10,000 years ago, and wild cattle 2000 years later, certainly made cheese from milk, or enjoyed cheese which was accidentally precipitated.

The Greeks used fig tree branches as a rennet substitute to bring about the coagulation of milk and the Romans added seeds and spices to their cheese. During the Middle Ages, monks furthered the development of cheese as a necessary meat substitute. Cheese-making was particuliarized from family to family and the methods passed from one generation to another. There are now, in fact, fewer cheese types than in former times, when cheeses were strictly local, and every farmhouse produced its own supply.

The dairy cow provides the bulk of the world's milk and cheese, but a significant amount of goat's and sheep's milk cheeses are made throughout Europe and the Middle East. In addition, cheese is made from the milk of reindeer in Lapland, the yak and zebu in China and Tibet, the buffalo in the Philippines, India and Italy, and from the camel in Afghanistan and Iran, where, it is rumored, nomad tribes occasionally make cheese from the milk of mares and donkeys.

Categorizing cheese

A cheese type is distinguished by its flavor: bland, like Edam, or powerfully strong, like Provolone. It is also categorized according to texture as listed below:

Fresh cheese: unripened curd eaten shortly after it is made.

Soft cheese: briefly ripened, easy to spread, and containing a high percentage of moisture and fat.

Semi-hard cheese: matured with less moisture (may contain a high percentage of fat); easy to cut.

Hard cheese: long-matured with low moisture content but may contain up to 50 per cent fat. A good grating cheese but difficult to cut.

Cheese may be identified partly by the formation of the rind. Rinds protect the cheeses' interiors and allow them to ripen properly. Apart from those with a manufactured wax coating, such as Edam, Gouda and some matured Cheddars, there are those with a dry or natural rind, such as Stilton, Parmesan and Gruyère, or with a natural rind which is then dyed, such as Leiden cheese. Some cheeses – Gouda, for example – are bathed in a brine solution. This hardens the rind and improves the flavor of the paste or body. White rind cheeses have a mold flora (usually *Penicillium candidum*) as with Brie and Camembert; washed rind cheeses, where the cheese is regularly wiped, washed or sprayed with water to encourage the growth of bateria molds, gives a cheese a sharper, richer taste. Examples are found with such cheeses as Limburger, Romadur and Tilsit, all with a red/orange rind of coryne bacteria mold; some cheese is distinguished by the absence of any rind, as with most fresh cheeses.

The paste further categorizes cheeses. In the early stages of cheese-making, the curd is a white flavorless mass. If the cheese-maker desires a soft cheese, such as Camembert, the curd may simply be left to drain. With a firmer cheese, such as Emmenthal, the curd is cooked, then pressed into molds. Some cheeses have a semi-hard body containing many holes of various sizes, caused by gas-producing bacteria during ripening. Emmenthal is one type, Samso another. Blue-veined cheeses are those where the blueing is either induced by the application or inoculation of a bacteria culture as with Stilton and Danish Blue, or occur naturally, as in the paste of Blue Cheshire. There are several basic techniques in cheese-making recipes, where the consistency and flavor of the paste is determined by the cooking and treatment of the curd. Emmenthal curds are heated to 91°F (32.5°C), finely cut, then heated again to 127°F (52.5°C), and finally pressed in molds. Cheddar is heated to 86°F (29.5°C), cut, stirred and heated again to 104°F (38.5°C), the curd stacked to promote cohesion and acid formation, finely milled, salted and pressed. Gouda curds are cooked to 95°F (35°C), the curds are then cut, stirred, molded and pressed, after which the cheeses are steeped in a brine bath. The curd of Caciocavallo cheese is toughened by immersion in hot whey and water; it is then kneaded and shaped. All these techniques are basic to cheese-making, but equally important are the infinite variety of traditional recipes, which may demand the addition of certain mold cultures, or herbs such as chives, sage and rosemary, or the wrapping of cheeses in chestnut or vine leaves.

Finally, cheese is also categorized by the type of animal that produced the milk – goat cheese like Banon, or a sheep cheese like Roquefort – and by the shape of the finished product: cheeses come in various shapes – wheels, loaves, pyramids, hearts, cylinders and squares.

Cheese in the kitchen

Cheese can be used in soups, soufflés, pastry, sandwiches, salads, pies, pizzas, tarts, on toast, as a garnish and for many other applications. The choice of the cheese may depend on the nationality of the dish, but also on the cheese's behavior during cooking. Some cheeses, such as Emmenthal, are inclined to draw threads and become stringy, whereas Gruyère and Sbrinz cheeses do not. On the other hand, this stringiness is desirable in some dishes – the Swiss when cooking fondu use a mixture of Emmenthal and Gruyère, and twirl the threads around cubes of bread. Cheese should also be chosen for its melting/spreading qualities: Cheddar or Dunlop cheese for Welsh and Scotch rarebit; Fontina or Gruyère for *fonduta*; Mozzarella for *calzone* and *mozzarella in carrozza*; firm or crumbly cheese, such as Greek Feta, Cheshire, and Roquefort, for salads and dressings. One of the most useful combinations for versatility is a mixture of grated Parmesan and Gruyère, the former giving the piquant, strong flavor, the latter the smooth, binding qualities suitable for cheese sauces, and for the base for soufflés and quiches.

Storing cheese

Storage can be a problem, if you need to keep your cheese for any length of time. A cool room or cellar is ideal, but the cheese should be wrapped in aluminum foil or waxed paper, to prevent it from drying out. One good method is to wrap each piece in foil or paper, then in a plastic bag for storage in a temperate part of the refrigerator – the salad crisper compartment, for instance. Remove the cheese to adjust to room temperature before serving – about 1 hour, depending on the type of cheese and the size of the piece. Parmesan should be freshly grated and used at once. Don't keep grated cheese in a jar, otherwise it will soon turn moldy, but wrap and store it as described above.

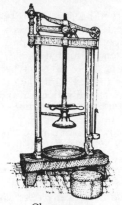

Cheese press
Iron cheese presses, dating back to the early 19th-century, use a screw method to squeeze the whey from the curd – part of the process in cheese-making.

Cheese shapes

Ball   Flat cylinder   Wheel

Cylinders

Oval   Blocks

Log   Blocks

The cheeses listed below are made with cow's milk unless stated otherwise.

FRESH CHEESE See also pp. 46–8

Cottage □
A predominantly American cheese type with many variations, it is an unripened, low fat, skim milk product with a granular curd. It is used in salads and sandwiches, often mixed with fruit. Pressed into solid curd and cut in cubes, it is eaten in India's *mattar pannir*.

Cream □
Prepared in much the same way as cottage cheese, but with full cream milk. There are several types: **double cream** cheese is made with a 50 per cent fat content, **single cream** cheese with a 20–30 per cent fat content. **American** cream cheese is made with a hot cream/milk mix, the curd being mechanically separated from the whey, and may often have a fat content as high as 73 per cent. French **petit-suisse** cheeses are small, paper-wrapped products with a 60–75 per cent fat content; **demisel** has a lower fat content (40 per cent) and is salted, as its name suggests. There are in addition many other versions throughout the world. The **Kesong Puti** of the Philippines, and **Surati Panir** of India are both made with buffalo milk. Sheep and goat milk cheeses are made throughout the Middle East, and are sold as **Jupneh** (Saudi Arabia) and variously as *Lebbeneh* or *Labneh*, while Latin America has its **queso blanco** cheeses, made from cow's or goat's milk.

Mascarpone
An Italian dessert cheese made from fresh cream and sold unripened; it may be flavored with liqueurs, and is sometimes sold mixed with candied fruits.

Mozzarella □
A famous Italian cheese traditionally made from buffalo milk, but now made from cow's milk. A similar cheese, made from goat's milk, is **caprino**. Mozzarella curds are scalded then lightly kneaded to obtain the firm consistency. Used as the pizza cheese, in *calzone*, and the fried cheeseballs called *suppli al telefono*.

Quark; Frischkäse
A sharper and more acidic continental-style cottage cheese, usually found as a solid-packed mass. It is a skim milk cheese. **Speisequark** contains more fat, and is sold plain or mixed with fruit, **Rahmfrischkäse** has additional cream, **Doppelrahmfrischkäse** has the highest fat content of 85 per cent, and **Schichtkäse** is made in curd layers.

The cheeses also vary in the amount and type of starter used, and the use of rennet. **Labfrischkäse** is made with little or no starter, mainly rennet. In Austria, **Topfen** is a quark cheese made from whole milk and skim milk, and may be mixed with butter, eggs and spices. Quark cheeses are widely employed in cooking, and to accompany other dishes. The cheese is used in pastry, and in such recipes as *quarksahnetorte*, *quarkschnitten* and quark soufflé.

Ricotta □
An Italian cheese made from whey. The albumen in whey coagulates when heated, and with a proportion of the milk fat and minerals in the whey, makes a type of cheese. The milk used varies from cow's milk in **Ricotta Piedmontese**, or **Ricotta Vaccina**, to sheep's milk in **Ricotta Piedmontese**, or the regional types **Ricotta Romana**, **Sarda** and **Siciliana**.

There is also a Maltese version, **Rkotta**, made from a mixture of cow's milk and sea water. Used as a stuffing for ravioli, cannelloni and pancakes.

Scamorza
An old Italian cheese related to Mozzarella, it was originally made from buffalo milk though today cow's milk is used. It is a drawn curd cheese of an oval shape, yellow in color with a firm but supple texture. It is used in pizzas.

SOFT CHEESES See also pp. 46–8

Barberey; Fromage de Troyes
A French cheese, salted, molded and ripened for about 3 weeks. Sometimes unripened and sold as a fresh cheese. Ripened cheeses resemble Camembert.

Bel Paese
A relatively modern Italian cheese invented in 1929, its name means "beautiful country". It is a dessert type with a short ripening period. Bel Paese is a flat, round cheese with a slight red rind flora.

Beli Sir
Both farmhouse and factory versions exist of this Yugoslavian, sourish cheese, brine-ripened for about a month, and pressed in rectangular molds.

Brenza; Bryndza
A soft and buttery cheese, it is sometimes used as a basis for Liptauer spread. It is made in Hungary, Romania and in the Carpathians from goat's or sheep's milk.

Brie □
Made by Briard farmers since the 8th century, it was served to Charlemagne in 774. It is a French cheese formed in the shape of a wheel and made with layers or curd. The cheese is sprinkled with *Penicillium candidum*, acquiring a white crust with reddish edges. It is ripened on straw mats for about 4 weeks at a controlled temperature.

Caboc □
A slightly sourish but rich creamy cheese from Scotland, made in cylinder or log shapes and coated in oatmeal.

Camembert □
A famous French cheese, made with unpressed curds in flat cylinder or half-moon shapes. The cheese is sprayed with *Penicillium candidum*, and acquires a white crust of mold flora. It is brine-dipped and ripened for about 3 weeks.

Chabichou
A goat's milk cheese from Poitou, France, in the form of a cone or cylinder, and with a natural, dry rind.

Chaource
A French, aromatic and slightly sourish cheese with a white mold flora rind. The cheeses are cylindrical and about 2½in. (6.5cm) high.

Epoisses
A small, cylindrical French cheese, it is a specialty of the Burgundy region, and the washed rind develops the orange smear of coryne bacteria. It may

Edam

be spiced during manufacture, or dipped in *marc de Bourgogne* before sale.

Feta □
A Greek cheese made variously with goat's and sheep's milk, or a mixture. Its roughly cut, pressed curd is ripened in its own whey, salted beforehand. Feta is used in many Greek recipes and Greece has the distinction of being the world's leading consumer of cheese (some 38lb [15kg] per head).

Leiderkranz
An American, Limburger-type rectangular cheese with a very soft paste and mild flavor. The washed rind has the red smear of coryne bacteria.

Liptauer
A Hungarian cheese spread made from sheep's and cow's milk. Liptauer is a factory product based on a sheep's milk cheese called *liptó*. Variations exist where butter, capers, onions, mustard and spices may be added.

Livarot
A strong, rectangular cheese from Normandy, France, with a red mold rind.

Munster □
A French cheese from the Vosges, Camembert-shaped in varying sizes. Munster has an orange-red rind, a very soft paste and distinctive flavor that had made it a popular and much imitated cheese. The Germans make Munsters, so do the Swiss and Americans.

Neufchâtel □
A lightly pressed and salted French cheese, which may be sold as fresh or ripened. It has a white mold flora rind when ripened, and comes in a variety of shapes including squares, rectangles and hearts.

Stracchino
There are several versions and types of this Italian cheese, originating in Lombardy. **Taleggio** and **Robiolo** are very soft, delicate cheeses with a red/orange rind flora, that results from their having been brined during ripening. They are uncut, unpressed cheeses. **Stracchino Cresenza** develops no rind flora.

Vermont Cheddar

Tomme de Savoie
A French mountain cheese with a softish paste and either a washed or dry rind. The cheeses are ripened in caves, and may be brushed with *marc* brandy, or coated with crushed, dried grape skins and pips. This latter type is called **Tomme au raisin**, □ or *Fondu au raisin*.

SEMI-HARD CHEESES
See also p. 51
Appenzeller
A Swiss cheese, cylindrical in form; its name originally derives from the Latin for "abbot's cell". These cheeses ripen from 3–6 months, during which time they are regularly turned, and washed with a mixture of white wine, water, and herbs.

Bellelaye; Tête de moine
A Swiss cylindrical cheese with a red rind flora.

Brick
A native American cheese first made in Wisconsin in the 1870s and named for its shape. It is a surface-molded cheese with a reddish-brown rind which can be waxed. The interior contains small holes and is yellow-white. It is a mild, tangy cheese used in sandwiches and in toasting.

Caerphilly □
Once a Welsh regional cheese but now manufactured all over Britain. The cheese is buttermilk flavored with a soft paste, and hardly ripens at all.

Cantal □
A French cheese from the Auvergne mentioned by Pliny the Elder and Diderot. It is a cylinder-shaped product with a natural rind and firm, uniform paste. Cantal possesses a fine flavor and aroma and can be used in place of Cheddar for many recipes since it melts easily and does not tend to draw threads.

Cheddar □
Cheddar cheeses are now made throughout the world, usually in a large, cylinder shape with a natural rind. A very versatile cooking cheese, since it doesn't draw threads, Cheddar can be used in sauces, soufflés, salads and pizzas.

Cheshire □
A famous cheese from Cheshire

county in England dating back to the 12th century, it has a crumbly texture and slightly salty tang. Usually fast-ripening, there are two types, **white** and **red**, □ the latter being colored with annatto dye.

Chevret
Literally the name means "goat" cheese, and there are many variations.

Colby □
A mild, American cheese whose curd is regularly washed in water to encourage rapid maturation – usually about 3–4 weeks. It has a Cheddar-type paste and natural rind, and is used in salads and snacks.

Coon
An American Cheddar-type cheese made by a patent process which includes scalding.

Danbo
A Danish cheese with long-lost Emmenthal origins, matured for 18 months to 2 years. Danbo is sometimes flavored with caraway; it is square in shape.

Derby
An English cheese from the county of Derby. It has a natural rind, firm paste, mild flavor, and comes in cartwheel shapes weighing about 35lb (14kg). Used as a toasting cheese, it is sometimes flavored with fresh sage leaves, which give green streaks to the cheese. In this form it is **Sage Derby**.

Dunlop □
A Scottish Cheddar-type cheese, bland and usually briefly ripened, it is said to have originated from an Irish recipe. It is a natural rind cheese.

Edam □
A mild, bland, buttery cheese with a thin natural rind and red wax coating usually matured 3–4 months. It is a slightly harder cheese than Gouda due to its low fat content. Edam is sometimes spiced with cumin seed and more mature versions are available.

Emmenthal □
Its name means "valley of Emme", the river which runs through central Switzerland. The 250lb (100kg) cartwheel, when cut open reveals the large

holes or "eyes" throughout the paste. The cheese has a natural rind and is softer and blander than Gruyère, and draws threads on being cooked.

Esrom
A Danish cheese based on the French Port Salut, with a washed red flora rind. It is used in *smorgasbord* recipes.

Fontina □
A fine-quality cheese from Italy's Piedmont region with a smooth paste containing a few small holes. The cheese has a natural, brown rind and is used in *fonduta*, a fondue of truffles, eggs and cheese.

Gammelost
A rapidly ripening Norwegian cheese that develops a unique mold growth on the rind. This is regularly pressed into the paste, and gives the cheese its characteristic sharp and tangy flavor. The paste is soft and dark brown in color.

Gloucester and Double Gloucester □
Full-cream cheeses once made from the produce of cows native to Gloucester, England. They have a rich, creamy color and mellow flavor and are made in cylinder shapes which weigh 10–34lb (4.5–15kg). They are used in sandwiches and salads.

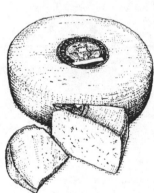

Leyden

Gouda □
An excellent, mild-flavored Dutch cheese with a soft, buttery paste. Allowed to mature for over a year, Gouda develops an excellent flavor to become one of the world's great cheeses. After brining the cheese develops a natural rind.

Gruyère □
Gruyère is a Swiss cheese, but variations are produced in France. France and Switzerland argued over the right to the name, which was finally granted to both by the Convention of Stresa, in 1951. Swiss Gruyère has a smooth, uniform paste with only a very few pea-sized holes, and a dark-brown natural rind. Some confusion arises with the French Gruyères: the paste or body of **Gruyère de Comte** carries larger holes, while **Gruyère de Montagne**, or **Beaufort** is similar to the Swiss type. Gruyère is a fine dessert

cheese, and is also used in a variety of recipes, since it does not draw threads.

Havarti
A Tilsit-type Danish cheese with an open, lace-like paste and a natural or washed rind – the dry rind gives Havarti a sourish taste, the flora on the washed rind makes it taste sharper. Havarti was the name of the farm of the cheese's developer, Mrs Hanne Nielson.

Jarlsberg □
A Norwegian cheese originating in Oslo in 1959, it is made in wheel shapes with a thick, natural rind covered with yellow wax. Its interior contains irregularly shaped rounded holes and it has a sweet, nutty flavor similar to Emmenthal.

Lancashire □
An English cheese with a white, softish, crumbly paste, made from milled, salted and pressed curd. It is similar to white Cheshire, and Cheshire is sometimes sold as "Lancashire". It matures in 2–3 months.

Leicester □
A firm-bodied English cheese with a mild flavor but distinguished by its bright orange color, due to the addition of annatto dye. It is used like the above Lancashire, as a melting and toasting cheese.

Leyden; Leiden □
A piquant, dryish cheese. Farmhouse Leydens are rubbed with a mixture of beestings or colostrum (first milk produced after calving), and annatto dye. Another unusual feature of this Dutch cheese is the addition of cumin seed to the curd.

Limburger
Once Belgian but now made in Germany, Limburger is a piquant, sometimes pungent cheese. The rind is washed with coryne bacteria and the cheese is ripened for a period of about 3–4 weeks.

Manchego □
A Spanish sheep's milk cheese made in large, cylinder shapes and matured for about a month. It has a hard, yellow natural rind, varies from white to yellow in color and its firm-textured interior paste may contain holes.

Monterey □
An American cheese derived from an old monastery recipe, and first marketed in 1916. The paste is creamy and soft, with numerous holes and a natural rind. One variety of Monterey has an unmilled, lightly pressed curd with a high moisture content, and is known as **Monterey Jack**. □ There is also a grating-type Monterey, which is very useful for cooking purposes.

Mysost and Gjetost □
Two popular Norwegian breakfast cheeses, **Mysost** is a whey cheese, made by evaporating the water until only the whey albumen and lactose remain as a brownish paste, giving the cheese a sweetish taste and firm consistency. Originally made from goat's milk, it was then known as **Gjetost** (*gje* = goat, *tost* = cheese). Genuine (*Ekte*) Gjetost is still made in limited quantities; Mysost may sometimes contain a proportion of goat's milk mixed with cow's milk.

Pont l'Evêque
A square-shaped, softish cheese, one of the oldest from Normandy, France, with a fairly strong taste and aroma. Pont l'Evêque cheeses have a washed rind and are packed in small chipwood boxes in the manner of Camembert.

Port Salut □
A mild French cheese with a firm paste and a washed rind. The small, round cheeses are made by Trappist monks from an ancient recipe and are named "Port of Salvation" as was their abbey when they returned from exile caused by the French Revolution. A similar type is the **Saint Paulin**.

Raclette □
Racler is a French word meaning "to scrape", for this cheese is the principal ingredient of a Swiss dish, prepared with grated melted cheese, and served with potatoes and gherkins.
There are several varieties, including **Gomser**, **Bagnes** and **Orsières**, all with a firm, spicy paste.

Reblochon
A French cheese from the Haut-Savoie, a mountainous region

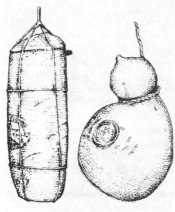

Provolone

where the cheese is ripened in caves. Reblochon is a rich, creamy cheese with a mild flavor and washed rind. Its name means "second milking" because the French herdsmen who originally made it used milk from a second, illegal, milking.

Samso
Originally a Danish copy of the Swiss Emmenthal and named Samso from the island on which it was made. Related cheeses have the suffix "bo" added to the name of the island or town of manufacture: **Danbo** is a square-shaped cheese with a natural rind, and sometimes contains caraway seeds; **Fynbo** is similar to **Samso**, but smaller in size, and the paste has smaller holes; **Elbo** has a more regular, firm paste with few holes and a natural rind; **Tybo** is a smaller, quite solid cheese with the same fat content; **Molbo** shares characteristics with Dutch Edam, being shaped like a ball with a red rind; **Maribo** is a Gouda-type cheese, but contains tiny holes and has a red wax rind.

Sauermilchkäse
A family of German cheeses made from low-fat milk, soured by a lactic acid starter, and without use of rennet. They vary considerably in shape, but all have a rind flora which gives them a color ranging from pale yellow to red-brown. The taste is sourish and sharp, and some cheeses have the addition of spices. Varieties include such cheeses as the **Mainzer, Harzer, Handkäse, Spitkäse** and **Stangenkäse**.

Tilsit □
Strongly flavored, usually wheel-shaped cheese with a washed rind first produced by Dutch cheese-makers living in Tilsit, East Germany. Now also produced in West Germany.

Wensleydale □
An English cheese from Yorkshire, once made from sheep's or goat's milk by Cistercian monks, but now factory-made using cow's milk. White Wensleydale is a lightly pressed, salted type with a buttermilk flavor and a natural rind. There is also a blue variety of this cheese. White Wensleydale is a traditional accompaniment to apple pie.

Wensleydale

HARD CHEESES See also p. 56
Asiago
An Italian cheese from the province of Vicenza in the northwest. There are two types, the **Asiago d'Allevio**, made from a mixture of skim and whole milk, producing a fairly piquant, grating cheese and the **Asiago Grasso di Monte**, with a smoother paste and a mellower flavor. Used in many recipes that require a grating cheese, such as soups, pasta dishes, and meat dishes.

Bergkäse
Large, cartwheel-shaped Austrian cheese with a smooth, uniform paste and mild flavor. The curds are finely cut, the cheese hard-pressed until a natural rind develops.

Caciocavallo □
Made by nomads, it means "cheese on horseback" since it is said to resemble saddle bags. This is an ancient, Roman cheese where the heated curd is kneaded and worked to a malleable paste, the finished product taking many shapes and forms. The cheeses are known as *formaggio di pasta filata*, and include Provolone.

Kefalotyri
A popular, hard Greek cheese, meaning "head cheese", made by finely cutting and stirring the curds, which are then heated before being pressed into molds – the resulting shapes often resemble skulls or hats. They are then dry-salted, and left to mature for several months. The cheese is used as a grating type in several national dishes.

Parmesan □
Parmesan cheese, or more correctly, **Parmigiano Reggiano**, is the noblest of a group of Italian cheeses known collectively as *formaggi di grana*, meaning hard cheeses with a grainy texture. The wheel-shaped, golden-colored cheeses are made of finely cut, carefully separated curd, which is then stirred and scalded to 137°F (58°C) before being pressed. The cheeses are salted over a period of weeks, after which they mature for 2–3 years, or even longer – they are categorized as *vecchio* (old); *stravecchio* (extra old); *tipico* (4 or 5 years old);

giovane (less mature, table cheese). Other *grana* cheeses include **Grana Padano**, made in considerable quantity throughout Lombardy; **Grana Lodigiano**, a low-fat cheese with an "eyed" paste of small holes; **Grana Lombardo** from around Milan. Grana cheeses are widely used as a grating type for typically Italian recipes, such as minestrone, or pasta, and they may be incorporated in sauces.

Pecorino □
A variety of hard cheeses made from sheep's milk in central and southern Italy. **Pecorino Romano** is made by heating the milk, curdling with rennet, finely cutting the curd and pressing. The cheese matures in about 8 months. **Pecorino Sardo** is made on the island of Sardinia, while **Pecorino Pepato**, made in Sicily, has added peppercorns. They are used both as table cheeses, and for grating.

Provolone □
Now made from cow's milk, but originally from buffalo milk, it is a drawn curd cheese made in Italy, America and Australia. It is found in a variety of shapes such as pear, cone or cylinder and is hung by cords to mature and harden. All Provolones are smoked, the younger ones are milder, softer, and used as table cheeses, the older, more robust and harder cheeses are used in cooking.

Sapsago □
A hard, grating cheese from Switzerland where it has been made for over 500 years. It is made in cone shapes without a rind and has a hard, dry texture. Known also as *green cheese* due to its color, which it gets along with its aroma, from dried clover.

Sbrinz □
A Swiss cheese, made by finely cutting the curd and scalding at temperatures above 130°F (55°C). The cheese is pressed to form a flat disk or wheel, then brined and "sweated" at 68°F (20°C) for about 4 months. The cheese is then racked, and left to mature for about 2 years. Sbrinz is a piquant, aromatic cheese, used as a table variety, also for cooking, since it grates well, and is used for sauces and soufflés.

BLUE CHEESES See also pp. 57–8

Bavarian Blue □
A very rich, high-fat (70 per cent) cheese with a mildly sour taste from Germany. It has a molded surface with blue veining and is made in wheels.

Bleu d'Auvergne
A small (4–5lb [2kg]) cheese from the French Auvergne region, and made by inoculating the curd, or sprinkling the surface, with *Penicillium glaucum* mold. The cheese is first washed, then dry-salt rubbed and pierced with needles to encourage mold formation.

Bleu de Bresse ⊔
A French cheese from the region that lies between Saone-et-Loire and the Jura, it is softish, mild-flavored and weighs about 4–5lb (2kg). It has a slightly higher fat content (50 per cent) than most blue cheeses, and is one of the ingredients in *fromage cardinal*. A larger and creamier blue cheese from the same region in nearby Ain is **Pipo Crem'** □.

Bleu de Corse
A white sheep's milk cheese produced on the Corsican plains it develops interior mold to become "blue". Other cheeses of this type are sent to mature in the Roquefort caves.

Bleu de Gex
A cheese from the Jura mountains with a firm paste, mild flavor and delicate blue veining; there is a very similar cheese from neighboring Septmoncel, the **Bleu de Septmoncel**. Both weigh from 12–15lb (5–6kg).

Bleu de Laqueuille
A fairly modern French cheese from Puy-de-Dome, introduced in 1850. Like most French blue cheeses it is quite small in size (5–6lb [2–2.5kg]), has a dry rind and mellow flavor.

Bleu de l'Aveyron
A French cheese matured in the natural caves of the Massif Central, a feature which it shares with **Bleu de Causses** and the famous Roquefort. This small, local blue cheese has a fine, delicate flavor and softish paste.

Bleu de Sassenage
Similar to Bleu de Gex (see above) but firmer in texture and much smaller in size. It is made in the Isère region of France.

Blue Cheshire □
A large, cylindrical blue version of the dyed Cheshire cheese, and one of the finest of all blues. The cheese ripens and "blues" only accidentally, although cheese-makers try and encourage the mold by pricking the cheese with needles and maturing it in a favorable atmosphere.

Blue Shropshire □
A newcomer, and smaller variation of the Blue Cheshire (above), made not in Shropshire, but in Scotland.

Danish Blue; Danablu □
Lacking a national blue cheese, Danish cheese-makers in the early 19th century began experiments with mold cultures and came up with a selection of excellent blue cheeses, of which Danablu is the most renowned. It has a white paste with blue veining. It is popular in open sandwiches. **Mycella** is another Danish blue cheese type, with a milder taste, and is produced by a different mold culture. **Blucreme** is an internal-mold cheese with added cream that is smoother and creamier than Danablu and is made in 10lb (4kg) loaves.

Dolcelatte □
Literally "sweet milk", this is an Italian blue cheese with a very soft paste, creamy texture, and greenish-colored veining throughout. It is a factory-made version of the famous Gorgonzola.

Fourme d'Ambert □
A strongly flavored, closely veined blue cheese from the Haute-Savoie region of France.

Gorgonzola □
Gorgonzola, Roquefort and Stilton are the three premier blue cheeses, with Blue Cheshire a close runner up. In the manufacture of Gorgonzola, the mold culture *Penicillium gorgonzola* is added to the curds with the starter. The curds are cut and packed into molds, then the unripe cheese is salted, pricked with needles and left for 3 months to develop the veining. Used for stuffing pears, and in

mousse au fromage, also salads. The cheese is pleasantly sharp in flavor, with a softish, white paste and greenish veins. It is slightly fatter in texture than Roquefort and moister than Stilton.

Roquefort □
A noble blue cheese from the southern Massif Central in France, and made of sheep's milk. It was praised by Pliny the Elder in the 1st century AD. White Roqueforts are also made from the milk of Corsican sheep in the Pyrenées. The cheese is sent to Roquefort where it eventually matures and turns blue. The success of Roquefort cheese is due to the unique, very humid environment in the complex of local caves. The cheeses are made in very much the same manner as Gorgonzola – the cut curd is packed into molds, brushed with salt and pricked with needles. The unripe Roqueforts are left to mature in the caves of Combalou mountain, where the moisture-laden air freely circulates spores of *Penicillium glaucum*, var. *roqueforti*, and in about 6 weeks, the cheeses start to "blue". Roquefort has a white paste with blue-green veins, and a fairly strong flavor. It is used for *tartelettes au Roquefort*; also in a well-known salad dressing.

Stilton □
Stilton is a relative newcomer to the great blue cheeses. Gorgonzola and Roquefort cheeses have been made for a thousand years or more, but Stilton first drew public attention in the early 18th century. Legend says that the cheese was first produced in Leicestershire, England, by a Mrs Paulet, and supplied to the Bell Inn at Stilton.

Stilton is a rich, milk cheese, made with finely cut curds, unpressed, salted, and left to mature. **White** Stilton is sold when fairly young, but the blue requires about 6 months to develop. Steel needles are driven into the cheese, and the cheese is left in a carefully controlled environment to ripen. It developes a natural rind, brown and crinkly. It is sold in tall cylinders which help to distinguish it from Gorgonzola and Roquefort.

Stilton

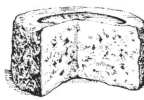

Roquefort

Eggs

Eggs, one of the most essential and versatile foods used in cooking, have been eaten and enjoyed since the beginnings of civilization. Often venerated as a symbol of life and fertility, many ancient philosophers saw eggs as a symbol of the world and the four elements, since they held that the shell represented earth; the white, water; the yolk, fire; and air was found under the shell at the round end of the egg. To early Christians, eggs were a symbol of rebirth and were hard-boiled, decorated and given as presents at Eastertime.

The eggs most often used today come from the domestic hen – either the farmyard or "free range" variety, or the modern "battery" variety; battery-produced eggs are normally sold in supermarkets. There is no nutritional difference between free range and battery eggs and none between brown and white eggs, since the shell color is related purely to the breed of hen. As far as culinary purposes are concerned, however, free range eggs do deteriorate more quickly.

Composition of the egg

The egg is made up of the *outer shell* (about 12 per cent of its total weight); the albumen, or *white* (about 58 per cent) and the *yolk* (about 30 per cent), which is held in place by a rope-like strand of material called "chalza", which is usable (as is the small, dark fleck often present – an indication that the egg is fertilized. This should be removed only if the eggs are being used in a light-colored sauce.) There is also an air space, known as the *air chamber*, at the rounded end of the egg. This gradually expands as the egg loses its freshness.

Egg white proteins, when whipped, break and expand, forming elastic walled cells that trap air, which in turn expands when subjected to heat (as in the oven). This is what makes egg whites such a valuable leavening agent. Yolk proteins, on the other hand, bind and thicken. They are less stable than those of egg whites, and, when exposed to excessive heat, harden and separate from the yolk's fat and water molecules – causing the yolk to curdle. This is why egg yolk mixtures should be heated gently.

Choosing eggs

All eggs are classified according to size, and common terms include extra large or jumbo, large, standard, medium and small. They are also graded for quality and, if packed in cartons, these are stamped with the date of packing. The grades include AA (sold no more than ten days after inspection), A, B and C. In practice, only top-quality eggs are sold in Europe and America; the less expensive B and C are used by catering and baking industries.

Fresh egg white should be firm, thick and support the yolk. A less than fresh egg has a thin white that spreads away from the yolk and a yolk which breaks easily.

Eggs in the kitchen

Eggs are extremely versatile. Apart from their endless uses in main dishes, soufflés and baking, they can be used for a number of general culinary purposes; to thicken, emulsify, coat, bind or glaze other foods and to provide a foamy base. They can be boiled, poached, baked, fried or pickled, though some, because of their size, may be less suited to general cooking (see listing below). Unless a recipe specifies otherwise use a large egg; two small ones can always be substituted.

Egg whites are more easily foamed when the eggs are at room temperature and at least three days old. Fat, even the merest trace from the yolk or any grease on the beater or bowl, will prevent foaming; salt acts similarly. A tiny amount of acid (such as cream of tartar) will make the foam stiffer and give greater bulk, while sugar keeps the proteins supple. Sugar or acid should be added when the egg white is just beginning to foam; otherwise it will remain as gritty particles. For cakes, soufflés, mousses and soft meringues, beat the foam until glossy peaks form a slight bend when the beater is removed. For hard meringues and chiffon cakes, the foam should be very white and glossy and form peaks that stand straight up. Do not overbeat or the foam will become dry and lose air.

Storing eggs

Refrigerated eggs keep fresh for 3 to 4 weeks, but should be kept away from strong-smelling foods since they absorb odors. Eggs spread less while still cold, so, unless separating or frying them, it's best to bring them to room temperature before cooking. Store eggs with the pointed end downwards so that the yolk rests on the white rather than on the air chamber. Do not freeze eggs unless separated as their shells crack at low temperatures. Eggs can be frozen up to nine months, but allow them to thaw completely in unopened containers before use.

Chicken □
Mass-produced to use in all aspects of cooking, chicken's eggs are the familiar standard by which other eggs are compared. They are often sold dried or hard-boiled, shelled and pickled in vinegar. When drained, these are served with cold meats and salads or beer and potato chips.
Bantam eggs □, which come from a breed of chicken, come in a variety of colors and are often hard-boiled and served in their decorative shells.

Duck □
Slightly larger and richer-tasting than chicken's eggs, these

should be eaten very fresh and are not suitable for meringues.

Goose □
Similar in size and taste to duck's eggs, goose eggs taste slightly oily and should always be served very fresh.

Guinea hen or fowl □
Flecked with brown, these are best medium or hard-boiled for 3–5 minutes, cooled, shelled and tossed into green salads.

Gull □
Valued for their fishy flavor, gull's eggs are slightly smaller than chicken's eggs. They are

usually hard-boiled for 5 minutes, cooled and eaten cold with a little celery salt.

1,000 year old □
A Chinese delicacy cured for 100 days, these duck eggs are grayish in color due to being coated in a mixture of lime, salt, tea, ashes and charcoal. The eggs are usually shelled, sliced, steamed and served cold.

Ostrich □
Eight to ten times larger than a chicken's egg and thicker-shelled, one egg can feed a family of 4. Use in the same way as chicken's eggs.

Egg rack

Egg basket

Partridge □
Tiny in size, these are cooked and enjoyed like guinea hen or quail's eggs.

Pheasant □
These eggs are small with a pale rosy color, about the size of quail's eggs, and can be used in the same ways.

Plover
Like quail's eggs, these are considered to be a delicacy.

They are usually served lightly boiled.

Quail □
Speckled beige, one-third the size of a chicken's egg, these are usually medium or hard-boiled; shelled and used in salads; pickled or set in aspic.

Turkey
Creamy-colored, specked with brown and sometimes twice the size of a chicken's egg, turkey

eggs are similar in flavor and may be used in place of chicken's eggs.

Turtle
Sea turtle eggs are imported from South America, the Caribbean, Africa and Australia. Rarely available, this soft-shelled delicacy is prized by connoisseurs for its rich, slightly oily flavor.

Vegetables

Vegetables, like fruits, are the edible products of certain plants. They share several characteristics: they are savory rather than sweet; we add salt to them; and, in most countries, they are associated with poultry, meat or fish as part of a meal, or as an ingredient. Some vegetables are botanically classed as fruits: tomatoes are berries, and avocados are drupes, but both are commonly used as vegetables because they are not sweet.

Some people would also add the distinction that vegetables are usually cooked, while fruits are eaten raw, but this is a very loose definition since we eat salad vegetables raw, and many dishes call for cooked fruit.

All our cultivated vegetables have derived from primitive varieties whose origins are, in some cases, unknown, but we do know that many of our present-day vegetables were cultivated in prehistoric times. The tribes of hunter-gatherers that eventually learned the value of agriculture recognized the importance of food crops, and we have evidence that peas were grown in Turkey by 6500 BC, from the wild pea (*Pisum elatus*).

In the New World it is thought that gourds, lima beans and perhaps maize were grown in Mexico before 5000 BC. It is also possible that the potato was then being harvested, and probably the tomato, too. The early Peruvians slit and sun-dried their potatoes, calling the product *tunta*. By 1000 BC the Incas had a similar but more advanced technique: they first froze the potatoes in the snows of the Andes, then allowed them to thaw, and usually squeezed out the juice until they were dry. This *chuno* would have been a staple when potatoes were out of season; it predated the modern freeze-dry technique of food preservation by a period of three thousand years.

There was probably a spontaneous genesis of primitive vegetable farming in widely separate parts of the world – in China, the Middle East and South America. By 3000 BC the farmers in Mesopotamia were growing crops of turnips, onions, broad beans, peas and lentils, leeks, garlic, radishes. The Chinese grew cucumbers, turnips and radishes – the men building the great wall of China in the third century BC were given a regular supply of fermented vegetables, including cabbage, beets, turnips, and radishes. These would have been in place of meat which was always in short supply – the Egyptians who built the pyramids fared no better, and left evidence of their diet, which included radishes, beans, garlic

and onions. In fact the onion was so highly thought of, the Egyptians elevated it to the status of a deity.

From this early cultivation of food crops in western Asia, varieties began to spread towards Europe. The Greeks and Romans encouraged vegetable production on a fairly large scale and, in the wake of the Roman armies, local farmers began to grow the crops which the Romans had introduced – carrots, leeks, artichokes, cauliflower, garlic, onions and lettuces. The Islamic invaders of Spain, thrusting northwards towards France, paused long enough to plant rice, spinach, eggplants, carrots and citrus fruits.

By the Middle Ages, extensive vegetable farming was carried out in Europe, especially in the Low Countries, where market gardeners were able to export a proportion of their harvest. Following the Spanish conquest of South America in the late fifteenth century, there was an important exchange of crops between the Old World and the New. Throughout the sixteenth and seventeenth centuries crops were gradually established in both continents. From the Americas came maize, potatoes, sweet potatoes, tomatoes, peppers, kidney beans, pumpkins, Jerusalem artichokes, and French beans. Settlers from Europe introduced to America broad beans, chick-peas, black-eyed peas, radishes, carrots, cabbages, okra, and yams – black-eyed peas, okra and yams being brought on the slave ships from Africa.

Over the centuries, different vegetables have found their individual place in our diet according to their particular characteristics: cooks did not quite know what to do with the tomato when it was first introduced – was it a vegetable or a fruit? The Italians called it *pomo d'oro* (a corruption of "apple of the Moors"), and likened it to the apple; the French called it *pomme d'amour*.

The introduction of chili peppers to India gave added fire to their already spiced dishes; capsicums were converted to paprika by the Hungarians; and as far as the potato was concerned, while the Irish took readily to it elsewhere it was a slow starter. Only in the mid-eighteenth century did the potato become acceptable in England, where it added a new dimension to the diet of the poor which consisted of onion broth, "water gruel", bread and roots (carrots and turnips), bread and cheese.

The production of vegetables for the table became a well-developed industry, especially in France, when the chemist Nicholas Appert pioneered canned foods at the end of the eighteenth century. Appert's technique was soon to revolutionize the marketing of vegetables, and was not to be equaled in importance in this field until the American physicist, Clarence Birdseye, introduced a new process of freezing foods in 1929.

Composition of vegetables

Flavor accounts for a very small percentage of a vegetable's composition. Most contain at least 80 per cent water, the remainder being carbohydrate, protein and fat. Squashes, in particular, contain a high percentage of water while potatoes contain a great deal of starch, used by the vegetable as a reserve food supply. Invert sugars are also a food source, and sucrose is present in corn, carrots, parsnips, onions, and so on. When vegetables age, the woody lignin increases, water evaporates, and sugars become concentrated: old, raw carrots appear to be sweeter than young ones. But sugars change as soon as the vegetable is separated from the plant. (A good example is corn, which is often rushed straight from the stalk to the pot in order to preserve its taste.)

Protein accounts for about 1 per cent of a vegetable's composition but can be as high as 4 per cent in corn and 8 per cent in legumes. Vegetables are also a useful source of vitamins, which can vary according to the time of day, the temperature, and when the vegetables were harvested. Sunshine increases the vitamin C in turnips, which also have more vitamin B if harvested in the morning; cabbages grown at 50–60°F (10–15°C) have a greater concentration of B vitamins, and a higher nutritive value when freshly harvested. These nutrients tend to concentrate in the outer leaves, more than the inner leaves and stem.

Each vegetable owes its unique character to the arrangement of cells and the various substances it contains. The cell walls are made of cellulose and lignin – a cell-building substance that produces such textures as fibrousness (globe artichokes), stringiness (celery) and crispness (carrots); crispness also depends on the amount of lignin and water content. Cells are cemented together by pectin, a form of carbohydrate. Common factors in vegetables are water and starch; most contain a substantial amount of water, in particular squashes and vegetable marrows.

The familiar qualities of some vegetables are due to small amounts of chemical compounds, such as sulfur in brassicas – hence the far-reaching smell of boiled cabbage – while onions contain an enzyme which brings tears to the eyes. In addition there are lipids or fats, organic acids, and pigments such as the green chlorophyll (cabbages), the yellow and orange carotenoids (carrots and pumpkins), and the purple or blue anthocyanins (broccoli and red cabbage).

Vegetables in the kitchen

When choosing vegetables you should obviously avoid those that are limp and wilting, discolored or damaged by harvesting. Leaf vegetables need careful picking over, to avoid serving garden pests on the plate. Vegetables should be prepared for the pot as simply as possible. Wash them just before cooking, don't soak them as they lose nutrients through peeling and cutting, they should only be peeled thinly. Vitamins are usually found just under the skin.

We cook vegetables in order to break down the starch and cellulose, and render them more digestible; heat achieves this, however we apply it. Ideally, most vegetables should be cooked as briefly as possible, to preserve their character, taste and freshness. Although boiled vegetables lose a quantity of their nutrients – cabbage can lose 40 per cent of vitamins C and B_6, especially when quartered or shredded – the actual volume of cooking water makes no difference, once the vegetable has been immersed. The cooking water of vegetables often contains valuable minerals and vitamins and is useful for soups. A good alternative to boiling or stir-frying, is to cook vegetables in a steamer, while both pressure-cooking and microwave cooking preserve the maximum amount of nutritive elements present in vegetables.

On contact with air certain vegetables tend to discolor, regardless of whether they are cooked or raw. This is because certain enzymes cause oxidization. This activity can be halted by the addition of an acid, which is why cooks plunge celeriac – and apples – into acidulated water (water with a little lemon juice added) after peeling them.

Blanching helps to preserve color, especially in green vegetables but some vegetable dyes are lost in the cooking process. Purple broccoli contains both chlorophyll (green) and anthocyanin (purple), the latter being water-soluble, so cooked broccoli always looks green. Red cabbage reacts like litmus paper – it turns blue in the presence of an alkali (the lime in tap water), so you need to add a dash of acid, such as vinegar, to preserve the color.

Vegetables can be classified according to their botanical family, such as the brassica (cabbages) group, or by identifying the edible part: root, leaf, shoot and stem or bulb.

LEAVES See also pp. 62–4

Calalou (*Colocasia*, spp.)
The West Indian and Creole name for the tops of the taro plant, or Caribbean spinach "callalloo greens". In the West Indies the leaves are used like cabbage.

Celtuce (*Lactuca sativa*)
Originating in China, celtuce is a sort of hybrid lettuce with a celery texture and taste. It can be used raw or cooked and is available in the spring and summer.

Chicory (*Cichorium endivia*)
A bitter-tasting curly-leaved salad plant originating in Asia or Egypt. There are several varieties, including **batavia** and **escarole**, both broad-leaved types. Used mainly in salads, they can also be braised. They are available winter and summer.

Dandelion
(*Taraxacum officinale*)
A wild meadow plant with a bright yellow flower. The blanched leaves are used for salads, especially in France, where it is cultivated, and in the American south, where it is used with pig weed, turnip green and land cress, to make poke salad. Dandelions should be eaten before they flower as they become bitter. The roots make a coffee substitute, and are used in Japan as a vegetable.

Garden cress (*Lepidium sativum* and *Sinapis alba*) □
A combination of cress and mustard sprouts, used in sandwiches and also as a garnish. It is available all year round.

Good King Henry (*Chenopodium bonus-henricus*) **Goosefoot** □
A wild plant which was formerly cultivated and used as a green vegetable, it is a perennial herb used as a spinach substitute.

Lamb's lettuce (*Valerianella olitoria*) **Corn salad**
A wild plant (which is also

Dandelion

cultivated) indigenous to Europe. The leaves are used in salads. It is a winter vegetable.

Land cress (*Barbarea verna*) **American cress; Winter cress**
A wild (but also cultivated) plant indigenous to Europe and America. It has a slight peppery taste, is available in winter, and is used in salads.

Lettuce (*Lactuca sativa*) ☐
Cultivated since ancient times in the Middle East, there are now several varieties: **cabbage** ☐ or *roundhead*, **romaine** ☐ or *cos* lettuce and **crisphead**, of which **Iceberg** ☐ is the most famous. Cabbage lettuces vary from the very soft-leaved to the robust; romaine lettuce has tall, crisp leaves, and crisphead is tightly formed. Although it may be braised or used in soups, lettuce is normally used for salads. Lettuce hearts are an ingredient in *petit pois à la français*.

Nettle (*Urtica dioica*) ☐
This is a prolific European weed used as a vegetable. Scottish and Irish cooks have made soups from the young, springtime tops of nettles for generations. The stinging hairs, containing formic acid, are destroyed by cooking. It can also be cooked in the same way as spinach.

Samphire
There are two unrelated samphires – **rock** samphire (*Crithmum maritimum*), and **marsh** samphire or *glasswort* (*Salicornia europaea*) (so-called because it was used in glass manufacture). These are wild plants indigenous to Europe. Marsh samphire is used in summer salads, or cooked as a vegetable; rock samphire is also cooked as a vegetable, and can be pickled.

Sorrel ☐
There are several varieties but the main ones are **wild** sorrel (*Rumex acetosa*), and **French** sorrel (*Rumex scutatus*). *Acetosa* implies its acid character, mainly from oxalic acid. This can be reduced if mixed half-and-half with spinach or spinach beet. Many people regard sorrel as a herb, though the leaves can also be used for salads, soups,

Brussels sprouts

sauces, in quiches and egg dishes. It is available mainly winter to springtime.

Spinach (*Spinacea oleracea*) ☐
Originally a Persian vegetable, *aspanakh*. Like sorrel it has a pleasant acidic taste due to oxalic acid. Spinach is obtainable all year round, and used in many recipes, including *oeufs Florentine*, soups, quiches and soufflés. **New Zealand** spinach (*Tetragonia expansa*) is not botanically related to spinach, but is prepared in the same way. It is thought to have been discovered in New Zealand by Captain Cook, hence its name. It is a summer vegetable.

Swiss chard (*Beta vulgaris*, var. *cicla*) **Seakale beet** ☐
This is related to beetroot, which it resembles. There are other varieties, including **rhubarb chard**, and **spinach beet**, which resemble spinach in flavor. The plants are valued for their firm, white stems, although the tough green leaves may also be used. They are available from winter to spring.

Vine leaf (*Vitis vinifera*) ☐
Sold fresh or packed in brine, they are used in salads and for *dolmades* (stuffed vine leaves). They are also wrapped around game and used decoratively in fresh fruit dishes.

Watercress
(*Nasturtium officinale*) ☐
Watercress was normally gathered from the wild; its cultivation began in the early 19th century. High in vitamins, the clean, fresh peppery taste of watercress greatly recommends it for salads. It is also used in soups, in Chinese and Japanese stir-fried dishes and as a garnish. Watercress is native to Europe, and is cultivated throughout the northern hemisphere. It is available all year round.

BRASSICAS See also pp. 66–8
These are all members of the *Cruciferae* family, the flowers of which are four-petaled and cruciform. The brassicas described below are all of the *Brassica oleracea* variety.

Broccoli ☐
Related to cauliflower, there are several varieties: **purple**

sprouting; **purple hearting** ☐ – like a cauliflower in size; **white**, and **green** ☐ (Calabrese). Broccoli was enjoyed by the Romans, and still has its Italian connection: the word *brocco* means "sprout". It bears a resemblance to asparagus, and is thus excellent served with melted butter, with Hollandaise sauce or Béarnaise sauce. Broccoli is also used for hors d'oeuvres, and in soups. It is available all year round.

Brussels sprouts ☐
These are presumed to have originated in the thriving market gardens of the Low Countries in the Middle Ages. A type of miniature cabbage, Brussels sprouts grow from tall, woody stems, and should ideally be harvested as small buds, and cooked just long enough to retain some firmness and bite. At best they are a winter vegetable, but the season stretches from August through April. Recipes include cooking sprouts with chestnuts or walnuts; they can be creamed, sautéed, or made into soup. The leaves from the top of the main stalk can be used as a vegetable, in the same way as cabbage.

Cabbage ☐
Probably developed from the wild cabbage, native to northern Europe and the coasts of Britain. Cabbages are classed according to season: spring, summer, autumn and winter varieties; and to type: semi-hearted, green-hearted, hard white, red. **Spring** cabbages are smooth-leaved, loose and small hearted. Green-hearted may have round or conical hearts, and include the **Savoy**, with dark, crinkly leaves; the **Drumhead, January King**, and **Primo**. Hard whites are the **Dutch, Danish** and **Winter White**.

Savoys are used as a cooked vegetable and are very good raw, sliced in salads. Hard whites are used for coleslaw and sauerkraut. Cabbage can be stuffed, made into soups and stews. **Red** ☐ cabbage is pickled in Britain; the Dutch, Danes and Swiss treat it more kindly, and stew red cabbage with apples and spices.

Two Chinese cabbages are **Pak-choi** (*B. chinensis*) ☐ and **Pe-tsai** (*B. pekinensis*) ☐ (known

Garlic

in Japan as *hakusai*). Pak-choi has dark green leaves and broad white stalks, like chard. Pe-tsai is the tall, compact and crisp-leaved type. Both feature in numerous Oriental dishes, quickly stir-fried, with meat.

Cauliflower □
The dense, white flower head gave the plant its Old English name – *coleflower*, or cabbage flower. It was first cultivated in the Middle East, and known in Europe by the 13th century. Cauliflower can be braised with olives and tomatoes; served with a Béchamel sauce, *au gratin*; covered with cooked egg yolks and buttered bread crumbs, *à la polonaise*. The florets can be dipped in batter and deep-fried, or served raw in salads, in a *bagna cauda*, or with mayonnaise.

Kale and **Collard** □
The names "kale" and "collard" derive from the Old English *cole* or cabbage. They are closely related members of the cabbage family, and probably originated in the eastern Mediterranean, where they have been cultivated for 2000 years. Kale was once a staple in Scotland, and was made into kail brose, a soup. Collard greens are a traditional dish, with pork, in the southern states of America.

Kohlrabi □
Its name is German for "cabbage-turnip", and the plant was probably developed in northern Europe. Like Brussels sprouts, kohlrabi is a cabbage mutant. It can be cooked in the same manner as turnips. It is used in a macédoine of vegetables; in Germany it is often steamed, then sliced and served with the cooked leaves. It is mainly found in winter.

SHOOT VEGETABLES
See also p. 70
Asparagus □
(*Asparagus officinalis*)
Although probably native to Europe, it is thought to have originated in the Middle East and been re-introduced into Europe in the late Middle Ages by the Arabs. There are about 20 varieties, but the most common is **green** asparagus (a weedier version is known in England as "sprue"), followed by the fat, **white** asparagus,

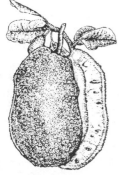

Jackfruit
A large fruit native to India, it can be eaten boiled, fried or raw; it is sometimes used in preserves. The seeds can be roasted

preferred by the French and Italians. Asparagus is served hot with butter, or cooked and served cold with vinaigrette. It is also used in soups, quiches, soufflés, in hors d'oeuvres and as a garnish.

Bamboo (*Bambusa vulgaris*) □
The conical shoots of species of bamboo are sold fresh in Far Eastern markets, but canned, in water, almost everywhere else. Shoots emerge from the ground and are cut when about 6in. (15cm) long, then stripped of their outer covering. They are used raw or just lightly cooked.

Cardoon (*Cynara cardunculus*)
A thistle related to the globe artichoke, it is indigenous to the Mediterranean region. Its root and stalks are similar to celery, and are eaten raw or braised as a vegetable.

Celery (*Apium graveolens*) □
Developed by Italian gardeners in the 16th century from wild celery to the pleasant-tasting, crunchy vegetable we know today. The distinctive flavor of celery is used in celery salt. There are two varieties of celery: **Pascal**, or heavy green-ribbed celery, with large green leaves and **golden**, which is blanched, having white ribs and yellow leaves. Celery is used in salads; as a vegetable; in hors d'oeuvres, and in soups and stews.

Endive (*Cichorium intybus*) □
Confusion reigns over the naming of chicory (p. 238) and endive, and the matter remains unsettled: the Belgians called it *witloof* ("white leaf"); the French and Americans call it "endive"; the British "chicory". Used mainly as a salad vegetable it can also be braised. It is available from autumn to early summer.

Fennel (*Foeniculum vulgare*) □
A celery-like shoot with the faint, sweetish flavor of aniseed. Fennel leaves are used as a herb to flavor fish and the plant is used raw in salads and hors d'oeuvres. It is also used in soups and as a vegetable. It is available all year.

Fiddlehead fern (*Pteridium aquilinium*) **Bracken** □
The tightly curled young shoots

of a wild plant native to France and abundant in many areas of the world, they can be served cooked, like broccoli, with Hollandaise sauce, or raw in salads. They are available canned or fresh in spring and summer.

Globe artichoke
(*Cynara scolymus*) □
A plant of the thistle family similar to cardoon. Young, fresh artichokes can be eaten raw; older ones boiled and served hot or cold with a dressing such as vinaigrette, mayonnaise, Hollandaise sauce. They can also be stuffed or baked. Artichoke bottoms or *fonds* may be bought canned and are used for appetizers. Artichoke hearts are sold canned or frozen and can be served as a vegetable or an appetizer.

Seakale (*Crambe maritima*) □
A wild (but also cultivated) seashore plant indigenous to western Europe, and gathered for its white stems. Seakale is eaten like asparagus.

FRUIT VEGETABLES
See also p. 72
Akee (*Blighia sapida*)
History maintains that akee fruits were introduced to the West Indies by Captain Bligh of the *Bounty*, hence the botanical dedication. The outer pink covering of the fruit is poisonous but benign portions are used as a vegetable with salt cod in Jamaica. It is available canned.

Avocado (*Persea americana*) □
Grown in many tropical countries, this nutritious, buttery fruit, with its green skin (or warty black skin depending on the variety) is used as a salad vegetable, an hors d'oeuvre, in sauces, dips and mousses, or as the main ingredient in Mexican *guacamole*. There is a wild variety in the American southwest, *aguacate*.

Breadfruit
(*Artocarpus communis*) □
Like the akee, it is associated with Bligh of the *Bounty*, who introduced it to the West Indies. The large fruits contain a pulp used as a vegetable, generally roasted.

Capsicum (*Capsicum annuum*) □
The pepper family includes

sweet □ or *bell* peppers, or
pimientos, and the hot **chili** □
peppers. Peppers are found in
considerable varieties. The most
familiar are the sweet, green
peppers, which change from
green to red as they ripen. The
small red or green conical
peppers are the fiery chilis.
Sweet peppers are used in
salads, stews, sauces and can be
stuffed. Chilis feature in Indian
curries, Mexican and Latin
American dishes. The most
popular varieties are **serrano**
and **jalapeño**. Peppers are
available fresh all year, and may
also be found canned.

Eggplant
(*Solanum melongena*) □
A member of the nightshade
family, its origins are probably
Indian, and several varieties are
found in various colors. All are
used as a vegetable – fried,
stewed, stuffed, baked,
casseroled and pickled, and
their most well-known use is
in *moussaka*. Eggplants are
available all year round.

Plantain (*Musa paradisiaca*) □
Related to the banana, plantains
are generally larger, with green
skins. They are native to Central
America where they are used as
a vegetable.

Tomato
(*Lycopersicum esculentum*) □
Few vegetables can have had
greater culinary impact than the
tomato. It is, in fact, a berry
and a member of the nightshade
family, like the potato. A native
of South America, it was
originally raised as a decorative
plant since it was feared to be
poisonous. There are numerous
varieties of this attractive fruit
once known as the *love apple*,
including **green** tomatoes, **plum**
tomatoes, **beefsteaks** □ and
cherry □ tomatoes. Used in
countless recipes, in sauces
(such as the classic Napolitana
sauce), catsups, purées, soups,
stews, even in sweet dishes.
Certain varieties are available all
year; others, like the Mexican
green tomatoes, and continental
plum tomatoes, are scarcer.

SQUASHES See also pp. 74–80
Cucumber (*Cucumis sativus*) □
Although not generally thought
of as a squash, it comes from
the same family, *Cucurbitaceae* –

hence its inclusion here. It is an
ancient plant, cultivated for
thousands of years. Varieties
range from the small, ridged
(**ridge**) cucumber □, to the long,
smooth-skinned (**hot-house**)
cucumbers □. In India the
refreshing quality of cucumbers
is added to yogurt to make
raita, used to temper the curry
dishes. Northern Europeans
combine it with sour cream and
the French garnish cucumber
salad with salted whipped cream.
Cucumbers are pickled, salted,
used in soups; also in a sauce
(especially with poached
salmon), and, of course, in
salads. Slices should be salted
and pressed to remove water
before adding dressing.

Other squashes
Squashes and gourds share the
distinction of being native to
both the Old World and the
New, in nature and in name –
"squash" comes from the
American Indian *askutasquash*
"gourd" from the Latin
cucurbita. Squashes feature in
American and West Indian
cooking, in African and Middle
Eastern cooking, also in the
Orient. There are many different
varieties, including **golden
nugget** □, **butternut** □, **snake**
squash □, **spaghetti** □, **custard**
squash □.

Another type is the **chayote**
(*Sechium edule*), *christophene* or
chaci, whose name, from the
Aztec *chayotl*, reveals its Central
American origin. Varying
widely in size, shape, shade and
texture, chayote, in common
with other squashes and
gourds, has a high water
content: the bigger the vegetable
grows, the more insipid it
becomes. Chayote can be
prepared in the same ways as
smaller squashes. It is used in
chutneys, and can be baked or
stuffed. In most countries there
is no distinction between
zucchini □ and **marrow** □
(both *Cucurbita pepo*), since the
zucchini is harvested before it
has the chance to grow into the
huge vegetable so loved by
English gardeners. Both may be
stuffed; marrows are cubed and
served *au gratin* or made into
jam; marrow flowers are served
Italian style, dipped in batter
and deep-fried. Zucchini can be
baked, sliced and fried in batter
(the flowers dipped in flour and

fried); served with a sweet-sour
sauce, and made into soups and
stews. They may also form an
ingredient in ratatouille, the
Provençal vegetable stew. They
are available all year. The
pumpkin (*Cucurbita pepo*) □,
one of the largest, will serve
both as a fruit and a vegetable.
Pumpkin is puréed, made into
soup, roasted, fried and baked.
Small squashes can be stuffed,
or cooked as for zucchini
recipes, according to the type
and area, or in a vegetable stew
such as *colache*, from the
American southwest.

BULBS See also p. 82
Garlic (*Allium sativum*) □
A member of the lily family,
it probably originated in Asia
as both Chinese and Egyptians
were using it early in their
history. It is not used simply
as a vegetable, but compounds
the taste of an infinite variety of
savory dishes. One of the most
notorious is *lièvre à la royale*, a
French dish of hare that calls for
some 30 cloves of garlic; another
is a dish of chicken or duckling
casseroled slowly with 40
garlic cloves (cooked whole,
peeled but not pierced). Garlic
is available all year round.

Leek (*Allium porrum*) □
It possesses the character of the
onion family, but is less potent
and often more suitable for
soups and stews. Sometimes
referred to as the "asparagus of
the poor", leeks are also a
vegetable in their own right;
they can be braised, served with
sauces, *au gratin* and are a major
ingredient in the Scottish cock-
a-leekie. They are available from
autumn to spring. **Welsh
onions**, natives of Siberia, not
Wales, are small, leek-like bulbs
with a delicate flavor. They can
be used to flavor stews.

Onion (*Allium cepa*) □
Dubbed "The King of
Vegetables", because of its
dominant taste, long reign, and
widespread influence, it is
extremely versatile. In America
onions which are storable for
long periods, are classified as
dry. There are two general
types: mild-flavored, or pungent,
and two shapes: globe and
elongated. Popular types are
Creoles, Bermudas, Spanish
and **Italian reds**. Small-sized

Chayote
*A round or pear-shaped squash
which can be eaten raw or cooked*

Crookneck squash
*The bright yellow crookneck squash
is a summer variety and has a thin
skin. Younger squashes can be eaten
skin, seeds and all*

Tree onion or Egyptian onion
*Unlike other members of the onion
family, this variety grows in clusters
at the tops of the plant stems. Tree
onions have the same flavor as other
varieties and are used in the same ways*

varieties are particularly suitable for pickling. **Green** onions are very young onions and include leeks, shallots, chives and scallions. As **scallions** □, or *spring onions*, they play their part in salads, in Oriental cooking. The **shallot** (*A. ascalonicum*) □ is widely used in France, where there are gray, pink, and golden-brown varieties. Onions are available all the year. Shallots are most abundant in spring and summer.

ROOT VEGETABLES
See also pp. 84–6
Apio and **Arracacha**
(*Apios tuberosa*)
Members of the Legume family, they are native to North America and can be cooked like potatoes and in desserts. They are very similar in flavor and are interchangeable.

Arrowhead
(*Sagittaria sagittifolia*)
Tule potato, or *wappato* are other names for this water plant with arrow-shaped leaves. Leaves and root are used in Chinese cooking.

Beet (*Beta vulgaris*)
Beetroot □
Beet and its close relatives, chard, and spinach beets, all developed from *Beta maritima*, a European seashore plant whose root was cultivated in Germany in the Middle Ages. Other root varieties are the **sugar beet**, an important source of sugar, and the **mangold** or *manglewurzle*, a cattle food. Beet is an ingredient in the classic Russian soup *borsch*. It is much used as a salad vegetable, and is also pickled and canned. In America, small beets are served in orange juice, as Yale beets, and in a sweet-sour sauce, as Harvard beets.

Burdock (*Arctium lappa*)
A wild, thistle-like plant common to the northern hemisphere. Young leaf stems are used in salads; in Japan, where it is called *gobo*, the entire plant is used.

Carrot (*Daucus carota*) □
Thought to be native to Europe, wild carrots were cultivated by the Dutch in the Middle Ages. Carrots are believed to improve eyesight and for this reason were issued to Second World

Black radish
Unlike the more common radishes, the black winter variety is the size of a small turnip. It is used mostly as a winter salad vegetable

War British night fighter pilots. The carrot is now used throughout the world as a foundation vegetable – like the onion – in cooked dishes, soups, stews, casseroles, and raw in salads.

Celeriac (*Apium graveolens*, var. *rapaceum*) **Celery root** □
This turnip-rooted vegetable is used in salads, in hors d'oeuvres, puréed, in soups and stews. It is a winter vegetable.

Chinese artichoke
(*Stachys affinis*)
Native to China and developed in Europe by the French, this tuber can be grated raw into winter vegetable salad, used as an accompanying vegetable to meat dishes, and in Chinese mixed vegetable dishes. It is available in the late autumn.

Hamburg parsley
(*Petroselinum hortense*)
Turnip-rooted parsley
This plant is cultivated for its root – which is white, slender and like a carrot. Its popularity in eastern and northern Europe may help to account for its name. Used in soups and stews, it can also be an accompanying vegetable, like celeriac.

Horseradish
(*Armoracia rusticana*)
Native to southeast Europe and western Asia, this root is usually crushed and made into a sauce. It has a pungent flavor and is a popular condiment with roast beef and cold meats.

Lotus (*Nelumbium nuciferum*)
This sacred plant of India and China is used extensively in the cooking of the Far East, where it is indigenous. The cut root is perforated with holes, a decorative quality exploited in Chinese and Japanese dishes. It is available fresh or canned, and can be made into a starch, pickled, or steamed. The raw leaves are used in salads.

Parsnip (*Pastinaca sativa*) □
This long, sweetish root with a distinctive taste is used as a vegetable. Parsnips probably originated in eastern Europe but have long been in use in England. They bear some resemblance to sweet potatoes and are also used in American

cookery. They can be braised, boiled, pan-roasted, puréed, candied, or made into wine. They are available from autumn to spring.

Radish (*Raphanus sativus*) □
Grown since prehistory in the Middle East, radishes were a favorite in ancient Egypt. There are black, white and red-skinned varieties, which can vary in shape and size. In Japan, the white **daikon** □ radish is finely sliced and cooked with other vegetables, or used in soups. In Europe radishes are primarily salad vegetables, and make excellent hors d'oeuvres. They are available throughout the year.

Rutabaga (*Brassica napobrassica*) □
A heavy, coarse-skinned vegetable with orange flesh. They can be boiled and mashed and in this form are served in Scotland with haggis. In the American Midwest they are mashed and candied. In Finland they are casseroled, with cream and spices.

Salsify (*Tragopogon porrifolius*)
Oyster plant and **Scorzonera** □
(*Scorzonera hispanica*)
Closely related plants with long, tapering roots, these are members of the daisy family. **Salsify** has a white skin, **scorzonera** black. Native to Europe and Mediterranean, both plants can be used for soups, salads, as a cooked vegetable, puréed, in hors d'oeuvres or casseroles. On cooking, salsify can acquire a slightly glutinous and glossy appearance, which may explain why it was once likened to oysters.

Turnip (*Brassica rapa*) □
This root vegetable can vary considerably in size, shape and color: it can be round or cylindrical, yellowish or white. Turnips are cooked whole when young and small, with lamb, as in the French *navarin*. The Japanese cut it finely and use it as an ingredient in soups and mixed vegetable dishes. The green-leaved tops are used as a leaf vegetable.

TUBERS See also pp. 87–8
Cassava (*Manihot utilissima*)
Tapioca; Manioc
A starchy tuber used in the

Cassava

West Indies and Central America. It is used to make **tapioca** which is exported in pearl or flaked form (p. 257), and is used to make desserts and confectionery. Fermented, cassava is used in a liquor and the leaves can be boiled and eaten as a vegetable. Cassava flour is an ingredient in cakes and pies.

Jerusalem artichoke (*Helianthus tuberosus*) □ Indigenous to North America, and introduced to Europe in the early 17th century, it is related to the globe artichoke and the sunflower. It can be eaten raw, sautéed with parsley, or slowly boiled and fried. It can be used in salads, sauces and casseroles. Mainly a winter vegetable, it is available up till early summer.

Potato (*Solanum tuberosum*) □ A member of the nightshade family, indigenous to Central America. There are many varieties of potato, including purple, lilac, spotted and striped. Some varieties are cultivated for individual qualities, such as storage, early cropping, high yield, suitability for frying, chipping and so on. Commercially, potatoes are canned, dehydrated, mashed and diced and flaked; fried and deep-frozen, made into flour. American varieties include **Russet Burbank**, good for baking, French fries, chips and flakes; **Norland**, excellent for frying and boiling; **Red Pontiac** produces a very white boiled potato.

Sweet potato (*Ipomoea batatas*) □ Sweet potatoes, despite their name, are not related to potatoes, though potatoes and *batatas* hail from the same area – Central America. Sweet or "Spanish" potatoes arrived in Europe before the common potato, and were highly regarded. They are usually elongated, though there are some round varieties. The flesh is usually white, and the outer skin may be white or reddish. Sweet potatoes are cooked with apple and served with ham, made into pies, puddings (in Creole cookery); baked whole, and boiled and then candied, sometimes with marshmallow. They are traditional at

Corn

Garden peas

Thanksgiving and are available from autumn to early summer.

Taro (*Colocasia antiquorum*) □ This tuber contains fine-grained and digestible starch and is used as a vegetable in West Indian cookery. The corm is the edible part, and is cooked in the same way as potatoes. In the West Indies the leaves are also eaten, like cabbage.

West Indian Yam (*Dioscorea*, spp.) □ There are many varieties of this potato-like tuber, the principal being *D. alata*, which is indigenous to Africa and Asia. Yams are high in starch but contribute little else to the diet. The Chinese variety (*D. esculenta*), features in many Oriental vegetable dishes. In Africa, yams are mashed, peppered and spiced to make *foufou*, a dish of the Ivory Coast; *kalajoum*, a chicken stew with peppers and coconut. They may also be candied.

PODS AND SEEDS
See also p. 90
Bean sprouts (*Phaseolus aureus*) □ The tender young sprouts of the germinating mung bean are used in the East as a vegetable in cooked dishes. They are also often used raw in salads.

Corn (*Zea mays*) **Sweetcorn; Maize; Indian corn** □ Corn was indigenous to America, but is now grown throughout the world. It was a staple food of the Indians and they traded it to the early English settlers who called it "Indian corn". Corn is used as a vegetable, briefly boiled or roasted and eaten with butter. It is always used young – picked before the grain is ripe. Also used in soups, it can be puréed, made into fritters, and cornmeal (p. 257).

Fava beans (*Vicia faba*) □ This seed has been grown and eaten throughout Europe and the Middle East since prehistoric times (see Dried Pulses, p. 244). It is the one variety unknown in the New World before Columbus. Upper class Greeks and Romans regarded them as harmful to their vision and there is some evidence today

that a hemolytic disorder among Mediterranean people known as *favism* is related to broad beans. A brown, Egyptian variety provides the staple *ful*. They may be creamed, served with a sauce or puréed and are the traditional complement to ham or bacon. Broad beans are found frozen or canned, and are fresh in the summer months.

Green beans (*Phaseolus vulgaris*) □ Native to Central America, like the potato they were brought to Europe and their preparation perfected, hence their European name, "French". There are a great many varieties, eaten for the pods and seeds together, including **wax pod** beans, **scarlet runners**, **haricot** and **lima** beans. Most are sold canned, frozen and fresh.

Okra (*Hibiscus esculentus*) **Lady's Fingers; Gumbo** □ The immature seed pod of a plant of the hibiscus family, native to Africa. When cooked it becomes sticky, and syrupy. It is widely used in the southern states of America, in okra soup and dishes with rice. It appears in Indian cooking as *bindi*; as *bamia* in the Middle East, cooked in a lamb stew. Okra is available canned, and fresh from summer to early autumn.

Pea (*Pisum sativum*) □ Possibly the earliest of all cultivars it was first domesticated from the wild pea in the Middle East. Peas were eaten as a meat substitute in early Lenten times. In England, up until Tudor times *peason* (the Old English version of peas) were always eaten dried. The varieties which are in common use are **garden** peas □, which, harvested young give us the tender **petit pois** □; **mange tout** □, *sugar peas* or *snow peas*, cultivated for their tender pods; **asparagus** peas (*Lotus tetragonolobus*), not of the pea family, but eaten like mange tout, when small. Garden peas are canned, dried, puréed, used in soups (*potage St Germain* is a classic pea soup), stews, and as a cooked vegetable. Chinese cooking makes much of "snow peas" in stir-fry dishes. They are available from early summer to autumn.

Dried Pulses

Pulses are the edible seeds of certain plants of the legume family and include beans, peas and lentils. Some, like green beans, fava beans, lima beans and green peas are eaten fresh; others are eaten dried and in this form have been a staple food in many parts of the world for thousands of years.

Archeological research into plant origins has shown that beans were among the first plants cultivated when agriculture began. The "common bean" (which includes kidney and its many varieties such as pinto and black) was first cultivated in Mexico; lima beans in Peru; fava beans and chick-peas in the Middle East; soy- and aduki beans in China, and black-eyed peas and pigeon peas in Africa. Pulses have become widely naturalized outside their native regions, however, so that today most of them are available worldwide.

Pulses remain as popular as ever in the cooking of the Middle East, Asia, the Caribbean, Mexico and Central and South America, while in America and Europe there is an ever-growing interest in them due in part to the high cost of meats and to the increasing popularity of vegetarian cooking.

Methods of processing

Beans are dried as quickly as possible after picking to preserve their flavor, plumpness and texture. They are then graded and any stones removed before picking. Most pulses are now artificially dried and graded by machine.

Dried beans, peas and lentils are in some cases also available cooked and canned and a few types are fermented or processed into some other form, such as flour, oil, fresh pressed bean curd or dried bean curd sheets.

The fermentation processes which are used vary considerably. In China black beans are fermented in salt, and in Africa in wood ash. The process may continue for months, as for the soybeans used to make soy sauce.

Mung beans and soybeans may also be sprouted for their shoots, which are eaten as a fresh vegetable.

Dried pulses in the kitchen

Most pulses are widely available and the lesser known varieties can usually be found in stores specializing in Oriental and health foods.

They keep well and are easily reconstituted but should be stored in a cool, dry place and used within 6 to 9 months or they will begin to shrivel and harden.

Beans, peas and lentils may be used whole in casseroles, salads and vegetable dishes, puréed in soups or ground and used for croquettes and dips. All types of beans and lentils are high in protein and 30 per cent more is released if they are eaten with a cereal; this is why there are many dishes around the world in which pulses are served with rice or bread.

In many recipes, one pulse can be successfully substituted for another, but variation in flavor and texture should be taken into account since this makes some pulses much more suitable than others for certain dishes. Those beans, peas or lentils which become very tender with cooking will absorb other flavors well and are particularly good in spicy or herby casseroles, while those with a firmer texture are the best to serve whole as a vegetable or in salads.

Remember that most pulses need soaking and cooking, the exact times depending on the particular type and quality of the bean. Pick over the beans before washing and soaking them to remove any stones or pieces of grit and add salt towards the end of cooking time to make the beans soften more quickly.

PEAS AND LENTILS
See also p. 92

Chick-peas (*Acer arietinum*) □
Also known as *garbanzos, ceci* (Italy) and *chana dal* (India). These large peas, shaped like hazelnuts, are usually beige or golden although there is also a small, dark brown variety. They have a nutty flavor and slightly crunchy texture. They are a staple food in the Middle East and are milled into flour, roasted whole, or ground after cooking and used as the main ingredient of *hummus*, a savory dip, or *felafel*, deep-fried patties. Chick-peas also appear in many European and Oriental dishes.

Lentils (*Lens esculenta*) □
There are many different varieties of lentil, usually identified by and named after their color, which may be **green, orangey-red, brown, gray, yellow** or **black**. Some are best known by their Indian names, as various types of *dal*. They all have the same flattish round shape, rather like a small

Lentils

pea, but vary in size and may be sold split or whole. Lentils play an important part in Indian cookery, where they are usually served as a main or side dish with curry, and the split red ones are a staple food throughout the Middle East, often served with rice. The familiar green and split red lentils cook to a soft purée and also make good soups, but the brownish and gray continental ones retain their shape and may be served as a vegetable. They are the only pulse which may not require soaking before being cooked.

Peas (*Pisum sativum*) □
Dried peas include the whole marrowfat or "blue" peas that tend to have tough skins and a soft floury texture, and the skinless yellow or green split peas which cook to a soft purée. Split peas have the sweeter flavor – the green ones are similar to frozen garden peas.

Dried peas were an important vegetable before frozen peas appeared, but they have now lost much of their popularity. In Germany, however, whole dried peas are still baked with sauerkraut and sour cream and English cooks use them to make the traditional pease pudding served with salt pork – a complementary combination that is also successful in split pea soups made with a ham bone and vegetable dishes.

BEANS See also p. 94
Aduki beans (*Phaseolus angularis*) **Adzuki beans** □
These small dark red or black beans are very tender when cooked and have an unusually sweet, quite strong flavor. They originated in the Far East where they are valued for their medicinal properties and have been eaten in rice dishes and soups for thousands of years. Their sweetness has also made them an ingredient in Oriental confectionery.

Black-eyed peas (*Vigna sinensis*)
Cowpeas; Black-eyed beans □
These small, whitish beans with

Sacks of dried beans and peas

Soybeans

a distinctive black or yellow "eye" become tender with cooking and absorb other flavors well. Black-eyed peas are very popular throughout the southern states of America, where they have given their name to the classic dish of salt pork and beans cooked with Tabasco. In China they are stir-fried and mixed with meat or fish to make *chiang ton chia*.

Black fermented Chinese beans (*Glycine max*) □
Smallish black beans – usually soy – which, in China are often fermented in salt and added to meat and vegetable dishes.

Black kidney beans
(*Phaseolus vulgaris*) □
A shiny black variety of the common bean, tender with a sweet flavor, they are a staple food throughout the Caribbean, Central and South America and Mexico. Fried black beans and rice are the national breakfast dish of Costa Rica, known as *gallo pinto*, while *feijoada completa*, a dish of mixed meats and black beans served with cassava meal (*farofa*), diced oranges, hot fresh pepper sauce and collard greens is the national dish of Brazil.

Borlotti beans
(*Phaseolus vulgaris*) **Saligia beans**
A pinkish Italian variety with red speckles, which come from Italy, they are baked in spicy casseroles or served cold in salads.

Cannellini beans (*Phaseolus vulgaris*) **Fasiola beans** □
Another version of the common bean, they are creamy white, slightly larger than the American white bean and with a fluffier texture. They appear mainly in Italian cooking and are often mixed with tuna fish to make the dish *tonno e fagioli*.

Fava beans (*Vicia faba*)
Broad beans □
Fava beans are eaten both fresh and dried; the dried ones have a fine texture and are whitish, beige or brown.

Ful medames
(*Lathyrus sativus*) □
Sometimes called simply *fool* or *ful*, this is a small, light brown

variety of fava bean, known by its Egyptian name. Dried fava bean patties or *taamiya* are eaten throughout the Middle East and *ful medames* have given their name to one of the national dishes of Egypt, in which they are baked with eggs, cumin and garlic. They are also good eaten as a vegetable.

Green beans (*Phaseolus vulgaris*)
Flageolets; Green haricots □
A pale green variety of common bean with a slightly elongated kidney shape. They have a fresh texture and very delicate taste so they are especially good eaten as a vegetable. In France, they are traditionally served with roast lamb, and are also eaten in salads.

Lab-lab beans
(*Dolichos lablab*) □
Hard-skinned black beans from the hyacinth plant, which originated in India but are now eaten throughout Asia and the Middle East, particularly in Egypt. From this they have been called the "kidney bean of Asia" or Egyptian bean.

Lima beans (*Phaseolus lunatus*) □
There are two sizes and several varieties of these kidney-shaped beans which are eaten both fresh and dried. They are usually pale green or cream, which accounts for the fact that they are sometimes referred to as *butter beans*. They are also known as *Madagascar beans* because they are grown there so extensively, although they were originally found in South America. Dried limas retain their shape well and are often served by themselves as a hot vegetable or in salads.

Mung beans
(*Phaseolus aureus*) □
Also known by their Indian name *moong dal*. These tiny olive green beans have a good flavor and very high vitamin content. They are available split, whole and skinless. Mung beans are widely used in China, where they are sprouted for their sweet, tender shoots and processed to make *fen tiao* noodles, and in India where they are curried. The shoots are delicious eaten raw in salads as well as cooked in Oriental dishes. The beans are used in stews.

Pigeon peas (*Cajanus cajan*)
Gunga peas; Toor dal □
These beige beans take their name "pea" from their shape and size and have a sweetish flavor. They are a staple food in the Caribbean and are used there in a large number of rice dishes and soups, such as *jug-jug*, from Barbados, said to be a corruption of haggis brought by Scots exiles after the Monmouth Rebellion, and pigeon pea soup from Trinidad.

Pinto beans (*Phaseolus vulgaris*)
These are kidney-shaped and beige dappled with brown flecks. They lose their color but not their flavor when cooked.

Red kidney beans
(*Phaseolus vulgaris*) □
These vary from pink to maroon and have a floury texture and fairly sweet flavor. They are the basic ingredient of chili con carne, the hot spicy Texan and northern Mexican dish, and also of *frijoles refritos*.

Rice beans
(*Phaseolus calcaratus*) □
So-called because their taste is reminiscent of rice. Grown in China and India.

Soybeans (*Glycine max*) □
Soybeans are small and oval in shape, ranging in color from **yellow, green** and **red** to **black**. They are very high in nutrients, especially protein, and have been an important part of Oriental diets for many years. They are used for making bean curd (which may be fresh or dried and is known in Japan as *tofu*), delicate noodles called *harusame* and a sweet confectionery paste.
The beans are also fermented and used to make flavoring pastes and condiments, notably soy sauce (called *shoyu* in Japan), *tempeh* from Indonesia and *miso* from Japan. More recently, soybeans have become the most important commercial pulse in the world, used for making a variety of basic Western foodstuffs, as well as for industrial purposes such as the manufacture of plastics. They provide an important oil (p. 220), can be ground to make a flour (p. 257) and are the basis of most meat substitute chunks and granules. Soybeans are also used for their milk.

Soybeans are very hard and need long preparation for cooking, but a pre-cooked variety known as *soy splits* is also available. The green beans, fresh and dried bean curd and soy flavorings are used in many Chinese and Japanese dishes. The beans may also be sprouted for their long, crisp shoots, which are best cooked. They have a floury texture and sweetish flavor.

White beans
(*Phaseolus vulgaris*) □
A variety of the common or haricot bean which varies considerably in size but is always the same plump kidney shape. The American white bean is also known as *navy bean* because it featured among the bulk provisions of the navy in the early 19th century; it may also be found under the names of *pea bean*, *Michigan bean*, or

Great Northern, or named after a particular growing area, such as the very large **Soissons** beans from France.

White beans are usually eaten canned in tomato sauce, but are also an ingredient of classic casseroles, such as Boston Baked Beans from New England and cassoulet, a French dish of beans with sausages and smoked goose.

Mushrooms and Truffles

Confusion exists over the terms "mushrooms" and "fungi". Here we use the term "mushroom" to describe all forms of edible fungi. Mushrooms can be wild, domesticated, fresh, canned, pickled and dried. They are made into sauces and catsup and are used in a great variety of dishes in most countries throughout the world. Mushrooms contain about 80 per cent water, 8 per cent carbohydrate and 1 per cent fat. They are also a source of protein, riboflavin and thiamine, iron and copper, potassium and phosphates.

Wild varieties of mushroom have long been in use; they were recognized by the Sumerians in 3500 BC and the Greeks gathered and exported their edible varieties, which the Romans incorporated in their recipes. The French used the wild *cèpes*, *chanterelles* and *morels* of the forests and regarded the mushroom as a delicacy worth cultivating.

Mushrooming is a favorite pastime in many countries, though the mushrooms sought are different. In America alone there are about fifty edible wild species. However, not all mushrooms are edible. Certain mushrooms of the *Amanita* family are deadly, indeed *Amanita phalloides* is known as *death cap*, or, more picturesquely, *death angel*. Mushrooms of the *Psilocybe* species found mostly in Mexico are hallucinogenic and were once regarded as sacred. Amateur mushroom hunters are urged to gather only those easy to identify, among them the morel, held to be the finest of all mushrooms, the shaggymane and the puffballs. In America, membership of one of the many mycology societies takes care of the problem with expert identification; in France local pharmacists give the same kind of expert help.

Cultivating mushrooms

Ignorance about the growth and life-cycle of mushrooms was widespread until the French botanist Marchant in 1678 demonstrated that mushrooms grew from spawn, appearing on a lace-like structure, the mycellium, just beneath the surface of the soil. Market gardeners in Paris swiftly put theory into practice and transplanted the "roots" of the wild mushroom to a bed of horse manure, and thus bred the ancestors of a remarkably successful product.

In the 1890s, French scientists finally consolidated their long monopoly by developing a pasteurized spawn, and therefore more dependable crops. American growers, who had first raised mushrooms in New York City and Long Island, adopted the French technique in the late nineteenth century. Pennsylvania is now the center of the mushroom industry in America.

Elsewhere, the cultivation of mushrooms remains a local industry on a limited scale, mainly in China and Japan, although wild mushrooms have a ready market in Europe. Russia's *Lactarius deliciosus* is gathered in conifer forests and sold in dried form, likewise the boletus, and chanterelles in France, Italy, Poland, and Germany, where over 300 species of edible mushrooms are sold. Five types of mushroom are now cultivated: the common mushroom; the French and Italian truffle; China's padi-straw mushroom and Cloud Ear fungus, and Japan's shiitake. The matsutake, from Japan, while not cultivated, is extensively gathered and canned for export.

Mushrooms in the kitchen

Some mushrooms may need parboiling first, especially chanterelles. Large varieties can be sliced, dipped in egg and breadcrumbs, and fried in bacon fat, while young mushrooms are excellent sliced raw in salads. Dried mushrooms are a useful standby ingredient, and they keep for over a year. They are dried on wire trays in a current of air maintained at 130°F (54°C). Unless their skin is tough and discolored mushrooms need not be peeled. Wipe the caps with a damp cloth or paper towel. If they are very dirty or sandy and must be washed, do it quickly without letting them soak. Wild specimens should be carefully sorted and checked for insects and grit. Cook as soon as possible after gathering. Dried mushrooms will need soaking in warm water until soft – about 15 minutes. To store fresh mushrooms, put them in an open, plastic bag in the refrigerator, where they will keep for four or five days; dried mushrooms keep for at least a year. Three ounces (85g) of dried mushrooms when reconstituted are equal to one pound (450g) of fresh mushrooms.

CULTIVATED VARIETIES
Matsutake
This type of mushroom grows on the *matsu* (pine) tree. A

cousin of the European **blewit** (*Tricholoma matsutake*) is a delicate, finely tasting mushroom which is collected

wild, and sold canned or fresh (in Japan). It is used in several Japanese dishes, including steamed chicken, *tori mushiyaki*.

Mushrooms □
The cultivated mushroom (*Agaricus bisporus*), is usually harvested young, either as a **button** □ mushroom, with pale pink gills, or as a **cup** □ mushroom, where the cap or pileus has partially opened. The mature, or **flat** □ mushroom has dark brown gills.

Most growers use stable manure, machine mixed with gypsum and cottonseed or barley, being rich in nitrogenous compounds. The compost is pasteurized by steaming, and laid in a controlled environment to receive the spawn. A layer of "casing" soil then covers the spawn, which is left for about 3 weeks at 65°F (18°C), while the compost is regularly kept moist. Mushrooms appear after the first month, and continue to crop for a further 3 or 4 months. One third of a grower's crop will be sold fresh, a third for canning and the remainder is used for soup.

Oyster mushroom
A wild mushroom with a bluish-gray cap, it is eaten fried, broiled or grilled. It is popular in France

Padi-straw mushroom
(*Volvariella volvacea*)
These small, conical mushrooms are grown on wet rice straw beds, and sold fresh or dried. The local industry, from Canton, is probably quite old. They feature in such recipes as the vegetarian dish *sushi-chin*, and steamed or fried chicken dishes.

Shiitake (*Lentinus edodes*) □
These are the most widely used mushrooms in Oriental cooking and are grown in China and Japan on the wood of dead deciduous trees. *Lentinus edodes* takes its name from the *shii* tree (*Pasania*), but also grows on the oak and hornbeam. The spawn is planted into holes or wedges cut in the logs, and crops last for 3–6 years. *Shiitake* are dried by sun, or artificial heat. Dried ones should be soaked in warm water for 20 minutes.

Truffles □
These are tubers that grow near the roots of oak or beech trees – they are cultivated inasmuch that oak groves are planted to encourage them. The two main varieties, and the most highly prized in cuisine, are the black **Périgord** □ truffle (*Tuber melanosporum*) and the white **Piedmontese** □ truffle (*T. magnatum*) of Alba, Italy, both

expensive luxuries. There is also the **red-grained black** truffle (*T. aestivum*), which grows in England but is largely ignored, and the **violet** truffle of Europe (*T. brumale*). Fresh truffles are gathered in the autumn, and are only marketed locally, so most of us are obliged to buy them cooked and canned, when they have lost some of their characteristic aroma.

White truffles have a powerful taste and aroma. They are usually grated, raw, on pasta, risotto or egg dishes, although one classic recipe suggests cooking them with Parmesan cheese. Black truffles can be used as a decorative garnish, in *pâté de foie gras*, aspic dishes, or cooked with scrambled eggs, as in *brouillade de truffe*.

Wood or Cloud ear
(*Auricularia polytricha*) □
A distant cousin of the European **Jew's ear**, this Chinese mushroom is cultivated on wood, or gathered wild from tree trunks on which it grows. Dried, it forms a gelatinous, tough product that needs reconstituting in several changes of warm water for about 30 minutes. It is used in soups, chicken and fish dishes.

WILD VARIETIES
There are many types of edible wild mushroom in Europe and America. Here we list a few better known varieties. It is important to have wild mushrooms identified by a reputable source before eating or cooking them.

Boletus (*Boletus edulis*) Cep
A superior-tasting mushroom widely eaten in Europe. The Greeks and Romans used the term *bolites* to describe the best edible mushrooms, but this term has since been applied only to the *Boletus*. Found in woodland clearings in late summer and autumn, usually under coniferous trees, they are distinguished by their stout stalks with delicately raised white veins running towards the top, and by the vertical tubes underneath the cap in which the brown spores are produced.

Chanterelle
(*Cantharellus cibarius*) □
Commonly found in beech

woods from July to December. The funnel-shaped, yellow cap hides a paler flesh and the stalk is delicately ribbed, running up to the under edge of the cap. Chanterelles cannot be artificially cultivated but are available dried or canned in food stores. They have a delicious flavor and are often used in French cooking.

Field mushroom
(*Agaricus campestris*) □
Found in meadows from late summer to autumn, the well-known white cap of the field mushroom is abundant in food stores throughout the year.

Giant puffball
(*Lycoperdon giganteum*)
All true puffballs are edible but can only be eaten when they are young, firm and white. The giant puffball can be found in woods and meadows from August to October.

Horse mushroom
(*Agaricus arvensis*)
Similar to the field mushroom in habitat and taste, the horse mushroom has a yellow-tinted cap and grayish gills.

Morel (*Morchella esculenta*) □
Not a true mushroom, the morel is easily recognizable by its brown, sponge-like cap, pitted with hollows in which the spores are produced. It can be found in woodland clearings during spring and early summer and can also be bought, dried or canned, in specialty food stores.

Parasol mushroom
(*Lepiota procera*) □
The parasol mushroom can be found in sandy meadows and roadsides from July through to November. The genus name *Lepiota procera* derives from the latin words *lepis*, meaning "scale" and *procerus*, meaning "tall". An adequate description for this elegant mushroom with tiny scales on the cap. Although this is an excellent tasting mushroom, the stalk should not be eaten as it is tough and fibrous.

Fruit

Attempts at the cultivation of fruit date back over 8000 years. Evidence of carbonized apples was found by archeologists in ancient dwellings in Turkey; and neolithic sites in Denmark and Switzerland have yielded the fossilized remains of fruits such as sloes, blackberries, raspberries, strawberries, bilberries and crab apples. These apples were larger than the wild types found today, so it is assumed that they were at an early stage of cultivation.

We cannot pinpoint the exact provenance of fruits, nor precisely when they began their gradual migration, for written records are scanty, or vague, but certain facts are available.

Apricots and peaches were grown in China some 3000 years ago. Their cultivation gradually spread westwards, the apricot becoming so well established in Armenia that the Romans called it *armeniacum*, "the Armenian apple", but there it lingered, for it did not reach Palestine until post-biblical times.

Armenia, northern Persia and the foothills of the Caucasus were the finest orchards of the ancient world. Here was the home of the vine, the quince, the medlar, pomegranate, and probably also the plum and the bullace. It is thought that the Phoenicians took the vine from Armenia to Greece and Rome, and that the Romans in turn planted vines in southern France, and along the steep banks of the Rhine. The cultivation of fruit also spread southwards to the "Fertile Crescent" of Assyria and Babylonia, where farmers grew crops of pomegranates, apples, cherries, peaches, mulberries and figs.

Oranges, native to China, are thought to have appeared in India during the first century AD, and from there went first to the east coast of Africa, then to the Levant. Roman horticulturists planted orange groves in Italy and may have introduced the orange to Spain, although the Spanish orange is also ascribed to the Moslem invaders who introduced the lemon. Oranges made their way to the New World in the sixteenth century, and were finally established in California in 1769. Bananas followed a similar route, though somewhat earlier; they reached India in about 500 BC, and from there migrated to the Canary Isles and the West Indies via Africa.

By the seventeenth and eighteenth centuries there was considerable exchange of fruits between Europe and America. One of the most welcome contributions from the New World was the American cultivated strawberry, which was first introduced in 1660.

American apples were being sold in London's markets in the 1770s, along with bananas from the West Indies, and a new, bright pink plant that nobody knew how to cook. It had come from Central Asia, probably Uzbekistan, where it was, and still is, eaten raw. This sour and acid-flavored fruit was called "rhubarb", and eventually became popular with the British, who stewed it with sugar.

The pineapple was the only fruit from Central America to gain international status, until the modern trend for the avocado. It had been cultivated in Brazil and Peru at least a thousand years earlier, sharing its domestication with the guava, papaya, avocado, star apple and sour sop. All these fruits spread to the Caribbean islands, to mingle with those that were indigenous.

Southeast Asia has a bounty of interesting and succulent fruits such as the banana, mango, carambola, durian, rambutan and mangosteen. The rambutan is unlikely to be found outside its native Malaysia, but the mango, which was transported to the Caribbean in the seventeenth century, has since become known throughout the world.

Fruit, in spite of its widespread cultivation, however, was regarded with suspicion; it was thought to provoke gastric disorders, a view first expressed by the Greek physician Galen. It was a belief that was to persist until the late nineteenth century. Even then, the demand for foreign fruits was maintained only by the wealthy, for imports were expensive.

Varieties and hybrids

The willingness of some fruits to "marry" with others and to respond to selective crossbreeding has inspired horticulturists ever since the Romans first tried grafting plum trees.

The development of fruits has come about by way of two botanical systems, variation and hybridization. Variations are produced by two parent plants of the same species, that have different characteristics or qualities. Crossing two varieties of apple such as Worcester and McIntosh Red produces a third variety: "Tydeman's Early Worcester". This variety combines the best qualities of both parents.

Crossbreeding between parents that are genetically unalike, or distinctively different, results in a hybrid. Crossing a grapefruit with a tangerine produces a fruit which bears some of the characteristics of both species, in this case the tangelo. Of all fruits, the citrus family has responded best to hybridization. A few examples are the ugli fruit, a cross between a tangerine and a grapefruit; the clementine, a hybrid of the tangerine and the sweet orange; and the citrange, resulting from a cross between a citron and an orange. Attempts to create progeny from the kumquat, a citrus-like fruit native to China, created the orangequat, limequat, and citrangequat.

Many of these hybrids may turn out to be mere botanical curiosities with little commercial application, but some are becoming popular in the world market. The Jamaican ortanique, a cross between the orange and one of the tangerine varieties, probably the satsuma, is an example of this.

Some seasonal varieties of fruit have an attractive quality or unusual appeal; examples are blood oranges, pink grapefruit and red bananas with pink flesh. Blood oranges, such as the Moro, Tarocco and Dobelfina varieties contain a red pigment, anthocyanin, which gives the blush to the flesh of the orange, while the Thompson variety of the pink grapefruit owes its color to a carotenoid pigment called lycopene.

Commercial uses of fruit

All citrus fruits have aromatic oils in their skins – oils which are used in cooking, in liqueur-making and which are also essential to the perfume industry. Lemon oil is widely used as a flavoring agent, and the skin of bitter oranges, such as the bergamot orange and the Seville or bigarade, produces oil of neroli and oil of bergamot for use in scents.

Countless fruits are used as a flavoring for liqueurs and brandies, some of the more famous being Curaçao, based on the orange and kirsch, based on the cherry.

Citric acid, found mainly in the pulp of the fruit, is a useful by-product of lemons. Prepared in crystalline form it is used for flavoring cordial drinks and confectionery. Enzymes of papaya and pineapple are used in meat tenderizers because they help to break down protein.

Many fruit flavors, such as bananas, pears, oranges and pineapples, have been synthesized for the food industry (p. 215) and these are particularly useful in the manufacture of ice cream and soft drinks.

Buying and storing fruit

When buying fruit watch out for soft spots or bruises. If possible, buy produce that is displayed openly, rather than depending on prepackaged fruit; also, buy in season for reasons of both flavor and economy. Methods of testing for ripeness, however, vary with each individual fruit.

Unless you plan on eating the fruit immediately, it is best to buy produce that is slightly underripe and let it ripen at home over a two- to three-day period. Most ripe fruit should be stored in the refrigerator, while underripe fruit can be stored at room temperature. All fruits have individual characteristics and it is impossible to give an overall rule on when fruit is ready to be eaten.

Fruit in the kitchen

Fresh, canned or dried fruit can be put to a variety of uses in the kitchen. It can be eaten raw in salads, as a dessert with cheese, or can be cooked with meat or on its own.

The sugars and acids in fruit contribute greatly to the flavor and ultimate purpose to which the fruit will be put – whether for cooking or as fresh, dessert fruit. Plantains, for example, contain a lot of starch and are less sweet than their close relative, the banana. Therefore they are used mainly as a vegetable. Cooking apples are also lacking in sugar, but are high in malic acid; they pulp easily when cooked, while dessert apples remain firm. Cooking varieties are also the most suitable for baking. Use dessert apples for braised red cabbage, and *à la Normande* dishes and where pieces of apple that retain their firmness are required, as in some types of apple pie.

Citrus fruits as part of a salad or compote should be peeled with a knife to remove the "pith". Ideally, the inner core, seeds and segment membranes – known as the *rag* – should also be removed. When shaving off the zest from the skin of citrus fruits, use a potato peeler and take off the top layer only. If you need a large amount to flavor a dessert, take off the whole peel, string the pieces together and blanch them several times. Then dry them and leave them in syrup to sweeten. If you want to use citrus peel as a sweetener, rub a sugar lump over the peel before adding it to the dessert.

Don't sugar strawberries in advance, as the sugar absorbs the water content and the fruit goes mushy. Red currants, blackcurrants and the rarer white variety will need to be destalked, a tedious job but less so if a fork is used to strip the fruit from the stems. Most berries yield a fair amount of water; add sugar and cook briefly to keep them whole.

Melons, especially charentais, should be prepared just before serving; otherwise they lose some of their fine aroma and flavor.

Bananas, apples and pears all darken on exposure to air when peeled, and should be dipped in acidulated water (water with a squeeze of lemon juice, or a teaspoonful of tartaric or ascorbic acid).

If you are preserving fresh fruit, it is best to use slightly underripe fruit as the pectin content will be at its highest (see Jams, Marmalades and Jellies, p. 227).

PITTED FRUITS

See also p. 98

Apricot (*Prunus*, spp.) □
A fruit that originated in China but is now widely available. It is eaten fresh and used in pies and compotes. It is also available canned and dried – the latter is often stewed.

Cherry (*Prunus*, spp.) □
Popular varieties of sweet cherries are **Black Tartarian** and **Napoleon**. The best varieties for cooking derive from the **Morello** with **Montmorency** being usually the most favored. These are excellent for pies and jams. Cherries are also available canned and are used in liqueurs.

Date (*Phoenix*, spp.) □
Principally cultivated in the desert oases of southern Algeria and Tunisia, dates are also grown in South Carolina and Arizona. The date varieties now cultivated in America – **Medjool** and **Deglet Noor**, among others – are all, as their names imply, of Arab origin. Dates can be bought fresh or dried and can be served as a garnish for a fruit tray or may be stuffed with cream cheese. Dates also freeze well and so may be kept for an extended period.

Loquat (*Eriobotrya japonica*)
Japanese medlar
It belongs to the same botanical family as the apple. A native of China and Japan it has been quite widely cultivated in Mediterranean countries. The yellow pear-shaped fruit is the size of a crab-apple. It can be eaten fresh or stewed and is also made into jam.

Medlar (*Mespilus germanica*)
A fruit the size of a small apple with a brown skin and firm flesh, it is thought to be native to Oriental countries and is grown extensively in the southern states of America. It is generally eaten fresh but can also be used to make preserves.

Nectarine (*Prunus*, spp.) □
A smooth-skinned variety of peach, it can be eaten fresh like a peach or cooked and made into jams.

Peach (*Prunus*, spp.) □
A fruit with more than 2000 varieties, peaches are usually classified as *freestones* and *clingstones*. The former are popular for eating fresh and for canning and drying. The latter, which have paler-colored flesh, are useful for poaching.

Plums (*Prunus*, spp.) □
Many different varieties are available. **Bullace** is a type of plum related to the damson. Native to Europe and rare in America it is used in jams. The **damson** □ is a European plum which, unlike other varieties, is not suitable for eating raw. It is very dark and tart and has a thick skin. It makes excellent preserves. The **greengage** □ (known as the *Reine Claude*) is a plum with a yellowish-green skin. It is one of the sweetest and best-flavored plum varieties. The **mirabelle** is a small golden yellow plum; it is eaten stewed, made into jam (p. 42) and is also made into a liqueur of the same name. The **sloe** is not an edible variety of plum because of its sourness. In one area of France it is distilled to make a liqueur and elsewhere it is grown for jam. Most plums can be eaten fresh and all can be used in jam-making and for

Date palm

compotes to be served as desserts. American plums, such as the **red plum** and the **wild goose** are generally smaller than their European cousins. Their flesh is yellowish-orange and they are often used for jams and desserts. Plums are available fresh, canned and dried.

BERRIES See also p. 100
Arbutus (*Arbutus unedo*)
This rather tasteless berry is the fruit of the strawberry tree. It is mainly used in preserves, for the extraction of alcohol, and in a drink similar to cider.

Blackberry (*Rubus fruticosus*) □
Available in the late spring and summer, this nutritious fruit is commonly eaten fresh or can be made into preserves, pies and syrups. Blackberries are also thought to aid diseases of the mouth and throat.

Blackcurrant (*Ribes nigrum*) □
This sweet, black fruit is best known for its use in the making of the liqueur cassis, but can also be cooked in desserts or made into jams. It is also thought to have therapeutic properties in cases of arthritis. It is a summer fruit.

Blueberry (*Vaccinium*, spp.) □
This small, dark blue fruit is in season from late spring to early autumn. It can be eaten fresh or stewed with sugar. It can also be cooked in pies and desserts or made into preserves.

Boysenberry (*Rubus*, spp.)
Similar in appearance to the loganberry, this fruit can be eaten fresh or used in preserves.

Sloe berries
The tiny, dark blue plum-like fruit of the sloe or blackthorn is used mainly in the manufacture of gin; also in preserves

Buffalo berry (*Shepherdia argentea*) **Buffalo currant**
A tart yellow fruit the size of a currant and containing one seed, it is used in making pies and preserves. It is native to America.

Cape gooseberry
(*Physalis peruviana*)
Similar in appearance to a ground cherry, this yellow berry can be eaten raw but is more likely to be made into preserves.

Cloudberry
(*Rubus chamaemorus*)
A small, golden-colored fruit which grows in large areas of open moorland. It can be used in desserts or jams.

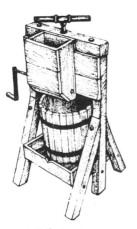

A fruit press

Cranberry
(*Vaccinium oxycoccus*) □
This acid-tasting fruit is almost always used to make cranberry sauce. Fresh berries are in season from early autumn to early winter, but frozen and canned cranberries can be purchased throughout the year.

Dewberry (*Rubus caesius*)
A small, black berry with a white blush to the skin, the dewberry is usually cooked in desserts or used for jam-making.

Gooseberry (*Ribes grossularia*) □
Sweet-tasting gooseberries can be eaten raw, but the sour-tasting varieties are mainly used in jams and preserves and are also made into wine. Available in early summer.

Ground cherry (*Physalis pruinosa*) **Strawberry tomato; Dwarf cape gooseberry**
A sweet, but slightly-acid tasting fruit enclosed in a lantern-shaped husk, the ground cherry is usually made into preserves but can also be eaten raw.

Hawthorn (*Crataegus*, spp.)
The *haws*, or berries of this plant are used in the making of jams and jellies. In Britain, a wine is made using the haws and the flowers of the plant.

Honey berry (*Rubus*, spp.)
A close relative of the raspberry, the honeyberry can be eaten raw or can be cooked for use in desserts and preserves.

Huckleberry
(*Vaccinium myrtillus*)
Bilberry; Whortleberry
Acid-tasting when raw, this berry is used mainly in desserts, preserves and confectionery. It is also made into a wine in central Europe, both for drinking and for medicinal purposes. It is available throughout the summer.

Loganberry
(*Rubus loganbaccus*) □
This dull red fruit is a hybrid of a blackberry and a raspberry. Loganberries are available canned, or fresh in the mid-summer months.

Mulberry (*Morus*, spp.)
There are various species of this fruit, but the **white** mulberry

(*Morus alba*) and the **black** mulberry (*Morus nigra*) are the most common. They are generally eaten fresh, or used in jams and wines, but can also be used to make a mildly astringent syrup.

Naseberry (*Achras sapota*)
Sapodilla; Chickoo
The pulp of this brown-colored fruit is embedded with black, inedible seeds and is palatable only when ripe. The flavor, however, is delicious, resembling the taste of brown sugar.

Phenomenal berry
(*Rubus*, spp.)
Similar to the loganberry in both parentage and appearance, this fruit is usually cooked in jams and preserves, but can also be eaten raw.

Raspberry (*Rubus idaeus*) □
White, red □ and **black** raspberries are in season in the peak of summer. This richly flavored fruit is available fresh or frozen and can be eaten fresh, or used in desserts, drinks and preserves. Raspberries are also considered to have excellent diuretic properties.

Red currant (*Ribes rubrum*) □
A red, translucent berry with a rather sour taste. Red currants can be eaten fresh, but are more often used in the making of preserves, syrups and currant wine. They are also considered to be a refreshing medicinal essence. They are available during the summer.

Salmonberry (*Ribes spectabilis*)
The salmonberry is an American wild raspberry or bramble. The name derives from the large berries that are salmon-red or wine-red when fully ripe. They can be eaten fresh or cooked in pies and desserts. They are sometimes made into preserves.

Strawberry (*Fragaria*, spp.) □
A native of America, strawberries are available fresh and frozen and are delicious eaten alone or with cream. They can also be made into preserves, fruit soups, pies and many desserts. Their peak season is in late spring and early summer, though they are available all year. The **wild** strawberry □ is a smaller, richer-tasting version of

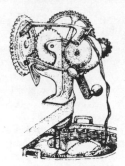

A 19th-century mechanical apple peeler

the cultivated strawberry. It can be used in similar ways and does not have to be hulled before being eaten.

Tangleberry
(*Gaylusacia frondosa*)
This is a type of huckleberry that grows wild in some parts of America. The sweet-tasting berry may be eaten fresh or cooked in pies and desserts.

Veitchberry (*Rubus*, spp.)
A close relative of the loganberry, this fruit can be used in similar ways.

White currant (*Ribes sativum*)
Less acid-tasting than the red currant, this berry can be eaten on its own or used in preserves.

Worcesterberry
(*Ribes divaricatum*)
This is actually an American species of the gooseberry. The small black fruit was first sold in Worcester when it was thought to be a hybrid of a gooseberry and a blackcurrant. It can be used in similar ways to the gooseberry.

APPLES □ See also p. 106
The many varieties of apple (*Malus communis*) can be divided into two groups: *dessert* and *cooking*. Dessert apples – those to be eaten fresh – include **Golden** □ and **Red Delicious** and **Newtown Pippin**. Some of those which are good for eating raw and for most cooking purposes are **Northern Spy, Jonathan, Stayman, Winesap** and **McIntosh** □. Usually recommended for baking are **Spitzenburgs, Northern Spys** and **York Imperials**. Dessert apples can be bought dried, to be reconstituted and served with cereals or for baking. Fresh apples are often served cut up in fruit salads or whole with cheese. Cooking apples are made into purées, baked whole or used in pies.

GRAPES □ See also p. 108
Grapes (*Vitis vinifera*) are either white or black and different varieties of both are grown in many parts of the world for eating fresh, for wine-making and for drying into raisins. American favorites include **Flame Tokay** and **Thompson Seedless** □ from California; **Concord**, grown in the eastern

states, and the smaller spicy muscadine type such as **Golden Muscat** from the southern states. The flesh of the Tokay is solid and it is known for its excellent keeping qualities. As well as the Thompson, other varieties of seedless grape have been developed – making them easier to prepare if they are being included in baking.

PEARS □ See also p. 105
There are many varieties of pear (*Pyrus communis*) throughout the world differing in size, color and texture. They are eaten fresh and used for cooking and pickling. The best known American varieties for eating fresh are **Max Red Bartlett** in the summer months and later in the year **Comice** □, **Anjou** and **Bosc**, among others. One of the most popular types used for cooking and pickling is the **Kiefer**. Pears are also available canned and can be served as a dessert with cream or other fruits. Eaten fresh, they can be served whole with cheese or cut up and added to fruit salads. They can be stewed and puréed.

CITRUS FRUITS
See also pp. 102–104
Citron (*Citrus medica*) □
Unlike other members of the citrus family the citron is not cultivated for its flesh or juice but for its thick, fragrant rind, which is candied and used in cakes and confections, it is also used in the preparation of candied fruits and liqueurs.

Clementine (*Citrus*, spp.) □
Regarded by some as a variety of tangerine, and by others as a cross between the tangerine and sweet orange. Mainly produced in North African countries, it is practically seedless.

Grapefruit (*Citrus paradisi*) □
A popular species of the citrus family, it is native to the West Indies, but now grown mostly in America. Often served as a breakfast appetizer, it is thought to contain an enzyme which stimulates the metabolism – hence its frequent use in slimming diets. Many varieties have been developed, including the **Florida Duncan** □, which is particularly good for juicing, and the **Texan Pink** □, so sweet

that it can be eaten without additional sugar. Often available in the form of canned segments, grapefruits can be eaten raw or broiled with brown sugar. They are also used in the preparation of juices and marmalades.

Kumquat (*Fortunella*, spp.) □
A small, oval, orange-like fruit with sweet skin and juicy, slightly bitter flesh. It can be served fresh and eaten with the skin, but is also available bottled in syrups. Kumquats are sometimes used in preserves.

Lemon (*Citrus limon*) □
Widely grown in Mediterranean countries, its acid taste makes it unpleasant to eat as a fruit, but it has many culinary uses, particularly in baking and confectionery and in the preparation of lemon juice and sugar for lemonade. It is also often added to fish dishes.

Lime (*Citrus aurantifolia*) □
One of the smaller of the citrus fruits it is cultivated mainly in tropical countries. It is used for its juice, and its grated zest of peel is often used in sherbets and ice cream. It is also used in preserves and curries.

Mandarin and **Tangerine** (*Citrus reticulata*) □
Generally thought of as being the same thing, although biologists are still confused by their nomenclature, these fruits are smaller than oranges, and have very loose skin which is easy to remove. They are available fresh or canned, and can be eaten on their own or used in fruit salads. They are also sometimes candied and glazed, or used in the preparation of liqueurs.

Orange □
The best known of the citrus fruits, this, like other members of the citrus family, is native to China and Southeast Asia. There are both bitter and sweet oranges. The two main varieties of bitter orange are the **Bergamot** (*Citrus bergamia*), used mainly for perfumery and essential oils, and the **Seville** □ orange (*C. aurantium*), which bears bitter-tasting fruits unsuitable for eating raw. The fruit itself is used mainly for making marmalades, though the

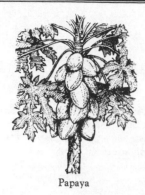

Papaya

Cherimoya
The pulpy fruit of a Peruvian tree, it is a member of the custard apple family. Also known as the sherbet fruit, it can be eaten raw, without the seeds, or used to make drinks and ices

rind is used for its oil which is extracted and used in liqueurs such as Curaçao; also for orange flower water (p. 25). Seville oranges are sometimes added to meat and fish dishes for extra piquancy. Sweet oranges (*Citrus sinensis*) are mostly consumed as fresh fruit or used for preparing orange juice drinks; they can also be used in salads and fruit salads. They are extensively grown in Florida and California, where they are usually classified as *normal*, *blood* and *navel*. The most common type of normal orange are **Valencias** □ – good for juicing and slicing for use in salads and fruit salads. Other varieties are **Pineapple Oranges, Parson Browns, Hamlins** and **Florida Temples**, which taper slightly at the stem end. The latter, though marketed as oranges, are in fact, a cross between the tangerine and the sweet orange. They peel easily and can be used in salads. Navel oranges, so-called because they have a circular mark at the stem end resembling a navel, have a thicker skin than normal oranges, which makes them easier to peel and segment. They are, therefore, well-suited for use in salads. Blood oranges are small, with slightly rough skin, and have sweet, juicy flesh with flecks of red. They are usually eaten on their own, though they can also be used in salads. The **ortanique** is another variety of orange – flattened in shape.

Pomelo (*Citrus glandis*)
Shaddock
The largest of the citrus fruits, it has a thick skin and a bitter fibrous pulp similar to the grapefruit. It is usually eaten on its own.

Satsuma (*Citrus*, spp.) □
Similar to the tangerine, it has a loose skin and contains no pips. It can be used in preserves, but is usually eaten fresh.

Tangelo (*Citrus*, spp.)
A cross between the tangerine and the grapefruit, it tapers slightly at the stem end. It is good for juicing, eating as a fresh fruit, or in salads.

Ugli (*Citrus*, spp.) □.
A rough-skinned fruit which is a hybrid between the grapefruit and tangerine, it is native to the

East Indies. Its flesh is sweeter than grapefruit, although it is often substituted for it. Sometimes used in preserves, it is also eaten baked.

MELONS □
See also pp. 110–12
There are several types of melon (*Cucumis melo*), but broadly speaking there are three groups defined by form and color. There are *musk* or *netted* melons (with a "network" pattern on the skin); *winter* melons, which are quite smooth-skinned; and *cantaloupe* melons, which have a warty exterior. There is also the **watermelon** □ (*Cucumis citrullus*), with a dark green skin and bright red flesh. Musk melons have a flesh of a yellowish green color; the flesh of winter melons is greenish-tinged – the best known types are **casaba** and **honeydew** □. The flesh of the cataloupe is orange-colored. A new melon in this category is the **ogen** □ (developed in Israel), which has greenish flesh.

Melon is eaten in its natural state either at the beginning of a meal as an hors d'oeuvre or at the end as a dessert. It should be served chilled and is often seasoned with ginger. In America it is sometimes also served as a breakfast starter.

TROPICAL FRUITS
See also p. 114
Custard apple
A term covering a group of fruits which includes the **cherimoya, sweet** and **sour sop** and the **bullock's heart** (*Anona*, spp.). They are tropical fruits which rarely appear in temperate zone markets. The cherimoya has a pineapple flavor while the sweet sop, which is particularly popular in the West Indies, has a sweet, custard-like flesh. The flesh of the sour sop is white and more acid than the others in the group. The flesh of the bullock's heart is more solid and sweet and it gets its name from its shape and dark brown color.

Feijoa (*Feijoa sellowiana*)
Pineapple guava □
Although native to South America it is a fruit that is now grown mainly in New Zealand. A dark green fruit with white flesh it is delicious raw in fruit

salads but is principally used for jams and other preserves.

Guava (*Psidium guajava*) □
A fruit that varies in size from that of a walnut to an apple, it is one of the most commonly planted tropical fruits. When ripe the skins are light yellow in color, the pulp is juicy and contains small seeds. The flesh varies in color from white to yellow to pale pink. Guavas are eaten raw or stewed and they are made into pies and jams. They are also available canned. Guavas are noted for their high vitamin C content; in some varieties it is higher than that of citrus fruits.

Kiwifruit (*Actinidia sinensis*)
Chinese gooseberry □
This fruit is grown largely in New Zealand. It is the size of a small plum, has a hairy brown exterior and bright green flesh. Kiwifruit, which is rich in vitamin C, may be served fresh or poached and garnished with lemon juice.

Mango (*Mangifera indica*) □
A fruit that is an important source of vitamin A. It is mainly eaten fresh but is also made into chutneys and jams and is sometimes canned. India is the biggest producer, although it is grown in many tropical climates. Mangoes look rather like elongated peaches and have a juicy pulp and a large seed. They can be sliced and served with ice cream and other desserts.

Papaya (*Carica papaya*)
Pawpaw □
It is widely cultivated in all tropical countries. A large berry varying in weight, it has a yellowish rind and yellow to salmon-colored flesh with a large central cavity containing many seeds. Papayas are used for antipasto (in the same way as melons) and their juice makes a pleasant drink. An enzyme (papain) from their leaves is used as a meat tenderizer while the black seeds, which contain pepsin, are sometimes used as a garnish. Underripe fruits may be used for cooking and can be treated in the same way as summer squashes. When served raw, papayas should be chilled

and sprinkled with lemon or lime juice.

Passion fruit (*Passiflora edulis*) **Purple granadilla** □
Purple in color the fruit is about the size of an egg. The sweet juicy pulp is eaten raw and in the countries where it is grown the juice is bottled and makes a popular drink. When at its best passion fruit is slightly wrinkled.

Pineapple (*Ananas comosus*) □
A fruit that is grown in most tropical and subtropical countries. It has a high sugar content – more than 15 per cent – and is one of the finest table fruits. Attractive as well as tasty, fresh pineapples are often used as a table decoration. Available fresh, canned or candied, the flesh should be eaten uncooked and can be sliced and eaten on its own as a dessert or added to ice cream or other dessert dishes.

OTHER FRUITS
See also p. 116
Banana (*Musa*, spp.) □
Native to tropical countries, bananas are usually eaten raw – often on their own or incorporated in fruit salads – although they can also be gently baked or flambéed with rum. The skin of the fruit is green when unripe changing to yellow when ready for eating. They are nutritious and rich in vitamin A.

Durian (*Durio zibethinus*)
A fruit native to Southeast Asia

and much enjoyed there. Its main characteristic is a highly unpleasant smell which probably accounts for the fact that it has never attained a wider popularity. It has a dull yellow skin when ripe and its pulp, which is eaten raw, is creamy.

Fig (*Ficus carica*) □
There are several varieties of **white, purple** and **red** figs and their cultivation today is extensive, particularly in the Mediterranean countries. They are usually eaten fresh, some are canned or used in relishes and many are dried. These are excellent in baking and desserts and are also good when stewed.

Persimmon (*Diospyros kaki*) **Kaki fruit** □
There are several varieties but the principal ones are **North American** and **Oriental**. The ripe fruit is quite soft and a golden orange. They can be eaten fresh in fruit salads or stewed and puréed and combined with ice creams.

Plantain (*Musa*, spp.) □
Native to the Tropics this fruit is a relative of the banana. It has a higher starch and lower sugar content than dessert bananas. Unsuitable for eating raw it is used widely in West Indian cooking in soups and stews.

Pomegranate (*Punica granatum*) □
Probably a native of Persia originally it is now grown in

many other areas including California and Florida. The size of a large orange, it has a thin but hard rind and the seeds are red sacs of juice. Pomegranate juice is used as a flavoring addition to summer drinks and in parts of the Middle East it is included in soups. In the West Indies it is used widely in cooking and in preserves.

Prickly pear (*Opuntia ficus-indica*) **Indian fig** □
This fruit is a cactus native to America but grown in other countries now. The fruits are either red or yellow and covered in spines. Internally the pale pink or whitish pulp encloses hard seeds. The fruit is eaten raw (in America the spines are often singed off) but it can also be stewed.

Quince (*Cydonia vulgaris/oblonga*) □
Although one of the earliest known fruits it is not one that has a widely popular appeal. Rarely eaten uncooked, it is used principally in preserves and confectionery and turns pink when cooked.

Rhubarb (*Rheum rhaponticum*) □
Technically it is a vegetable but it is used as a fruit. It is widely available and can be bought fresh or canned. When fresh it is stewed with sugar and used for pies and jams.

Prickly pear
The prickly pear or Indian fig is the fruit of a type of cactus. The plants bear the fruits at the tips of their jointed stems, and the pulp is contained within their spiny outer skin

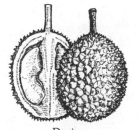

Durian
A fruit of a Southeast Asian tree it can weigh up to 20 lb (9kg). The large seeds are roasted and eaten like nuts

Dried Fruit

If a ripe fruit is dried it loses most of its moisture, accumulates natural sugars, and keeps almost indefinitely. This fact has been known to Middle Eastern people for over 5000 years. They have always preserved dates, figs and apricots by sun-drying, which is still the most favored technique, although some fruits are now artificially dried.

Medieval Europeans put their apples into warm ovens, then peeled, cored and threaded them onto strings, and suspended them from the kitchen ceiling. In the monasteries, however, monks dried their plums, grapes and apples on stone, straw-covered floors.

Dried fruits were introduced into America by the settlers, who also brought with them apples, nectarines, grapes, peaches, quinces and apricots, to add to the indigenous plums, cherries and persimmons. Today, California is the main producer of dried fruit.

Methods of processing
Six pounds (2.6kg) of fresh fruit produce only one pound (450g) of dried fruit. The fruits are harvested by hand, the stalks and pits removed. They are then fumigated and graded before being spread out in the sun to dry. While sun-drying gives fruit a golden, translucent appearance which cannot be achieved mechanically, it has many disadvantages, principally that of cost, which makes mechanical dryers more popular. Most fruits are picked when ripe (except pears, which are picked while still green and left to ripen on trays). They are then chemically treated with either sulfur smoke or an alkali dip, depending on the fruit. Both methods accelerate drying, but the latter is preferred for whole fruits, such as prunes or grapes. The methods described in the alphabetical listing below are those used in California.

Dried fruit in the kitchen

Dried fruit is sweeter and richer than fresh fruit, which makes it invaluable in baking and desserts. It is most often used in fruit cakes and cookies and occasionally in stuffings. It can be eaten on its own; candied, as a confectionery item; on cereals, or topped with cream, yogurt or custard.

Drying fruit

Packets of ready-mixed dried fruit can be bought in most supermarkets and health food stores, but the fruit can also be bought separately. Currants, raisins and sultanas are usually sold washed and ready to use; other dried fruits may need washing and soaking, preferably overnight. Keep the liquid in which they were soaked and use it to cook the fruit.

Apples □
Main varieties used are **Baldwin, Delicious, Jonathan, Winesap** and **King**.

Apples attract moisture and so have a shorter shelf life than other dried fruits. They can be eaten alone or used in baking.

Apricots and peaches □
Apricot varieties used are **Moorpark, Royal** and **Blenheim**; peach types are **Muir, Alberta** and **Lovell**. They can be eaten on their own and are also used in Middle Eastern recipes with meat.

Bananas □
These are peeled and dried whole or sliced lengthwise. They are then sulfured and sun-dried or machine-dried.

The vaccum-dried purée of the ripe fruit produces a type of flour; dried bananas are also used in baking.

Currants, raisins and sultanas □
These are all types of dried grapes: **currants** (the word is derived from the Greek "Corinth" grape) are a small, seedless type; **raisins** and **sultanas** (known in America as *golden raisins*) are large, succulent and often seedless grapes related to the Spanish muscatel. The main varieties are **Thompson Seedless** and **Muscat**.

The most popular use of all three types is in baking and desserts.

Dates □
These are classified into *dry*, *semi-dry* and *soft* types, of which the latter is the most popular. The main varieties used are the Middle Eastern **Deglet Noor, Hallawi** and **Khadrawi**.

They are eaten on their own or used in baking.

Figs □
The most famous varieties are the **Smyrna** fig from Turkey and the **Black Mission** from America; also the **Calimyrna**, a hybrid of the Californian and Smyrna.

Figs can be eaten on their own or with Parma ham. They can also be processed into paste and jam, and, in the Middle East are used in confections.

Pears □
The most popular type used is **Bartlett**. They are halved, sulfured and sun-dried.

They are eaten on their own or used in baking.

Prunes □
These are whole, dried plums. In California and Oregon the prime varieties for drying are the **Agen**, the **Robe de Sergeant**, and **Imperial**, from France; also the **Italian** prune and the **Sugar** plum from America.

Prunes can be eaten on their own or used in cakes, puddings, sauces, and the Arab stew *tadjub ahmar*; also as a filling for dumplings and fritters. They can be canned or preserved in brandy or vinegar, and are sold pitted and unpitted.

Red dates
Although called "dates", these are in fact jujubes (olive-sized fruits native to China but also cultivated in the Mediterranean area). Usually sun-dried, they are used in Oriental and Indian cooking as flavorings for both sweet and savory dishes.

Nuts

Botanically, nuts are single-seeded, dry, hardshelled fruits that have to be cracked to open them, such as chestnuts and filberts. However, the term "nut" is also used for any seed or fruit with an edible kernel in a hard or brittle shell; for example peanuts – strictly speaking a legume – or almonds, walnuts and coconuts. Since the earliest times nuts have been used as source of food and oil. They were collected by food-gathering peoples before the birth of agriculture, were used extensively by the Greeks, and cultivated by the Romans: there is evidence that, as early as the second century BC, sugared almonds were distributed by the Romans on occasions of rejoicing like births and marriages. Nuts are also an important feature of Middle Eastern cookery. In fact, medieval Europe learned the use of nuts in cooking from the Arabs, who not only used them in sauces with meat and poultry, but in marzipan, nougat and other sweetmeats.

Spain, occupied for almost eight centuries by the Moors, also adopted the use of nuts in cooking, and took the technique to the Americas after the Conquest. They found the Aztecs already using pumpkin seeds and peanuts, and probably pecans, as thickeners for poultry and fish and shellfish sauces. Almonds are used extensively in Scandinavian cooking – it is said that whoever finds the almond in the Swedish Christmas Eve rice pudding will be the first of the group to get married – and they are also important in Indonesian, Far Eastern and African cooking. In fact, the use of nuts is universal: they are present in every aspect of cooking from hors d'oeuvres through to desserts.

Using nuts

Some nuts, such as pecans and Brazil nuts, can be shelled more easily if they are allowed to stand in boiling water for

15 to 20 minutes. To remove the thin, inner lining of shelled nuts such as almonds, pistachios and walnuts, pour boiling water over them and then follow immediately with a cold rinse. Filberts need to be put under the broiler for a few minutes before peeling. Nuts are more easily chopped if they are warm and moist.

Roasting or toasting nuts brings out their flavor and once shelled and shucked (if desired) they can be placed in a medium oven (350°F [175°C]) for 10 to 20 minutes.

Storing nuts

The length of time nuts will keep varies according to the type: unshelled nuts are protected from heat, air, light and moisture, and therefore will keep almost indefinitely anywhere; shelled nuts, on the other hand, do not keep as well, and should be stored tightly covered in a cool, dark, dry place or freezer. Both salted and unsalted nuts should be refrigerated although, of the two, unsalted nuts last longer.

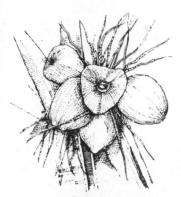

Coconuts
The fruit as it appears on the tree before it has been stripped of its outer green covering

Cashew nut
The cashew tree bears a tart, reddish pear-shaped fruit (left), from the bottom of which grows the kidney-shaped nut (right)

Water chestnut
The floating leaves of the plant are visible while the young fruit grows beneath the surface of the water. An enlarged detail of the fruit is shown right

Almond (*Prunus dulcis*) □
This is one of the most popular nuts worldwide. There are two types: **sweet** □ and **bitter** □. The latter contains prussic acid and is never eaten raw but its essence can be distilled and used as a flavoring. Sweet almonds are used whole for baking and confectionery; ground into a paste for butters, pralines, fillings, and nougat; chopped, diced and shredded for coating and garnishing; roasted; salted and sugared. Sugared almonds may be covered in sugar, syrup or honey.

Earth almonds □ (*Cyperus esculenta*) are tubers which are very starchy and are eaten raw or cooked or made into a flour.

Brazil nut (*Bertholletia excelsa*) □
A rich and nutritious food containing 66 per cent fat and 14 per cent protein. Brazil nuts are eaten raw as snacks or toasted and used in cakes.

Cashew nut
(*Anacardium occidentale*) □
The cashew grows as a single, hard protruberance beneath a fleshy apple-like fruit. While both the soft covering and the kernel are edible, there is a toxic oil in the nut's shell which must be removed by roasting before eating. Kajú, a liquor, is made from the fruit but the nuts themselves are used in baking or in cashew butter or are eaten as a cocktail nut.

Chestnut (*Castanea sativa*) □
The sweet chestnut has been grown for many centuries and used in soups, cereals, stews and stuffings. It is the only nut which is treated as a vegetable – because it contains more starch and less oil than other nuts it can be cooked differently. It can be eaten whole, either roasted, boiled, or steamed. Once shelled they are preserved whole in sugar or syrup as marrons glacés; (p. 128);

chopped and used in stuffings, or with vegetables; or ground into a flour.

There are two types of **water chestnut**: *Trapa natans* has an edible seed and a floury texture and is eaten raw, roasted or boiled in Central Europe and Asia. A related aquatic plant, **ling** (*Trapa bicornis*), is grown in China, Korea and Japan. Its seeds are eaten boiled, or preserved in honey and sugar or used for making flour.

The **Chinese water chestnut** or *pi tsi* is a tuber which is cultivated in the East Indies, China and Japan. It is used sliced as a vegetable and is usually bought canned outside Asia.

Coconut (*Cocos nucifera*) □
All parts of the fruit are used, but only the milk and meat as food. Coconut milk is a refreshing and nutritious drink, and can be used as an additive to curry sauces. Coconut meat can be eaten fresh or dried and used as desiccated coconut for baking and confectionery (p. 128). Most coconut meat, however, is dried to form *copra*, from which coconut oil is extracted. The sap of the coconut palm can be fermented to produce palm tree wines or *arrack*.

Filbert (*Corylus maxima*) and **Hazelnut** (*Corylus avellana*) □
Both are fruits of the hazelnut or cobnut bush; filberts refer to the cultivated and more robust nuts. Filberts are named after St Philbert, a French abbot whose feast day in August coincides with their ripening time. Both filberts and hazelnuts are rich in oil and are used in butters, confections and desserts.

Lychee (*Litchi chinensis*)
Although normally considered a fruit (p. 248), lychees are also commonly referred to as nuts. They are eaten fresh, canned or preserved in syrup. The "nuts" are prepared by drying the fruit,

in which case the pulp acquires a nutty, raisin-like taste.

Macadamia nut; Queensland nut (*Macadamia ternifolia*) □
It is mainly eaten as a cocktail nibble but is occasionally used in confectionery. The nuts are usually exported from Hawaii ready-roasted and salted.

Peanut (*Arachis hypogaea*) **Groundnut; Monkey nut** □
A highly nutritious underground legume, the peanut can be eaten raw or roasted and is used primarily for peanut butter and peanut oil. Peanut butter is made from ground, roasted nuts (the skin and germ are removed). Peanut oil is used for frying and salads.

Pecan nut (*Carya illinoensis*) □
This North American nut is eaten in large quantities as a dessert nut, plain or salted. Pecans are also used in the famed pecan pie, nutbreads, candies, ice creams and in vegetarian dishes.

Pine nut; Indian nut (*Pinus pinea*) □
The seed of the stone pine, these are eaten raw or roasted and salted like peanuts. In Italy they are used in sauces and soups and to make the famous pesto sauce; in the Middle East they are popular in *dolmas*.

Pistachio nut (*Pistacia vera*) □
Prized for their pleasant, mild flavor and ornamental color, pistachios are used in stuffings and sauces as well as in confectionery, baking and ice creams. They can be eaten salted as a cocktail or dessert nut and are sold with dyed bright red shells or in their natural tan ones. To preserve their brilliant color, they should be shelled and then boiled in water for a few minutes and their skins removed.

Walnut (*Juglans regia*) **English walnut; Persian walnut** □ The walnut can be used when immature or ripe, and dried or toasted. Young green nuts are pickled in vinegar; immature walnuts are an important ingredient in the Mexican national dish, *chiles en nogada* (peppers in walnut sauce); ripe walnuts are eaten as a dessert nut and are used in confectionery, baking, in salads, and in vegetarian cooking. A liqueur, brou, is made from the shucks or casings of the nuts. Walnut oil which has a pronounced flavor is used for salad dressings. **Black or American** walnuts (*Juglans nigra*) have thick, hard shells and are usually larger than European walnuts. Stronger-tasting than the latter, they are used in confectionery and ice creams. **Butternut** (*Juglans cinera*) also known as *white walnut* has a rich and pleasant flavor and is used in confectionery.

Cereals

Cereals are named after Ceres, the Roman goddess of agriculture, and comprise edible grains such as wheat, oats, corn, and foods prepared from such grains. When agriculture (generally thought to have been started by women) first began in the Middle East, Central and South America in about 7000 BC, cereals figured prominently – wheat and barley are Middle Eastern crops, corn is Mexican.

The starchy carbohydrates which are provided by cereals are essential in human nutrition. Rice is a staple food for half the world's population, the remaining half cultivating wheat, oats, corn, barley, millet and so on, depending on soil and climate. There is a wealth of starchy dishes in every cuisine in the world, including Mexico's corn *tortillas*, made from *masa harina* (literally dough flour, made from cooked corn kernels), Italy's *pasta* in its myriad forms, and Brazil's *farofas*, made from cassava (manioc) meal.

Cereals come from the cultivated grasses (*Graminaceae*) wheat, corn, rice, oats, barley and rye. In addition there are other crops that are good starch providers, including tapioca and cassava meal from the root of the cassava plant and sago from the sago palm. Fecula or "flour" products also come from the roots of such plants as the lotus, arum lily, bracken, potato – and other tubers.

From the cereal grasses we harvest the valuable grains – which are actually the fruit of the plant – and the way we use these grains depends on their individual structure and their behavior as foodstuffs.

Rice

There are about 7000 varieties of rice (*Oryza sativa*). Probably native to India and Indo-China, it comes in many forms. *Brown* rice is simply the rice plus bran, which is removed during the secondary stage of milling (or "pearling") to give us the familiar white *polished* grain. The bran in brown rice offers additional protein, plus traces of iron, calcium and vitamin B, but takes longer to cook. Not all rice varieties are white when polished: Carolina and some Italian rices are amber-colored.

Rice is divided into three groups: long, short and medium-grain. *Long-grain* rice is four to five times as long as it is wide and, when cooked, the grains are separate and fluffy. It is used in salads, curries, stews, chicken or meat dishes. *Short-* and *medium-grain* rice have short, plump grains which cook tender and moist with the grains clinging together. Each type of rice is suited to traditional cooking styles: Indian cooks prefer a dry rice, especially for pilaus; Japanese and Chinese cooks use short-grain rice which can be shaped by the fingers, and easily handled with chopsticks.

Under the general classification of long-grain rice are the American Carolina, and the delicate Basmati from Pakistan. The short-grain rices include Japan's *kome*, and the stubby round Italian rice. There is also wild rice, which, despite its name, is a water grass, not a grain. Native to North America and known to botanists as *Zizania aquatica*, it is long-grained and gray-brown in color, with a "nutty" flavor. Wild rice is used mainly for stuffing game and poultry.

Converted, *precooked* or *prefluffed* brand-name rice is a commercial product that has been parboiled then dried, and though its cooking results are more easily determined, there is some loss of flavor.

Rice in the kitchen

Rice will keep almost indefinitely, a fact only important to Western households that do not use rice as a staple food. In cooking, long-grain rice will absorb 1½ times its bulk in liquid, depending on the type of grain. Basmati, for example, will absorb less water than Patna or Carolina. To cook long-grain rice, use 1½ cups of water for each cup of rice, in a tightly covered pan over a very low heat for 20 minutes. Short-grain rice will absorb over four times its bulk in liquid, or 1 cup to about 4 or 4½ cups of liquid, according to the recipe.

Rice can be cooked separately or processed to make rice flour, flaked rice and ground rice, for use in puddings, cakes and as a thickening agent for sauces, soups and stews. As the chief ingredient in fermented drinks, rice makes some very potent Chinese spirits, and the famous Japanese *sake*.

Wheat and flour

Wheat is a cereal grass, and was probably first cultivated in Mesopotamia. There are two main varieties, bread wheat (*Triticum aestivum*) and hard wheat (*T. durum*), used for making pasta (p. 259) and semolina.

Bread wheat is the world's most important cereal crop; its unique quality is due to the high gluten content of the wheat berry. Gluten is a muscular substance of great elasticity that strengthens the cellular structure of bread. When yeast liberates carbon dioxide gas during "proving", and water releases steam during baking, the gluten helps the bread to expand – without gluten our bread would be flat and heavy.

The wheat berry, and the way it is milled, gives us our flours in different varieties and grades. The berry consists of the outer husk or bran, the endosperm, containing most of the starch to make flour, and the inner core or wheat germ embryo. When the entire grain is milled we obtain a brown flour rich in nutrients and protein. In America this flour is known as *Graham* or *whole-wheat flour*; in Britain it is wholemeal flour. The "brownness" of the flour depends on the amount of bran included, white flour being the product of the endosperm only.

Strong, hard or bread flour is milled from certain varieties of bread wheats, while all-purpose, soft, plain or cake flour has less gluten, and comes from soft types of flour. Self-raising flour contains an aerating agent incorporated in the flour.

Flour in the kitchen
Flour provides the basic structure of bread, cakes, batters, and pastry, but the structure is further dependent upon the type of flour, and the raising agent. Bread flour must be aerated by yeast, although brown flour can be leavened either with yeast or with baking soda. Bread also requires kneading to strengthen the gluten. The soft flour in cakes is raised by the dispersal of air or gas, by baking powder and/or whisked eggs. Steam is liberated in oven-cooked batters by whisked eggs, while pastry owes its textures to the plasticity of fat, and steam released by water in the dough depending on the type of pastry. Soft flours produce a softer, spongier texture – you cannot beat air into bread flour, but soft flours are easily leavened by thorough beating which introduces aerating.

GRAINS See also p. 122
Barley □
Native to Mesopotamia, where it was milled to make bread, and fermented to make beer. **Malting** barley is used in Scotland in the production of whisky, gin and beer. In countries where barley and rye crops flourish, you will find barley porridge and barley bread. It is not, however, usually used to make bread flour. The husked, polished berry is **pearl barley** □, and is added to soups.

Buckwheat □
Probably native to China, its seeds are roasted and made into a flour which is used for pancakes, crisp thin cakes, and noodles called soba in the Far East. Buckwheat groats, or kasha, are used in soups.

Corn; maize □
Native to Mexico, corn has been cultivated for thousands of years, both as a vegetable and a source of meal. The dried grains, when coarsely ground, are known as hominy, and when medium-ground become grits. Bourbon whiskey is a product of fermented corn and the grain is also used in the manufacture of corn syrup and corn oil.

Millet □
Native to Asia, millet was once the principal cereal of Europe, rivaling barley. Millet has as high a protein content as wheat, but is inferior for baking. Millet flour is used for flat breads and griddle cakes. The grains can be mixed with pulses and vegetables, and used in soups and stews.

Oats □
Native to Central Europe, oats are a Scottish staple, and are milled to varying degrees of fineness. Cooked with water, oats become porridge; **oatmeal** is an ingredient in haggis, oatcakes, and the whisky drink Athol Brose.

Rice □
Native to India and Indo-China, there are countless varieties, including **glutinous** □, **converted** □ (parboiled to remove surface starch), Italian **arborio**; **kome**, from Japan; **Basmati** □, from Pakistan; American **Carolina** □; **pudding** rice □ and **brown** rice □ (which includes the bran).

Rye □
This is an important cereal crop in Europe, where it is milled to make bread flour. In Germany, rye flour is used in the dark pumpernickel bread. Apart from their conversion to bread flour, rye grains are fermented to make rye whiskey in America. Because of the gluten deficiency, rye flour is usually mixed with wheat flour in bread recipes.

Sorghum; Kaffir corn; Egyptian rice corn; Guinea corn; African corn □
A type of millet cultivated in Africa and Asia, the seeds when ground are made into porridge, flat cakes and are used in soups. Other varieties of sorghum produce a sweet syrup.

Wheat □
Native to Mesopotamia, there are two main varieties: **bread** wheat, used mainly for bread flour, and **hard** wheat, used for making pasta and semolina.

CEREAL PRODUCTS
See also p. 124
Cornmeal; polenta □
This is the finely-milled grain; **cornstarch** is the pulverized starch extracted from the meal. As polenta is deficient in gluten, wheat flour is sometimes mixed with it, and baking powder acts as the aerating agent.

Cracked wheat; Burgul; Bulghur □
This is obtained by boiling and drying the grains, and finally grinding them. A prominent staple food throughout the Middle East, it features in the tabbouleh salad, is pounded into a paste with lamb to make the Lebanese kibbi.

Sago □
The dried, starchy granules obtained from the sago and other palm trees growing in the Far East, it is used as an invalid food, in milk puddings, and as an ingredient in some Scandinavian dishes, such as the Danish sagosuppe.

Semolina; Semola □
Particles of the endosperm from hard durum wheat, it is used in puddings and, when mixed with water and formed into minute pellets, becomes "couscous".

Tapioca □
Pellets made from manioc or cassava flour, they form the basis of nursery milk puddings, and are used also to thicken soups and stews.

Wheatgerm □ and **bran**
Bran helps to provide the roughage in a diet, and can be added to white flours, or to whole-wheat flour. Wheatgerm is rich in proteins and may be used in soups and stews as a thickening agent.

Other cereal products
Several flours can be used alone or in conjunction with wheat flour for baking or thickening. Examples are **lotus root** □ flour, **potato** flour □ and **soy** flour □.

Rice
A cultivated grass plant, a detail of the grains is shown left

Baking Goods

Some ingredients, though unobtrusive, play a vital role in baking; others are more decorative. In the first category are the raising and thickening agents – the ingredients responsible for the "inside" chemical changes in baking. In the second, are those that provide the additional touches, the colorings and the confections.

Yeast and baking powder are two examples of raising agents in breads and cakes, while gelatins and arrowroot are thickeners of aspics and sauces. Marzipan and colorings are examples of the more decorative ingredients.

Uses in the kitchen

Yeast is used to raise the strong, gluten flour of bread doughs and baking powder is used for most cakes and some breads. Fresh yeast should be grayish-brown and crumble easily. When old, the brownish shade darkens. It should be dis-solved in warm water before being combined with other ingredients. Dry yeast should be sprinkled on the water and greater heat and more moisture are needed than with fresh.

Many thickeners, such as arrowroot and cornstarch – so important in gravies and sauces – are used in baking as well, while gelatin, sold in powder and in sheets, is used to set both aspics and gelatin-based desserts. Generally, dried baking goods, such as yeast, baking powder and cornstarch, will keep indefinitely stored in tins, in a cool, dry place.

There is a wide range of confections and colorings for the pastry cook to call upon. Many of the traditional coloring dyes, such as chlorophyll and cochineal, are being replaced and augmented by synthetic colors which give a huge range of availability. There are also many commercial products available in hard and soft candy as well as candied fruits.

Pastry cutters

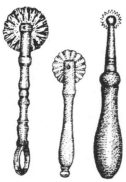

Antique dough wheels
These early examples were used to press the edges of pies and tarts

RAISING AND THICKENING AGENTS
See also p. 126

Agar-agar; Macassar gum □
A gelatinous product extracted from dried seaweed. Sold in threads or powder form, it is only partially soluble in water, unless boiled. It is used in ice cream, jellies and marshmallows.

Ammonium bicarbonate
The predecessor of modern leaveners. It renders non-fermented dough spongy.

Arrowroot □
A fine white flour from a West Indian tuber (*Maranta arundinacea*), used as a thickener for puddings.

Baking powders □
There are three kinds. **Tartrate**, a combination of cream of tartar and tartaric acid, reacts as soon as it comes into contact with liquid. **Phosphate** is slower to react but gives up the greater part of the carbon dioxide in cold dough; the remainder may be released when the mixture is baked. **Double acting** also starts to work in the cold dough but the main rising does not begin until the dough contacts heat.

Baking soda; Sodium bicarbonate □
Used on its own, it has no leavening power but combined with an acid ingredient such as sour milk it produces a reaction.

Cornstarch □
The starch extracted from corn-meal, used to thicken sauces.

Gelatin □
A setting agent sold in powder form or as leaf gelatin – a transparent sheet.

Cream of tartar □
A substance found in grape juice after fermentation; it reacts with baking soda to produce carbon dioxide to leaven batters.

Gum arabic
A product obtained from the *Acacia senegal* tree. It prevents the crystallization of sugar and is used to glaze marzipan fruits.

Gum tragacanth
A gum used in making pastillage gum paste for sugar flowers and cake decorations. From a plant found in the Middle East.

Kuzu; Kudzu □
A thickener often used in Oriental cooking; it comes from a tuberous root.

Pectin □
A substance occuring in many fruits, it is used mainly in jam- and jelly-making to set the gel.

Yeast □
A plant with active living cells which feed on sugars and produce alcohol and carbon dioxide. **Compressed** and **dried** □ are used in baking and act at different temperatures. **Fresh** □ should be used as soon as possible but will keep for 2–3 days wrapped in paper in the refrigerator. Dried will keep 6 months in a sealed tin. There is also **brewers'** yeast □ used mainly in brewing beer, and **red** yeast □, used in Oriental vinegars.

COLORINGS AND CONFECTIONS See also pp. 127, 128

Alkannet
A red or blue coloring from the root of *Anchusa tinctoria*.

Annatto
An orange dye from the seeds of the West Indian *bixa orellana*.

Candied fruits □
Cherries, angelica stalks, citrus fruit peel, or whole fruits coated in syrup and dried. Used as decorations or chopped in cakes.

Carotene
A yellow pigment linked to vitamin A, found in carrots.

Chlorophyll
Green pigment from leaves, such as spinach and nettles.

Chocolate □
Available in several forms: unsweetened or baking; sweet or semi-sweet either for eating or as a baking ingredient.

Cochineal
A pink pigment obtained from a female of an insect species, *Dactylopius coccus*, found in Mexico and Iran.

Hard candy decorations □
These are usually commercial products made of either boiled, hard sugar or royal icing.

Marrons glacés □
Best-quality chestnuts are boiled, packed in syrup then glazed.

Marshmallow □
Basically a mixture of gelatin, sugar and syrup. Originally made from the roots of the marshmallow plant which contained oils, starch and gelatinous substances.

Marzipan □
Believed to have originated in the Middle East, it is a mixture of egg white, almond paste and confectioners' sugar.

Nougat
Of European origin, nougat is made of sugar, syrup, egg whites and often includes nuts and candied cherries.

Pastillage
A gum paste used on cakes. It is prepared with icing sugar, gum tragacanth or gelatin and cornstarch. It may be colored, rolled flat, cut, pressed and molded.

Rice paper □
A very fine paper made from the pith of an Oriental tree. It is used to coat the undersides of macaroons and nougat.

Pasta

Pasta – the word simply means "dough" – is the staple diet of Italy, essential to the Italian kitchen and far more popular than its rivals, bread, polenta (corn meal) and rice. Pasta, or to give it its official title, *pasta alimentari*, falls into two main types: the factory-made flour and water paste, called *pasta secca* – "dry" pasta, as sold in packages, and the fresh paste made with flour and eggs called *pasta all'uovo*, or *pasta fatta in casa* – "home-made" pasta. (Although this latter normally *should* be home-made, there is also now a factory-made *pasta all'uovo*, which is sold in packets.)

Pasta secca begins as a springy dough of flour, salt and water which is then cut, pressed or molded into a variety of shapes, sizes and designs which include tubes, ribbons, spirals, shells, bows and wheels, to provide a versatile foundation for an equally bewildering number of sauces. Even the Italians find the study of pasta confusing, since names and shapes vary from province to province.

Pasta uses the flour milled from the hard, translucent *Triticum durum* wheat, although there is also a type which is made with buckwheat. Durum produces fine, gritty particles of amber-colored semolina flour, which is more durable than bread flour. When mixed to a dough with water this makes a nutritious paste that can be dried and kept indefinitely; you can test for good-quality pasta by running your finger along the surface – it should be silky smooth and quite pliant, rather like celluloid.

Strictly speaking, home-made *pasta all'uovo* should also be made with semolina flour, but all-purpose flour is a good substitute, and with the addition of eggs, salt, and perhaps a little water or oil to soften the dough, makes a good-quality *sfoglia*, as the rolled-out sheet of finished pasta is called.

Some pasta-makers, especially from the region of Emiglia-Romana, color their paste with spinach purée which, not unnaturally, turns the pasta green – *lasagne verdi* or *tagliatelle verdi* are such examples. There are also whole-wheat versions (see below) which result in a darker-colored product.

Pasta's origins and development
Historians will always argue over the provenance of pasta. It is probably indigenous to Italy, having been developed by the Etruscans from a Greek recipe, a dough cake cut into strips and called *laganon*, from which the word *lasagne* is ultimately derived. Yet one of the earliest words for pasta was *tri*, from the Arabic *itriyah*, "string", which, as a description of spaghetti (literally "little threads") hints at an Arabic origin.

By the fifteenth century, pasta was known as *vermicelli*, or "little worms", and in Sicily as *maccheroni*, a word of disputed origin. Today, *macaroni* is a generic term for all types of *pasta*

secca, and recipes and sauces have swollen the ranks of pasta into a confused legion of nearly 600 different shapes.

But how has pasta managed to diversify to an extent that eclipses even France's varieties of cheese? This was, in part, brought about by the days of flourishing trade at the time of Italy's Renaissance, when there was ever-increasing rivalry between such great pasta firms as Buitoni in Tuscany, Pezzullo in Salerno, and Pittalunga in Genoa, each with a specialist catalog of pasta designs.

Also, the Italians, artists in the kitchen, found that some shapes were particularly suited to certain sauces; that *spaghetti* from Naples complemented the meat *ragu* of Bologna; that delicate *fettucine* noodles went best with a cream and mushroom sauce; and that the ribbons of pasta called *trenette* were the life partner to the Ligurian *pesto* made with basil and pine nuts.

The majority of pasta shapes are, however, successfully interchangeable with the infinite variety of sauces – the spirals of pasta called *fusilli* or *archimede* are just as companionable to *vongole* clams as is the traditional *spaghettini*.

Some shapes are particularly well suited to oven cooking and to stuffing. The tubes of *cannelloni* and *rigatoni* are filled with meat, or minced vegetables, covered with a cheese-flavored béchamel sauce and finally baked *al forno*. *Lasagne*, the large sheets of pasta, are alternately layered with minced meat and béchamel, and then baked as before. Smaller shapes, such as *ravioli*, hats (*cappelletti*) or half-moons (*tortellini*) are stuffed and may be cooked *in brodo*, or water.

Reviewing the long history of this simple ingredient, pasta, one might reasonably conclude that its evolution had finally come to rest, having reached the peak of its development. Yet an entirely new type of pasta has recently been introduced. A British manufacturer has actually succeeded in selling spaghetti to the Italians, the invader being a whole-wheat type made with durum wheat milled by a special process.

In the world of pasta the manufacturer constantly looks towards improving the versatility of his product with new recipes and designs (a *pasta secca* in the shape of flying saucers – *dischi volanti* – is one such example) in the hope that today's novelty will become tomorrow's traditional dish.

Pasta in the kitchen
The basic types of pasta, dry or fresh, can be further divided into categories according to their use: *pasta asciutta* and *pasta in brodo* or *pastina*.

Briefly, the term *pasta asciutta* describes all those substantial daily dishes such as the familiar spaghetti or macaroni served with a sauce; pasta stuffed with meat, cheese or puréed vegetables, such as *ravioli* or *cannelloni* (*pasta ripieni*, meaning "stuffed"); pasta dishes baked in the oven – *al forno* – such as *lasagne*.

Pasta in brodo, the second category, is pasta in miniature; tiny shapes of pasta (*pastina*) that find their natural element in soup – *in brodo* – such as wheels (*ruote*), shells (*conchiglie*), butterflies (*farfalle*), stars (*stelle*) and a host of other motifs. Thrifty cooks sometimes employ broken scraps of *pasta secca* that have dropped to the bottom of the grocer's bin or sack, to make a rustic dish of pasta, cheese and tomatoes called *tuoni e lampo* or "thunder and lightning".

Whereas opinions might vary about which pasta goes best with which sauce, everyone is united on the topic of how pasta should be cooked. *Pasta asciutta* needs plenty of salted, boiling water, roughly 4qts (4.5 l) to each lb (0.5kg) of pasta

(and 2 tablespoons salt to every lb pasta), otherwise the pasta goes gluey since the water cannot cope with the excess starch. Some experts demand that salt be added after the pasta, otherwise a slight aroma of phenol is liberated, but the majority of cooks ignore such finesse, merely insisting that pasta should be cooked to a precise minute – give or take a second or two.

Cooking times vary according to the pasta, but the end result should be "*al dente*" – in other words, not soft but with firmness to the bite. Some people like their pasta firmer, even hard; the term for this is "*fil de ferro*" – "wire". Pasta should not be drained too thoroughly, otherwise you will find that it sticks together, especially lasagne. As a further precaution, cooks may add a teaspoon of oil to the pasta while it is still boiling to prevent sticking.

Noodles and Dumplings

The Chinese, pioneer inventors that they were, must have discovered the value of starch pastes early in history, and celebrated noodle reports followed Marco Polo's visit to China in 1270. We may assume that pasta was an independent invention: vermicelli was a staple in the Italian diet long before the thirteenth century.

Since there has been domestication of cereals for over 8000 years it can be assumed that the production of noodles is quite ancient. Familiarity with cereals would have proved that grains make flour, and flour plus water produces a pliable paste that can be cut and dried and kept.

The word "noodle" derives from the German, Bavarian and Austrian words for dumplings – *nudeln*, *knödl* and *knödel* and dumplings seem to have originated from the practice of nipping off pieces of uncooked dough or bread (*croûtons*), and dropping them into soups or stews; variations on this theme exist from Hungary across Europe to Britain.

Types of noodles
While noodles and pasta have much in common they fall into different categories. Noodles are defined as a food paste made of flour, water and eggs which may be sold and used either dried or fresh. Most Italian pasta (p. 259), when made commercially, contains no eggs and is made from durum wheat flour in a variety of traditional shapes. In many Western countries, particularly in Germany and America, noodles must include eggs, unless sold as "plain noodles". Noodles are also referred to as "vermicelli", regardless of whether they come from Italy or Hong Kong, and the main

areas of production are Central Europe, America and the Far East.

The Germans are credited with being the first to make a noodle dough with eggs, and in the familiar ribbon-shape of commercial noodles. This type of egg noodle paste is also popular with the Italians and the Chinese. Asian noodles, however, may be based on a number of different flour pastes, with or without eggs, including the flour of mung beans, soybeans, buckwheat, seaweed, corn, chick-peas, rice and durum wheat, and sold in skeins of fine threads that are typically Eastern. The Japanese have an impressive range of *menrui* (noodles) made of white wheat or golden buckwheat such as *soba*, *somen*, and *udon*. Japan shares with China a fondness for bean-gelatin or cellophane noodles, called, in Japan, *harusame*. Another popular Japanese noodle is *shirataki*, made from *konnyaku* (devil's tongue or snake palm plant), a member of the arum family.

Noodles in the kitchen
Commercially made noodles will last almost indefinitely, kept in a cool, airy place. Noodles should be cooked according to the recipe or instructions on the package. Presoaked noodles need less cooking than dried ones, and they are usually soaked to facilitate cooking in stir-fried dishes – 5 minutes is usually sufficient. *Harusame* noodles, and Chinese cellophane noodles may need presoaking for 30 minutes.

Straight from the package, *soba* noodles need about 7 minutes, *somen* 7 minutes, *udon* 20 minutes. Unlike vermicelli, they are preferred soft, and not *al dente* in the Italian style.

EGG NOODLES
See also p. 138
Chinese
These vary considerably, but typically they are ⅓in. (6mm) wide, and sold like loosely tangled balls of wool. Noodles are *mein* or *mee* in Chinese cooking, and feature in chow mein dishes, incorporated with meat and vegetables.

Chinese wok
A Chinese pan with shallow, sloping sides, used mainly for stir-frying vegetables and noodles

Commercial
These are made from about 12lb (5.5kg) fresh eggs to every

96lb (44kg) semolina flour. The dough is mixed, kneaded, rolled, laminated, cut and dried, all by machine.

European egg
These may have ultimately derived from the *spätzle* (little sparrows) of Wurttemburg, where egg dough is forced through the holes of a colander into boiling water. They accompany veal, cabbage, or are mixed with chopped meat or herbs and served as a salad.

EGG DUMPLINGS
Csipetke
These are Hungarian egg-flour dumplings. They are scraps of dough, dropped into boiling water and served with soups and goulash.

Kasnudln
From Austria, these are a variety of Uszka (below), made either with a savory filling such as cheese or meat, or with a sweet filling such as fruit and spices.

Uszka

This is a type of ravioli from Poland. It is an egg-flour dough stuffed with mushrooms and dropped into soup. *Uszka* means "little ears" and is named after the shape of the dumplings.

OTHER NOODLE TYPES

See also p. 140
These include noodles made from different flours, or dumplings without egg.

Bijon

These noodles are produced commercially in Southeast Asia from corn kernels. The kernels are steeped from 4–7 days in water to encourage the fermentation of butyric acid, then mashed and formed into "dumplings" with cornstarch. The dough is extruded into long strands, parboiled for 2 minutes, then sun-dried for about 4 hours.

Other noodle types from the same area include: **Canton** noodles made from wheat flour, duck eggs, salt and vegetable oil; **miki**, made with wheat flour, eggs, soda ash; **misua**, fine wheat noodles like the Japanese **udon sotanghon**, a version of cellophane noodles. These noodles would be served with such typical dishes as *laksa*, a fish and coconut milk soup.

Bread dumplings

Bavarian **knödl**, Austrian **knödel,** and Czech **knedliky,** are all made with stale bread or yeast dough, and may be sweet or savory. The English **Norfolk** dumpling falls into this category, being a boiled yeast dough that accompanies meat broths and stews, or is served with sugar, honey or treacle as a sweet.

Shirataki ("white waterfall")

These noodles are made from the starch of the devil's tongue plant (*Amorphopallus rivieri*), cultivated in China and Japan from the tubers, which are dried to make *konnyaku* flour. They feature in the well-known *sukiyaki* dish.

Soba

These are Japan's most popular type, made with golden buckwheat, and served in the many *soba-ya* restaurants. The noodles may be presented in *zaru* bowls, accompanied by *nori* (seaweed) and horseradish.

Somen

Thin, very fine, white wheat noodles which are often served cold as a summer dish.

Transparent noodles

Chinese and Japanese transparent noodles are made with mung bean paste or wheat flour. In Japan they are known as *harusame* ("spring rain"), and feature in *yosenabe*, a kind of chop suey of fish and vegetables in broth. In India, transparent noodles are *sevian* or "China grass" and are used to make sweet dishes.

Udon

Very narrow, ribbon-like white wheat noodles, served in hot soups, and in mixed meat and vegetable dishes.

Fish

Marine and freshwater fish were an important part of man's diet long before prehistoric societies learned to cultivate vegetables and domesticate animals. Fish provided protein and vitamins, and were easy to catch and prepare – it is even likely that a large proportion of fish and shellfish were eaten raw (a much smaller proportion is eaten raw today).

In Egypt fish was abundant and cheap – cheaper than bread. Apart from sea fishing, the Egyptians had fish ponds where the stock was fattened for the table. The fish were spit-roasted over charcoal and served with eggs on top. Fish such as carp, barbel, bleak and loach were supplied by rivers and lakes; gray mullet and tuna by the sea. Even in early history the people of the Iberian peninsula were catching anchovies, sardines and cod, salting them, and exporting their *bacalao* as far away as Asia Minor.

In Europe, pike provided both sport and feast, while in Scotland salmon was so common in the seventeenth century that a law was passed forbidding employers to give it to their servants more than three times a week. Carp – freshwater fish that often attained formidable proportions – were reared in ponds and lakes throughout Europe, the Middle East (they still feature in Jewish cooking) and in China and Japan, where they provided inspiration for poets and cooks alike.

The commercial prominence of certain species must have been firmly established by the time the fishermen learned to navigate the open seas. Nations argued over who had the rights to fish for what and where. It is certain that the most valuable fish of all time is the herring, which still supplies one-third of the world's catch – some 20 million tons. Such was the abundance of herring, that the commercial and economic history of northern Europe is founded on the bright, silvery, oily fish: it is said that Amsterdam is built upon herring bones. Today, cod, mackerel and tuna follow closely behind herring.

Fish in the kitchen

Fish are a good source of high-grade protein and most fish are low in fat. They can be cooked in a variety of ways, including frying, sautéeing, baking, broiling or grilling, steaming and poaching. Salmon, the king of fish, is enjoyed fresh poached, marinated as gravad lax, cold in aspic and in pastry as *kulebiaka*.

Dover sole is chosen as the basis for a remarkable number of classic, French dishes, such as *filets de soles Joinville*, and Escoffier's *timbale*, but is perhaps best when simply broiled, or prepared *à la meunière*. Turbot should be poached or steamed, and served with an appropriate sauce, while the drier halibut may be braised, broiled and served with melted butter, or baked in the oven, or poached in white wine, as *à la dieppoise*, garnished with shrimp and mussels. Brill can be treated the same way. Other flatfish, such as dab, lemon sole and flounder, plaice and megrim, should be eaten as fresh as possible, either broiled, or served *à la meunière*.

Choosing fish

Fresh fish has bulging eyes, firmly adhering scales and firm flesh; it should never have an offensive odor. Some fish are skinned before sale – the dogfish, for example; others are skinned and decapitated – the anglerfish, for example. Fish should be cooked as soon as possible as they decompose very quickly. They can be kept refrigerated for no more than a day and should be frozen if they are not to be cooked within that time.

Types of fish

There are more than 20,000 species of fish in the seas of the world, yet we exploit a mere fraction of this huge, potential harvest. Admittedly, at least 50 per cent are commercially unacceptable – the tiny, rainbow-hued coral fish, and species that favor the deep waters – but of the remainder only about a dozen different fish regularly appear in European markets. The Portuguese and Japanese are exceptions. In the Tokyo market over sixty species are sold each day, and Japanese fishing boats scour the oceans to bring home the national daily average – about 7000 tons of fish, most of which will be eaten raw, as *sashimi*.

Elsewhere in the world tastes are more conservative. The bulk of the European catch consists mainly of cod, hake, herring, mackerel, pilchard and anchovy, if only because they are so abundant; about a dozen species, out of a possible 160 types of fish inhabiting the Mediterranean and Atlantic, are regularly in demand. Americans are fortunate in having a large number of saltwater fish available year round. They include salmon, flounder, cod, halibut, trout, perch and bass.

It is not possible within the scope of this book to give a detailed list of the many fish eaten but a selection of the most prominent ones are described below. For a fully comprehensive list of fishes and their uses, readers are advised to refer to the *Multilingual Dictionary of Fish and Fish Products* (United Nations).

FRESHWATER FISH
See also pp. 142–5

Carp ☐
Carp originate in China, where they are steamed or baked, often with a sweet and sour sauce; in Europe they can be stuffed and jellied. Other members of the carp family include **roach, dace, chub, tench, gudgeon, barbel** and **bream**, all with a somewhat muddy flavor except for the gudgeon and carp itself.

A fish kettle

Catfish
Most varieties are freshwater and include **blue, channel, yellow** or *goujon*, **spotted** or *fiddle*, **bullhead** or *horned pout*. There are a few species of sea catfish: **wolf fish** and the **spotted catfish**. These are caught in northern coastal waters of Europe, also off Newfoundland. Catfish is usually sold as fillets, which can be baked or fried.

Eel ☐
Spawned in the Sargasso Sea, it travels to fresh water to mature. It is skinned before cooking.

Grayling
A beautiful, silvery fish with a thyme-like scent, hence its Latin name *Thymallus*. It is also an excellent table fish, best prepared *au bleu*, or stuffed with herbs, and baked. It is caught in the northern hemisphere.

Pike ☐
Caught in the fresh waters of Europe, pike are traditionally stuffed and baked with oysters, anchovies, butter and herbs.

Salmon ☐
A fish that is usually caught in fresh waters of North America and northern Europe, but also spends a large part of its life in the sea. There are many varieties including the **humpback**, also known as the *pink salmon*; **chum, chinook, coho,** and **sockeye**. There are many fine recipes for this fish, such as the Russian *kulebiaka*, a salmon pie. It can be broiled, or poached in *court-bouillon*, and served, hot or cold, with an appropriate sauce. Salmon is also sweet-cured, smoked, and canned.

Salmon trout ☐
Also called *sea trout*, it bears characteristics of both fish – it is larger than other trout, has the pinkish flesh of salmon, and is prepared in the same way as salmon.

Trout ☐
There are many sub-species; the most familiar are **brown** trout, **rainbow** or *steelhead* trout, **cutthroat, brook, lake** trout and the **arctic char**. All these fish can be prepared *au bleu, à la meunière, en papillote*, baked, broiled, and potted. Many forms are also smoked.

Whitefish
These are herring-like freshwater fish found in lakes throughout the northern hemisphere. Other species and sub-species include the **houting, powan, vendace, northern white**. They can be successfully substituted for trout.

SEAWATER FISH
See also pp. 146–55

Argentine
There are several varieties, the **lesser** argentine or *silver smelt*; the **larger** argentine or *great silver smelt*; the **eastern, deep** sea argentine of Japan.
Argentines are often wrongly called "smelt", and "smelt" is also the name sometimes given to the **atherine**, which looks more like the lesser argentine (in fact, smelt is from a different family). All these small, silvery fish, however, may be broiled, grilled or fried. The fish are aptly named (*argentum*, the Latin for silver) since a product from the scales, guanine, is used to make artificial mother-of-pearl. It is found in the North Atlantic and Mediterranean.

Blue fish
Caught on the Atlantic coast of America, and in the Mediterranean. It can be broiled, fried, or baked with tomatoes, onions and herbs.

Bonito
Caught in Atlantic, Pacific and Mediterranean waters, bonito are of the family of tuna fish, and are generally marketed cut into steaks. They are also salted.

Brill ☐
Caught in the North Sea, Mediterranean, and Black Sea it is cooked in the same way as sole.

Cod ☐
Cod can grow to considerable size and weigh up to 80lb (35kg), but the flesh of codlings (scrod) is firmer and sweeter. There are several varieties, including the **Pacific, Greenland** and **polar** cod. Cod can be stuffed, baked, steamed, and fried.

Coley; Saithe; Pollock ☐
This is a close relative of the pollack and is usually salted in Scandinavia; in Germany, where it is known as *seelachs*, it is

Perch

Shad

smoked, and canned in oil. It is caught off the coasts of Newfoundland and Europe.

Conger eel
Although it can be stuffed and baked it is best used for soups and stews. It is caught off the Atlantic coast of Europe, Africa, and the Mediterranean.

Croaker and Meagre
The croaker is found in the Eastern waters of America, the meagre in Atlantic and Mediterranean waters. They can both be cooked as for bass.

Dab □ and Sand dab
A small flatfish, the dab is caught in North Atlantic waters off the coast of Europe. The American sand dab is of finer quality. Sold whole or in fillets, they can be broiled or fried.

Dolphin fish; Lampuga; Dorado
A large golden fish, caught in warm waters, it is usually bought as fillets or steaks, which can be broiled, baked, or fried.

Flounder □
Similar to plaice, it is caught in European Atlantic waters, and there are sub-species in the Mediterranean. It can be fried or steamed.

Garfish; Garpike; Sea eel
Its slightly oily flesh is sometimes compared to that of the mackerel. It can be fried, broiled or grilled.

Gray mullet; Striped mullet; Black mullet □
A firm-fleshed, well-flavored fish, it can be stuffed and baked, broiled and fried.

Greater and lesser weaver
Caught around the shallow coastal waters of Europe, the spines and venom sacs have to be removed before cooking. They are used in *bouillabaisse*: broiled and deep-fried.

Grouper
A common Mediterranean fish, especially along the North African coast. The steaks are grilled, broiled or baked.

Gulf hake; Forkbeard
There are two, the lesser or *tadpole* fish and the greater

Anchovy

forkbeard. The lesser is black-skinned, the greater resembles a small pollack. It is cooked in the same ways as hake.

Gurnard; Sea robin
Armor-plated, spiny fish, including the **red** gurnard, and the **ray** gurnard. There are also several Mediterranean species. Gurnards can be baked or braised.

Haddock □
Haddock is widely used for smoking (p. 267), and is also filleted and deep-frozen. It is caught in the North Atlantic off Newfoundland, and Europe.

Hake □
Suitable for baking, steaming or poaching, hake is also salted and dried.

Halibut □
The largest of the flatfish, varieties include the **Greenland** halibut, and sub-species. Halibut are caught from Newfoundland to Norway, also the Barents Sea.

Herring □
A small 7–16in. (18–40cm) oily fish, whose flesh and roes are valued for food. Herring can be canned, smoked (p. 267) and pickled. Caught mainly in the North Atlantic, they are usually stuffed and baked, broiled, or fried, casseroled, marinated, and made into salads. There are several herring-like fish, such as **sea** herring, in the Pacific. There is even a freshwater variety.

John Dory
It is suited to recipes for turbot or sole and is caught along the coasts of Europe and Africa, there are related species elsewhere.

Ling □ and Tusk
These are closely related to the hake. Cooking applies as for hake. There are many varieties of both.

Mackerel □
Scomber is the true mackerel caught in the Atlantic and Mediterranean, although there are several related species. These include the **chub** or *Spanish mackerel* and the **scad** or *horse mackerel*. There are also the **amberjack, Jack** mackerel and

pompano of American and Southeast Asian waters. Mackerel should be broiled. They are also cooked with white wine.

Monkfish; Anglerfish □
A large-headed, ugly fish, for which reason it is decapitated before sale. Caught on Atlantic coasts of Europe and in the Mediterranean. It can be poached, steamed or fried.

Needlefish; Skipper; Saury
It closely resembles the garfish, but is plumper. It can be fried, broiled or grilled.

Ocean perch
Other related species are the **Norway haddock**; and the **blue mouth**. They are caught in the Atlantic, and the Mediterranean, though there is also a freshwater European variety. They are rather coarse, and best used in soups and chowders.

Opah; Kingfish; Sunfish; Moonfish
A large, beautifully colored fish, with a plump, oval body. It can be fried and, in Japan, is eaten raw. It is available worldwide.

Plaice □
It is caught off Spanish and Portuguese coasts. Smaller fish can be broiled or grilled whole; fillets can be fried.

Pollack □
It can be baked and fried, but is best for soups and stews. In America the **Alaska** or *walleye pollack*, is salted, dried or pickled.

Pompano
Caught in Atlantic and Caribbean waters, and in the Gulf of Florida. Pompano fillets are baked, broiled and cooked *en papillote*.

Red mullet □
It is also known as the *sea woodcock*, since, like the game bird, it is cooked and eaten ungutted. It should be fried, broiled or baked.

Red snapper □
Found in the Gulf of Mexico, small fish can be baked whole while larger ones provide fillets and steaks.

Rockling

There are several types – the **three- four-**, and **five-bearded** rocklings, so-called for the barbels around the mouth. Found among the coasts of Europe and off Newfoundland. Cook as for whiting.

Sardine □ and Pilchard

Called "sardine" when young, "pilchard" when mature. They are sold fresh, smoked, and canned in oil or tomato sauce. When fresh they are broiled.

Sea bass; Striped bass □

Caught in the North Atlantic and Mediterranean but freshwater bass such as the **largemouth**, **smallmouth**, **rock**, **white** or *silver* and **yellow** bass are also available. They are broiled or grilled; stuffed with herbs, and baked.

Sea bream □

A family of over 200 species, including the **scup** and **porgy** (American varieties) and the **red**, **black**, **gilt-head** or *daurade*, and **Pandora** bream (European varieties) and the **Japanese** bream. Best broiled or baked, in the Mediterranean it is often served on a bed of dried fennel stalks.

Shad

There are several varieties, the **allis** shad or *rock herring*; the **twaite** shad; the **American** shad. Shad are a larger, plumper type of herring, mostly caught in rivers, where they come from the sea to spawn. Shad can be treated like herring. They are also smoked, or canned in brine or oil. Found in the Atlantic, Mediterranean and Pacific.

Skate □

Only the "wings" are used as food. A classic French recipe serves skate with capers and black butter sauce. Skate are caught in the North Atlantic and Arctic.

Smelt □

It is found in the Baltic and around Britain; another type is caught in the Gulf of St Lawrence. Smelts are usually fried.

Sole □

Dover □ sole is caught from southern Norway to the coast of North Africa, and in the Mediterranean. Another variety, **lemon** □ sole, is caught off the coasts of Europe. Both are sold whole or in fillets, and can be poached, fried or broiled.

Sprat; Brisling □

These are oily like the herring, and should be broiled, grilled or fried. Caught along the coasts of Europe they are also available smoked or canned.

Sturgeon

The fish is famous for its roe, made into caviar (p. 267), but less known for its flesh, which is also of good quality. Caught in the Caspian, Black Sea and Danube.

Swordfish

Caught in warmer seas it is usually sold as steaks, occasionally smoked. May be baked with tomatoes or broiled.

Tilefish

A large, deep-water fish which can weigh up to 30lb (13.5kg). It is best cooked like cod.

Tuna; Tunny; Bluefin tuna; Albacore; Longfin

Familiar to most people as canned tuna, but also sold fresh, when it can be broiled, baked, or braised with wine, tomatoes and herbs. Tuna also features in *salade Niçoise*.

Turbot □

A flatfish caught on the Atlantic coast of Europe, the Mediterranean and the Black Sea, it can be poached.

Whitebait □

These are the fry (young) of the sprat and herring. They are usually eaten whole, and deep-fried. Also sold deep-frozen.

Whiting; Silver hake □

There are two other varieties of whiting, the **Norway trout** and the **blue whiting** fished in the North Atlantic and Mediterranean.

Tuna

Swordfish

Seafood

Julius **Caesar** is the first emperor recorded to have served a variety of seafood at a state dinner, but the oyster and mussel shells found in prehistoric dwellings throughout the world are enduring evidence that seafood has been a prime source of food since earliest times.

Seafood consists largely of "shellfish" – the term includes edible freshwater and marine animals without backbones, the crustaceans and molluscs. Crustaceans, such as lobsters and crabs, have a hard jointed exoskeleton or "crust" which they periodically shed and replace as they grow. Molluscs inhabit shells that are either hinged, like oysters and clams, or single, like the abalone, whelk, and winkle. In zoological terms, hinged-shelled molluscs are bivalves or *lamellibranchiata*; single-shelled molluscs are univalves or *gastropods*.

For culinary purposes, other molluscs – such as land snails and the shell-less marine animals squid, cuttlefish and octopus – as well as edible frogs, turtles and terrapins are traditionally considered as seafood.

The shells of some crustaceans are renowned for a dramatic color change when cooked. This is because they contain red and yellow pigments called *carotenoids*, bound to molecules of protein, that create the familiar blue-gray color in lobsters, some crabs and shrimps. When these creatures are boiled, they turn orangey-red or pink because heat breaks the pigment-protein link and the carotenoids are no longer obscured.

Shellfish are prized for their tender, fine-textured flesh which can be prepared simply in a variety of decorative and delicious ways, but they are notorious for rapid spoilage. The reason for this seems to be that shellfish contain quantities of certain proteins, amino acids, which encourage bacterial growth. Eating shellfish from polluted waters can also have unpleasant consequences. It is essential that they be extremely fresh or, if frozen, be consumed immediately on thawing, and come from unpolluted waters.

Fresh shellfish are available all year round, but their availability reflects seasonal and regional demands which for most shellfish reach a peak during the salad days of summer. For instance, crabs shed their shells many times before reaching maturity and in some places, from mid-spring to mid-autumn, they are in demand as young "peelers" or "soft-shells". As they have just emerged from their latest shell, they are smaller, more flavorful and so tender that almost every part of the crab (except the "face", thin upper shell, and inner spongy material) can be eaten. Oysters, on the other hand, are traditionally eaten during cold weather when they are fatter and have more taste.

Choosing seafood

To ensure freshness and best flavor, it is preferable to choose live specimens and cook them yourself. This is often possible as there is a brisk trade in live seafood air-freighted to world markets. Freshwater crawfish, lobsters, rock lobsters, and crabs should be very active and a rock lobster or lobster's tail should curl up under its body when picked up. Fresh shrimps and prawns, usually only available in fish markets near the sea, should be crisp and dry; stale ones are limp and dry.

Live mussel, clam, and oyster shells should be tightly closed. Any open ones which do not clamp shut when tapped sharply are stale or dead and should be discarded. Scallops, however, may be alive when their shells are open – touch the inner membrane and it will move. Like snails, whelks and other gastropods will recede into their shell when touched.

Once cooked, mussel, clam and oyster shells should open. If any do not, discard them. Some people, however, think that bivalves, especially oysters, are best eaten raw when the shells have just been opened by hand (and the aid of a sharp oyster knife). It's often possible to buy them like this on the half-shell or to buy them shucked, in containers, with shells to eat them on, but they should be eaten promptly.

Crustaceans are often sold cooked and they should smell fresh and pleasant. Shrimps, especially, are usually boiled on board ship or on reaching port as a precaution against spoilage. A freshly boiled lobster or rock lobster should have a dry, bright shell with no cracks or holes in it and the tail will be tight and springy if the animal was alive when it was cooked. A stale bodied lobster or rock lobster has a limp tail and legs which smell unpleasant. The same generally applies to crabs, which may also have a bleached appearance. Select a cooked lobster, rock lobster, or crab, that is heavy for its size as it means it will have grown into its latest shell.

When molluscs are not sold fresh, they are usually pickled in vinegar or brine, or canned. When pickled, they are usually eaten raw with beer or other beverages, but if used in salads or similar preparations they should be rinsed first with cold water. Canned molluscs and crustaceans are already cooked and should be added to dishes which need little or no cooking. Commercially frozen crustaceans may require cooking.

Preparing shellfish

A lobster or rock lobster should be prepared for broiling or grilling by being laid on its back and having a heavy, sharp knife inserted between the body and tail shell to sever the spinal column and kill the animal. The shell is split lengthways and the inedible bits removed. Lobster claws should be cracked. Lobster and rock lobster should be placed meat side up under the grill (about 4in [10cm] away from heat), cooked for 10 to 12 minutes, and basted frequently with melted butter. Crabs should be put into warm water, around 70°F

(21°C) for 30 minutes before boiling – a crab dropped straight into boiling water will shed its claws – covered tightly, brought to a boil and simmered 8 minutes per pound (450g) and left to cool in the water.

Raw or cooked shrimps, jumbo shrimps, and freshwater crawfish, are prepared by having the head, upper shell (carapace), legs, tail section and dark intestinal vein running down the back removed. If raw, they are added to boiling water, steamed for 3 to 4 minutes or dipped in butter and deep-fried for 2 to 3 minutes or until golden. Every part of a lobster, rock lobster, and crab can be eaten except the grayish gill, aptly named "dead men's fingers", the hard stomach behind the eyes and, in the lobster, the black intestinal vein running through the body. The lobster's tan-colored liver or "tomally" (which turns green on cooking) can be left in the animal or removed and added to sauces.

The male lobster and rock lobster are slightly larger and have more meat than the female, but a female sometimes contains the coral or eggs, sometimes called "berry", which is not only delicious to eat when cooked in the animal but can also be used as a garnish for other dishes as it turns red when cooked. Female crabs similarly have smaller claws than males and may contain brown eggs, also called berry.

All molluscs should be washed well and be left in several changes of fresh water (clams overnight) to help rid them of saltiness and sand before cooking. Scallops should have the membrane or mantle around the white meat discarded, but both the meat and red roe can be eaten. Oysters and scallops are shucked before cooking – oysters only need heating through, about 1 minute; scallops are boiled, steamed or sautéed 1 to 2 minutes depending on size. Mussels should have the "beards" – the threads they use to anchor themselves to rocks – removed and may also need thorough scrubbing. Mussels and other molluscs are usually steamed or boiled in their shells for 1 to 2 minutes depending on size.

Freezing shellfish

Shellfish may be frozen if freshly caught, but they must be absolutely fresh and be kept frozen only up to one month. Scrub and remove molluscs from their shells, wash in salted cold water, drain, pack in rigid containers with the strained juices (leaving room for expansion), cover, label and seal. Once thawed, they are best used in soups and sauces, added towards the end of cooking. Shrimps, jumbo shrimps, and freshwater crawfish may be frozen with their heads removed, either raw or lightly boiled and cooled, sealed in plastic bags, and labeled. Lobster and rock lobster should be cooked, cooled and frozen the same day they are caught. Crabs should be cooked and cooled, and the meat removed from the shell and packed in containers.

Preparing squid, cuttlefish and octopus

Fresh squid (calamari) and cuttlefish are prepared by having their tentacles and head pulled from the tail, or body, section. Any intact ink sac is removed from the head (only in very fresh animals) and may be reserved for use in cooking. The tentacles, head and inner organs are discarded. The thin cuttlebone is pulled from the tail section, the bone discarded and then the animal washed and rubbed under cool running water so that its reddish-violet membrane is removed.

Once prepared, squid whose tail sections are less than 3in. (7.5cm) long can be poached, grilled, or sliced into rounds, leaving the tentacles in one piece, battered, and fried quickly in oil. Larger squid and cuttlefish are usually sliced and stewed as they need longer, slower cooking to become tender, but they, like octopus, can also be stuffed with a mixture of chopped tentacles, beaten eggs and herbs and braised with wine.

Octopus is prepared by having its beak-like mouth and anal portion cut away. The ink sac can be reserved, if desired. The body is turned inside out and the internal organs, suckers and tips of the tentacles are removed. After cleaning, unless the octopus is young (under 2lb [900g]), the flesh should be softened by pounding and stewed for 2½ to 3 hours or until it can be easily pierced with a knife. Towards the end of cooking, the ink can be mixed with a little flour and used to thicken, color, and flavor the stew.

Preparing snails
Snails are widely available already prepared and frozen or, more usually, canned, but they can be prepared at home using either the common garden snail (*Helix aspersia*) or the more succulent variety used in France (*H. pomatia*). Before the

creatures can be prepared, however, they must be starved for two days then fed on lettuce for two weeks to purge them of any poisons they might have ingested. Their shells are then scrubbed and rinsed in several changes of water mixed with vinegar and salt. Snails whose heads do not come out should be discarded; the remainder should be dropped in *boiling* water and cooked for 5 minutes. Once drained and cooled, the snails are removed from their shells, their intestinal sacs pulled away and discarded and the snails simmered in a *court bouillon*, until tender. The shells are boiled briefly in water and bicarbonate of soda, drained, scrubbed, and rinsed.

Frogs' legs
Farms have been established in many countries to provide this delicacy. Skinned and immersed in several changes of water to make the flesh swell and become whiter the legs are prepared for speciality shops or for commercial canning and freezing. Their delicate taste and texture go well with a variety of flavors and are often served with garlic butter.

Lobster fishing
Lobstermen transfer their catch to salt-water-filled pots for storage

Cockling
To gather the edible shellfish digging is carried out along the shore line

CRUSTACEANS
See also pp. 156–61
Crabs
Many species of this crustacean are found in American and European coastal waters. Atlantic coast favorites are the **blue** □, **Jonah**, **rock** and **stone** crabs, while the **Dungeness** and **king** crabs are renowned on the Pacific coast, especially towards Alaska. Popular European varieties are the **blue**, **edible** □ or *common* crab, the **shore** or *green* crab, and the **spider** □ crab. Sold canned and frozen, when fresh, crabs can have hard or soft shells.

Dublin Bay Prawn □
Known as "Norway lobster" in Atlantic countries, these small crustaceans with claws were often found in the nets of fishing boats looking for other catch and were sold locally in Dublin markets. Today, they are scarce and much prized and the early name has stuck; the Italians who fish them from the Adriatic call them *scampi*. Their tails, prepared like shrimps, are usually frozen and available only in good restaurants served in rice dishes or salads, deep-fried or broiled. In most recipes, however, jumbo shrimps or anglerfish can be substituted.

Freshwater crayfish □
Small freshwater crustaceans with claws, they are found in lakes and lowland streams and are prepared and cooked like jumbo shrimps and shrimps. They are the basic ingredient in French *bisque d'écrevisse*.

Lobsters
Largest of the crustaceans, lobsters are prized for their flavor and generous meat yield. Found in Atlantic coast waters from Nova Scotia to North Carolina, and Scandinavia to the Mediterranean, their flesh is finer-textured than rock lobster and at its best when the animal weighs 1–2lb (450–900g).

Rock lobsters; Langouste □
This crustacean is clawless but nearly lobster size. Found in warm coastal waters of the Atlantic, Mediterranean, Pacific, and Caribbean, it is prepared and cooked like lobster. It is usually available frozen.

Shrimps and Prawns □
The terms for these small clawless crustaceans vary from country to country, but in Europe "prawn" usually refers to those over 2–3in. (5–7.5cm), while in America "shrimp" is generally used for all sizes. When raw their shells are grayish, turning pink or brown on boiling.

MOLLUSCS
See also pp. 162–5
Abalone
Also called *St Peter's ear*, because of the shape of its shell, abalone has very firm flesh that needs softening before cooking. It is usually tenderized and canned for use in soups and Oriental dishes, but fresh abalone is sometimes available. When fresh, it is tenderized, cut into thin steaks, and eaten raw or sautéed a mere 45–55 seconds as it is easily overcooked.

Clams □
Found the world over in the wet sand of freshwater streams and sea coasts, clams are often cultivated alongside oysters. There are two main types: *soft shelled*, which includes round and long "razor" clams; and *hard-shelled* round ones. Both types can be eaten raw or cooked, but round clams are usually preferred raw as meat in the "neck" of long-shelled clams tends to be tough. The native American **Quahog** clam is sold under various names which can be used to differentiate sizes – **littlenecks** □ are the smallest followed by **cherrystones** □, **mediums** and finally, **chowders** □. Clams are also sold smoked and canned.

Cockles □
About 1in. (2.5cm) long, cockles are round marine molluscs mostly consumed in Britain. In America, along the northwest coast, they are often used in chowders but generally referred to as "clams". Unless by the sea, cockles are sold ready-cooked, shelled and packed in ice, or canned. They are good in salads, soups, and can be used in pasta dishes.

Limpets
Marine molluscs with a single tent-like shell, limpets cling to rocks around the world at low tide. Usually 1–2in. (2.5–5cm) long, they can be eaten raw, or used in soups, and oyster dishes.

Mussels □
Closely related to the clam, mussels are found the world

Conch
A pink-shelled, warm water mollusc eaten mostly in Florida and the Caribbean islands. It has a similar flavor and texture to scallops. Usually marinated and tenderized before cooking, it is used in salads and chowders

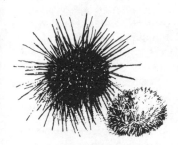

Sea urchins
The white variety on the right, also known as sea egg, is considered a great delicacy. Shown left is the black sea urchin

over on sea shores and estuaries. Varieties are usually specific to a certain area, but the **blue** mussel (*Mytilus edulis*) is found along the Atlantic coasts of both America and Europe where it is also bred commercially. Mussels are generally sold fresh in their shells and eaten raw, steamed in the famous dish *moules marinière*, or used in salads, soups and pâtés.

Oysters □
Native to the coasts of Europe and America, since Roman times the best and largest number of these molluscs have come from cultivated beds. Varieties of oysters vary in texture, size and flavor. Among the best known are the **Olympias** from the West Coast and the **Bluepoints** from east coast America, **Galway Bays** of Ireland; the **Whitstables** and **Colchesters** of Great Britain; the **Marennes**, **Belons** and the large **Portuguese** □ from France. Usually not sold in summer when spawning makes them thin and less succulent, most are at their best enjoyed raw, though the delicious large Portuguese and Bluepoints are less tender and usually cooked.

Scallops □
Named for the fluted shape of their shells, scallops are commonly found along the European and American Atlantic coasts. There are many species but two basic types: the delicately flavored *small bay* scallops and the larger *deep sea* scallops. Scallops can be broiled, floured and deep-fried, or poached and served in the shell with cream sauce.

Whelks and Winkles (Periwinkles) □
Both these small molluscs are plentiful along the marine coasts of America and Europe. Whelks are spiral-shelled, up to 3in. (7.5cm) long, and larger than winkles, which have round shells. Both are usually sold boiled and shelled to eat cold with lemon juice and bread.

Snails □
Edible snails are gastropod molluscs, gourmet fare since ancient Greece. Widely available canned or frozen, they are sometimes sold fresh. Allow 6–8 per person.

Squid, Cuttlefish and Octopus □
These cephalopods (meaning "head-footed" and denoting the way their limbs sprout from their heads) feature in the cuisines of many countries, especially in salads and stews. All are sold fresh, also canned, smoked and dried.

OTHER SEAFOOD
See also p. 162
Frogs' legs □
Only the hind legs of certain frogs (usually *Rana esculenta*) are used. The tender white meat is usually battered and deep-fried, or sautéed and served with sauce.

Sea urchins
Not a mollusc but an echinoderm, sea urchins are found off the coasts of America and Europe attached to coral. Salty-tasting, they have a texture like raw egg and a hard, spiny shell that must be cut open. They can be eaten raw or used to flavor omelets and sauces.

Turtles
The green sea turtle caught off Caribbean, Mediterranean, and Red Sea coasts is commercially considered as "shellfish". Most of the fatty meat is sliced into steaks and frozen or canned to use in soups.

Preserved Fish

The process of curing foods, and thus preserving them by methods of drying, smoking and salting, was a discovery of major importance and was, no doubt, due to the application of natural phenomena – fish trapped in coastal salt deposits would have been preserved. Today, several methods are used for preserving fish.

Unsalted fish are cleaned, headed and gutted, tied in pairs, and dried for about six weeks in a current of air. *Heavy salt-cured* fish are headed and gutted and their backbones removed. The split fish are piled in layers with a mixture of coarse and fine salt between each layer, about 30 lb (13.5kg) salt to every 100lb (45kg) of fish. The fish are then hung in a current of air, or machine-dried. *Light-cured* fish are headed, gutted, washed and split, and about one-third of the fish is salted with dry salt, using 8- (3.5kg) to 10lb (4.5kg) salt to every 100lb (45kg) fish. The fish are laid in tubs until the juices dissolve the salt and form brine, in which the fish remain from two to three days. They are then sun- or machine-dried.

Pickled-cured fish are cleaned, eviscerated, packed with plenty of salt into wooden barrels and left for ten days, when shrinkage takes place. The juices and salt form a brownish liquor called "blood pickle" which is drawn off, and then poured back to top up the barrel, the lid sealed and the barrel of fish stored.

Anchovies are cleaned, dry-salted, pressed to remove fat, and sprayed with their own brine liquor for several months at room temperature. Sardines are headed and gutted, then immersed in brine for about 15 minutes before being tunnel-dried.

There are two main types of smoke cure: *cold-smoking*, below 85°F (30°C); *hot-smoking*, at 250°F (120°C), which also cooks the fish. Smoke is generated in kilns by sawdust, which is regularly recharged to give uniformity to the product. Fish are given a preliminary brine bath before smoking.

Fish roes
The ova or eggs of the female fish are called "roe", and of the male fish "milt". Best roes come from the sturgeon and the salmon. Other roes include those of the carp, cod, pike-perch, gray mullet and herring. The roe of the sturgeon, caviar, is the most highly prized and expensive.

Preserved fish in the kitchen
Dried fish, such as stockfish and salt cod, require a prelimnary soaking in water for a day, to soften the fish and remove some of the salt. As *bacalao*, salt cod is transformed into such dishes as the French *brandade de morue*. In Spain and Portugal it is braised, stewed, fried, and eaten raw in salads. Smoked fish may be pounded to make a savory paste or butter, used in

pátés, or in soufflés. Smoked fish have limited keeping properties that vary according to type. As a general guide, smoked fish will keep for up to five days at normal temperatures and up to fourteen days at below normal temperatures.

Pickled and canned fish once opened should be refrigerated if not consumed at once. Anchovies are used in salads, sauces, in anchovy butter and paste. In Scandinavia, pickled fish are commonly used in everyday cooking and in the *smorgasbord*.

Smoking fish

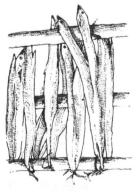

Bombay duck
The fish is shown being sun-dried on bamboo racks; it can be curried, fried or pickled

PRESERVED FISH
See also pp. 167–72

Anchovy □
A tiny, very fatty fish with a powerful flavor, it is cured by having most of its fat content removed by pressure and fermentation. Canned anchovies are usually packed in oil.

Arbroath smokies □
Haddocks or whiting weighing about ½lb (225g) are headed and gutted but not split, and tied in pairs. The fish are brined.

Bismarck herring
German herrings from the Baltic which are simply filleted and marinated in vinegar with onion rings, for 2–3 days.

Bloaters
First developed at Yarmouth, England, in 1835, bloaters, which are prepared whole, are said to owe their special flavor to the activity of gut enzymes. The fish are dry-salted for about 12 hours, washed to remove surplus salt, threaded on metal "speats", and stacked in the kiln to smoke.

Block fillets; Golden cutlets
Haddock or whiting split and gutted, with the head and backbone removed, leaving 2 joined fillets. They are brined, then dyed to make them a bright yellow. They are then smoked.

Bombay duck; "Bombil" □
A well-known Indian condiment made from dried bummaloe. Once dried, Bombay duck loses its fishy taste and adopts instead a curious flavor, rather like burnt oil or fat. It is used as a condiment with curries.

Buckling
Hot-smoked herring, originally from Schleswig-Holstein in Germany. In Britain they are headed and gutted, but with the roe left intact. Buckling are brined and smoked.

Finnan haddie; Findon haddock □
The fish are headed, gutted and split down the backbone. They are then immersed in brine.

Dyes are not added. The haddocks are then threaded on spears, the protein gloss allowed to develop, and they are smoked.

Glasgow pales
So-called because they are lightly smoked and undyed. They are first split and gutted, then brined and smoked.

Katsuoboshi
A Japanese dried fish which can also be smoked.

Lutefisk
The reconstituted unsalted cod from Norway known as *stockfish* or *stockfisk*. It is usually prepared in the early spring. In Sweden there is a smaller version made with dried ling.

Kippers □
These are made from good-quality fresh herring. The fish are split and gutted by machine, soaked in brine, and dyes are added to the solution. The fish are hung on tenter hooks or sticks for 1 hour and then smoked.

Matjes herrings □
These are young Netherlands herring caught in the spring, before they become too fatty. They are lightly salted and barrel-stored for a few days only, just sufficient to ferment the gut enzymes.

Migaki-nishin
Japanese dried fish fillets and abalone.

Oysters
They are steamed, brined, dipped in oil, then hot-smoked before being packed in oil, in sterilized jars.

Pedah
A partly dried fish with a fine red color, that owes its unique taste to methyl ketones. It is produced in Thailand.

Red herring
Named for the color their skins turn after smoking. Whole fish, dry-salted or heavily brined, and smoked intermittently.

Rollmops □
Herring fillets, rolled and served with wooden skewers, and packed in spiced brine.

Sardine □
The scales are left on the fish, which must be thoroughly gutted before processing. They are cooked either by frying in peanut oil or steam cooking.

Smoked eels □
Eels are gutted, headed and brined then dry-salted. They are then washed, dipped in boiling water, and hung up to smoke.

Smoked salmon □
The fish are headed, gutted and filleted, and string is passed through the lug bones to facilitate hanging. The skin is scored with a sharp knife, and the fillets dry-salted with fine salt according to size. Some curers use traditional mixtures such as brown sugar, saltpeter and rum. The salmon is washed in cold water before being hung to dry for a day then smoked.

Smoked sprats □
The most famous are the *Kieler Sprotten* – sprats from the port of Kiel in Germany. The fish are washed and brined.

Smoked trout □
Rainbow and brown trout are used, gutted but the heads are left on. The fish are brined, speared on rods, smoked, then hot-smoked.

CAVIARS AND ROES
See also p. 173

Caviars □
Beluga □ comes from the large Caspian sturgeon which have been known to live for over seventy years, and reach a length of 12ft (3m). **Botargo** is a Sardinian delicacy, of compressed and salted mullet roe. **Danish** is tiny black grains of lumpfish roe. **Osetr** is taken from the Danube sturgeon, a fish also found in the Caspian. **Sevruga** □ comes from the small, Caspian sturgeon.

Roes □
Cod's □ roes are washed and

dry-salted for 6–8 hours, then rewashed, dipped in boiling water to swell them. They are then smoked. Japanese preserved roes include: **hontarako**, a salted and dried cod's roe; **karasumi**, made from the roe of the gray mullet or tuna, salted, pressed and dried; **tarako** or *momojiko*, the salted roe of the Alaskan pollack.

FISH PRODUCTS
Bagoong
From the Philippines, this is a shrimp paste, but may also be made from small fish. These are cleaned, mixed with salt in the proportion of 1 part salt to 3 parts fish, and pressed into vats and colored with dyes. **Nam pla**, from Thailand, is a distant cousin.

Nuoc-mam □
A clear brown liquid with a cheesy smell and salty taste. It is prepared in Vietnam from small fish such as the clupeids (herring and sprats). The whole fish are pressed into tubs, salted and tightly sealed, and left for about 12 weeks when the liquid is

drained off. Salting is heavy and caramel, molasses, rice or boiled corn may be added as extra flavorings. **Petis** and **nuoc-mam roc** are variations.

Prahoc
A fish paste from Cambodia. Prahoc is made with eviscerated fish, scaled, washed and pressed under banana leaves. The fish are then mixed with coarse salt, and sun-dried in order to lose some of their moisture, before being pounded to a paste. The product is then left to ferment.

Trassi; Trasi udang
A cured shrimp paste made in Sumatra from shrimps mixed with 10–15 per cent salt. The mixture is spread out in the sun for a few days, and it is then kneaded and dyes are added until a sticky, red mass is obtained. Other ingredients may be included – potato peel, for example, and rice bran. Mature trassi keeps indefinitely and when cooked and mixed with chili peppers becomes *sambal goreng*, a popular condiment.

SEAWEEDS See also p. 166
Carrageen moss; Irish moss □
The source of agar-agar – a thickening agent used in sauces but in Scotland it is made into a type of milk jelly.

Dulse
A red-colored, broad-leaved weed used either as a vegetable or to flavor soups.

Laver □
A red seaweed, gathered along the coasts of Britain and Eire for centuries. One type, **sea lettuce**, is used in salads, sauces and soups. A fine, silky plant, it is mashed and boiled and then sold as laverbread. The Japanese laver *Porphyra tenera* is gathered and dried to a thin, flexible, dark-brown sheet called *hoshinori* and *askusa nori*. It is used in sauces, soups, sandwiches and a vinegared rice dish.

Mekabu □
A Japanese seaweed available in the form of curled, dried strands. It is used mainly in soups and salads and as a garnish. **Kombu** is another popular type.

Poultry

The word "poultry" is used to describe all domestic birds which are bred especially for the table, and covers chickens, turkeys, ducks, geese, guinea hens and domestic pigeons or squabs. Our chickens are descended from the old jungle fowl *Gallus gallus* of the pheasant family *Phasianinae*, which were bred in the Indus valley some four thousand years ago. Records show that the farmers of ancient Mesopotamia bred ducks, and that geese were already popular in Germany by 1000 BC. It is generally assumed by zoologists that all our varieties of domestic duck are descended from the wild mallard (*Anas platyrhyncha*) – except the Muscovy duck, which originated in South America – and that geese owe their ancestry to the graylag (*Anser feras*).

The turkey we buy today is not the wild turkey the pilgrims found in 1620 (*Meleagris gallopavo silvestris*). It is a descendant of *Meleagris gallopavo gallopavo*, the turkey domesticated by the Aztecs of Mexico and taken from there to Spain by the conquistadors. From Spain the turkey reached England. About a century ago it crossed the Atlantic to America.

Over the years poultry farming has developed enormously. Gradually the demand for selective breeding for meat and eggs has led to automated production techniques, and today poultry is more popular than the meat from any other animal or bird. In the past forty years production in America alone has soared from 30 million broilers to over 300 million.

Choosing and buying poultry
In America, the standard and quality of poultry is closely supervised by the US Department of Agriculture, and grades are given. "Grade A", for example, indicates that the bird in question is of a very high quality, as regards both appearance and meatiness; the circular mark means its been approved.

Generally poultry can be bought either whole or in a variety of individual portions – legs, wings, thighs, drumsticks, halves and quarters. It can also be bought fresh or frozen, with or without giblets (which are often used to make gravies and stuffings). Chicken and turkey are also frequently smoked as gourmet items (p. 285).

Cooking poultry
Chicken especially is a delicate meat, and needs considerate cooking since it has a rapid rate of shrinkage in high heat, but much depends on the age of the bird: tender, young poultry can be barbecued, fried, broiled or roasted; old birds need long, slow braising or stewing; traditional dishes such as the Scottish cock-a-leekie, and the French *coq au vin* are unlikely to have been prepared with cockerels but with capons or boiling hens. The age and the type of poultry therefore determines the method and ultimately the recipe. As a general guide, cut-up fryers should be cooked in deep fat at 300–325°F (148–162°C)

in a thick-bottomed pan for about 20 to 25 minutes. Broiled chicken pieces need to be 7 to 9 inches (17–22cm) from the source of heat, until well-browned and tender.

To roast a chicken, brush with oil or fat and, if it is to be stuffed, pack the stuffing loosely just before roasting; tightly packed stuffing will go soggy. Never stuff ahead; a chicken that, for convenience, has been stuffed the previous day may encourage bacterial activity. Birds that are roasted in aluminum foil, or in a ceramic "chicken brick" are in fact cooked by steam and not by radiant heat – they will need a final 20 to 30 minutes browning, uncovered. As a general guide, a 2 to 2½lb (900g–1kg) broiler will take 1 to 1¼ hours at 400°F (200°C). To test whether the bird is cooked, pierce the thigh or drumstick to the bone with a sharp pointed knife or fork. If the juices run clear and free of blood, or if the joints sever easily when pulled, the chicken is ready for serving.

Chicken that is to be sautéed should first be cut up, the pieces seared in hot fat to seal off the surfaces, then seasoned. Sautéed chicken must be slowly cooked, along with the appropriate vegetables and herbs, in a covered oven dish without moistening; any sauce, egg or cream binding must be added at the finishing stage. Turkeys are usually roasted, and a meat thermometer will be a useful aid to this: a 12- to 17lb (5.4–7.6kg) bird will take about 3 to 3¾ hours uncovered, or until a meat thermometer inserted in the leg shows 185°F (85°C). A turkey of comparable weight, covered with foil and roasted at 450°F (230°C) cooks in 2½ to 3 hours. To roast a

duck or goose, pierce the skin in several places during cooking to allow the excess fat to run off into the pan. A 3- to 5lb (1.4–2.3kg) duck takes 2½ to 3 hours, uncovered, at 325°F (170°C), a goose of 4- to 8lb (1.8–3.6kg) needs 2¾ to 3½ hours at 325°F (170°C).

When roasting guinea hens, choose young birds of about 1½lb (675g). Older (and probably tougher) birds of 2½ to 3lb (1.1–1.4kg) are more suited to casserole cooking and braising. Guinea hens are usually roasted covered with strips of pork rind, or bacon, to keep the breasts from going dry. A 1½lb (675g) bird will need about 1½ hours at 350°F (180°C). Squab should be roasted for about 45 minutes – at 425°F (220°C) for the first 20 minutes and at 350°F (180°C) for the final 25 minutes. Cover the breasts with bacon or pork rind.

Storing poultry

Fresh, uncooked poultry should be used within two or three days of purchasing provided it has been kept in a refrigerator. Once cooked it should be kept in the refrigerator, loosely wrapped, and re-used within a few days. The meat can also be frozen, if separated from the stuffing and the gravy (which can be frozen separately).

When thawing frozen poultry it is best to do so gradually in a refrigerator, allowing about 15 hours for a 3lb (1.4kg) bird; alternatively it can be thawed by placing the bird in a sink and covering it with cold water (the water should be changed regularly until the bird thaws).

Chicken brick

Turkey
The native American bird re-introduced to its birthplace via Ireland and the English

Capon □
Capons are neutered male chickens, especially bred for their good-flavored meat. They average 6–10lb (2.7–4.5kg) in weight, and are excellent roasted.

Chicken □
There are many hundreds of varieties of hens: the **White Cornish** and the **White Rock** in America; the **light Sussex** in England; the **Faverolles** and **Bresse** in France; and the way that these breeds have been developed is a closely-guarded secret. Birds are rated by their performance – how many days it takes to reach a certain weight – the American **Cobb 500** will reach 4½lb (2kg) in 5 weeks, and Britain's **Ross 1** a thumping 5lb (2.3kg).

Chickens are available throughout the year, fresh or frozen, and are usually sold oven-ready. Generally they can be cooked cut up (broiled, fried or stewed), or whole (roasted, braised, boiled or casseroled).

They are also sold under different names, normally according to their age and weight. For example: **poussins □** (baby chickens, 4–6 weeks old and weighing up to 2lb (900g); most popular in England and parts of Europe, and used for

roasting or barbecueing); **Rock Cornish game hens** (a cross between Cornish and White Rock hens, and weighing up to 1½lb (675g); most popular in America, and used for baking, broiling and roasting); **broiler-fryers** (weighing 1½–3½lb (675g–1.6kg) mostly used for frying or broiling); **roasters □** (weighing usually about 3½–6lb (1.6–2.6kg); ideal for roasting, barbecueing or frying); **hens, fowl** or **stewing chickens □** (weighing from 2½lb [1.1kg] upwards, they require long, slow cooking).

Duck □
Some farmers still produce old-fashioned kinds on a small scale; duck lovers rear the **Long Island**, **Aylesbury** and **Peking** types. The most famous breed of duck in America is certainly the Long Island duckling, first brought to New York from China by a Yankee clipper captain in 1873.

Duck is not as meaty as chicken and, because of its tendency towards fattiness, is best roasted. It is available fresh or frozen and, on average, weighs 4–6lb (1.8–2.7kg). **Ducklings**, or young ducks, weigh 3½–4lb (1.6–1.8kg) and are best roasted.

Goose □
There are many varieties, including the **Emden** goose, originating in Germany and the Low Countries, the **Chinese** goose, the **Roman** and **Brecon Buff** – all are reared for Christmas and Michaelmas. The French **Toulouse** goose is bred for its contribution to *pâté de foie gras*, the **Strasburg** for *confit d'oie* (cut-up pieces of goose preserved in goose fat). By and large, while table geese are expensive, and their meat yield low by comparison to the turkey, goose is considered by many to be the best poultry. It is a fatty bird and has a slight "gamey" flavor. It is available fresh or deep-frozen, usually weighs from 6–12lb (2.7–5.4kg), and is best roasted.

Guinea hen □
This is related to the pheasant and was once considered a game bird. Now, however, it is bred for the table and is regarded as poultry, although like game it is best hung for 2 or 3 days before plucking, dressing and cooking.

Guinea hens are bred on a large scale in France, and are suitable for roasting, casseroles, braising, and, in general, any recipe suitable for pheasant.

Squab and **Pigeon**
A squab is a young pigeon especially bred for the table. It is normally about 4 weeks old, and weighs between 12 and 24oz (350–675g). Popular breeds include the **Homer**, **Mondain**, **Carnean** and **King**. It is tender, and can be roasted, sautéed or broiled.

Turkey □
In America, 70 per cent of those turkeys that reach the table on Thanksgiving are special strains produced by the Nicholas Company, probably bred from such famous types as the **Bronze** turkey and the **Beltoville White**. They are sold whole or in pieces, and fresh or frozen. Their weight can range from 6–30lb (2.7–13.5kg) though the usual weight is between 10 and 14lb (4.5–6.3kg). The younger birds are best used for roasting; older ones are usually used in stews and soups.

Game

The word "game", for culinary purposes, is used to describe all birds and animals which are hunted for food, and although several types – such as pheasants, partridges, quails and rabbits – are now being reared domestically, they are still classified as game.

Animals regarded as game vary from country to country. Some of them do not exist outside the Americas. Among them is the Mexican pheasant of Yucatán, the curassow, now rare, raccoon (coon), opossum, Canadian snipe, squirrel (a favorite in Brunswick stew), woodchuck, beaver, muskrat, moose, wild turkey, and reindeer, which are also eaten in northern Europe. In France thrushes are very popular especially in the Ardennes. They are cooked in many ways, roasted, or stewed, but most popularly as *pâté de grives*, thrush pâté. In Italy there is a category of small birds called *uccelletti* which includes thrushes, larks, robins, blackbirds, bullfinches, quail, ortolan, snipe, woodcock and figpeckers. They are usually roasted or grilled. In many countries, game is protected by legislation that permits hunting only during specific seasons and dates – usually from late winter to early spring. In some cases, hunting is completely outlawed. In Britain, for instance, the thrush is a protected bird.

Basically, game is divided into two types: feathered and furred. Hares are decidedly game animals, but many people don't think of rabbits and pigeons as game, even though they are wild animals hunted for food. Game is further distinguished by the characteristic texture and taste of its meat, which differs from that of poultry and farmyard animals: it is generally darker, stronger-tasting, and often tougher, according to the age and type of animal.

Wild animals, because of their diet and general lifestyle, have certain enzymes in their tissues – more abundant in game than in poultry – which break down, or *metabolize* meat proteins. These enzymes, which become active about twenty-four hours after the animal has been killed, soften the meat, making it gelatinous and palatable, and giving it that "gamey" flavor. While the enzymes are at work, the game carcass hosts *anerobes*, micro-organisms which also help to break down the protein, forming non-toxic ptomaines. Provided that there are no dangerous *staphylococci* present the bacteria that affect game meat are harmless; it is curious that game and certain types of fish can be safely eaten and enjoyed at a stage of advanced putrefaction, when many white meats, notably pork, are positively dangerous.

Although hanging game is traditional, it is a mistake to think that game must be mature, and there is historical evidence to suggest that it may not always have been eaten when well matured. Apicius, the Roman who wrote on cuisine in the reign of Tiberius, suggested that birds should be boiled with their feathers on to prevent them from going bad. The Egyptians preserved their game birds by salting them, a practice observed in fourteenth-century England: in 1387, King Richard II gave a dinner which included 3 tons of thirst-provoking, salted venison, plus 400 rabbits, 12 boars, 50 swans, and 150 pheasants, curlews and cranes.

Choosing game
The most important factor when buying game is to know its age, since this will determine its method of cooking (see below). Indications of age are by no means infallible, but there are some general guidelines when buying young birds. Look for clean and soft-textured feet, pliable breastbones and rounded spurs. Also, young partridges have a pointed flight feather (the first large feather of the wing), while in older birds the feather is rounded. When buying game animals, bear in mind that the ears of young hares (leverets) and rabbits split easily and are soft-textured. In general, however, the grading of game is a specialized business, best left to experts.

Hanging game
Game bought from a dealer will probably have been correctly prepared and hung, but you can, of course, order in advance and specify your requirements. Here are some approximate hanging times for freshly killed game: grouse, 3 to 4 days; pheasant, 6 to 14 days; partridge, 7 to 8 days; wood-pigeon, 2 to 3 days; snipe and woodcock, 7 to 10 days; hare and rabbit, 2 to 3 days; venison and boar, up to 3 weeks. Quail does not need to be hung at all.

Game should be hung in a cool, dry, airy place and protected from flies. Although there is no real need to hang game if you object to the taste, as a general rule, you should hang a carcass until you detect the first whiff of tainting – in birds this is around the crop or vent. Game is usually left intact during hanging, except venison, hares and rabbits, which may be paunched straight away.

In Britain, birds are usually hung by their heads, and rabbits and (particularly) hares with the head down. (The blood of hares is usually collected in a receptacle as it drains off, and is used to thicken the sauce in jugged hare.)

Cooking game
Game meat responds best to roasting. Young game birds, in particular, should be roasted, and it is traditional to leave them unstuffed. In practice, however, large birds such as pheasant and ptarmigan may be stuffed with seasoned ground beef, which helps to keep the flesh moist. Older, tougher game should be casseroled, braised or made into pies, pâtés

and terrines. Marinating in a mixture of oil, vinegar, wine or beer, with herbs and spices, helps to make tough meat tender, and enhances the taste.

The oven should be set at 400°F (200°C) for the first 10 minutes, then at 350°F (180°C) for the following times: grouse, 30 minutes; partridge, 30 minutes; pheasant, 45 minutes; pigeon, 60 minutes; ptarmigan, 45 minutes; quail, 25 minutes; snipe, 45 minutes; duck, 45 minutes; woodcock, 30 minutes. Roast a hare or a young rabbit at about 425°F (220°C) for about 45 minutes; venison should be roasted at 425°F (220°C) for 20 to 25 minutes, then at 350°F (180°C) according to the weight – a haunch takes about 1½ to 2 hours.

Teal duck
One of the smallest of the wild ducks, the teal is highly regarded by gourmets. It can be used in all recipes for wild duck and is usually roasted, broiled or grilled

American bear

Reindeer

FEATHERED
See also pp. 178–80
Duck □
The most famous variety is the **mallard** □, from which all domestic varieties are descended. There are several other types, including **teal**, **widgeon**, **shoveler**, **pochard** and **scaup**. It is not, as a rule, very meaty, but what there is makes good eating. It is best prepared by roasting.

Grouse □
The grouse family includes many varieties: the **red** grouse of Scotland, the **blackcock** or *black grouse*, the **capercaillie** or *wood grouse*, and the **ptarmigan** of northern Europe. Several American game birds bear the name of grouse, but are not related to the family – examples are the **sage** grouse, the **ruffed** grouse and the **prairie chicken**. Generally speaking, grouse keeps well. It can be roasted, broiled or grilled if young; older birds should be served casseroled or braised.

Partridge □
This is related to the pheasant, and there are many different species, including the **French** or *red-legged partridge* and the **rock** partridge. In France, it is cooked with cabbage and other vegetables and made into a decorative mold called a *chartreuse*. Otherwise, young birds are best roasted; older birds braised or casseroled.

Pheasant □
There are many varieties all over the world and the type was imported as a game bird from Shanghai to America in the late nineteenth-century. Perhaps the most popular game bird, it responds well to hanging. Farm-reared birds are sold oven-ready, fresh or frozen. It is best served roasted.

Pigeon
Pigeon is sometimes tough, and therefore best suited for stewing or braising. In North Africa, pigeons feature in a delicate pie, made with fine pastry, sugar and nuts, called a *bstilla*.

Quail □
Like the partridge, the quail is related to the pheasant. (In America there is some confusion over the names for quail and partridge; the **American** quail or *bobwhite* (*Colinus virginianus*) is also known as *partridge* or *massena quail*.) There are several other varieties, including the **Californian** quail and the **European** quail, which is reared on quail farms and sold as a gourmet item to restaurants. It can be roasted, sautéed or broiled, and features in many *haute cuisine* dishes, especially when it is served in aspic.

Snipe □
This is best roasted. It is often cooked with its entrails, which are regarded as a delicacy.

Woodcock □
This is related to the snipe. It is best roasted or braised and, like the snipe, is often cooked with its entrails.

FURRED See also p. 181
Bear
The **European** bear (*Ursus arctus*) and the **American** bear (*Ursus americanus*) are occasionally enjoyed for their steaks, but bear paws are considered to be the prime part. Bear is most popular in German and Russian cooking.

Boar
The **European** wild boar (*Sus scrofa*), although plentiful on the continent and in some parts of America, is still best known for its medieval associations.

Only the meat of the young boar is really tender; older animals need to be hung for 2 or 3 days, and the flesh marinated before cooking. It is usually roasted, and is popular in German and Russian cooking.

Deer
The meat of any animal from the deer or *Cervidae* family is called "venison", a word that derives from the Latin *venari*, to hunt, for at one time all game was "venison", the prize of the hunt. Venison is one of the most popular game meats, but needs to be hung and marinated, unless the animal is very young. The best meat is taken from the buck, in its second year, and the most popular cut is the haunch, although the loin and fillets also make good eating. Deer, in general, are eaten for their meat and liver, and the **elk** in particular (*Alces alces*) has a plentiful supply, while smoked elk tongue is a delicacy. Young, tender venison may be broiled or grilled, or larded with pork fat and roasted (some cooks prefer to pour sour cream over the meat before roasting).

Hare □
Hares, though they belong to the same family as rabbits, are "gamier". They are also larger, their flesh is darker and stronger-tasting. The **European** hare and the **blue mountain** hare are particularly popular in northern Europe.

Young hares do not need hanging and can be fresh roasted; older animals of 2 years upwards should be hung and the meat made into casseroles, stews and pâtés. Its main use, of course, is in jugged hare, and it is also used in the German casserole with red wine, *hasenpfeffer*, and in the French dish *lièvre à la royale*.

Rabbit □
The meat of rabbits is generally tender, and the animals do not need to be hung. Curiously, it has never become an *haute cuisine* ingredient, but has always been a countryman's dish, and countless recipes for rabbit pie and stew testify to this trend.

Meat

From the earliest times, man has been a carnivorous animal. Because meat provides so much protein and essential vitamins, early people could spend less of their time eating and could successfully turn their energies to activities which in time placed them above their peers. Meat was from the first equated with life and early hunting magic was designed to supply a plentiful amount of animals. Though today there is a re-appraisal of the importance of meat in the diet – whether its drawbacks like cholesterol and high price outweigh its value as a protein-provider, or, in the case of vegetarians, an ethical consideration – meat is still the most expensive item on the budget and a great deal of thought should be put into choosing and using it wisely.

The meat which we use in our recipes comes from the three main types of domestic farm animals – cattle, sheep and pigs, giving us beef and veal, mutton and lamb, and pork. While regional preferences, religion and climate may have certain influences, these meats feature in the majority of national cuisines, and may be supplemented by other domestic types, such as horsemeat, goat and reindeer.

National and regional preferences for the meat of certain types of animal – pork in China, mutton and lamb in the Middle East, beef in Europe and America – are partly due to ancient origins: sheep and goats were domesticated in Mesopotamia at the dawn of civilization; pork traditionally began the feast of the Chinese New Year; beef was eaten by the Greeks and the Romans, and has latterly become the prime meat of western Europe and America.

Butcher's meat today is largely a product of selective breeding and feeding techniques, whereby animals are carefully reared to reach high standards and specific needs: the present-day demand is for lean and tender meat – modern cattle, sheep and pigs are well-fleshed yet compact creatures compared to their forebears of a century ago. Animals have only been reared exclusively for food during this century; during the last century, our beef and mutton was tough, fatty, expensive, and probably strongly flavored. Candles were made from beef and mutton fat so that fatty animals were preferred. Moreover, sheep were bred primarily for their leather and wool (they were only slaughtered after the fleece was no longer productive, and the yield of mutton was by then tough and stringy) and cattle or oxen raised primarily as beasts of burden. Before road and rail transport had been developed, and animals could be swiftly conveyed to distant markets, cattle and pigs were herded on foot along the drove roads, often for hundreds of miles – another contributory factor to toughness.

Breeding techniques

Animal breeders seek to produce superior food animals through the contributions of various strains with specific and desirable qualities; the good qualities in each breed are combined in their offspring so that heavier, meatier animals are produced, with a higher proportion of lean meat (between 50 per cent and 70 per cent of the body weight) to fat and bone. Because the most tender and lean meat is found along the backbone and including the rump, breeders try and produce animals with broad backs and heavy hindquarters, carcasses that will yield steaks and roasts. Young male animals are often castrated (whence they become "steers"): the absence of male hormones induces rapid growth and plumpness, thus providing larger quantities of tender meat; the Greeks and Romans were among the first who practiced this technique. The age at which animals are slaughtered has been considerably reduced to meet the increased demand for smaller cuts of meat for roasting (and so for smaller carcasses). Beef cattle raised on cereals such as soybeans and ground nuts or barley attain a desirable weight within ten to twelve months, against the two years of grass-fed animals.

Cuts of meat

The consumer's requirements (affected by social and economic trends), the animal's anatomy, and religious custom influence the way in which the butcher cuts his carcasses. Regional climates, family occupations, and the use of local ingredients, such as herbs, fruits and vegetables influence cooking methods and therefore demands for cuts. Butchering techniques vary considerably, not only between countries, but even within cities and towns. The names given to the cuts vary too, except in America, where regional variations were standardized in the 1970s. In Britain, names may vary to such an extent that a particular cut – the thick flank of beef, for example – has as many as twenty-seven local names, including bedpiece, Pope's eye, rump, mouse, crown, broil, top piece, and soft side.

Meat from specific parts of an animal may be cut and cooked according to local custom, and, more strictly, by religious observance – especially in Jewish kosher and Mohammedan *halal* butchery, which stipulates the killing of the animal by an authorized person of the religion, total voiding of the blood by draining, soaking and salting, and the consumption of the meat within seventy-two hours. Kosher dietary laws further demand that only the forequarters of permitted animals – goats, sheep, deer and cattle – may be used.

Choosing meat

Meat is a natural and therefore not a uniform product, varying in quality from carcass to carcass, while flavor, texture and appearance are determined by the type of animal and the way it has been fed. There is no reason to think that flavor is only obtained in meat which possesses a proportion of fat although it does give a characteristic flavor to meat and helps to keep it moist during roasting. The color of meat is also no guide to quality. Consumers are inclined to choose light-colored meat – bright red beef, for example – because they think that it will be fresher than an alternative dark red piece. Freshly butchered beef is bright red because the pigment in the tissues, myoglobin, has been chemically affected by the oxygen in the air. After several hours, the color changes to dark red or brown as the pigment is further oxidized to become metamyaglobin. The color of fat can vary from almost pure white in lamb, to bright yellow in beef. Color depends on the feed, on the breed – and to a certain extent, on the time of the year.

The most useful guide to tenderness and quality is a knowledge of the cuts of meat and their location on the carcass and the relevant grading system. The US Department of Agriculture rates meat as Prime, Choice and Good; the higher the quality of the grade, the more tender, tasty and juicy the meat. Cuts are described under their respective headings, but in principle the leanest and tenderest cuts, the "prime" cuts come from the hindquarters. The "coarse" cuts, or meat from the neck, legs and forequarters, those parts of the animal that have had plenty of muscular exercise and where fibers have become hardened, provide meat for braising and stewing. Many consider these cuts to have more flavor. The meat from young animals is generally more tender and since tenderness is a prime factor, animals may be injected before slaughter with an enzyme, such as papain, which softens the fibers and muscles. But this merely speeds up a natural and more satisfactory process: meat contains its own proteolytic enzymes which gradually break down the protein cell walls as the carcass ages. That is why meat is hung from ten to twenty days in controlled conditions of temperature and humidity before being offered for sale. Meat which is aged longer becomes more expensive as the cost of refrigeration is high and the meat itself shrinks because of evaporation and the trimming of the outside hardened edges.

Meat in the kitchen

Meat is an extremely versatile product that can be cooked in a multitude of ways, and matched with practically any vegetable, fruit and herb. The cut (shin, steak, brisket), the method of heating (roasting, braising, broiling) and the time and temperature all affect the way the meat will taste. Raw meat is difficult to chew because the muscle fiber contains an elastic protein (collagen) which is only softened by mincing – as in steak tartare – or by cooking. When you cook meat, the protein gradually coagulates as the internal temperature increases. At 171°F (77°C) coagulation is complete, the protein begins to harden, and further cooking makes the meat tougher.

Since tenderness combined with flavor is the aim in meat cookery, much depends on the ratio of time and temperature. In principle, slow cooking retains the juices and produces a more tender result than does fast cooking at high temperatures. There are, of course, occasions when high temperatures are essential: you need to broil a steak under a hot flame for a very limited time in order to obtain a crisp, brown surface and a pink, juicy interior – using a low temperature would not give you the desired result. But in potentially tough cuts, such as brisket, and where there is a quantity of connective tissue (shin, neck of beef), a slow rate of cooking converts the tissues to gelatin and helps to make the meat more tender. Meat containing bone, by the way, will take longer to cook because bone is a poor conductor of heat. Tough or coarse cuts of meat should be cooked by braising, pot-roasting or stewing. Marinating in a suitable marinade, such as wine and wine vinegar, helps to tenderize the meat, and imparts an additional flavor. Searing meat in hot fat, or in a hot oven before roasting or stewing helps to produce a crisp exterior by coagulating the protein but does not, as is widely supposed, seal in the juices. However, if the external temperature is too high, and cooking prolonged, rapid evaporation and contraction of the meat will cause considerable loss of juices and fat. Salt sprinkled on meat before cooking will also hasten loss of moisture since salt is hygroscopic and absorbs water.

Meat bones are useful for giving flavor to soup and stock, especially beef ones with plenty of marrow. Veal bones are gelatinous and help to enrich and thicken soups and sauces. Fat can be rendered down for frying, or used as an ingredient when suet or lard is called for.

Cooking meat

Briefly, meat cookery can be broadly divided into the following categories: quick cooking at moderate to high temperatures, as when broiling, barbecuing and frying – suitable for such prime, tender cuts as steaks, chops, veal scallops, and kabobs; slow to moderate cooking, as when roasting or using a rotisserie – suitable for prime, tender joints such as beef sirloin, leg of lamb, cuts of pork and veal; slow cooking in a liquid, as when stewing, braising or pot roasting – suitable for coarse cuts such as thick flank, leg, shin and neck cuts. One big advantage to pot-roasting or braising, and stewing meat is that any quantities left over can be easily re-heated. In fact, many dishes are improved by allowing them to "mature" and then re-heating. Roasts, on the other hand, are less adaptable, and cold roast meat is not suitable re-heated, since it lacks the essential moisture.

When you are preparing meat for cooking, never wash it, simply wipe the surface with a damp cloth. Use a meat thermometer when roasting; many are graded with temperature scales and also scaled according to the type of meat and the cut. They record the internal temperature of the meat. Meat that requires carving should rest for fifteen minutes so that it loses its springiness and is easier to carve, and juices do not escape so readily. Always carve on a nonslip surface, and one where the juices can be collected. Use a sharp knife, otherwise the meat will simply tear along the grain, and a guarded carving fork.

Beef

Domestic cattle, from which we derive our beef, have been gradually developed over thousands of years. Their ancestors were the wild aurochs, *Bos primigenius*, first domesticated in Anatolia and Greece in about 6000 BC. The lineage of this ancient breed was so enduring that the last known specimen of aurochs was recorded in Poland in 1627. The Greeks, and later the Romans, prepared their beef dishes with an abundance of pepper and other spices, not because the meat was less than fresh, or that it lacked flavor, but because spices were an expensive item, and so was beef. Such fine ingredients were employed on special occasions, and denoted the wealth of the household.

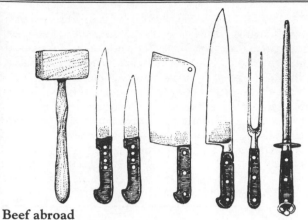

Beef abroad

Beef has always been an expensive meat. During the Middle Ages, the infrequent fare of the common man was salt pork and mutton and beef the privilege of the wealthy. In Britain, farmers maintained herds of cattle and sheep, only slaughtering a part of their stock as winter approached, and grazing ended. Beef would then be eaten fresh, the remainder salted for the coming months. Yet by the eighteenth century the English had a reputation as a nation of beefeaters. Tables were burdened, one observer noted, "with large dishes of meat", and boiled beef "besieged with five or six heaps of cabbage, carrots and turnips". Massive roasts were cooked on spits before the open fire. This might imply that butchering was rather primitive, and smaller cuts unknown or ignored. But in London an event took place that was, in some respects, a culinary revolution – the introduction of the beefsteak. Steak became so popular that clubs were formed to "study beef under the most favorable circumstances". One such club was the "Sublime Society of Beefsteaks", established in Covent Garden in 1735. Their motto was "Beef and Liberty", and their emblem was the gridiron upon which the steaks were broiled.

The ready availability of beef was partly due to the unique experiments conducted by Lord Townshend – "Turnip Townshend" as he was known – who had shown that livestock could be kept through the winter by feeding them on turnips. Townshend's efforts later inspired Robert Bakewell, who became England's first commercial stockbreeder; he recognized that hardier, weightier and more productive stock were needed in order to produce better beefsteaks.

In France, the *bifteck* had been noted by the epicure Brillat-Savarin. Here, as in London, butchering techniques were gradually improving, yet only city butchers could be relied upon to cut a steak for the grill: "It would seem", wrote one steak fancier, "that country butchers have not learned the secrets of proper cuts". Steaks became implemented in the *grande cuisine*, especially during the *belle époque* at the end of the nineteenth century. A *chef de cuisine* invented a recipe for strips of fillet steak with mushrooms and sour cream, and dedicated it to Count Stroganoff. In the Café Anglais the composer Rossini was honored with *tournedos Rossini*, filet mignon served with a truffle and a *sauce Madère*.

Beef in America

Beef has always been the most sought-after meat in America and steak was established as the favorite by the mid-nineteenth century. It was often served to travelers at coach stops or "porterhouses". At this time, too, the reflector oven was introduced; this replaced the spit as the principal cooking apparatus for roast beef. This small, rounded metal piece reflected heat from a coal fire onto a piece of meat placed between it and the fire. The roast itself rested on a trivet or muffin rings and required frequent basting for proper cooking.

Other favorite American beef dishes had even earlier antecedents: corned beef was eaten by generations of Americans who otherwise would have been without meat in winter; meat pies introduced by early English settlers made good use of leftover roasts and could be baked in large, outdoor ovens; pot roasts were named for the vessels in which they were cooked, notably the Dutch ovens of the early New Englanders or the *étouffades* of the French immigrants; and even the ubiquitous hamburger is a twentieth-century update of the minced beef first eaten by the early colonials without benefit of forks.

The early American desire for beef was met by the successful transplantation of Spanish cattle to Texas. Bred to withstand the heat and lack of water in Andalusia, the Texas Longhorns even overcame the rigors of being herded for up to 1000 miles to the railroad centers for shipment to destinations east. And if the cattle supplied Americans with their favorite meat, the cowboys who herded them popularized a favorite way of cooking it – the barbecue. Although the Texas Longhorns, the staple of the American meat economy, have long been displaced by meatier breeds from Great Britain, today it is America, and not Britain, that has become a nation of beefeaters – Americans eat and import more beef than any other country in the world, consuming some 65lb (29kg) per head of the population every year, in the form of barbecued sirloin steaks, hamburgers, broiled T-bone and porterhouse steaks, New England boiled dinner with corned beef, and the Southwest's chili con carne.

Choosing and using beef

The cuts of beef vary considerably from the very tender fillet steak, to the tough brisket or shin and there is a greater variety of cuts in beef than in other meat. In America meat is graded according to quality and yield and such factors as marbling, maturity, color, firmness, texture and the ratio of usable meat to fat and bone are the primary considerations.

There are seven primal cuts from a side of beef, each one composed of muscle, fat, bone and connective tissue. The least-developed muscles, usually from the inner area, yield cuts that can be roasted or broiled, while leaner and more sinewy meat is cut from more highly developed external muscles. An exception to this are rib and loin cuts which come from external but basically immobile muscles.

Knowing where the cuts come from helps to determine the cooking method. The forequarter, which normally weighs from 155 to 190lb (70–86kg) produces four primal cuts: chuck, rib of beef, brisket and short plate. Chuck comes from the neck and shoulder – one of the most mobile sections. Cuts from this portion are likely to be sinewy with a large amount of connective tissue. Moist cooking such as braising, stewing or pot-roasting produces the best results but some small, tender chuck steaks can be produced which are suitable for frying and broiling. Rib of beef is an immobile primal cut from the center of the back and yields the tenderest steaks and roasts – all suitable for roasting and broiling. Brisket is cut from above the leg and being a fibrous portion requires long, slow moist cooking. Curing, as for corned beef, can also produce more tender meat. Short plate, part of the breast bone, produces cuts which need moist cooking or grinding. However, skirt steak – a more tender cut – is produced from the same area.

The hindquarter comprises 48 per cent of the carcass but produces the largest amount of steaks and roasts. It weighs between 145 to 180lb (65–81.5kg) and is made up of three cuts: full loin, whole flank, round of beef. Full loin is the tenderest part of the carcass and produces porterhouse, sirloin and filet mignon as well as tenderloin roast. From whole flank, London broil is cut, as well as chopped meat trimmings. Round of beef, the hind leg, is a lean mobile section comprising the rump (requiring moist cooking) and six other roasts. These include the tender side of round and top round, and the less tender bottom round, edge of round, and the shank and heel which are more suitable to moist cooking or grinding.

BEEF CUTS

Rib roast small end
Taken from the small end of the primal rib, this is a roasting cut.

Rib eye roast; Delmonico pot roast
This is the large center muscle of the rib. All other muscles, bones and seam fat are removed. It is used for roasting.

Round tip roast cap off
This comes from the hindquarters. If high quality, it can be roasted, otherwise braised.

Chuck short ribs
These are pieces of layered meat and fat and contain rib bones. They are usually braised.

Chuck eye roast boneless
This contains meaty inside muscles of blade chuck, and is used for braising.

Chuck arm pot roast
A braising cut taken from the fore end, it contains round arm bone but is also sold boneless.

Round rump roast
A boneless roast that is usually tied. It can be braised or roasted.

Bottom rump round roast
An irregular thick cut from the hindquarters. It is used for braising.

Flank steak; London broil
This cut comes from the tail end of the loin, and can be pan broiled or pan fried.

Chuck blade steak
This contains the blade bone, backbone and rib bone, and is braised or pan broiled.

Chuck 7-bone steak
Taken from the center or nearer the rib end of chuck, it is usually pot-roasted.

Shank cross cut
Taken from hindshank or foreshank perpendicular to bone, it is used for braising.

Top loin steak
A boneless cut from the short loin, it used for broiling.

Porterhouse steak
The best short loin steak, it contains top loin, and tenderloin, and is pan broiled, or pan fried.

Pin bone sirloin; Sirloin steak
This contains top sirloin and tenderloin muscles. It is broiled or pan broiled.

Rib eye steak; Delmonico steak
It is cut across the grain from rib eye roast. It is broiled, pan broiled or pan fried.

Top round steak; Inside round steak
This comes from the hindquarters. It can be braised, broiled or pan broiled.

Veal

Veal is the meat from dairy calves usually slaughtered at three months of age. Today this meat is in short supply – due to more efficient dairy production from fewer animals – and expensive: young animals have a coddled upbringing and many are completely milk-fed. The association of milk and veal goes back at least to Norman times, when chefs prepared *blancmange* – veal cooked with milk and almonds – and taught English cooks to make *veel bukkenade* with veal, eggs, milk and spices, a medieval version of *blanquette de veau*.

In countries where livestock, and especially cattle, were considered a valuable commodity, veal was usually the outcome of calf mortality. Nevertheless, in France and Italy it was a highly prized meat; François I was said to have demanded veal for the table daily. It is likely that the popularity of French veal was partly due to the influence of Italian cooking, introduced to the Court by Catherine de Medici, wife of King Henri II.

One particular cut of veal, the scallop, has had a curious, military history. It probably originated in Spain, and was introduced to the city of Milan, when Milan was a part of the Spanish Empire in the sixteenth century. The *scallopine Milanese* may have been named after the scallop shell, the emblem of Spain's patron saint, St James, and featured in Milan homes as a delicacy brought to Italy by the scallop-bearers, the troops of Charles V.

When Milan was later occupied by Austrian soldiers under Marshal Radetsky, the Marshal introduced the *scallopine* to the Imperial kitchens of Emperor Franz Josef in Vienna, where it became the famed *wiener schnitzel*.

Not much veal is eaten in America but it is important in many other countries. Romanians mince veal and make a casserole, while the Bulgarians stew it with horseradish. French dishes include the provincial *blanquette de veau*, and the grand *selle de veau Orloff*. Italy, already replete with *scallopine*, is known for its cold veal with a sauce of tuna fish – *vitello tonnato*; the Tuscan stew *stufatino*; veal olives; and the famous *ossobuco*, where pieces of veal knuckle are gently stewed with tomatoes.

Choosing and using veal

Veal is graded as to formation, finish and quality in three grades, Prime, Choice and Good. Unlike beef, veal may be judged by the color of the meat. The whiter it is, the greater proportion of the calf's diet has been milk, and the meat is likely to be tender with a delicate flavor. Mature veal is pink or rosy pink, the fat creamy white. A dry, brown or mottled appearance indicates staleness. Veal is, however, inclined to dryness, as there is little internal fat, and for this reason it is often pot-roasted or braised, and larded with pork fat.

The veal carcass is divided into two portions – foresaddle and hindsaddle. There are six primary cuts of veal and the three from the foresaddle are the shoulder (chuck); rack and breast, and foreshank. The shoulder is not very tender and may be cut into roasts, chops, steaks and shoulder cutlets. Most cuts should be moist-cooked, but dry cooking is possible with extra fat. The rack is usually cut into chops or scallops for sautéeing or braising but may be roasted whole as a crown roast. The breast and foreshank are usually best braised and are the least desirable cuts. The hindsaddle provides the majority of the better cuts from its three divisions: the legs and hindshanks, the loin and the flank. The leg is usually divided into roasts with or without bone and the hindshank and any of its smaller cuts should be braised. The loin provides expensive chops for braising or sautéeing. It is also sold with the bone as a roast; the flank meat is usually cubed or ground.

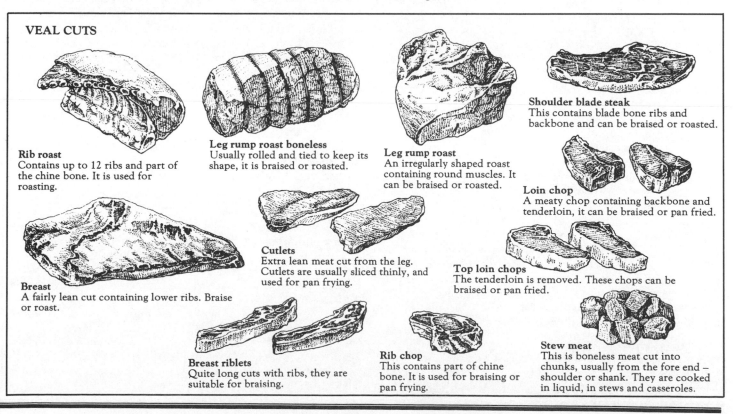

VEAL CUTS

Rib roast
Contains up to 12 ribs and part of the chine bone. It is used for roasting.

Leg rump roast boneless
Usually rolled and tied to keep its shape, it is braised or roasted.

Leg rump roast
An irregularly shaped roast containing round muscles. It can be braised or roasted.

Shoulder blade steak
This contains blade bone ribs and backbone and can be braised or roasted.

Breast
A fairly lean cut containing lower ribs. Braise or roast.

Cutlets
Extra lean meat cut from the leg. Cutlets are usually sliced thinly, and used for pan frying.

Loin chop
A meaty chop containing backbone and tenderloin, it can be braised or pan fried.

Top loin chops
The tenderloin is removed. These chops can be braised or pan fried.

Breast riblets
Quite long cuts with ribs, they are suitable for braising.

Rib chop
This contains part of chine bone. It is used for braising or pan frying.

Stew meat
This is boneless meat cut into chunks, usually from the fore end – shoulder or shank. They are cooked in liquid, in stews and casseroles.

Lamb

Sheep and goats have an ancestry that certainly predates cattle and pigs, going back to around 9000 BC. The earliest evidence of animal domestication comes from northern Iraq, where long-haired, mouflon sheep (*Ovis orientalis*) were kept for their fleece and eventually slaughtered for their meat. They probably shared their domestication with the bezoar goat (*Capra hircus aegagrus*), whose remains have been found at Jericho. The bezoar still exists in southwest Asia, and a handful of mouflon sheep remain in Corsica and Sardinia. Direct descendants of these ancient breeds are the Soay of Scotland, and probably such strains as the Merino, the Drente of Holland, and Britain's Norfolk Blackface.

Through selective breeding, sheep have lost their long hair to the woolly fleece, and modern breeders are now concentrating on a nearly naked but virile type, the Wiltshire horn ram – fat, meaty and used for crossbreeding. Like cattle, which yield both milk and meat, sheep have a two-fold purpose to provide wool and meat, and of the two yields, meat is by far the most important.

Lamb is the meat from a sheep under a year old; above that age the animal is called a *hogget*, and its meat becomes mutton. The demand for lamb in preference to mutton is partly due to the fact that the lamb carcass provides smaller cuts of more tender meat. Mutton needs to be well ripened by long hanging before cooking and, as it is usually fatty, it needs a good deal of trimming as well.

The best domestic lamb is marketed when it is between five and seven months old, and is known as "spring", "summer" or early lamb. Much of the flavor of lamb has now been sacrificed to productivity – a deep-frozen leg of lamb bears no comparison with a leg of fresh, spring lamb but the latter is in short supply and is expensive. But whatever the source, the demand is for lamb, and very little mutton is now sold on the market.

Mutton was at one time more popular than lamb because of the larger size of the roasts. For centuries, all over Europe, people had been used to huge cuts of meat roasting before an open fire. Furthermore, because of the practice of serving many courses all at the same time, a large roast was less likely to get cold on the table, a common problem with soups and fish. Lamb was a strictly seasonal luxury. Later on, mutton was in many countries associated with poverty. In fact this idea was largely erroneous: the poor rarely enjoyed meat of any kind, their diet consisted of bread, cheese and root vegetables, and occasionally broth, salt pork, or bacon.

Lamb in America
In America, lamb and mutton have never become widely popular, because of the preference for beef. Mutton especially is held to have a very strong flavor and its lack of popularity has little to do with a lack of suitable grazing, but a lot to do with tradition, and of course, affluence. Lamb-and-lima bean casserole may be indigenous to America, but foreign and immigrant influences have bestowed most of the lamb dishes eaten today, such as Irish stew, England's crown roast, Middle Eastern lamb with lentils. The recent popularity of kabobs and shashlik have given rise to the term "kabob meat", which many people use interchangeably with lamb.

In spite of these influences, however, the demand for lamb in America seems to be steadily declining; most lamb sold in America is "yearling lamb" and is older and less tender than the baby lamb found abroad. There is a limited production of home-produced meat, and most of the lamb and mutton consumed is imported from New Zealand and Australia. In contrast, France's own home-produced lamb, and in particular the prized *pré salé*, or salt marsh lamb, cannot meet its home demand, and prices there are high. *Pré salé* lamb or mutton comes from herds that have grazed on the coastal pastures, and the meat is reputed to take on a salty tang, with a hint of iodine. Britain has its salt marsh lamb, and the Dutch rate very highly their pedigree Texel breed, which originated in the Frisian Islands and are now found in Britain, France, South America and South Africa.

Lamb in the kitchen
In Middle Eastern and North African cooking, lamb features as the whole, spitted and roasted carcass called *mechoui*, or as *shish kebab*, which in fact means "skewered lamb". It is cut in slices and packed on a rotating spit as *shawarma*, or *doner kebab*. Everywhere, minced lamb with cracked wheat is eaten, either raw, as in *kibbi nayya*, or cooked as with the Lebanese specialty *kibbi*. In Iran, mutton is stewed; in Tunisia it is cooked with spices and raisins. The French are particularly fond of roasting the leg. Their *gigot* may be stuffed and cooked in pastry (*gigot en croûte*), or casseroled for many hours (*gigot à sept heures*). Lamb, or originally mutton, created the immortal Irish stew, and the Lancashire hot pot.

Lamb is well suited to certain fruits and adjuncts: mint sauce with lamb and caper sauce with mutton are favorites in Britain. Algerians cook it with prunes and almonds, Moroccans with lemons and olives, the Belgians with endives, the Swedes with dill. Other herbs include rosemary, marjoram, coriander and juniper berries.

Lamb cuts are smaller and tenderer than most other meats and they should be cooked so that they are still pink – and carved very thinly. Recipes for leg or shoulder of lamb also work well with mutton.

Choosing and using lamb
Good-quality lamb should have a fine, white fat, with pink flesh where freshly cut; in mutton the meat is a deeper color. Lamb has a very thin, parchment-like covering on the carcass, known as the fell, which should not be removed before cooking. Lamb is best when young as it's more tender and flavorful. A good way to judge age is through weight – especially with legs of lamb; the highest quality is about 5lb (2.2kg) and never more than 9lb (4kg). Smaller chops are also more tender and therefore more expensive. Lamb is graded as per other meats and is marketed as Prime, Choice and Good. Mutton is rarely sold, and if it is, it is always much less expensive than lamb.

A lamb carcass weighs between 45 and 60lb (20.4–27.2kg) and is divided into halves – the foresaddle and hindsaddle. The foresaddle contains the chuck, rack, foreshanks and breast. Chuck, although it is cut from the mobile neck and shoulder, is tenderer than for other meats since the animal is less developed. The neck meat is usually ground but shoulder and loin chops and kabob meat is obtainable. The rack produces desirable meat in the form of lean rib chops and is also roasted whole as a crown roast. The front legs, or foreshanks, provide inexpensive meat which is usually braised. The breast can be de-boned, ground or used as riblets and braised. The hindsaddle is made up of the flank and two desirable cuts: loin and leg. Most of the flank is ground as it is quite stringy. The loin is the tenderest and is usually cut up and sold as chops for broiling. The leg is the meatiest part and can be roasted whole or as two parts – the shank or rump, the shank being meatier. Two legs still attached are known as a *baron*.

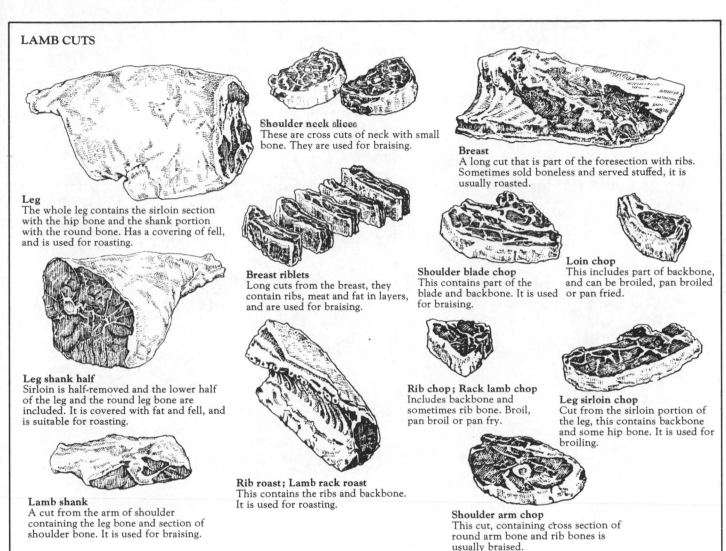

LAMB CUTS

Shoulder neck slices
These are cross cuts of neck with small bone. They are used for braising.

Breast
A long cut that is part of the foresection with ribs. Sometimes sold boneless and served stuffed, it is usually roasted.

Leg
The whole leg contains the sirloin section with the hip bone and the shank portion with the round bone. Has a covering of fell, and is used for roasting.

Breast riblets
Long cuts from the breast, they contain ribs, meat and fat in layers, and are used for braising.

Shoulder blade chop
This contains part of the blade and backbone. It is used for braising.

Loin chop
This includes part of backbone, and can be broiled, pan broiled or pan fried.

Leg shank half
Sirloin is half-removed and the lower half of the leg and the round leg bone are included. It is covered with fat and fell, and is suitable for roasting.

Rib chop; Rack lamb chop
Includes backbone and sometimes rib bone. Broil, pan broil or pan fry.

Leg sirloin chop
Cut from the sirloin portion of the leg, this contains backbone and some hip bone. It is used for broiling.

Lamb shank
A cut from the arm of shoulder containing the leg bone and section of shoulder bone. It is used for braising.

Rib roast; Lamb rack roast
This contains the ribs and backbone. It is used for roasting.

Shoulder arm chop
This cut, containing cross section of round arm bone and rib bones is usually braised.

Pork

The first people to taste roast pork were probably the Chinese, and Neolithic sites excavated in China show that pigs, used as food, were the only domestic animals.

In the eighteenth century an Asian variety, *Sus scrofa vittatus*, was introduced. It was found easier to handle and confine and had potentially good prospects for cross breeding. Today, most of our modern pig strains have descended from this Asian stock.

One of the most controversial aspects of pork is the fact that it is taboo in certain religions. It has been variously proposed that pork is basically unhygienic, and in hot climates presents a health hazard, or that the pig was once a tribal emblem (a totem), and thus sacrosanct. One theory suggests that pork has similarities to human flesh – cannibals have sometimes referred to man (as an ingredient for the pot) as "long pig". The pig, like man is omnivorous, and is subject to some of man's diseases and it is possible that as religion grew out of primeval rites, the pig became associated with primitive, human sacrifice and was then condemned as a food; in ancient Turkey pigs were associated with death.

Be that as it may, pork is greatly esteemed by many nations as a prime and tender meat. The pig's later associations with man have been very close. For centuries the European peasantry existed on little else but an occasional dip into the barrel that contained their meager supply of salt or pickled pork; navies rationed it to their seamen who grew to despise it, and so did the aristocracy, who viewed pork as the food of the poor. Pigs were a feature of every homestead, however humble; pigs went with the settlers to the New World, and became so prolific that pork was a main item in American cooking long before beef took command, so that pork dishes feature among America's earliest recipes. The pigs were left to fatten in the woods and then, as today, they were utilized to the last ounce, and nothing was rejected, including the head, entrails and trotters (Variety Meats, p. 281, Sausages and Preserved Meats, p. 282). Today, pork is America's second favorite meat after beef.

Pigs as everyone knows, will eat almost anything – they are nature's vacuum cleaners, omnivorous and greedy, but pig farmers have to control their diet to produce the right combination of fatness, weight, and carcass quality. Pigs cannot eat grass alone, and are fed cereals, proteins, minerals and compound vitamins; diet influences the flavor of the meat, and it is likely that the free ranging, ancestral pigs, though probably tougher and fattier than today's breeds, had a more natural flavor.

Pork in the kitchen

The pig's hardy, omnivorous, scavenging nature is the quality which has made it so enduring in a wide variety of climates and conditions. Pork does not feature, as does lamb, beef and veal as meat of classic cuisine, but it is one of the most universally satisfying. Perhaps because of its long association with salt, pork is often cooked with, or served with fruit: England, and many countries in Europe serve it with applesauce; Danish cooks stuff pork with prunes, so do the Germans, who also stew pork in beer, serve it with sausages and potatoes, or with sauerkraut. In Greece and Turkey pork is an ingredient in moussaka; in Russia, Italy, Greece and Poland suckling pigs are spitted whole and spit-roasted –

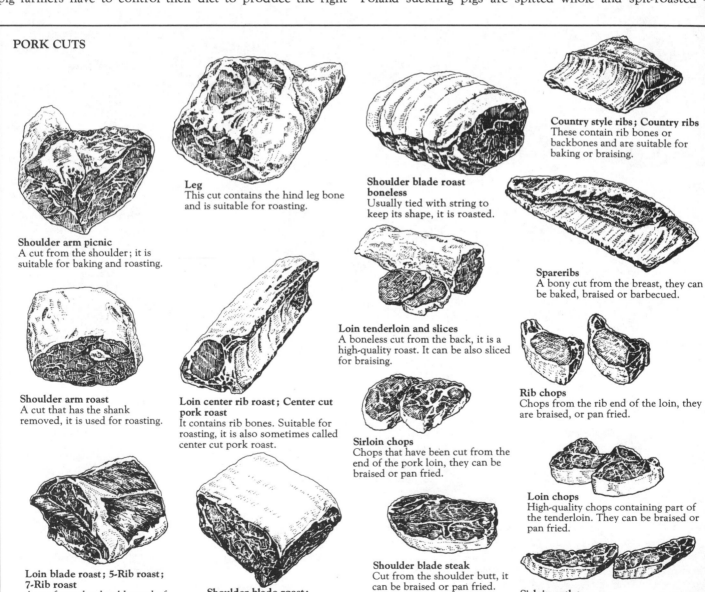

PORK CUTS

Leg
This cut contains the hind leg bone and is suitable for roasting.

Shoulder arm picnic
A cut from the shoulder; it is suitable for baking and roasting.

Shoulder arm roast
A cut that has the shank removed, it is used for roasting.

Loin center rib roast; Center cut pork roast
It contains rib bones. Suitable for roasting, it is also sometimes called center cut pork roast.

Loin blade roast; 5-Rib roast; 7-Rib roast
A cut from the shoulder end of the loin, it is used for roasting.

Shoulder blade roast; Boston butt
This is the top of the shoulder and is used for roasting.

Shoulder blade roast boneless
Usually tied with string to keep its shape, it is roasted.

Loin tenderloin and slices
A boneless cut from the back, it is a high-quality roast. It can be also sliced for braising.

Sirloin chops
Chops that have been cut from the end of the pork loin, they can be braised or pan fried.

Shoulder blade steak
Cut from the shoulder butt, it can be braised or pan fried.

Country style ribs; Country ribs
These contain rib bones or backbones and are suitable for baking or braising.

Spareribs
A bony cut from the breast, they can be baked, braised or barbecued.

Rib chops
Chops from the rib end of the loin, they are braised, or pan fried.

Loin chops
High-quality chops containing part of the tenderloin. They can be braised or pan fried.

Sirloin cutlets
Tender boneless cuts which are suitable for braising.

suckling pig is an essential part of the Polish Easter festivities. But it is the Chinese who really excel with a wide variety of pork dishes – they have had centuries of practice: pork is shredded and stir-fried, braised with mushrooms or spiced with star anise and ginger.

Choosing and using pork

The age of a pig at slaughter will determine its category: a 16- to 18-week-old pig that has attained a carcass weight of around 112lb (50kg) ("porker"), will be sold as fresh pork. At six months, having gained extra weight (and more fat) they are "baconers", used for producing bacon and hams. Pigs of a higher weight will be slaughtered for manufacturing pies, sausages, salami, and a variety of other pork products.

Pork should be pale pink with firm, white fat. Nearly all cuts of pork are prime, that is, they can be broiled or roasted because porkers are slaughtered at a young age and the meat is therefore tender throughout. The majority of cook books, even recent ones, recommend that pork be well done to the point of dryness, thus minimizing the danger of the parasite trichina. However, scientists have now recommended a new, safe internal temperature for pork at 170°F (76°C), so that the pork remains moist and tender.

Fresh pork is divided into seven primal cuts but only four are in general use by the consumer. The belly and jowl are sold to processors to become bacon, and the feet are sold as offal. The four consumer cuts are the leg, loin, breast and shoulder. Leg of pork (known as fresh ham) is sold whole, deboned or as two roasts, shank and butt. Ham steaks can be cut from here. The loin produces more bony or fatty roasts and chops. The breast is sectioned into ribs, whole rib sections are known as "slabs". The shoulder yields less tender and lean roasts than the leg. Picnics, butts and ham steaks are cut from this section.

Variety Meats

Variety meats or offal – literally the "off-fall" or off-cuts from the carcass, have been alternatively enjoyed or condemned for centuries, condemned because certain items such as the brain and heart were thought to provoke melancholy, while the head – and especially the boar's head – has been invested with symbolic significance of victory, similar to the fox's brush after the hunt.

Many people are still reluctant to eat brains, sweetbreads and tripe, and many more are unable to actually identify or pinpoint the location of caul, mesentery and chitterlings. Some forms of variety meats are unpopular for social, economic and religious reasons; others have always been in considerable demand, especially liver and kidneys – and particularly those of the calf.

Variety meats in the kitchen

All variety meats should be purchased as fresh as possible; if stale they are usually dark in color with a dry appearance.

Brains, sweetbreads and tongues need a preliminary soaking. Brains should be soaked in cold water until all the blood is leached away and the arteries and fibers should then be removed. Sweetbreads require soaking for an hour or more, then blanching (parboiling) in acidulated water (about 7 minutes for lambs'; 10 for calves'). Tongues should be soaked in acidulated water if fresh for an hour, or in plain water overnight if salted. Small tongues should be blanched for 10 minutes; larger ones for 30 minutes, and they should then be plunged in cold water before removing the skin.

Beef and pork kidneys can be soaked in acidulated water for about 30 minutes. Other items, such as liver, tripe, trotters and calves' feet, hearts and heads are usually prepared by the butcher.

Apart from the more popular items, listed below, a tour around the anatomy of an animal will reveal some of the less familiar cuts – beginning with the head.

Calves' and sheeps' heads may be boned or left whole. They may also be served whole – but more often than not divided into pieces – with appropriate sauces, the garnish being the sliced tongue and the brain. Pig's head is used mainly for charcuterie, in head cheese and sausages. Pigs' and calves' ears are usually broiled or stuffed. Calves' feet and pigs' trotters are highly gelatinous, and used to thicken stocks. They are also boned, stuffed, fried, and used in head cheeses.

Tails can be braised or boiled; sheeps' tails are made into a pie. Oxtail, which is rich in gelatin and has plenty of flavor, responds to long, moist cooking, in casseroles and soups.

Many variety meats come from the inside of the animal. Examples are the spleen (the pig's is used as a sausage ingredient; that of the ox and calf can be stuffed) and intestines (pigs' intestines are used as casings for sausages, and chitterlings or "chitlins" are famous in the southern states of America served with collard greens). Calf's mesentery (part of the peritoneum) is also a sausage ingredient, but may be fried or prepared in the manner of tripe, while the lungs or "lights" are for stewing. Pig's caul (the lace-like membrane around the paunch) is the binding for *crépinettes* (small sausages).

Caul
Pig's caul, the lace-like membrane around the paunch, is the binding used for *crépinettes*, small forcemeat sausages.

Chitterlings
Pigs' intestines which are used in sausage-making, they are famous in the southern states of America where they are served with collard greens.

Feet □
Calves' feet □ and **pigs' trotters** □ are highly gelatinous, and used to thicken stocks. They are also boned, stuffed and fried and used in head cheese.

Heads □
Pig's head □ is used mainly in charcuterie, in head cheese and sausages. When chopped with spices it is the basis of

Pennsylvania Dutch scrapple. **Calves'** □ and **sheeps'** □ **heads** may be boned or left whole and are usually prepared by the butcher. May also be served whole but usually divided into pieces and served with a sauce. **Bath chaps**, the smoked cheeks of the pig, are usually boiled and eaten cold like ham. **Calves' brains** □ are the most popular. They are served with black butter sauce or fried and cooked in batter. **Pigs'** and **calves' ears** can be broiled or stuffed. In China, pigs' ears are cooked with spices. **Sheeps' eyeballs** □ are eaten in some Middle Eastern countries. **Beef tongue** □ has an excellent flavor, fresh or salted. Salted tongue is used cooked, pressed and sliced cold. Fresh tongue is braised with wine, or boiled and served with various garnishes. **Veal** □ and **lamb tongues** are more tender but can similarly be salted and pressed.

Hearts □
Oxheart □ is tough and requires long, moist cooking, or parboiling before long, slow roasting. **Calves'** and **lambs'** □ hearts are more tender. Both are suitable for stuffing.

Kidneys □
Veal □ kidneys are usually more tender than others. The French prepare them as *rognons sautés au Madère*; in Belgium they are cooked with gin and juniper berries. In Britain they are an essential part of steak and kidney pie or pudding. **Lamb** □ kidneys are stronger in flavor than **veal** kidneys. Remove the fine skin before cooking. They can be sliced, then broiled or fried. **Beef** □ kidney is stronger flavored and coarser, and can be used to advantage in pies. Like lamb kidneys in shape **pork** □ kidneys are larger and more strongly flavored. They can be grilled, or used in stews.

Lights □
These are the lungs. They are not very substantial or nutritious but are sometimes included in stews.

Liver □
Veal □ liver is generally held to be the finest in quality and flavor, therefore the most expensive. It should be finely sliced and broiled or fried briefly, otherwise it hardens. **Lamb** □ liver is more strongly flavored and often less tender yet suitable for broiling or frying. It is spit-roasted in the Middle East. **Beef** □ liver is inexpensive, with a strong flavor, but usually tough. It is suitable for braising and stewing while **pork** □ liver is also strongly flavored, and largely used in charcuterie, where it is one of the ingredients in *pâtés*.

Marrowbone □
Shoulder or thigh bones of oxen or calves contain marrow – a soft substance extracted from the bones when they are cooked. It is used in sauces and stews.

Melt □
This is the spleen. **Pigs'** □ melts sometimes go into sausages; **ox** and **calves'** melts can be stuffed.

Mesentery
This is a membrane – part of the peritoneum. Calf's mesentery is a sausage ingredient but may be fried or prepared in the same way as tripe.

Sweetbreads □
The pancreas and thymus glands are known as sweetbreads or, in France, *ris de veau*. Recipes for **veal** □ and **lamb** sweetbreads are more or less interchangeable. The thymus gland is located in the throat, the pancreas in the viscera near the stomach; they are generally referred to as *stomach* and *throat sweetbreads*. The former is plump and rounded, the latter elongated. Sweetbreads are eaten with black butter sauce.

Tails □
These can be braised or boiled; **sheeps'** tails are made into a pie. **Oxtail** □, which is rich in gelatin and has plenty of flavor, responds to long, moist cooking, in casseroles and in soups.

Testicles; Fries; Animelles
Lambs' and **calves'** testicles can be fried in batter, sautéed or cooked in a *court-bouillon* and served with vinaigrette.

Tripe □
There are two kinds of tripe coming from the viscera of oxen and cows. Ruminants possess two stomachs – the rumen is the first, and provides **plain** tripe, the reticulum is the second, and gives us the **honeycomb** tripe, generally the more tender. Tripe has been processed by the butcher before sale, but it still needs slow cooking. Perhaps the most famous recipe is the French *tripe à la mode de Caen*.

Sausages and Preserved Meats

Early on in history it was discovered that meat would keep for an extended period if the moisture content could be reduced by drying, salting or smoking. In this way regular year-round supplies of meat became available and a new era that was eventually to see hams, bacon and sausages take their place as a staple part of our diet began.

Inhabitants of hot climates pounded meat to release the juices and dried the strips in the sun or over a fire. The South African *biltong* is an example of this technique. In North America, the Red Indians invented *pemmican* – dried, lean buffalo meat, pounded and mixed with fat, vegetables and fruit (usually cranberries), then packed in hide skins and sealed with tallow. Sealing meat in fat is still a technique used in the preparation of pâtés and terrines.

In Mexico and Central America, buffalo meat was cut into strips and sun-dried. This *charqui* was later made by the pioneers, who knew it as "jerky" or "jerked beef". The peasants of Europe, and in particular those of Britain, lived for centuries on a diet of bacon, bread and beer – and bacon was often a luxury. Most of the beef that came to the table was powdered with dry salt. Ships' victuallers bought it by the ton for the British fleet.

Cooking techniques were devised to offset the saltiness; these included adding cereals such as barley to absorb the salt, or a variety of vegetables: the *pot-au-feu* of France, and the boiled beef dinners of New England were dishes born of expediency. Spices, especially ginger and pepper, played an important role in masking the taste of salt meat and, during one period in the seventeenth century, piles of oranges were maintained in the kitchens of wealthy households, so that the juice could be added to cooked meat dishes.

Although salt beef and sun-dried buffalo meat certainly played an important role regionally, much of the tradition of preserved meats actually rests firmly on the pig. French butchers, particularly, have a long history of charcuterie – the hams of Gaul were so famous that they were even exported to Rome – and it is the French who must be accredited with developing the sausage.

Originally an ancestor of the sausage (the word comes from the Latin *salsus* meaning "salted") was made by primitive peoples, using the paunch of an animal to contain other parts of the viscera, which would then have been cooked over a fire; Scotland's haggis is a probable descendant. The Greeks and Romans encouraged sausage-making and it is believed that the Germans, who claim to have invented the sausage, learned their skills from the Romans, but it was left to the French to develop the idea so imaginatively – the range and variety they have devised over the years is staggering.

Following France, the most varied contributions to sausage-making come from Germany and Italy, with several other European countries providing a significant share.

The European ways with hams and sausages spread to America – the French inspired the Creole-Acadian *boudins* and *andouilles*; the Italians the bologna and salami of New York; the Germans inspired the frankfurters and knackwursts of Milwaukee; Spain and Portugal originated the *chorizos* of Latin America.

The American diet of the nineteenth century consisted largely of salt pork. Utility and poverty saw that every scrap of the animal was used, preferably salted and smoked, so that the products could last the months following pig-killing time – usually November. The tradition of using every part of the animal is still maintained: sausages, liver sausages and blood puddings employ the inexpensive cuts, while the choicer portions – the belly, loin and legs – are reserved for the smoking and curing processes, to produce bacon and ham.

Processing

The word "cure" simply means that meat is cured of its propensity to putrefaction. In the past, dry-salting was often unsatisfactory because salt was coarse and unrefined, and could produce uneven results. Sugar, which helps soften the meat and adds flavor, was used only by the few that could afford it. Meat was thus dry, hard and very salty but in the late eighteenth century some attempt was made to refine curing techniques.

Types of sausages and hams vary because local tastes, ingredients and techniques vary. Hungarians add paprika to their sausages; German utilize the wild juniper that flavors Westphalian hams. Brine recipes vary too and so do smoking techniques. The following are the most commonly used.

Brine cure: This is also known as *pickle* and, if sugar is added, it becomes a "sweet pickle". Most pickles are sweet – an exception is that used for Bayonne ham. Some brines are spiced and may contain juniper, coriander, ginger, and other spices. Saltpeter is added because it keeps the meat attractively pink – bacteria in the meat convert the salt to a nitrite (or nitrite is added to the brine). Nitrites stabilize the red pigment myoglobin in the blood, retaining the characteristic color of the meat.

Dry cure: Dry salt is rubbed into the meat, special attention being paid to the area around the bone, if any. The salt is moisture-absorbing and draws out the juices to form a brine which then penetrates the meat.

Smoking: This doubtless came about from drying meat over a fire. Wood smoke contains several antiseptic tar products, and meat is usually smoked over hardwood logs and sawdust. Duration of smoking varies considerably, according to the product and the recipe.

Corning: In the sixteenth century the word "corn" was synonymous with "grain", and meat rubbed with grains of salt was thus corned. In New England saltpeter was omitted from the cure and the resulting gray color of the meat is still preferred. In Britain, corned beef refers to a product of cured, boiled, pressed and then canned beef.

Hams, bacons and other cured meats

Ham is the cured and smoked hind leg of pork while bacon is usually the cured belly of pork which accounts for its high fat content. Canadian bacon, however, is cut from the loin of the animal and is consequently much meatier.

There are perhaps a hundred or more different hams, each country contributing to the selection, but most are cured in more or less the same manner – dry-salted or brined, smoked and matured. Bacon is available smoked and unsmoked in two forms, either sliced or as unsliced slab bacon. Other meats such as mutton and beef are sometimes cured.

Sausages

Sausages are made from the minced meat of pork, veal, beef, chicken, mutton, rabbit, even horseflesh and armadillo. Some countries add a quantity of cereal to the mixture, notably Britain, while other countries, such as Germany, forbid it. A rich variety of ingredients is used in sausage-making: eggs, cream, beer, wine, pigs' blood, tripe, breadcrumbs, oatmeal, potato flour, onion and garlic, herbs and spices, salt and pepper. Some sausages are precooked, others fresh, others cured, air-dried and smoked.

Sausage skins, or casings, are made of the intestines of sheep and pigs and there are also artificial casings. Those sausages to be smoked are first air-dried, then smoked over hardwood chips or sawdust, either cold-smoked or hot-smoked depending on the product.

There are literally thousands of sausages – Germany alone boasts nearly 1500 varieties, not to mention the legion of Italian salamis. Germany categorizes sausages into *bruhwurst*: lightly smoked and scalded fresh sausages, to be cooked by the purchaser; *rohwurst*: salami-type sausages, raw, cured, air-dried and smoked; *kochwurst*: ready-cooked, used for spreading, or slicing and eating cold. French types are divided into large *saucissons*, which may be smoked, *saucissons fumées*; fresh *saucisses* and *saucisses fumées*, and the boiling sausages *cervelat*.

The most diverse and varied of all sausage types must certainly be the Italian salami. The characteristic of this type of sausage is that it is brine-pickled, smoked, or both, and is made of raw ingredients.

SAUSAGES See also pp. 190–99

Andouillette ☐
A French sausage which, like the larger **andouille**, is made of pork and/or tripe, chitterlings, calf mesentery, pepper and perhaps wine, onions, and spices. Sometimes smoked, it can be broiled or fried.

Berliner
A pork and beef sausage mildly flavored with salt and sugar.

Bierschinken ☐
A German sausage containing ham, or ham fat and sometimes peppercorns and pistachio nuts.

Whole smoked meats

Bierwurst □
A German pork or pork-and-beef sausage flecked with fat and smoked.

Blood sausage;
Black pudding □
There are many versions of this sausage or pudding made with pigs' blood. The British one has oatmeal, onions and spices. The German one is **blutwurst**; the French **boudin noir**; the Spanish **morcilla** □; the Irish **drisheen**; the Italian **biroldo**. They are usually sliced and fried.

Bockwurst
A delicately flavored, highly perishable German white sausage, consisting of fresh pork and veal, chopped chives, parsley, eggs, and milk.

Bologna □
There are a number of versions but it is usually a mixture of cooked smoked pork and beef. **Polony** is the English version.

Boudin blanc
Unlike *boudin noir* this is a fresh sausage made with white meat and may also include pork, eggs, cream, seasonings and spices. It is eaten hot, poached or broiled.

Bratwurst □
A German *bruhwurst* type which can be either broiled, grilled or fried. It is made of minced, spiced pork/veal.

Braunschweiger
A cooked, smoked liver sausage containing eggs and milk.

Breakfast sausage □
A small, finely minced fresh pork sausage which may contain a variety of spices; it can be fried or boiled.

Butifara □
A Spanish pork sausage with garlic and spices. It is preboiled and air-dried and may be eaten cold but features in the Catalonian cooked dish *cazuela a la Catalana*.

Cambridge sausage
An English sausage containing pork, herbs and spices.

Cervelat; Cervelas □
The name originated from the Latin word for brains but

nowadays it contains pork, and is usually seasoned with garlic. A Swiss version is the **land jaeger** – a black, wrinkly and heavily smoked sausage. The **goettinger** is a German cervelat made with spiced beef and pork and the **saveloy** □, containing saltpeter which gives it a reddish tinge, is the English version.

Chorizo □
A Spanish (and Latin-American) spicy sausage made with pork, cayenne (or other hot pepper) usually in narrow casings. Some chorizos are fresh, but most are dried and smoked. **Longaniza** is a Portuguese version.

Cotechino □
An Italian, lean and fat pork sausage. In Italy they are made fresh, but a part-cured, part-cooked type is commercially distributed and exported. The fresh needs several hours cooking, the commercial sausage only about 30 minutes. It is often served hot with beans.

Crépinette □
A general term for a small minced meat sausage – some contain lamb; others pork. Wrapped in caul, they are coated with melted butter and breadcrumbs.

Cumberland sausage □
An English sausage made of coarsely chopped pork, with pepper. Stuffed in a long casing.

Extrawurst □
A lightly smoked sausage of minced beef and pork from Germany. It is poached or broiled.

Frankfurter □
An ancestor of the ubiquitous hot dog it is made of lean pork, very finely ground, filled in narrow casings and smoked. American frankfurters contain beef and pork. **Vienna sausage** is a small "cocktail" frankfurter. **Knackwurst** is a small, plump lean-meat frankfurter containing pork and beef.

Haggis
A Scottish sausage, served hot on festive occasions (and other times of the year). Haggis is made from the liver, lungs and heart of a sheep, chopped with onions, oatmeal, parsley and

seasonings, the mixture is then stuffed into the paunch. It needs long cooking, but commercial ones are precooked and only require about 30 minutes.

Jagdwurst □
There are various types of this "hunter's wurst", some large and round, others narrow and flat. They contain pork and spices and are smoked. *Schinken jagdwurst* □ contains ham.

Kabanos □
A Polish sausage made of minced pork.

Kalbwurst
Generally a German veal smoked sausage, it may also contain pork, pork fat and pistachio nuts.

Katenrauchwurst □
Containing smoked pork, it is firm and dark-skinned.

Knoblauchwurst □
A German garlic sausage, made with fat and lean pork flavored with spices and garlic. It can be broiled or poached.

Kolbasa and **kielbasa** □
The first is Russian, the second Polish, and both words mean "sausage". Made with beef and pork, well spiced and either fresh or smoked.

Lap cheong □
A Chinese sausage of chopped pork, cereal, soy and paprika.

Linguic
A Portuguese pork sausage cured in brine, seasoned with garlic, and spiced with cinnamon and cumin.

Link sausages □
A general term covering fresh sausages, which may contain pork or pork and beef or venison and seasonings. There are many varieties from different countries available under many names listed here. **Skinless sausages** consist of sausage meat sold without casings. They are sometimes shaped in patties.

Liverwurst; Leberwurst □
A German liver sausage of which there are many kinds. Most are made of pork, and pork or veal liver and may also contain truffles, peppercorns,

flecks of back fat. They are usually finely minced and lightly smoked and are ready to eat, as slices or a spread.

Luganeghe □
A pure pork Italian sausage in a continuous casing, it can be boiled or broiled.

Merguez □
A spiced sausage from North Africa made from goat or mutton and flavored with *hrisa*, a mixture of hot pepper and cumin. It is usually broiled.

Mettwurst/Metwurst □
A German spreading sausage of pork and beef often containing paprika. They vary in texture and are bought ready-to-eat as a spread or in slices.

Mortadella □
A large, bland sausage from Bologna, it is made of pork, garlic and sometimes flavored with coriander seeds. Ready to eat it should be thinly sliced.

Oxford sausage □
An English sausage containing veal, pork, beef suet and herbs and spices.

Paprika sausage □
A coarse-textured sausage, made of lamb and beef and containing paprika and other seasonings.

Pepperoni □
An Italian pork and beef sausage, flavored with red pepper and spices.

Plockwurst □
German beef or beef/pork *rohwurst* type. There are several varieties, including the **pfeffer-plockwurst** □ with peppercorns.

Salamelle □
The name given by the Italians to a type of spiced sausage.

Salami □
There is a vast range of salami sausages available. These include **Birnenformige** □, **Edel** □, **Land** □ and **Netz** □ from Germany; **Alesandre, Calabrese, Cotto** □, **Felinetti** □, **Genoa** □, **Milano** □, **Napoli** □, **Easter Nola** and **Toscana** □ from Italy and there are versions from America, Denmark, Hungary as well as French types such as

Sliced smoked meats

Arles. All are made with uncooked meat which may be pork, beef or a mixture and variously flavored. Some are decorated with pistachio or peppercorns or coriander seeds. **Kosher salami** is an all-beef type flavored with garlic, mustard, coriander and juniper. Salami may be air-dried or smoked or both. It is ready to eat, thinly sliced and eaten cold although chopped slices find their way into many Italian cooked dishes. **Salamini** are smaller versions of the usually large sausage.

Salsiccie □
Italian pork sausages also known as *salsiccie casalinga* when they are home-made. They are usually flavored with garlic and peppercorns and may be poached, broiled or fried.

Saucisson fumé □
Saucissons are large and can be air-dried or smoked. The *saucisson fumé* is typically pork, with flecks of back fat or bacon, peppercorns and garlic and herbs. Some are coated with dried herbs.

Schinken kalbfleischwurst □
A variety of sausage made from ham, ham fat, mixed with pork and sometimes flavored with peppercorns and caraway seeds. It is sliced and eaten cold.

Smokies
Smoked, cooked links of pork and beef spiced with pepper.

Strassburger
A liver and veal sausage containing pistachio nuts.

Teewurst □
A German *rohwurst* type, finely minced pork or pork/beef, spiced and lightly smoked. Teewurst is a spreading sausage.

Thuringer
A pork sausage that may also contain some beef or veal. It can be either fresh or cooked.

Toulouse sausage □
A sausage from Toulouse in France, made of pork and pork fat, coarsely chopped and flavored with pepper and a little sugar. These sausages feature in several French recipes, especially the cassoulet of Toulouse.

Weisswurst
A mildly spiced German sausage made of pork and veal.

Zampone □
An Italian sausage from Modena where the meat is stuffed into a boned pig's trotter.

Zungenwurst □
A large, German smoked sausage made of pork fat, large pieces of pork tongue, sometimes liver and blood.

OTHER MEATS See also p. 200
Bauernspeck
Austrian belly and flank of pork is cured in brine with juniper berries, then cold-smoked.

Bünderfleish
Swiss dried beef, it is brined, rubbed with spices, then air-dried.

Corned beef; Salt beef
Cured and spiced brisket of beef. **Bresaolo** is a dried salt beef from Italy.

Dutch loaf
A cold cut comprised of pork and beef.

Fenelar
Norwegian smoked mutton. Leg is dry-salted with salt, saltpeter and sugar, rubbed with the mixture for several days, then brined in a sweet pickle after which it is smoked and air-dried.

Head cheese
A cooked meat specialty product containing small pieces of pork head bound together by gelatin.

Honey loaf
A mixture of pork, beef, honey spices and pickles.

Pastrama □
Romanian cured meat taken from either goat, mutton, beef, pork or goose. The meat is dry-cured with a mixture of salt, saltpeter, black pepper, nutmeg, paprika, garlic and allspice, before smoking. The American version, **pastrami** □, is cured, smoked plate of beef.

Scrapple
A specialty product of cooked pork and cornmeal flour.

Smoked turkey □
The meat is soaked in pickling brine and then smoked.

Souse □
Pieces of pork meat in a vinegar-spiked gelatin base to which dill pickles, sweet red peppers, and bay leaves are sometimes added.

Spinkganz □
German smoked goose. Only the breast is used, this is dry-salted with salt, saltpeter, sugar and pepper, then smoked.

Tongue □
Usually beef, it can be smoked, corned or pickled.

HAMS See also p. 202
Bayonne □
Cured at Orthez in southwest France, this is a raw ham type – a *jambon cru*. The brine contains red wine and rosemary and olive oil. After brining it is wrapped in straw and smoked.

Bradenham □
A black-skinned ham from Chippenham in England. The ham is dry-cured, then treated with spices and molasses.

Deviled □
A prepared product made of finely ground ham and seasonings.

Irish □
Usually dry-cured and smoked over peat. Limerick and Belfast are two well-known types.

Kentucky □
A dry-cured, country ham, treated with the cure throughout the maturing process.

Parma □
A fine-quality raw ham – *prosciutto crudo*, cured at Langhirano near Parma. Hams are rubbed with a mixture of salt, sugar, nitrates, pepper, allspice, nutmeg, coriander and mustard. They are packed together for 10 days, the process is then repeated. After maturing, the hams are pressed, steamed and rubbed with pepper.

Seager □
Ham from Suffolk, England,

cured by a sweet pickle of brine and syrup, the ham is dried, smoked and matured.

Virginia and **Smithfield □**
The hams are given two rubbings of salt and salpeter, washed, and smoked. They are then rubbed with pepper, and matured for up to 18 months.

Westphalia □
A raw ham type, like Bayonne and Parma. The hams are dry-cured with salt, sugar and saltpeter, kept for 2 weeks, then brined for a further 2 weeks and smoked.

York □
A typical brine uses salt, saltpeter, sugar, juniper berries and herbs. The hams are brined and smoked.

Coffee

The raw material
The green coffee beans are extracted from the ripe, red berries of the tree, each berry containing two beans or seeds. The red berries of the coffee tree ripen several times a year, and are usually hand-picked, although in inferior grades, the trees are sometimes shaken and the ripe berries are picked from the ground, or the branches are stripped of everything at once, and the ripe berries are picked out from a cluster of leaves, flowers and under-ripe fruit. The berries are then hulled by one of two processes: the *dry* method, in which the berries are sun-dried for three weeks, then hulled by machine, and the *wet* method, where the berries are washed and hulled by machine, and then partially fermented before being given a final washing. Some countries, notably Costa Rica, also polish their beans. It takes approximately 4000 berries to produce 2.2 lb (1kg) of coffee.

Coffee originated in Ethiopia, where *Coffea arabica*, one of the three main species, grows wild. The others, *robusta* and *liberica*, were later found in the Congo and Liberia respectively. The coffee tree requires a hot, moist climate and a rich soil. While *arabica* grows best at a high altitude – from 2000 to 6000 feet above sea level – the other species grow better at altitudes below 2000 feet.

The word "coffee" comes from the Arabic *quwah*, which, through its Turkish form *kahveh*, became coffee in English, *café* in French and Spanish, *caffe* in Italian and *kaffee* in German, all remarkably alike. *Arabica* was first cultivated about 575 AD but it was not until the fifteenth century in southern Arabia that the plant was extensively cultivated. From there it spread to countries bordering the Indian ocean and the Mediterranean. Though its early history is shrouded in legend, we do know that for a time there was disapproval of coffee in Christian countries – an attitude that was changed by Pope Clement VIII, despite opposition from the rest of the clergy. By the mid-seventeenth century it had reached all of Europe, where innumerable coffee-houses, forerunners of the modern club, sprang up. It reached North America by 1668 but did not supplant tea as a beverage until after the Boston Tea Party, when tea became unpopular. Early in the eighteenth century it was taken to the French West Indies and from there was introduced to Brazil and the rest of South and Central America. Coffee today is grown in the West Indies, Mexico, Central America, tropical South America, Africa, India and Indonesia. *Arabica*, *robusta* and *liberica* are all grown commercially and each has its own varieties.

Extracting the brew
Coffee beans are classified into three main types. The finest coffee comes from *Coffea arabica* and has a low caffeine content. *Coffea canephora*, which produces the *robusta*, is a strong, high caffeine type, but of inferior quality. Finally there is *Coffea liberica*, which is very productive but mediocre in taste.

Blending the many different varieties of bean grown throughout the world enables coffee merchants to achieve an infinite range of tastes, and it is upon their technique that reputations depend.

Taste and aroma are induced by roasting the raw, green

beans. The beans turn a pale yellow at around 212°F (100°C); at 300°F (150°C) they begin to swell and turn brown, and on reaching 450°F (230°C) they swell to almost double their volume, turn dark brown, and sweat oil on the surface, giving the beans an attractive glossy appearance.

There are four main types of roast. The *high* or *double* roast has a strong, bitter taste and should always be drunk black. The *full* roast has a slightly bitter taste but lacks the "burnt" taste of a high roasted bean. *Medium* roast produces a strong-tasting coffee without the bitter taste, while the *light* or *pale* roast allows the milder beans to develop a full, delicate taste and aroma which is good with milk.

Strong, black coffees, especially the *robustas*, tend to be more stimulating on account of the caffeine present. To produce decaffeinated coffees, the beans are steamed in order to hasten the solubility of the caffeine alkaloid, which is then further treated with a solvent such as dichloromethane.

The process of extracting an aromatic brew from roots and seeds has been thoroughly pursued since ancient times, and few plants have been ignored. The Turks and later the Viennese developed a fondness for fig-flavored coffee. French and Belgian coffee-makers found that the dried and ground roots of the chicory plant (*Cichorium intybus*) imparted a desirable taste when added to coffee. Other plants have been used as coffee substitutes, in particular the dried roots of the dandelion (*Taraxacum officinale*), a relative of chicory.

Coffee in the kitchen

Raw coffee beans will keep indefinitely in a cool, dry place. Once roasted and ground, the coffee should be used as soon as possible; the finer the grind, the more rapid the loss of taste. Pulverized Turkish coffee should be drunk fresh within twenty-four hours of purchase.

Brewing coffee is merely a matter of infusion or boiling and, although there are many types of equipment for coffee-making on the market today, all that is really needed is a jug or a saucepan.

Infusion, and in particular filtration, is the most popular method of brewing coffee in the West today. By this method, boiling water, which has been slightly cooled, is poured over the ground coffee, extracting the caffeine and aromatic constituents and leaving behind the bitter components.

Boiling coffee gives it a strong, bitter taste, as much of the aroma is steam-distilled from the brew and the bitter components are dissolved into it.

Coffee used in recipes should be made very strong and concentrated; or you can use instant coffee powder, with excellent results. Coffee is often used in confectionery, baking, desserts and ice cream and any recipe that includes the term "mocha" will have a predominantly coffee taste. Coffee also features in several drinks with an alcohol base. Apart from "Irish coffee" there are such liqueurs as Tia Maria, kahlua, crème de café, crème de mokka, and Bahia, mostly made from the pulp of the coffee berry.

Instant coffee

Instant coffees are available in powder form or granules, and have been in use since the 1930s, heralding the era of convenience foods. They are produced by brewing freshly roasted and ground coffee to obtain a strong concentrate. This is then passed through an atomizing spray into a stream of hot air which evaporates the water and leaves behind a fine residue powder.

Freeze-dried coffee is the most successful method of making an aromatic instant coffee. The coffee is brewed, frozen into slabs and ground into particles which are then put into a vacuum with a small amount of heat. This turns the ice directly into steam, leaving the ground particles dry, chunky and ready for use.

Colombian
A full-bodied coffee bean that has little acidity.

Costa Rican
Mild-tasting bluish-green *arabica* beans, that give a slight acidity.

Jamaican
A large yellow bean *arabica* coffee with a delicate flavor. One of the most famous varieties is the **Blue Mountain** coffee, very popular in Japan.

Kenyan
The pale green African *arabica* beans give a rich liquor with a sharp taste when roasted.

Mocha
An *arabica* type, originally from the old port of Mocha in Yemen, and one of the world's finest coffees. It is known for its slightly "gamey" or "cheesy" taste. Production is limited, so the label "mocha" can mean a blend, such as **Ethiopian**, real Mocha, **Honduras** and **Nicaraguan** coffees.

Mysore
East Indian *arabica*, bluish-gray beans, giving a liquor with a fine, strong taste.

Santos
Santos and **Rio** are similar types, both having green-yellow beans which give a liquor with a smooth, mellow taste and no acidity.

Turkish
Not a blend, but a pulverized coffee. Most Turkish is made in Cyprus, traditionally from Mocha, but now mostly from Brazilian beans. A typical blend might be one third each of Santos, Rio and **Victoria**, all Brazilian *arabicas*.

Tea

Tea is the world's most popular drink. It is the name given to the leaves of the tea plant *Thea sinensis*, an evergreen tree or shrub which grows in damp tropical or subtropical regions at altitudes of up to 7000 feet. It is closely related to the magnolia and would grow, like its relative, to a great height if it were not pruned to a bush, so the leaves can be easily picked. Though the plant may have originated in India it had reached China (where as *cha* it is the national drink), by 200 AD and Japan (where it was not only a popular drink but had reached great ritual significance in the *cha-no-yu* [tea] ceremony), by the eighth century. It was brought to Europe by the Dutch in 1610, reached England in 1644 where it has given its name to a light afternoon meal, and America, where a tax on it was partly responsible for the War of Independence, at the beginning of the eighteenth century. It has subsequently spread throughout the world. It is grown principally in China, Taiwan, Japan, India, Sri Lanka and Southeast Asia, and, to a lesser extent, in Africa.

There are two main types of tea, black and green, produced from different treatments of the leaves after they are picked. For black tea, which is amber-colored and strongly flavored, the leaves are fermented. For green tea, greenish-yellow in color and rather bitter in taste, this step is omitted. There is another category of tea – Oolong, grown in China, Taiwan and Japan which is partly fermented with a subtle flavor combining the characteristics of both black and green tea. Oolong is often perfumed and flavored with jasmine flowers.

The prime part of the tea shrub is the bud, enclosed by two downy leaves (*pekoe* in Chinese, means "downy"). Tea planters refer to the "two leaves and a bud", while the word "pekoe", or more accurately "orange pekoe" is employed to describe leaf sizes and grades. The leaves are plucked from the shrub by hand with great skill and remarkable speed and it takes about 4lb (2kg) of leaves to produce 1lb (450g) of black tea. In some regions the seasons have considerable influence on the quality of the final product – the teas of North India, for example, are picked from April to December, while the finest Ceylon teas have a short season in February and another in August – the remaining months produce teas of a less superior quality.

Processing the leaves

The plucked leaves are swiftly transported to the factory, where they are spread on racks to dry, losing about 50 per cent of their moisture content. After this "withering" process, the leaves are machine-rolled to break up the cellular structure, which releases the fermenting enzymes and encourages absorption of oxygen; the rolling technique was also designed to give a decorative twist to the leaf, imitating the original hand-twisted leaves of China. After rolling, the pulped leaves are left to ferment at about 82°F (27°C), and they gradually assume a coppery hue; fermentation is necessary to produce the characteristic taste and strength of tea. The fermentation

is checked by "firing" in chambers, that is, passing a current of hot air over the leaves for about 30 minutes, at a carefully regulated temperature.

Once fired, the black and broken leaves are sifted by machine to be sorted into two main grades – "broken and small leaf" teas, and "leaf" teas. It is generally true to say that the larger the leaf size the better the taste of the brew, while smaller leaves give stronger and darker brews.

Broken leaf teas are separated from the leaf teas by sifting, then further graded into broken orange pekoe; flowery broken orange pekoe; broken pekoe, and so on down to "fannings" and "dust"; while leaf grades are flowery orange pekoe; orange pekoe, and pekoe.

These orthodox grades apply to both China and India teas, but in recent years, Indian manufacturers have gone over to machine-cutting, called "legge-cut" leaves. Such teas are quick to infuse and thus are particularly suitable for use in the tea-bag industry.

Tea in the kitchen

Tea is used as a hot beverage, as iced tea or tea punch (with lime juice, sherry and rum). Ceylon tea is best for making iced tea or tea punch, since it is the only type that does not cloud. Black tea may be served with lemon and sugar or with milk, green tea with lemon and sugar or plain. In North Africa, tea is infused with mint leaves and a great deal of sugar added; in the Himalayas a kind of tea soup is concocted with yak butter and salt.

Tea is rarely used as an ingredient in recipes, but tea ice cream and tea soufflé are examples. However, the habit of taking soothing or stimulating beverages by infusion is universal, and probably arose from the medicinal application of brewed herbs. Tea, coffee, Paraguayan maté (*Ilex pape*), Yapon tea (*L. cassine*) and guarana bread (*Paullinia sorbilis*) all contain tannin, theine or caffeine, but the majority of infusions are free from stimulants. Such are the tisanes or herbal teas – camomile, agrimony, bergamot, vervain, tillene, and mint.

Tea should be made in china teapots as metal ones may affect the taste of delicate teas. Metal ones, however, help keep the tea hot. Tea must be kept in an airtight container or "tea caddy" for long-term storage.

Silver teapot
A Swedish-designed teapot made in the early 18th century

Assam □
A high-quality, full-bodied tea from Assam Province in northeastern India.

Ceylon
Delicate and fragrant teas grown in altitudes of over 4000 feet. High quality.

Darjeeling □
Considered the best and most delicate of all the Indian teas, it is grown around the town of Darjeeling in the State of West Bengal on the slopes of the Himalayas.

Earl Grey
A well-known, blended tea with a strong taste.

Green □
Unfermented tea made in China, Taiwan and Japan. Green teas include such types as **gunpowder** □, **chun mee** and **sow mee**, and part-fermented Oolong teas. They are characterized by a delicate taste and fine aroma.

Jasmine □
Tea that is blended with dried jasmine flowers.

Keemun □
Fermented tea with a large, black leaf, and said to possess "the fragrance of an orchid".

Lapsang Souchong □
Fermented black tea with a brittle leaf, and a "smoky"

taste. Lapsangs come from the Province of Fukien and Taiwan.

Scented Orange Pekoe □
Fermented black tea with a jasmine taste.

Wines, Beers and Spirits

The use of alcohol in recipes has only developed during recent times. It is true that the ancient Egyptians may have cooked with beer, flavored with mandrake root, and that the Greeks and Romans may have used wine in their recipes, in preference to water, or as a marinade for tough and salted meats, but spirits and liqueurs had not yet been discovered.

By 300 BC the Aztecs were brewing pulque from the agave cactus, though it is unlikely that they knew how to distill it. The happy discovery of distillation is credited to the Chinese, who were probably producing a type of rice spirit by 1000 BC. The use of the *alembic*, or still, was pursued only after an Arab chemist called Geber wrote about his experiments with distillation in 800 AD. The product was alcohol, a word deriving from the Arabic *al'kohl*, a black cosmetic (kohl) produced by a process similar to distillation.

Spirits and liqueurs

Geber's experiments were continued by European alchemists, who used alcohol medicinally, as a base liquor in which fruits and herbs were steeped. Distilling methods became more refined over the years until, by the twelfth century, the Russians and Poles were able to distill grain mash to make a type of vodka, or "little water" (probably from rye). At the same time, Irish monks began producing a spirit from barley, which they called *uisge beatha*, the "water of life". These "waters" had the harsh taste of unrefined and unmatured spirit and needed herbs to render them palatable. Even the *usquebaugh* of Scotland – later to be anglicized to "whisky" – had in those days the addition of licorice, raisins, cloves and ginger to the base spirit.

Herbs and spices were the physicians' stock-in-trade, and were eventually to inspire some of the finest spirits and liqueurs, whose origins can be traced back to the fifteenth and sixteenth centuries. The method of making liqueurs has remained virtually unchanged: they are still based on the extraction of essential oils from fruits and herbs. Liqueurs were the speciality of the monasteries. French monks of the Benedictine order produced the herbal elixir called Béné-dictine, while the Carthusians near Grenoble responded with the powerful green Chartreuse.

In southwest France, the wine-growers of the Garonne and Charente regions began distilling their wines to make *ayga ardenterius*, "burnt wines". These later became known as Armagnac and Cognac *brandies*, a word probably deriving from the Dutch *brandewijn*, the Dutch being particularly fond of it. In the sixteenth century Holland produced its own contribution to the growing family of spirits when a professor at Leyden university distilled an *eau-de-vie* from rye. The addition of spices and juniper berries created a unique and aromatic beverage that the Dutch called *jenever*, and the English abbreviated to "gin". Throughout Europe, fruit-growers saw the possibilities in distilling fermented fruit juices. In Normandy, Calvados was the issue of apples. Alsatian growers produced *eaux-de-vie* from pears; the Hungarians made *slivovitz* from plums. Following the slow introduction of the potato to Europe in the sixteenth century, Russians and Scandinavians were able to produce vodka and aquavit.

Spirits can be made from almost any plant – and almost every plant has been tried. Sugar cane, first brought to the West Indies in the seventeenth century, was an ideal source of the dark, potent rum. Settlers in the New World, who had tried everything from pumpkins to pears, found that they could make an excellent spirit from corn mixed with rye – and Bourbon whiskey was born.

By now the Chinese and Japanese had discovered their own wines and spirits (*pai chiu*), made from rice, millet, and wheat, and yellow Chinese rice wine and *sake* are still used extensively in Oriental cooking. Rice was also used in the East Indies to make *arrack* or *raki*.

Processing

Wines, ciders and beer are the products of fermentation. Cider is the product of fermented apple juice, and wine that of fermented grape juice, though in the East the Japanese and Chinese have produced wine from fermented rice grain. Red wines are made from black grapes by fermenting the complete fruit – skins, juice and pips altogether. White wines can be made from either color but if the black ones are used the skins are separated before fermentation. Champagne is a sparkling wine – one that has a double fermentation. It is fermented, bottled and fermented again. Generally, wines have a 10 per cent alcohol content.

Beer is the fermented mash of malted barley and hops. Basically there are three types: light-bodied, medium- and heavy-bodied. A great deal depends on the degree of heat used in the course of processing. Beers usually have about a 3 per cent alcohol content.

Fortified wines are those whose alcohol content has been raised to about 20 per cent – sometimes even more. Alcohol – often brandy – is added either during or at the end of fermentation.

Spirits are distilled from wines, fruits and cereals. Brandy-making involves two processes – fermentation and distillation – while whisky is made in three stages: conversion of the starch in the grain to sugar, fermentation, and distillation. Brandy is distilled from wine, rum from the juice of the sugar cane, and vodka from rye, malt or potato starch, while different whiskies are distinguished from one another in their manufacture and the grains from which they are made.

Liqueurs are extracts from fruits and herbs which are blended with a spirit, such as brandy, and may include honey or sugar syrups. Some better known ones are maraschino, an Italian liqueur made from cherries; Cointreau, with a distinctive orange flavor, and Bénédictine and Chartreuse.

Wines, beers and spirits in the kitchen

Recipes for spirits and liqueurs began to appear in early cookery books as housewives – skilled in the art of wine-making and brewing – were encouraged to install in the kitchen an alembic, or still. Modern recipes have inherited and improved upon the old culinary techniques of incorporated wines and spirits, especially in the wine-producing countries. France, in particular, has utilized her wines to such an extent that they are inseparable from the repertoire. For example, *coq au vin* and *boeuf à la bourguignonne* are Burgundian dishes using the local red wines; *marchand de vin* denotes simple foods such as steaks served with a red wine sauce. White wines feature in many fish dishes, and even red wines are sometimes used in such recipes as *sole bordelaise* from the claret region of Bordeaux. Sauces are flavored with brandy or Madeira, and liqueurs are prominent in *crêpes suzette* and *soufflé au Grand Marnier*.

Ordinary table wines such as claret, Burgundy, hock and Moselle are widely used but sometimes a more specific type is called for, such as champagne as a *court-bouillon* for salmon. On a more everyday level cider is often used as a cooking liquor for boiling hams, in rabbit stews and batters. In Far Eastern cooking, rice wines are popular: Japanese *sake* and *mirin* are used in *sukiyaki* and sauces, while Chinese rice wine is a principal ingredient in *tsui-chi* or "drunken chicken".

Beer has long been employed in German recipes, and beer soup was a sixteenth-century favorite; it features in the Flemish stew *carbonnade*. In Britain it is used, like cider, in a fritter batter, Welsh rarebit and in cakes and puddings. Stout or strong ale are traditionally used to moisten the Christmas pudding mixture. The body of the "made" or

fortified wines makes them important ingredients of British dishes. Sherry is used notably in trifle and syllabub – a concoction of sherry and cream – while port is combined with Stilton cheese. The center of the cheese is scooped out and the cavity filled with port. The French put their port in the cavities of Charentais melons. Madeira, too, with its characteristic, aromatic taste is a useful flavoring in sweets and sauces. Madère sauce accompanies ham, or kidneys in French cooking and can be used instead of sherry. Marsala features in sauces and in the Italian dessert *zabaglione*. Kirsch has an affinity with pineapple, cherries and strawberries and features in *pêches cardinal*. Liqueurs have a natural affinity with desserts. Maraschino, which, like kirsch, is made from cherries, may be used in place of kirsch and is an ingredient in Nesselrode pudding. Cointreau, with its orange base, is a favorite with orange-flavored dishes, especially soufflés, and *crêpes suzette*. Curaçao is used in *fraises Romanoff*.

Corkscrews
These early versions date back to the 19th century

Tequila production
The juice from the mature agave cactus, native to Mexico, is fermented and distilled to produce tequila, the Mexican national drink. One of the initial stages in extracting the juice is trimming the leaves and chopping the agave in half

LIQUEURS See also p. 206

Advocaat □
A Dutch liqueur made from brandy, egg yolks and sugar, it is drunk alone or with other drinks.

Amaretto □
An Italian fruit-based liqueur, it contains almonds and can be used with fruit and in desserts.

Aniseed-flavored liqueurs □
Varieties include the French **anisette** □, Spanish **anis** and Italian **sambuca** □. They are all used as liqueurs or in cocktails.

Bénédictine □
Made from a recipe combining herbs, honey and brandies, it can be added to coffee and is used for flambéeing fruits.

Chartreuse □
A French brandy-based liqueur containing honey, herbs and spices. Both yellow and green varieties are available. It is used in cocktails, cakes and chocolate.

Crème de cassis □
A blackcurrant-based liqueur made in many countries, though the French is the most famous. It is used in cocktails and desserts. Similar liqueurs are produced in other flavors, including **crème de banane** □, **crème de cacao** □ and **crème de mente**.

Drambuie □
A whisky-based liqueur tinged with herbs and spices, it can be used in coffee.

Galliano □
An Italian herb-based liqueur

used mainly in cocktails.

Kummel □
A caraway-flavored liqueur. Produced mainly in Holland, it is used as a flavoring in desserts.

Orange-flavored liqueurs □
These are based on the bitter bergamot orange, and often include the peel. There are several versions, all of which can be used in soufflés, pancakes and recipes for orange sauce. The most noted are **Cointreau** □, **Curaçao** □, **Grand Marnier** □.

Strega □
An Italian liqueur based on herbs steeped in spirit, it is used in desserts and cocktails.

Tia Maria □
A Jamaican liqueur based on rum and spices, it is used in desserts, chocolates and cocktails.

WINES See also p. 208

Fortified wines □
These are fortified with spirits during or after fermentation. Varieties include **Madeira** □ (from the island of the same name), **Marsala** □ (from Sicily), **Malaga** (from Spain) and **Tokay** – all used as dessert wines; **sherries** □ (sweet, medium and dry) and **port** □ (from Portugal) – red or white – all used as aperitifs. Some fortified wines, such as **Marsala** and **Madeira**, feature in desserts such as *zabaglione*.

Table wines □.
Usually the fermented juice of the grape, though varieties have been made from fruits such as

elderberry and rhubarb; also from rice, such as the Japanese **mirin**. Red wines include **claret** and **Burgundy**; white wines include **hock** and **Moselle** from Germany and **Sauternes** from France, and can vary in sweetness. **Champagne** □ is a white sparkling wine. Table wines are usually drunk as meal accompaniments; lesser-quality wines can be used in sauces and casseroles.

Vermouth □
Vermouth can be white, red or pink. It is a high-strength wine cooked with a number of different herbs and used as an aperitif and in cocktails.

SPIRITS See also p. 208

Brandy □
A spirit distilled from grape wines, the two main types are **Cognac** and **Armagnac**. Good brandies are often drunk as liqueurs as well as spirits; lesser quality brandies are used to *flambé* foods and in sauces and desserts. True **fruit brandies** are distilled from fruit wines. The best known is **Calvados** □ (apple brandy) – the American equivalent is **applejack**. Others are **mirabelle** and **slivovitz** □ (plum brandies) and **kirsch** □ (cherry brandy). They all have the same uses as brandy.

Campari
Made from herbs, the peel of bitter oranges and quinine bark steeped in spirit, it is usually mixed with other drinks.

Gin □
A colorless spirit distilled from maize, used mainly in cocktails.

Wine rack

Rum □
Rum is distilled from sugar cane and molasses. Produced mainly in the West Indies, colorless and dark varieties are available. Rum is used in baking, desserts and cocktails.

Vodka □
A colorless spirit distilled from rye, malt, or potato starch. It is made mainly in Poland and the USSR. Similar spirits: **aquavit**, **arrack □**, **mescal**, **ouzo □**, **pastis**, **pernod □**, **pulque**, **schnapps □** and **tequila □** – used mainly in cocktails.

Whisky; Whiskey □
There are various types: **Scotch** (spelt "whisky"), **Irish**, **American**, of which the most famous is **Bourbon**, and **Canadian rye** (all spelt "whiskey"). They are all based on varieties of grains, which may be malted, unmalted or blended.

BEERS AND CIDERS
See also p. 208
Beer □
Made from the fermented mash of malted barley and hops there are two main types: **lager □** and **ale □**. Ale can be divided into several types: light, bitter and heavy-bodied – an example of the latter is **Guinness □** (stout).

Cider □
Usually the product of fermented apple juice, another variety is made from pears. It is drunk on its own, used with pork, and in desserts.

INDEX

Lungo-vermicelli coupe **132**
Lutefisk 268
Lychee (*Litchi chinensis*) 255

M

Macadamia nut (*Macadamia ternifolia*) **121**, 255
Macaroni **135**, 259
Macassar gum *see* Agar-agar
Mace (*Myristica fragrans*) **19**, 214
Mackerel **150**, 261, 262, 263
Madagascar bean *see* Lima bean
Madeira **208**, 290
Mainzer 234
Maize *see* Corn
Maize meal *see* Cornmeal
Malaga 290
Malegueta pepper *see* Grains of paradise
Mallard duck **180**, 269
Malt extract **27**, 217
Malted milk 217
Malting barley 257
Malt vinegar **35**, 222
Manaliga *see* Cornmeal
Manchego cheese **50**, 233
Mandarin (*Citrus reticulata*) 251
Mandrake root 289
Mangetout *see* Snow pea
Mango (*Mangifera indica*) **114**, 252
Mango, dried **23**, 216
Mango chutney **28**, 218
Mango honey 226
Mango pickle **29**
Mangold 242
Mangosteen 248
Manichi *see* Rigatoni
Manioc *see* Cassava
Manuka honey **40**, 227
Maple syrup **39**, 225
Maraschino **206**, 289, 290
Maribo 234
Margarine **44**, 229
Marigold (*Calendula officinalis*) **9**, 211
Marjoram (*Origanum marjorana*) **13**, 212
Marmalades **43**, 227
Marmite 217
Marron glacé **128**, 258
Marron purée *see* Chestnut purée
Marrow (*Cucurbita pepo*) **79** 241
Marrow bones **185**, 282
Marsala **208**, 290
Marshmallow **128**, 259
Marzipan 259
Marzipan fruits **128**
Mascarpone cheese 231
Matjes herring **167**, 268
Matzoh meal **124**
Matsutake 246
Mayonnaise **36**, 223
Mazoum 229
Meagre 263
Medlar (*Mespilus germanica*) 249
Megrim 261
Mekabu **166**, 269
Melba sauce **37**, 223
Melons (*Cucumis melo*) **110–113**, 252
Melt **186**, 281, 282
Menrui noodles 260
Merguez **191**, 285

Mescal 291
Mesentery 281, 282
Mettwurst/Metwurst **194**, 285
Mexican tea *see* Epazote
Michigan beans *see* White beans
Migaki-nishin 268
Migonette pepper 214
Miki noodles 261
Milfoil *see* Yarrow
Milk **45**, 228
Millet **122**, 257
Milt 267
Mint (*Mentha*, spp.) **10**, 212
Mint jelly and Mint sauce **36**, 223
Mirabelle brandy 249, 290
Mirin 290
Miso **27**, 217
Misua noodles 261
Mocha coffee 287
Molbo 234
Molasses (light and dark) **39**, 225
Molluscs **162–165**, 266
Monguete **91**
"Monkey nut" *see* Peanut
Monkfish **153**, 262, 263 *see also* Anglerfish
Monosodium glutamate **26**, 217
Monterey Jack **51**, 233
Moonfish *see* Opah
Moong dal *see* Mung bean
Moose 271
Morcilla **192**, 284
Morel (*Morchella esculenta*) **96**, 246, 247
Morning glory honey 226
Mortadella **194**, **195**, 285
Moselle 290
Mostaccioli *see* Penne
Moutarde de meaux **30**, 219
Mozzarella cheese **46**, 231
MSG *see* Monosodium glutamate
Mulato pepper **22**, 215
Mulberry (*Morus*, spp.) 250
Mung bean (*Phaseolus aureus*) **93**, 245
Munster cheese 232 *see also* Petit Munster
Muscovy duck 269
Mushrooms **96–7**, 246–247
Mushrooms, dried **96**
Musk melons 252
Mussel **164**, 265, 266
Mustard **20**, **30–31**, 219
Mycella cheese **57**, 235
Mysore coffee 287
Mysost cheese 233

N

Nam pla 269
Napoli salami **199**, 285
Naseberry (*Achras sapota*) 250
Nasturtium (*Tropaelum majus*) **14**, 212
Natto 217
Navel orange **104**, 252
Navy bean *see* Boston bean
Neapolitan parsley *see* Parsley
Nectarine **98**, **99**, 249, 253
Needlefish 263
Nepal pepper 214
Neroli bigarade 216
Netted melons 252
Nettle (*Urtica dioica*) **64**, 239
Netz salami **197**, 285

Neufchatel cheese **49**, 232
New Zealand spinach (*Tetragonia expansa*) 239
Nicaraguan coffee 287
Nigella (*Nigella sativa*) **17**, 214
Non pareils *see* Sprinkles
Norfolk dumpling 261
Northern whitefish 262
Norway haddock 263
Norway lobster *see* Saltwater crayfish
Norway trout *see* Whiting
Nougat 259
Nuoc-mam 269
Nutmeg (*Myristica fragrans*) **18**, 214
Nuts **120–21**, 254–256

O

Oatmeal **124**, 257
Oats **122**, 257
Ocean perch 263
Octopus **163**, 264, 266, 267
Ogen melon **111**, 252
Okra (*Hibiscus esculentus*) **90**, 243
Olive oil **33**, 221
Olives **28**, 218
One-thousand- (1,000-) year-old egg **60**, 236
Onion (*Allium cepa*) **82–3**, 218, 241–2
Oolong tea 288
Opah 263
Orange blossom honey **40**, 227
Orange-flavored liqueurs 290
Orange flower water **25**
Orange mint **10**, 212
Orange pekoe tea 288
Orangequat 248
Oranges **102**, **104**, 251–252
Orecchiette **133**
Oregano (*Origanum vulgare*) **13**, 212
Orris 216
Orsières 233
Ortanique 248, 252
Osetr caviar 268
Ostrich eggs **61**, 236
Oswego *see* Bergamot
Ouzo **208**, 291
Oxford sausage 285
Oxtail **185**, 281, 282
Oysters **165**, 264, 265, 267, 268
Oyster plant *see* Salsify
Oyster sauce **36**

P

Pacific cod 262
Padi-straw mushroom (*Volvariella volvacea*) 246, 247
Pak-choi (*Brassica chinensis*) **69**, 239
Palm hearts **70**
Palm oil 221
Pandora bream 264
Papaw *see* Papaya
Papaya (*Carica papaya*) **114**, 252
Paprika (*Capsicum tetragonum*) **19**, 214
Paprika sausage **191**, 285
Parasol mushroom (*Lepiota procira*) **97**, 247
Parma ham **202**, 286

Acknowledgments

Dorling Kindersley Ltd would like to thank the following people: Ian Carr, Vic Chambers, Tony Wallace and Ron Williamson at Contact Graphics Typesetters Ltd; Michael Burman, Andy Butler, Derek Coombes, Gill Edden, Rosamund Gendle, Helen Sampey, Gail Slatter, Jill Squires, Kevin Summers and Michelle Walker. Thanks are also extended to the following suppliers: I. Camisa, Charles of Belgravia, Culpeper Ltd, Justin de Blank Ltd, W. Fenn, Fortnum and Mason Ltd, Thomas Goode and Co., Harrods Ltd, A. Myall and Sons Ltd, Neal's Yard Wholefood Warehouse, Paxton and Whitfield, Randall and Aubin Ltd, Richards Ltd, and the John Topham Picture Library